SOMETHING ABOUT THE AUTHOR®

Something about
the Author *was named
an* ***"Outstanding
Reference Source,"*** *the highest honor given
by the American
Library Association
Reference and Adult
Services Division.*

ISSN 0276-816X

something ABOUT the AUTHOR®

**Facts and Pictures about Authors
and Illustrators of Books for Young People**

volume 184

GALE
CENGAGE Learning™

Detroit • New York • San Francisco • New Haven, Conn • Waterville, Maine • London

Something about the Author, Volume 184

Project Editor: Lisa Kumar

Editorial: Dana Ferguson, Amy Elisabeth Fuller, Michelle Kazensky, Jennifer Mossman, Joseph Palmisano, Mary Ruby, Robert James Russell, Amanda D. Sams, Marie Toft

Permissions: Beth Beaufore, Barb McNeil, Sara Teller

Imaging and Multimedia: Leitha Etheridge-Sims, Lezlie Light

Composition and Electronic Capture: Amy Darga

Manufacturing: Drew Kalasky

Product Manager: Peg Knight

For product information and technology assistance, contact us at
Gale Customer Support, 1-800-877-4253.
For permission to use material from this text or product,
submit all requests online at **www.cengage.com/permissions.**
Further permissions questions can be emailed to
permissionrequest@cengage.com

Gale
27500 Drake Rd.
Farmington Hills, MI, 48331-3535

LIBRARY OF CONGRESS CATALOG CARD NUMBER 62-52046

ISBN-13: 978-0-7876-9933-8
ISBN-10: 0-7876-9933-0

ISSN 0276-816X

This title is also available as an e-book.
ISBN-13: 978-1-4144-3836
ISBN-10: 1-4144-3836-2
Contact your Gale sales representative for ordering information.

Printed in the United States of America
1 2 3 4 5 6 7 12 11 10 09 08

Contents

Authors in Forthcoming Volumes

Below are some of the authors and illustrators that will be featured in upcoming volumes of *SATA*. These include new entries on the swiftly rising stars of the field, as well as completely revised and updated entries (indicated with *) on some of the most notable and best-loved creators of books for children.

Julie Burtinshaw ❚ Burtinshaw's first novel for teens, *Dead Reckoning,* was nominated for several awards for its retelling of a nautical disaster involving a ship that sunk off the west coast of Canada. She draws on historical events in her native British Columbia in *The Freedom of Jenny,* which focuses on a family of former slaves who journey there from Missouri in the late 1880s. A contemporary tale of teen adventurers, Burtinshaw's novel *Adrift* is also set on the Canadian coast.

Jennifer Keats Curtis ❚ In her writing, Curtis introduces children to the ecology of the Maryland coastal region, where she lives. An outgrowth of her workshops and school presentations, her books *Oshus and Shelly Save the Bay, Turtles in My Sandbox,* and *Osprey Adventure* focus on the animals that live in the complex Chesapeake Bay estuary ecosystem, where freshwater flows into the Atlantic and mixes with the ocean's salt water.

*Sid Fleischman ❚ Regarded as a master of the tall tale as well as one of the most popular humorists in American children's literature, Fleischman is noted for writing action-filled adventure stories that weave exciting plots, rollicking wit, and joyous wordplay with accurate, well-researched historical facts. His Newbery Medal-winning *The Whipping Boy* features a spoiled prince and the stoical lad who takes his punishment, while other books are set against historic backdrops such as the California Gold Rush, seventeenth-century piracy, and rural life in the American Midwest. Illustrated by a variety of talented artists, Fleischman's many books for children include *The Giant Rat of Sumatra, Jim Ugly,* and *The White Elephant.*

Leonid Gore ❚ Gore was already a successful illustrator of children's book in his native USSR when he immigrated to the eastern United States in 1990. Along with such titles as *Jacob and the Stranger,* a story by Sally Derby that is set in the small town of Slavda, Gore's ornate style has been featured in numerous other books, among them Mary Packard's *I Am King!,* Anette Griessman's picture book *The Fire,* and an illustrated adaptation of Shakespeare's *Hamlet* by Bruce Coville. In 2007, Gore released his first self-illustrated book for children, *Danny's First Snow.*

Alan Katz ❚ A comedy writer, Katz has the ability to stay young at heart. Whether writing his "Silly Dilly" song books or working on cartoons for Disney or Nickelodeon, he uses his capacity to think like a child to make sure his silliness and jokes appeal to young readers. Along with his books, Katz is also the creator of the trivia game "That's Right, That's Wrong!" which is hosted by his fictional alter ego Dr. I.B. Wrongo and airs regularly on XM Radio. He also visits schools and libraries to do readings, sing, and tell jokes.

*Jim Murphy ❚ Murphy writes on a variety of topics, among them sports, transportation, inventions, dinosaurs, animal life, mechanical devices, and historical figures. In addition, he has created picture books such as *Fergus and the Night-Demon* and *Backyard Bear,* as well as novels such as *My Face to the Wind: The Diary of Sarah Jane Price, a Prairie Teacher.* A prolific writer, Murphy is best known for his books on American military history and natural disasters, among them *The Great Fire* and *The Boys' War,* both of which bring readers back to the nineteenth century.

*Terry Pratchett ❚ Winner of the prestigious Carnegie Medal for his novel *The Amazing Maurice and His Educated Rodents,* Pratchett is known primarily for his "Discworld" fantasy novel series. Including novels such as *Interesting Times* and *Wyrd Witches,* the "Discworld" books feature humorous parodies of the works of well-known science-fiction and fantasy writers such as J.R.R. Tolkien and Larry Niven. An irreverent writer, Pratchett is known to spoof politics and faith, universal fears of aging and death, as well as modern trends such as New Age philosophy.

Queen Latifah ❚ Queen Latifah is an American rap and hip-hop artist who has also gained acclaim as the first woman rapper to be nominated for an Academy award. Harnessing her talent, her natural charisma, and her commanding, energetic presence, Queen Latifah has expanded her audience through her work in films such as "Chicago" and "Hairspray." In her many public appearances, as well as in books such as her memoir *Ladies First: Revelations of a Strong Woman* and the picture book *Queen of the Scene,* she also works to inspires others to learn from her success.

Mary Ann Rodman ❚ Rodman is the author of *My Best Friend,* which garnered both the Charlotte Zolotow Award and the Ezra Jack Keats Award. A former school librarian, Rodman has also published the humorous chapter book *First Grade Stinks!* as well as the critically acclaimed middle-grade novel, *Yankee Girl.*

Cynthia von Buhler ❚ A sculptor, painter, performance artist, and children's book author, von Buhler has been recognized across a number of creative mediums. Her interest in writing and illustrating children's books was inspired by her own desire to get involved with the children that will comprise future generations. Her imaginative illustrations have appeared in a number of picture books, among them her original story *The Cat Who Wouldn't Come Inside,* which was inspired by von Buhler's experiences with a stray cat.

Introduction

Something about the Author (*SATA*) is an ongoing reference series that examines the lives and works of authors and illustrators of books for children. *SATA* includes not only well-known writers and artists but also less prominent individuals whose works are just coming to be recognized. This series is often the only readily available information source on emerging authors and illustrators. You'll find *SATA* informative and entertaining, whether you are a student, a librarian, an English teacher, a parent, or simply an adult who enjoys children's literature.

What's Inside *SATA*

SATA provides detailed information about authors and illustrators who span the full time range of children's literature, from early figures like John Newbery and L. Frank Baum to contemporary figures like Judy Blume and Richard Peck. Authors in the series represent primarily English-speaking countries, particularly the United States, Canada, and the United Kingdom. Also included, however, are authors from around the world whose works are available in English translation. The writings represented in *SATA* include those created intentionally for children and young adults as well as those written for a general audience and known to interest younger readers. These writings cover the entire spectrum of children's literature, including picture books, humor, folk and fairy tales, animal stories, mystery and adventure, science fiction and fantasy, historical fiction, poetry and nonsense verse, drama, biography, and nonfiction. Obituaries are also included in *SATA* and are intended not only as death notices but also as concise overviews of people's lives and work. Additionally, each edition features newly revised and updated entries for a selection of *SATA* listees who remain of interest to today's readers and who have been active enough to require extensive revisions of their earlier biographies.

Autobiography Feature

Beginning with Volume 103, many volumes of *SATA* feature one or more specially commissioned autobiographical essays. These unique essays, averaging about ten thousand words in length and illustrated with an abundance of personal photos, present an entertaining and informative first-person perspective on the lives and careers of prominent authors and illustrators profiled in *SATA*.

Two Convenient Indexes

In response to suggestions from librarians, *SATA* indexes no longer appear in every volume but are included in alternate (odd-numbered) volumes of the series, beginning with Volume 57.

SATA continues to include two indexes that cumulate with each alternate volume: the Illustrations Index, arranged by the name of the illustrator, gives the number of the volume and page where the illustrator's work appears in the current volume as well as all preceding volumes in the series; the Author Index gives the number of the volume in which a person's biographical sketch, autobiographical essay, or obituary appears in the current volume as well as all preceding volumes in the series.

These indexes also include references to authors and illustrators who appear in *Gale's Yesterday's Authors of Books for Children, Children's Literature Review,* and *Something about the Author Autobiography Series.*

Easy-to-Use Entry Format

Whether you're already familiar with the *SATA* series or just getting acquainted, you will want to be aware of the kind of information that an entry provides. In every *SATA* entry the editors attempt to give as complete a picture of the person's life and work as possible. A typical entry in *SATA* includes the following clearly labeled information sections:

PERSONAL: date and place of birth and death, parents' names and occupations, name of spouse, date of marriage, names of children, educational institutions attended, degrees received, religious and political affiliations, hobbies and other interests.

ADDRESSES: complete home, office, electronic mail, and agent addresses, whenever available.

CAREER: name of employer, position, and dates for each career post; art exhibitions; military service; memberships and offices held in professional and civic organizations.

MEMBER: professional, civic, and other association memberships and any official posts held.

AWARDS, HONORS: literary and professional awards received.

WRITINGS: title-by-title chronological bibliography of books written and/or illustrated, listed by genre when known; lists of other notable publications, such as plays, screenplays, and periodical contributions.

ADAPTATIONS: a list of films, television programs, plays, CD-ROMs, recordings, and other media presentations that have been adapted from the author's work.

WORK IN PROGRESS: description of projects in progress.

SIDELIGHTS: a biographical portrait of the author or illustrator's development, either directly from the biographee—and often written specifically for the *SATA* entry—or gathered from diaries, letters, interviews, or other published sources.

BIOGRAPHICAL AND CRITICAL SOURCES: cites sources quoted in "Sidelights" along with references for further reading.

EXTENSIVE ILLUSTRATIONS: photographs, movie stills, book illustrations, and other interesting visual materials supplement the text.

How a *SATA* Entry Is Compiled

SATA editors examine a wide variety of published sources to gather information for an entry. Biographical and bibliographic sources are consulted, as are book reviews, feature articles, published interviews, and material sometimes obtained from the biographee's family, publishers, agent, or other associates. Whenever possible, the author or illustrator is sent a copy of the entry to check for accuracy and completeness.

Entries that have not been verified by the biographees or their representatives are marked with an asterisk (*).

Contact the Editor

We encourage our readers to examine the entire *SATA* series. Please write and tell us if we can make *SATA* even more helpful to you. Give your comments and suggestions to the editor:

Editor
Something about the Author
Gale, Cengage Learning
27500 Drake Rd.
Farmington Hills MI 48331-3535

Toll-free: 800-877-GALE
Fax: 248-699-8070

Something about the Author Product Advisory Board

The editors of *Something about the Author* are dedicated to maintaining a high standard of excellence by publishing comprehensive, accurate, and highly readable entries on a wide array of writers for children and young adults. In addition to the quality of the content, the editors take pride in the graphic design of the series, which is intended to be orderly yet inviting, allowing readers to utilize the pages of *SATA* easily and with efficiency. Despite the longevity of the *SATA* print series, and the success of its format, we are mindful that the vitality of a literary reference product is dependent on its ability to serve its users over time. As literature, and attitudes about literature, constantly evolve, so do the reference needs of students, teachers, scholars, journalists, researchers, and book club members. To be certain that we continue to keep pace with the expectations of our customers, the editors of *SATA* listen carefully to their comments regarding the value, utility, and quality of the series. Librarians, who have firsthand knowledge of the needs of library users, are a valuable resource for us. The *Something about the Author* Product Advisory Board, made up of school, public, and academic librarians, is a forum to promote focused feedback about *SATA* on a regular basis. The nine-member advisory board includes the following individuals, whom the editors wish to thank for sharing their expertise:

Eva M. Davis
Youth Department Manager,
Ann Arbor District Library,
Ann Arbor, Michigan

Joan B. Eisenberg
Lower School Librarian,
Milton Academy,
Milton, Massachusetts

Francisca Goldsmith
Teen Services Librarian,
Berkeley Public Library,
Berkeley, California

Susan Dove Lempke
Children's Services Supervisor,
Niles Public Library District,
Niles, Illinois

Robyn Lupa
Head of Children's Services,
Jefferson County Public Library,
Lakewood, Colorado

Victor L. Schill
Assistant Branch Librarian/Children's Librarian,
Harris County Public Library/Fairbanks Branch,
Houston, Texas

Caryn Sipos
Community Librarian,
Three Creeks Community Library,
Vancouver, Washington

Steven Weiner
Director,
Maynard Public Library,
Maynard, Massachusetts

something about the author

AILLAUD, Cindy Lou 1955-

Personal

Born May 10, 1955, in Renton, WA; daughter of Ronald (a teacher) and Lola May (a cake decorator) Petett; married Whit Aillaud (a teacher), June 11, 1976; children: Jason, Brian. *Education:* Washington State University, Pullman, B.A. (education), 1977; Central Washington University, special education endorsement, K-12, 1989. *Hobbies and other interests:* Walking, hiking, photography, reading.

Addresses

Office—P.O. Box 1245, Delta Jct, AK 99737. *E-mail*—smiles99737@yahoo.com.

Career

Delta/Greely School District, Delta Junction, AK, elementary school teacher, 1979-82, 1989—. Cub Scout master, 1992-95; Delta/Greely Arts Council, member and officer, 1979-82; member of community choir, 1989-2001; chair of Relay for Life Children's Games, 2006-07. Member, Alaska State Science Consortium and Alaska State Writing Consortium.

Member

National Education Association (member of AK affiliate), American Alliance for Health, Physical Education, Recreation and Dance, Alaska Alliance for Health, Physical Education, Recreation and Dance, Fairbanks Arts Association, Alaska Photography Center.

Cindy Lou Aillaud (Courtesy of Cindy Lou Aillaud.)

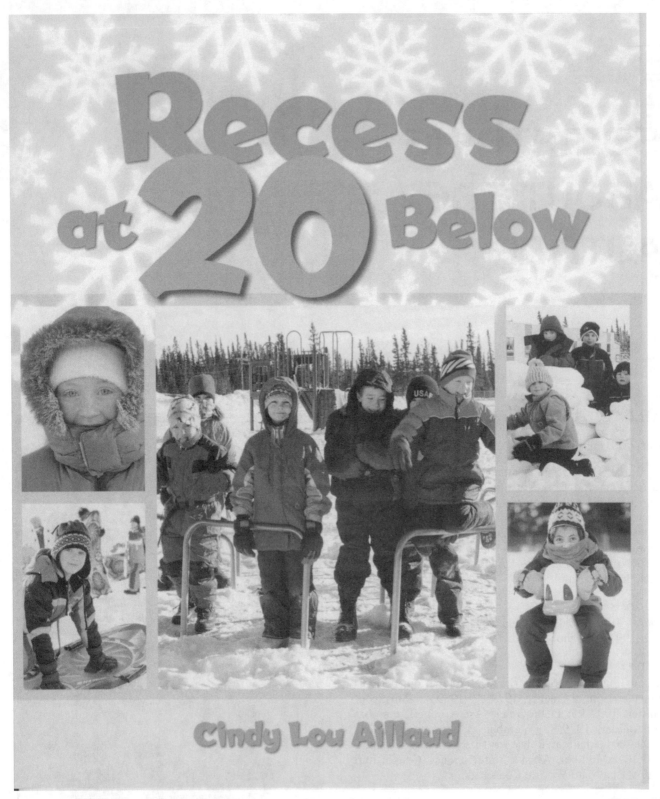

Cover of Aillaud's **Recess at 20 Below,** *which focuses on a child's school day near the North Pole.* (Alaska Northwest Books, 2005. Cover photographs © by Cindy Lou Aillaud. Reproduced by permission.)

Awards, Honors

Fulbright Memorial Fund Scholar to Japan, 2000; DisneyHand Teacher honoree, 2004; Notable Social Studies Trade Books for Young People designation, and International Reading Association Selector's Choice, both 2005, both for *Recess at 20 Below;* named Alaska Elementary Physical Education Teacher of the Year, 2006; named to *USA Today* Teacher Team, 2006.

Writings

Recess at 20 Below, Alaska Northwest Books, 2005.

Sidelights

Cindy Lou Aillaud grew up in western Washington, where the winters were rainy. Longing to play in the snow, she headed north after graduating from Washington State University, and has worked as a teacher in the region near the Arctic Circle since 1979. Aillaud has taught elementary students at almost every grade, including children with special-education needs. In her current job as a physical education teacher in Delta Junction, Alaska, she can claim every child enrolled in her school as one of her students.

Supervising a group of kindergarten students outside during recess one November inspired Aillaud's picture book *Recess at 20 Below.* Creating the photographs for the book tap into another of Aillaud's passions, and by including scenes from an actual school, both Aillaud and her students are able to illustrate for readers what life is like in the frozen north. At twenty degrees below zero, playing outside is an adventure that starts with bundling into numerous layers of clothing. The face still needs to be exposed to the cold, however, and one's breath freezes instantly and makes crystallized patterns on eyebrows, bangs, and eyelashes. With only three hours of daylight during the winter months, outside playtime is limited, and walks too and from school are made in the dark.

As Robin Smith wrote in her *Horn Book* review of *Recess at 20 Below,* the author's humorous photographs of snow-covered children are "sure to elicit a gasp of surprise and delight" from readers who are unfamiliar with living in such cold. Her "straightforward text misses no interesting detail," Smith added, and *School Library Journal* contributor Cassandra A. Lopez praised the book's "colorful, clear photographs" and engaging narrative. Writing in *Booklist,* Connie Fletcher concluded that in *Recess at 20 Below* Aillaud "gives a familiar school-day activity a whole new meaning in delightful, intriguing fashion."

A nationally respected teacher, Aillaud was selected from among 150,000 nominees as one of thirty-nine DisneyHand teachers of the year in 2004. As a Fulbright Memorial Fund scholar, she visited Japan to learn about Japanese culture, then brought her new understanding back to her students in Alaska. "Through my book, *Recess at 20 Below,* I am hoping to encourage children of ALL ages to go outside and play," she told *SATA.* "I would advise any aspiring writer to look in their own backyard for inspiration."

Biographical and Critical Sources

PERIODICALS

Booklist, December 15, 2005, Connie Fletcher, review of *Recess at 20 Below,* p. 48.

Horn Book, January-February, 2006, Robin Smith, review of *Recess at 20 Below,* p. 96.

School Library Journal, March, 2006, Cassandra A. Lopez, review of *Recess at 20 Below,* p. 206.

ONLINE

USA Today Online, http://www.usatoday.com/ (January 9, 2007), Abbie Stillie, "Alaska Gym Teacher Doesn't Let Elements Stop Exercise."

*   *   *

APOSTOLINA, M.
(Michael Apostolina)

Personal

Male.

Addresses

Home—W. Hollywood, CA.

Career

Author and screenwriter. Miramax Films, Hollywood, CA, formerly head of creative affairs; Vestron Pictures, Hollywood, former executive. Director and producer of short films, including *Kidnap Madonna's Baby,* c. 2006.

Awards, Honors

American Library Association Best Book nomination, 2006, for *Hazing Meri Sugarman.*

Writings

Hazing Meri Sugarman, Simon Pulse (New York, NY), 2006, published as *Meri Sugarman, Psycho Queen,* Simon & Schuster (London, England), 2006.
Meri Strikes Back, Simon Pulse (New York, NY), 2006.
Dark Cindy, Simon Pulse (New York, NY), 2007.

Author of screenplays, including *Planet Deb, Thornhill Prep, The Shop Teacher, Fear the Reapers,* (with Robert Sugalski) *Indecent,* and *Kidnap Madonna's Baby.* Contributor to magazines, including *Film in Review* and *Details.*

Sidelights

While growing up, M. Apostolina was always telling stories, sometimes writing them down, sometimes creating plays, and sometimes making short films. Entering the Hollywood film industry after college, he took a job

Cover of M. Apostolina's teen novel Hazing Meri Sugarman, *featuring a photograph by Michael Frost.* (Simon Pulse, 2006. Reproduced by permission.)

for Miramax Films, where he was responsible for helping screen writers develop their scripts. This film career ended when Apostolina realized that, instead of consulting, he wanted to be the one doing the writing. Beginning with his 2006 young-adult novel *Hazing Meri Sugarman,* his shift in career path has gained him fans who enjoy his humorous novels with their quirky brand of teen intrigue.

Hazing Meri Sugarman is a dark and eccentric novel about a college freshman and her initiation into a campus sorority at Rumson University. Cindy Bixby desperately wants to join Alpha Beta Delta, the same sorority her mother pledged to years before. Cindy's hazing experience with Alpha Beta Delta involves a series of humiliations dreamed up by beautiful, popular sorority president Meri Sugarman. Cindy endures the indignities, gains Meri's good graces, and ultimately becomes a sister. However, things undergo a drastic change when Meri's ex-boyfriend takes an interest in Cindy, causing the new sorority sister to experience Meri's wrath. In a review for *Publishers Weekly,* a critic characterized *Hazing Meri Sugarman* as an "offbeat debut" and concluded that, although the book is a "surprising, dark and ultimately uneven novel, . . . readers will likely find enough amusing and bizarre material" in Apostolina's story "to keep them going."

The relationship between Meri and Cindy plays out over the course of two more novels. In *Meri Strikes Back* Cindy is linked arm-in-arm with her new boyfriend and enjoying some peace with her friends at Alpha Beta Delta. Then Meri returns, dressed to the nines and out for revenge. Meri's revenge has extended to the entire sorority in *Dark Cindy,* but when Cindy discovers the diary of the former president, the playing field may be leveled. But is Cindy ready to stoop to the same depths?

Apostolina finds inspiration in "everyday life" as he explained in an online interview for TeensReadToo.com. "Just observing everything around me is enough to inspire me," the author added. In a separate interview for Publishers Marketplace online, Apostolina offered advice to young and aspiring writers, noting that "the best tip is to always outline your story before you begin writing your novel. . . . it's good to have a road map, so to speak, of what story you're trying to tell."

Biographical and Critical Sources

PERIODICALS

Booklist, March 1, 2006, Gillian Engberg, review of *Hazing Meri Sugarman,* p. 79.
Publishers Weekly, January 16, 2006, review of *Hazing Meri Sugarman,* p. 66.
School Library Journal, June, 2006, Stephanie L. Petruso, review of *Hazing Meri Sugarman,* p. 146.
Voice of Youth Advocates, April, 2006, Jennifer Rummel, review of *Hazing Meri Sugarman,* p. 37; February, 2007, Teri S. Lesesne, review of *Dark Cindy,* p. 518.

ONLINE

Publishers Marketplace Web site,, http://publishersmarket place.com/ (October 27, 2007), interview with Apostolina.
Simon & Schuster Web site, http://www.simonsays.com/ (October 27, 2007), "M. Apostolina."
TeenReadsToo.com, http://www.teensreadtoo.com/ (October 27, 2007), interview with Apostolina.*

*   *   *

APOSTOLINA, Michael See APOSTOLINA, M.

*   *   *

BALDACCI, David 1960-

Personal

Born 1960, in Richmond, VA; son of Rudolph (a trucking foreman) Baldacci; married Michelle Collin (a para-

David Baldacci (Photograph © by Jerry Bauer. Reproduced by permission.)

legal); children: Spencer, Collin. *Education:* Virginia Commonwealth University, B.A. (political science); University of Virginia, J.D.

Addresses

Home—Vienna, VA. *Office*—Reston, VA. *Agent*—Aaron Priest Literary Agency, 708 3rd Ave., 23rd Fl., New York, NY 10017.

Career

Writer. Trial and corporate lawyer in Washington, DC, for nine years. Board member of Virginia Foundation for the Humanities and Virginia Commonwealth University; Wish You Well Foundation, cofounder, 1999. National Multiple Sclerosis Society ambassador; volunteer for literacy and other causes, including Barbara Bush Foundation for Family Literacy, American Cancer Society, and Cystic Fibrosis Foundation.

Awards, Honors

Gold Medal Award for Best Mystery/Thriller, Southern Writers Guild, 1996, and W.H. Smith's Thumping Good Read Award for fiction, 1997, both for *Absolute Power;* Gold Medal Award for Best Mystery/Thriller, Southern Writers Guild, 1997, for *Total Control.*

Writings

FOR CHILDREN

Wish You Well (young adult novel), Warner Books (New York, NY), 2000.
Fries Alive!, ("Freddy and the French Fries" series), illustrated by Rudy Baldacci, Little, Brown (New York, NY), 2005.

The Mystery of Silas Finklebean ("Freddy and the French Fries" series), illustrated by Rudy Baldacci, Little, Brown (New York, NY), 2006.

NOVELS; FOR ADULTS

Absolute Power, Warner Books (New York, NY), 1996.
Total Control, Warner Books (New York, NY), 1997.
The Winner, Warner Books (New York, NY), 1997.
The Simple Truth, Warner Books (New York, NY), 1998.
Saving Faith, Warner Books (New York, NY), 1999.
Last Man Standing, Warner Books (New York, NY), 2001.
The Christmas Train, Warner Books (New York, NY), 2002.
Split Second, Warner Books (New York, NY), 2003.
Hour Game, Warner Books (New York, NY), 2004.
The Camel Club, Warner Books (New York, NY), 2005.
The Collectors, Warner Books (New York, NY), 2006.
Simple Genius, Warner Books (New York, NY), 2007.
Stone Cold, Grand Central Publishing (New York, NY), 2007.

Contributor to periodicals, including *Panorama* (Italy), *UVA Lawyer, Welt am Sonntag* (Germany), *Tatler* (United Kingdom), *New Statesman,* and *USA Today.* Also author of unproduced screenplays.

Baldacci's works have been translated into over thirty languages.

Adaptations

Absolute Power was adapted by William Goldman as a film starring Clint Eastwood and produced by Castle Rock, 1997. Rights to *Total Control* were sold to Columbia/TriStar. The 2002 USA cable-network pilot *McCourt & Stein* was based on a novel by Baldacci. Many of Baldacci's novels have been adapted as audiobooks.

Sidelights

Praised by legions of fans for his tantalizing premises and fast action, David Baldacci is the best-selling author of suspense novels such as *Absolute Power, Total Control,* and *Last Man Standing.* A former lawyer, Baldacci is frequently compared by critics to novelist John Grisham, although his more recent fiction has strayed far from the courtroom setting of his 1996 debut, *Absolute Power.* While sometimes panned by critics, Baldacci's rise to the best-seller lists has been characterized by many as meteoric, fueled by a screen adaptation of his first novel starring popular actor Clint Eastwood. "I never expected my writing to generate any monies," the author noted on his home page. "However, when success came, it came fast. I am an overnight success, but, being somewhat slower than others, it took me five thousand nights to get there."

An advocate of literacy, Baldacci has also written for children and teens, producing the novels in his "Freddy and the French Fries" series as well as the young-adult novel *Wish You Well.* In 1999 he joined his wife in founding the Wish You Well Foundation, which supports family literacy through developing and existing literacy programs throughout the United States. "Our stated goal is to eradicate illiteracy in the United States, particularly among adults," Baldacci told interviewer Marat Moore in the *ASHA Leader.*

An avid reader, Baldacci developed an early love for the written word and made countless trips to his local library with his mother. "Reading opened my eyes to the power of words—and showed me the world," the author remarked to Moore. "I thought then that if someone could capture my attention through language—symbols on a page—what power they had! We think in language, after all. How broad can your mind be if you can't conceive ideas using language, or think for yourself? Without that capacity, we are just spoon-fed our entire lives. The only reason I'm a writer today is because, as a child, I was such a reader."

Baldacci began writing regularly while in high school and college, trying his hand at short stories. As his collection of rejection slips grew, Baldacci turned his attention to screenplays and novels. After penning the opening chapter of a thriller, he contacted several agents and received nearly as many offers to represent him. Baldacci spent the next two years writing *Absolute Power,* working as a lawyer by day and writing from 10 p.m. to 3 a.m. When the manuscript was finished it was sold in just one day.

Featuring a plot described by a *Kirkus Reviews* critic as "the mother of all presidential cover-ups," *Absolute Power* mixes politics and petty theft. In the book, veteran thief Luther Whitney is robbing a billionaire's home when he is interrupted by the lady of the house, who is returning home with her lover, the president of the United States. As Whitney watches from a closet, the couple's sexual foreplay turns violent and the woman defends herself against the president with a letter opener. Angered, the president calls in the Secret Service men who have accompanied him to the house; they shoot and kill the woman. Whitney, who has witnessed all, remains undetected until he leaves the house in possession of the letter opener. Now he becomes the focus of a secret manhunt and while trying to save his own life, he attempts to seek justice for the dead woman, blackmail the president, and otherwise get his revenge. When he fears he may soon be discovered, Whitney involves lawyer Jack Graham, his daughter's former fiancée, to help prove that the president is a heartless villain.

While some critics identified faults in *Absolute Power,* the consensus was that the novel will please readers and film goers. In *Booklist* Gilbert Taylor wrote that, while the book "could stand some polishing in plot and story structure," its adaptability to film "ensures demand for a tale that is all action and no message." A *Publishers Weekly* critic dubbed the book a "sizzler of a first novel," adding that, while "Baldacci doesn't peer too

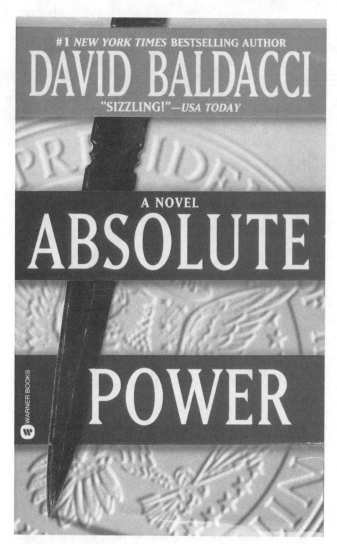

Cover of Baldacci's blockbuster thriller Absolute Power, *featuring artwork by Tony Greco.* (Warner Books, 1996. Reproduced by permission.)

deeply into his characters' souls . . . he's . . . a first-rate storyteller." A *Kirkus Reviews* contributor was disappointed that, despite its "arresting premise," *Absolute Power* ultimately distills into "an overblown and tedious tale of capital sins." Jean Hanff Korelitz came to a similar conclusion in the *New York Times,* but credited the problem to the novelist's relative inexperience. The thriller's "lack of suspense may result from the fact that Jack, its apparent hero, remains at the periphery of the story until it is nearly over," Korelitz maintained, concluding that Baldacci "brings an insider's savvy" to the story but lacks experience in plotting.

Baldacci's sophomore effort, *Total Control,* begins when lawyer Sidney Archer learns that her husband, Jason, has died in a plane crash. However, she later discovers that the death may have been a hoax and that Jason has disappeared in possession of high-tech corporate secrets. As the questions mount, Sidney loses her job and soon finds herself pursued by a group of assassins seeking an encrypted computer disk Jason presumably mailed to himself. Aided by an FBI agent who is her only trustworthy form of help, Sidney attempts to protect herself and her young daughter from a variety of evil competitors.

Total Control received the inevitable comparisons with Baldacci's blockbuster *Absolute Power*, a *Publishers Weekly* reviewer writing that the author's "windy thriller shows a slack authorial hand and generates only a fraction of the chills in Baldacci's bombastically effective debut." Kathy Piehl, reviewing *Total Control* for *Library Journal*, contended that the novelist "writes strictly for action, not wasting time developing characters or setting." In *Booklist* Donna Seaman, praised *Total Control* as more suspenseful than *Absolute Power,* and "also far more interesting in terms of the questions it raises about how much technology controls us."

Other thrillers have followed from Baldacci's pen, among them *The Winner, The Simple Truth, Last Man Standing,* and *Saving Faith.* In *The Winner* unwed mother Luann Tyler is offered the opportunity to share in a rigged one-hundred-million-dollar national lottery jackpot by a mysterious man named Jackson. Although she first declines, after she witnesses the murder of her drug-addict boyfriend and then kills the assailant in self-defense, she eventually uses Jackson's offer as a way of evading a murder charge. Although Luann agrees to leave the country permanently, she returns ten years later and becomes a target for murder. A man's wish to overturn his murder conviction is at the core of *The Simple Truth,* when felon Rufus Harms learns he was drugged at the time he supposedly murdered a young girl. When Harms' appeal to the Supreme Court is purloined by do-gooder law clerk Michael Fiske, the clerk becomes the target of the murderous conspirators that originally orchestrated Harms' imprisonment. *Saving Faith* finds whistleblower Faith Lockhart targeted by a hit man after she decides to reveal all she knows to the FBI, aided in her efforts to stay alive by a local private investigator who may or may not be trustworthy. The massacre of the FBI's elite Hostage Rescue Team takes center stage in *Last Man Standing,* when lone team survivor Web London joins forces with psychiatrist Claire Daniels to find out why he alone survived the deadly ambush. Not surprisingly, Web's investigation sparks further murders as his search takes him from the nation's capital to rural Virginia.

Characteristically, despite his continued position at the top of the *New York Times* best-seller list, Baldacci has earned mixed reviews for his work. In his *New York Times Book Review* of *The Winner,* Christopher Lehmann-Haupt complained that while the novel's text is "full of mixed metaphors and malapropisms," Baldacci's ending is full of the effective surprises that will make it an "inevitable" best-seller. Reviewing the same novel, a *Publishers Weekly* critic cited the story's "suspense, excitement and bankability," adding that although Baldacci reuses plot element from earlier books, "his strong characters and sheer Grishamlike exuberance

. . . will . . . thrust [*The Winner*] . . . toward the top of the charts." While a *Kirkus Reviews* contributor dismissed *The Simple Truth* as "a tiresome potboiler" and "just another big, silly book about lawyers," a *Publishers Weekly* writer maintained that, "for foxy plotting, [Baldaccci] is easily Grisham's peer." While *The Simple Truth* "isn't Baldacci's most original book," the critic added, ". . . it's his most generously textured, distinguished by delvings into family psychodramatics." Reviewing *Saving Faith,* a *Publishers Weekly* reviewer noted that while the plotting is somewhat overwrought, the storyline "moves fast . . . and its players and suspense are strong."

The nation's capital is the setting of *The Camel Club,* which introduces a cabal of four middle-aged men who have a shared suspicion of those who wield political power. Known by the pseudonyms Oliver Stone, Reuben, Caleb, and Milton, the members of the Camel Club keep pace with the news outside the mainstream, including conspiracy theories and back-room rumors. When members witness a murder on remote Roosevelt Island, they find themselves at the center of one of the most threatening intrigues they could imagine, and ultimately call on Secret Service agent Alex Ford to stop an apocalyptic event of international proportions. As *The Collectors* opens, the Camel Club has failed in its efforts to avert a national tragedy. Now the club's members are determined to stop further violence and plug a leak of information that compromises the safety of the nation. The murder of the director of the Library of Congress provides another clue to the puzzle, while the added help of a sexy con artist named Annabelle Conroy puts a potential wrinkle in the Camel Club's ongoing efforts. Calling the novelist "a master at building suspense," Huntley predicted that the high-octane ending of *The Camel Club* "will leave readers breathless," and *Library Journal* contributor Ken Bolton wrote that the novel's "terrifyingly vivid plot has more twists and turns than any conspiracy theorist could ever conceive." Reviewing *The Collectors, Booklist* contributor Allison Block cited Baldacci's "crisp, economical prose" and wrote that the novel's "cast of spies, misfits, and assassins" will prompt "even the most patriotic citizen question the American political system."

In *Stone Cold,* another Camel Club adventure, con artist Annabelle Conroy seeks the help of her old friend Stone after she scams a murderous casino owner. Meanwhile Stone, a former CIA assassin, finds himself targeted by a security expert hoping to settle an old score. "When Baldacci is on fire, nobody can touch him, and this is an exhilarating thriller," wrote *Booklist* contributor David Pitt. "Gripping, chilling and full of surprises," remarked a critic in *Publishers Weekly.*

Baldacci turns to murder in *Split Second* and its sequels *Hour Game* and *Simple Genius,* all of which feature former Secret Service agents Sean King and Michelle Maxwell. Retired from the service and working as an attorney, King returns to sleuthing when a colleague is found dead. Active agent Maxwell is drawn in to the

Cover of Baldacci's 2000 novel Wish You Well, *featuring an illustration by Franco Accornero.* (Warner Books, 2000. Reproduced by permission.)

hunt when the man she is assigned to guard goes missing, the target of kidnappers. As more victims surface, the two team up on a mystery that grows more complex with every new clue. In *Hour Game* King and Maxwell join forces to track down a serial killer with a timely signature: each victim is found wearing a wristwatch on which time has stopped. As the murders continue, the trail leads to the Battle family, a small-town, Virginia clan whose mysterious past is unearthed by the sleuths as they close in on the fastidious killer. In a *Booklist* review of *Split Second,* Kristine Huntley wrote that the "thriller is sustained by the pulse-pounding suspense [Baldacci's] . . . fans have come to expect," and a *Publishers Weekly* reviewer dubbed the sequel an "utterly absorbing, complex mystery-thriller that spins in unexpected directions." Noting that the villain's identity remains hidden until the novel's final pages, the *Publishers Weekly* reviewer added that *Hour Game* rewards readers with a "snappy surprise ending will have Baldacci's many fans remembering why they love this author so much." In *Simple Genius,* the duo investigates the death of scientist at Babbage Town, a top-secret think-tank connected to a CIA training center. Compli-

cating matters is Maxwell's puzzling, self-destructive behavior, which prompts a stay at a mental health facility. Though some reviewers viewed *Simple Genius* as the weakest of Baldacci's King and Maxwell novels, Gilbert Cruz, writing in *Entertainment Weekly,* noted that the author's "psychological look into a familiar character . . . marks the biggest departure" from his standard fare.

With *Wish You Well* Baldacci jumps genres, writing a coming-of-age novel that takes place in the 1940s. The story involves twelve-year-old Lou Cardinal and her younger brother Oz, who are sent from their home in New York City to live with an elderly relative on a farm in rural Virginia after their parents are injured in an automobile accident. After their father dies and the mother is rendered incapacitated, Lou and Oz struggle to adapt, both to their family's tragedy and the strange habits of their eccentric and single-minded great grandmother Louisa. Reviewing the novel for *Publishers Weekly,* a critic wrote that "Baldacci triumphs with his best novel yet," calling *Wish You Well* "an utterly captivating drama" that "has a huge heart." In *Kliatt,* Judith H. Silverman dubbed the young-adult novel as an "an excellent portrait of race and class distinction of the time and place," while Kathy Piehl predicted in *Library Journal* that "readers of historical fiction will welcome [Baldacci's] . . . debut in the genre."

Baldacci's first work for children, *Fries Alive!,* is part of the "Freddy and the French Fries" series concerning boy genius Freddy Funkhouser. When nine-year-old Freddy combines nanotechnology with his father's special brand of potatoes, he creates a rowdy gang of five life-size French fries. Freddy, his pal Howie Kapowie, and the fries join forces to compete in the annual Founders' Day Parade float contest. They take top prize from town bully Adam Spanker and his father, whose snazzy Patty Cakes restaurant has threatened to put the Funkhouser's Burger Castle out of business. "Baldacci's over-the-top action vaults at breakneck speed from one crisis to another," noted *Booklist* reviewer Kay Weisman. A mysterious apparition is at the center of *The Mystery of Silas Finklebean,* a sequel to *Fries Alive!* While preparing for a local science fair, Freddy and his group of spuds spot a ghostly spirit inhabiting a tunnel beneath the Burger Castle. When he discovers the lab of inventor Silas Finklebean, Freddy enlists the fries to help him duplicate the scientist's time-travel experiments.

Baldacci dedicates much of his time to his family, as well as to literacy and other social causes, and he serves as an ambassador to the National Multiple Sclerosis Society in honor of a sister who suffers from the debilitating illness. His first love, however, is writing. "I am always thinking about and seeking story ideas," the author remarked on his home page. "As a writer, you can never 'turn off' our passion for the written word and love of a great story. So I watch life, listen intently, and basically drive everyone around me a bit crazy as I absorb every environment in which I find myself."

Biographical and Critical Sources

PERIODICALS

ASHA Leader, October 16, 2007, Marat Moore, "A Passion for Literacy," p. 22.

Booklist, November 1, 1995, review of *Absolute Power,* p. 434; November 15, 1996, Gilbert Taylor, review of *Absolute Power,* p. 548; October 15, 1997, Donna Seaman, review of *Total Control,* p. 362; September 1, 1998, Gilbert Taylor, review of *The Simple Truth,* p. 5; October 1, 1999, Emily Melton and Gilbert Taylor, review of *Saving Faith,* p. 307; June 1, 2001, Whitney Scott, review of *Wish You Well,* p. 1908; November 1, 2001, Kristine Huntley, review of *Last Man Standing,* p. 442; November 1, 2002, Kristine Huntley, review of *The Christmas Train,* p. 450; September 1, 2004, Kristine Huntley, review of *Hour Game,* p. 4; July, 2005, Kay Weisman, review of *Fries Alive!,* p.

Baldacci turns to a younger readership with The Mystery of Silas Finklebean, *part of his "Freddy and the French Fries" series featuring artwork by Rudy Baldacci.* (Little, Brown, 2006. Reproduced by permission.)

1924; September 1, 2005, Kristine Huntley, review of *The Camel Club,* p. 5; July, 2006, Kay Weisman, review of *Fries Alive!,* p. 1924; September 1, 2006, Allison Block, review of *The Collectors,* p. 6; October 1, 2007, David Pitt, review of *Stone Cold,* p. 6.

Bulletin of the Center for Children's Books, September, 2005, Hope Morrison, review of *Fries Alive!,* p. 6.

Entertainment Weekly, April 27, 2007, Gilbert Cruz, review of *Simple Genius,* p. 144.

Kirkus Reviews, October 15, 1995, review of *Absolute Power,* p. 1444; September 15, 1998, review of *The Simple Truth,* p. 1302; October 1, 2002, review of *The Christmas Train,* p. 1411; July 15, 2003, review of *Split Second,* p. 921; August 15, 2004, review of *Hour Game,* p. 756; May 15, 2005, review of *Fries Alive!,* p. 584; September 1, 2005, review of *The Camel Club,* p. 929; July 15, 2006, review of *The Collectors,* p. 687; April 1, 2007, review of *Simple Genius.*

Kliatt, January, 2002, Judith H. Silverman, review of *Wish You Well,* p. 8.

Library Journal, January, 1997, Kathy Piehl, review of *Total Control,* p. 142; November 15, 1997, Joanna M. Burkhardt, review of *Total Control,* p. 88; April 1, 1998, review of *The Simple Truth,* p. 143; May 1, 2000, Michael Adams, review of *Saving Faith,* p. 170; September 1, 2000, Kathy Piehl, review of *Wish You Well,* p. 248; October 15, 2004, Ken Bolton, review of *Hour Game,* p. 52; January 1, 2007, Jeff Ayers, review of *The Collectors,* p. 51.

New York Times, December 11, 1997, Christopher Lehmann-Haupt, "The Lottery as Thriller: Hey, You Never Know," p. E12.

New York Times Book Review, February 25, 1996, Jean Hanff Korelitz, review of *Absolute Power,* p. 21.

Publishers Weekly, October 16, 1995, review of *Absolute Power,* p. 42; December 2, 1996, review of *Absolute Power,* p. 41; April 14, 1997, review of *Total Control,* p. 261; October 6, 1997, review of *The Winner,* p. 73; March 2, 1998, review of *The Winner,* p. 30; October 5, 1998, review of *The Simple Truth,* p. 78; November 8, 1999, review of *Saving Faith,* p. 16; July 17, 2000, review of *Wish You Well,* p. 171; November 5, 2001, review of *Last Man Standing,* p. 42; December 10, 2001, Jeff Zaleski interview with Baldacci, p. 47; August 18, 2003, review of *Split Second,* p. 58; September 20, 2004, review of *Hour Game,* p. 46; November 8, 2004, Daisy Maryles, "He Got Game," p. 14; May 30, 2005, review of *Fries Alive!,* p. 61; August 22, 2005, review of *The Camel Club,* p. 35; March 26, 2007, review of *Simple Genius,* p. 68; August 27, 2007, review of *Stone Cold,* p. 59; September 3, 2007, Melissa Mia Hall, interview with Baldacci, p. 36.

School Library Journal, June, 2005, Elizabeth Bird, review of *Fries Alive!,* p. 148; April, 2006, Elaine E. Knight, review of *The Mystery of Silas Finklebean,* p. 133; June, 2006, Elizabeth Bird, review of *Fries Alive!,* p. 148.

Times Literary Supplement, June 25, 1999, review of *The Simple Truth,* p. 37.

Washingtonian, August, 2007, Leslie Milk, "Mystery Man," p. 52.

Writer, June, 1997, Lewis Burke Frumkes, interview with Baldacci, p. 11.

Writer's Digest, January, 1997, Audrey T. Hingley, interview with Baldacci, p. 30.

ONLINE

David Baldacci Home Page, http://www.davidbaldacci.com (November 10, 2007).

Hatchette Book Group Web site, http://www.hachettebookgroupusa.com/ (November 10, 2007).*

*　　*　　*

BECKER, Bonny

Personal

Married; children: two. *Education:* Scripps College, B.A. (psychology); San Francisco State University, M.F.A. (English/creative writing).

Addresses

Home and office—Seattle, WA. *E-mail*—bjb@site7000.com.

Career

Author. Worked variously as a waitress, store clerk, substitute teacher, hotel maid, typist, photographer, journalist, editor and corporate communications manager.

Member

Society of Children's Book Writers and Illustrators.

Writings

The Quiet Way Home, illustrated by Benrei Huang, Henry Holt (New York, NY), 1995.

The Christmas Crocodile, illustrated by David Small, Simon & Schuster (New York, NY), 1998.

Tickly Prickly, illustrated by Shari Halpern, HarperFestival (New York, NY), 1999.

My Brother, the Robot (middle-grade novel), Dutton Children's Books (New York, NY), 2001.

Just a Minute, illustrated by Jack E. Davis, Simon & Schuster (New York, NY), 2003.

An Ant's Day Off, illustrated by Nina Laden, Simon & Schuster (New York, NY), 2003.

Holbrook: A Lizard's Tale, illustrated by Abby Carter, Clarion Books (New York, NY), 2006.

A Visitor for Bear, illustrated by Kady MacDonald Denton, Candlewick Press (New York, NY), 2008.

A Birthday for Bear, illustrated by Kady MacDonald Denton, Candlewick Press (New York, NY), 2009.

The Magical Ms. Plum, Knopf (New York, NY), 2009.

Sidelights

Bonny Becker's path to becoming a writer involved a number of job and career changes. Before earning her master's degree in English and creative writing, Becker worked as a waitress, photographer, journalist, and a corporate communications manager. As she noted on her home page, traveling her diversified career path took some time, but "it's been worth the wait. It's given me a lot of 'me,' to put in my stories." Even her wackiest story ideas come from ideas and experiences in real life, she asserted. Becker's work includes picture books for young readers such as *The Christmas Crocodile, Holbrook: A Lizard's Tale, Just a Minute,* and *A Visitor for Bear.* Featuring artwork by such noted illustrators as David Small, Abby Carter, and Kady MacDonald Denton, Becker's stories have been praised for their unusual storylines. As a *Publishers Weekly* contributor wrote of Becker's humorous picture book *Just a Minute,* which finds a boy carried into another time continuum while waiting for his always-tardy mom, the author's "over-the-top tale about pint-sized fear and loathing will likely have kids nodding and grinning in recognition." In addition, Becker has also written the middle-grade novel *My Brother, the Robot,* which finds a preteen faced with keeping pace with a perfect sibling. Problems arise when the boy's parents order a robot named Simon, hoping the mechanical boy will be a flawless son. The novel's "text is clever and comical," according to a *Kirkus Reviews* writer, the critic adding that kids should enjoy" *My Brother, the Robot* and its focus on self-acceptance.

Featuring illustrations by Carter, *Holbrook* tells the story of a lizard who is struggling to make it as an artist. In an attempt to gain respect among family and friends, Holbrook ventures out to the Golden City where he has dreams of making it big. Along the way, the lizard makes an assortment of friends but also learns an important lesson about trust. A *Kirkus Reviews* critic noted that *Holbrook* contains an "earnest message" but found the plot "predictable." In contrast, Robin Gioia wrote in *School Library Journal* that *Holbrook* is "a fun adventure that will capture the imagination" of young readers. Becker employs "storytelling techniques [that] yield . . . an amusing cast of rich characters," Gioia added of the illustrated middle-grade novel. Equally enthusiastic in her *Booklist* review of *Holbrook,* Carolyn Phelan noted that Becker's tale "moves along quickly, enlivened by dramatic situations, dry wit, and [Carter's] dynamic full-page illustrations."

Biographical and Critical Sources

PERIODICALS

Booklist, December 1, 1995, Hazel Rochman, review of *The Quiet Way Home,* p. 640; July, 1999, Ilene Cooper, review of *Tickly Prickly,* p. 1949; January 1, 2007, review of *Holbrook: A Lizard's Tale,* p. 96; September 1, 1998, Ilene Cooper, review of *The Christmas Crocodile,* p. 131.

Bulletin of the Center for Children's Books, February, 2007, Hope Morrison, review of *Holbrook,* p. 243.

Children's Bookwatch, March, 2004, Diane C. Donovan, review of *Just a Minute,* p. 6.

Kirkus Reviews, May 15, 2003, review of *An Ant's Day Off,* p. 745; September 1, 2003, review of *Just a Minute,* p. 1120; September 15, 2003, review of *My Brother, the Robot,* p. 1353; October 16, 2006, review of *Holbrook,* p. 1065.

Publishers Weekly, May 12, 2003, review of *An Ant's Day Off,* p. 66; September 15, 2003, review of *Just a Minute,* p. 64; September 28, 1998, review of *The Christmas Crocodile,* p. 58.

School Library Journal, January, 1996, Christina Dorr, review of *The Quiet Way Home,* p. 76; October, 1998, Lisa Falk, review of *The Christmas Crocodile,* p. 39; August, 1999, Ogla R. Barnes, review of *Tickly Prickly*; October, 2001, review of *My Brother, the Robot,* p. 148; July, 2003, Wendy Woodfill, review of *An Ant's Day Off,* p. 87; January, 2004, Rachel Fox, review of *Just a Minute,* p. 87; December, 2006, Robyn Gioia, review of *Holbrook,* p. 94.

ONLINE

Adams Literary Web site, http://www.adamsliterary.com/ (October 27, 2007).

Bonny Becker Home Page, http://www.bonnybecker.com (October 27, 2007).

   * * *

BERNARDO, Anilú
(Ann Reynold)

Personal

Born in Cuba; married Jim Reynold; children: Stephanie, Amanda. *Education:* Florida State University, B.A., 1971, M.A., 1980.

Addresses

Agent—c/o Reynold Public Relations, Inc., 7301 SW 7th St., Plantation, FL 33317. *E-mail*—anilu_bernardo@comcast.net.

Career

Author

Member

PEN American Center.

Writings

Un día con mis tías/A Day with My Aunts (bilingual picture book), illustrated by Christina Rodriguez, Piñata (Houston, TX), 2006.

FOR YOUNG ADULTS

Jumping off to Freedom, Piñata (Houston, TX), 1996.
Fitting In (short stories), Piñata (Houston, TX), 1996.
Loves Me, Loves Me Not, Piñata (Houston, TX), 1998.

Author's works have been published in Spanish.

Sidelights

Born in Cuba, Anilú Bernardo experienced first hand the difficulties of fitting in when her family fled Communist leader Fidel Castro's takeover in 1961 and moved to Miami, Florida. She spoke little English when she began school in the United States, but she wrote poems in Spanish and later expanded to writing fiction in both languages.

For Bernardo's first novel, *Jumping off to Freedom,* she interviewed *balseros,* Cuban men and women who made the voyage from Cuba on rafts, to develop the story of David. Unwilling to continue living under Castro, David's father builds a raft on which he, David, and another refugee can escape to the United States. As the three

Cover of Anilú Bernardo's novel **Loves Me, Loves Me Not,** *featuring artwork by Giovanni Mora.* (Illustration © 1998 by Arte Público Press/University of Houston. Reprinted by permission.)

are leaving, another refugee, Toro, demands to be taken along. *Jumping off to Freedom* tells a story of survival, as David faces sharks, storms, and both physical and emotional trauma. Eventually, he learns to trust Toro and that trust makes it possible for the group to reach Florida alive. In *Booklist* Anne O'Malley wrote that "survival story fans and readers looking for breath taking action will not be disappointed" in Bernardo's high-action tale.

Fitting In, a collection of short stories, draws on Bernardo's experiences after arriving in the United States: each of the five tales features a Cuban-American teen struggling to find a place among her peers. The stories "speak with a lively and authentic accent about the angst of bicultural, female adolescence," wrote Annie Ayres in *Booklist.* Esther Celis, writing for *Skipping Stones,* noted that, with effort, people can usually find something in common and in *Fitting In* Bernardo "communicates this with humor and eloquence."

Loves Me, Loves Me Not, a teen romance, "has depth in characterization and a recognizable Latino ambience," according to *Booklist* contributor Sally Estes. In the novel, Cuban-American teenager Maggie has a crush on cute basketball player Zach, whom she tutors in German. Maggie's friend Susie, trying to win over a boy named Carlos, suggests that she and Maggie double date, pairing up Maggie with Justin, the new boy at school. Although on the surface Bernardo's novel is about dating, it also deals with cultural misconceptions and prejudice and with Maggie's growing maturity and her realization that there is more to a person than what shows on the surface.

Along with her works for young adults, Bernardo has also penned a bilingual picture book for very young readers. *Un día con mis tías/A Day with My Aunts* is the story of a girl's day with her three aunts as well as a celebration of Cuban-American culture. From making empanadas to dancing the salsa, the narrator's day is full of family fun. "This story spills over with life, laughter, food, and music," noted Maria Otero-Boisvert in *School Library Journal.* A *Kirkus Reviews* contributor noted that "Bernardo's story is full of family activity," and added that recipes for the food featured in the book's text are included in both Spanish and English in the endpapers.

Biographical and Critical Sources

PERIODICALS

Booklist, May 1, 1996, Anne O'Malley, review of *Jumping off to Freedom,* p. 1498; December 15, 1996, Annie Ayres, review of *Fitting In,* p. 721; January 1, 1999,

Bernardo tells a bilingual story that draws readers into a close-knit Latino family in Un día con mis tías/A Day with My Aunts, *a picture book featuring artwork by Christina Rodriguez.* (Illustration © 2006 by Arte Público Press/University of Houston. Reprinted by permission.)

Sally Estes, review of *Loves Me, Loves Me Not,* p. 854; September 15, 1999, Stephanie Zvirin, review of *Loves Me, Loves Me Not,* p. 249.

Booklinks, January, 2005, Mayra Daniel and Chris Liska Carger, review of *Fitting In,* p. 54.

Book Report, September-October, 1996, Alma Marie Walls, review of *Jumping off to Freedom,* p. 35.

Kirkus Reviews, October 15, 2006, review of *Un día con mis tías/A Day with My Aunts,* p. 1065.

Publishers Weekly, September 16, 1996, review of *Fitting In,* p. 84.

School Library Journal, July, 1996, Gerry Larson, review of *Jumping off to Freedom,* p. 98; November, 1996, Melissa Hudak, review of *Fitting In,* p. 120; October, 2006, Maria Otero-Boisvert, review of *Un día con mis tías/A Day with My Aunts,* p. 144.

Skipping Stones, March-April, 1997, Esther Celis, review of *Fitting In,* p. 7.

Voice of Youth Advocates, June, 1996, review of *Jumping off to Freedom,* p. 92; April, 1997, review of *Fitting In,* p. 27; August, 1999, review of *Loves Me, Loves Me Not,* p. 182.

ONLINE

Arte Público Press Web site, http://www.arte.uh.edu/ (October 19, 2007), "Anilú Bernardo."

BRIGGS, Raymond 1934-
(Raymond Redvers Briggs)

Personal

Born January 18, 1934, in London, England; son of Ernest Redvers (in milk delivery) and Ethel Briggs; married Jean Taprell Clark (a painter), 1963 (died, 1973); partner's name Liz (a retired fteacher). *Education:* Attended Wimbledon School of Art, 1949-53; received National Diploma in Design, 1953; attended Slade School of Fine Art, 1955-57; University of London, D.F.A., 1957. *Politics:* "Green." *Hobbies and other interests:* Reading, gardening, growing fruit, modern jazz, secondhand bookshops.

Addresses

Home and office—Weston, Underhill Lane, Westmeston, Hassocks, Sussex BN6 8XG, England.

Career

Illustrator and author of books for children, beginning 1957. Brighton Polytechnic, Sussex, England, part-time lecturer in illustration, 1961-87; teacher at Slade School of Fine Art and Central Art School. Set designer and playwright. Member of British Campaign for Nuclear Disarmament, beginning 1982. *Military service:* British Army, 1953-55.

Member

Chartered Society of Designers (fellow), Society of Industrial Artists, Dairy Farmer's Association, Groucho Club.

Awards, Honors

British Library Association Kate Greenaway Medal, commendation, 1964, for *Fee Fi Fo Fum,* winner, 1966, for *Mother Goose Treasury,* and 1973, for *Father Christmas,* and high commendation, 1978, for *The Snowman;* Spring Book Festival Picture Book honor, *Book World,* 1970, for *The Elephant and the Bad Baby;* Children's Book Showcase, Children's Book Council, 1974, for *Father Christmas;* Art Books for Children citations, Brooklyn Museum and Brooklyn Public Library, 1975, for *Father Christmas,* and 1979, for *The Snowman;* Francis Williams Illustration Awards, British Book Trust, 1977, for *Father Christmas,* and 1982, for *The Snowman; Boston Globe/Horn Book* Award for Illustration, Premio Critici in Erba, Bologna Book Fair, Lewis Carroll Shelf Award, and Dutch Silver Pen Award, all 1979, and *Redbook* Award, 1986, all for *The Snowman;* Other Award, Children's Rights Workshop, 1982, for *When the Wind Blows;* British Academy of Film and Television Arts Award for Best Children's Program—Drama, 1982, and Academy Award nomination for best

Raymond Briggs (Photograph © by Allen Daniels. Reproduced by permission.)

animated short film, 1982, both for *The Snowman;* most outstanding radio program, Broadcasting Press Guild, 1983, for *When the Wind Blows.*

Writings

SELF ILLUSTRATED

The Strange House, Hamish Hamilton (London England), 1961.

Midnight Adventure, Hamish Hamilton (London, England), 1961.

Ring-a-Ring o' Roses (verse), Coward (New York, NY), 1962.

Sledges to the Rescue, Hamish Hamilton (London, England), 1963.

(Editor) *The White Land: A Picture Book of Traditional Rhymes and Verses,* Coward (New York, NY), 1963.

Fee Fi Fo Fum: A Picture Book of Nursery Rhymes, Coward (New York, NY), 1964.

(Editor) *The Mother Goose Treasury,* Coward (New York, NY), 1966.

Jim and the Beanstalk, Coward (New York, NY), 1970.

Father Christmas, Coward (New York, NY), 1973.

Father Christmas Goes on Holiday, Coward (New York, NY), 1975.

Fungus the Bogeyman, Hamish Hamilton (London, England), 1977.

Gentleman Jim, Hamish Hamilton (London, England), 1980.

When the Wind Blows, Schocken (New York, NY), 1982, reprinted, Penguin (London, England), 2005.

Fungus the Bogeyman Plop-up Book, Hamish Hamilton (London, England), 1982.

The Tin-Pot Foreign General and the Old Iron Woman, Little, Brown (New York, NY), 1984.

Unlucky Wally, Hamish Hamilton (London, England), 1987.

The Bear, Random House (New York, NY), 1994.

The Man, Random House (New York, NY), 1995.

Ethel and Ernest, Knopf (New York, NY), 1999.

Ug: Boy Genius of the Stone Age and His Search for Soft Trousers, J. Cape (London, England), 2001, published as *Ug: Boy Genius of the Stone Age,* Knopf (New York, NY), 2002.

Ivor the Invisible, 4 Books (London, England), 2001.

The Puddleman, Cape (London, England), 2004.

"SNOWMAN" SERIES

The Snowman, Random House (New York, NY), 1978, reprinted, Dragonfly (New York, NY), 2006.

Building the Snowman, Little, Brown (New York, NY), 1985.

Dressing Up, Little, Brown (New York, NY), 1985.

Walking in the Air, Little, Brown (New York, NY), 1985.

The Party, Little, Brown (New York, NY), 1985.

The Snowman Pop-up, Hamish Hamilton (London, England), 1986.

The Snowman Storybook, Random House (New York, NY), 1990.

The Snowman Flap Book, Random House (New York, NY), 1991.

The Snowman Tell-the-Time Book, Hamish Hamilton (London, England), 1991.

The Snowman: Things to Touch and Feel, See and Sniff, Random House (New York, NY), 1994.

The Snowman: A Fun-shaped Play Book, Random House (New York, NY), 1999.

ILLUSTRATOR

(With others) Julian Sorell Huxley, *Wonderful World of Life,* Doubleday (New York, NY), 1958.

Ruth Manning-Sanders, *Peter and the Piskies,* Oxford University Press (Oxford, England), 1958, Roy (New York, NY), 1966.

Barbara Ker Wilson, *The Wonderful Cornet,* 1958.

A. Stephen Tring, *Peter's Busy Day,* 1959.

Alfred Leo Duggan, *Look at Castles,* Hamish Hamilton (London, England), 1960, published as *The Castle Book,* Pantheon (New York, NY), 1961.

Alfred Leo Duggan, *Arches and Spires,* Hamish Hamilton (London, England), 1961, Pantheon (New York, NY), 1962.

Meriol Trevor, *William's Wild Day Out,* 1963.

Jacynth Hope-Simpson, editor, *The Hamish Hamilton Book of Myths and Legends,* Hamish Hamilton (London, England), 1964.

William Mayne, *Whistling Rufus,* Hamish Hamilton (London, England), 1964, Dutton (New York, NY), 1965.

Elfrida Vipont, *Stevie,* Hamish Hamilton (London, England), 1965.

Ruth Manning-Sanders, editor, *Hamish Hamilton Book of Magical Beasts,* Hamish Hamilton (London, England), 1965, published as *A Book of Magical Beasts,* T. Nelson (Nashville, TN), 1970.

James Aldridge, *The Flying Nineteen,* Hamish Hamilton (London, England), 1966.

Mabel Esther Allan, *The Way over Windle,* Methuen (London, England), 1966.

Bruce Carter (pseudonym of Richard Alexander Hough), *Jimmy Murphy and the White Duesenberg,* Coward (New York, NY), 1968.

Bruce Carter, *Nuvolari and the Alfa Romeo,* Coward (New York, NY), 1968.

Nicholas Fisk, *Lindbergh: The Lone Flier,* Coward (New York, NY), 1968.

Nicholas Fisk, *Richthofen: The Red Baron,* Coward (New York, NY), 1968.

William Mayne, editor, *The Hamish Hamilton Book of Giants,* Hamish Hamilton (London, England), 1968, published as *William Mayne's Book of Giants,* Dutton (New York, NY), 1969.

Michael Brown, *Shackelton's Epic Voyage,* Coward (New York, NY), 1969.

Elfrida Vipont, *The Elephant and the Bad Baby,* Coward (New York, NY), 1969.

Showell Styles, *First up Everest,* Coward (New York, NY), 1969.

James Reeves, *Christmas Book,* Dutton (New York, NY), 1970.

Ian Serraillier, *The Tale of Three Landlubbers,* Hamish Hamilton (London, England), 1970, Coward (New York, NY), 1971.

Virginia Haviland, editor, *The Fairy Tale Treasury,* Coward (New York, NY), 1972.

Ruth Manning-Sanders, editor, *Festivals,* Heinemann (London, England), 1972, Dutton (New York, NY), 1973.

James Reeves, *The Forbidden Forest,* Heinemann (London, England), 1973.

(With Mitsumasa Anno) *All in a Day,* Philomel (New York, NY), 1986.

Allan Ahlberg, *The Adventures of Bert,* Farrar, Straus & Giroux, (New York, NY), 2001.

Allan Ahlberg, *A Bit More Bert,* Farrar, Straus & Giroux, (New York, NY), 2002.

Also illustrator of a book of Cornish fairy stories for Oxford University Press, 1957

MEDIA ADAPTATIONS

The Snowman (animated film), TV Cartoons, 1982.

When the Wind Blows (stage play; produced in London, England, 1983, then New York, NY, 1988), Samuel French (New York, NY), 1983.

When the Wind Blows (radio play), British Broadcasting Corp., 1983.
Gentleman Jim (stage play), produced in Nottingham, England, 1985.
When the Wind Blows (animated film), TV Cartoons/Meltdown Productions, 1987.
Father Christmas (animated film), 1991.
The Bear (animated film), 1999.
Ivor the Invisible (animated film), 2001.
Fungus the Bogeyman (animated film), 2004.

The Snowman and *Father Christmas* were released on DVD in 1993 and 1997 respectively, and were released together on DVD, with material from *Father Christmas Goes on Holiday,* in 1998.

Adaptations

Michelle Knudsen and Maggie Downer adapted *The Snowman* as *Raymond Briggs' The Snowman,* Random House, 2003.

Sidelights

Raymond Briggs is an award-winning author and illustrator of popular books for children and of darkly satirical works for adults. He has also drawn hundreds of pictures for collections of traditional nursery rhymes and fairy tales, revisited old favorites like "Jack and the Beanstalk," and written his own award-winning stories. One of these, *Fungus the Bogeyman,* is a cartoon-style look at a repulsive yet humane imaginary world full of filth and wordplay. Another, *The Snowman,* is a wordless story, poignant and more softly illustrated, while *When the Wind Blows,* a devastating, understated cartoon-style work geared for adults, portrays a middle-aged working-class couple before, during, and after a nuclear war. The characters and settings in each of Briggs's books often reflect elements of the author/illustrator's past.

Briggs had "an uneventful but happy childhood and home life," as he told Lee Bennett Hopkins in *Books Are by People.* "My parents were happily married. Their faces turn up constantly in my illustrations but quite unconsciously." "I hated school for there was too much emphasis on teamwork, competition, sports, science, and mathematics—all the opposite interests of an 'arty' type," he recalled of his experiences as a student at the Rutlish School for Boys. Briggs drew constantly and as an only child he was somewhat indulged by his parents. When, at age fifteen, he said he would like to study art, he did not receive the usual parental objection "that I didn't want to learn a useful trade," as he later explained in a *Publishers Weekly* interview. As Briggs revealed in *Designer,* the principal of the school Briggs hoped to attend was dismayed that the boy wanted to be a cartoonist, however. "He told me it wasn't an occupation for gentlemen. It was a great shock to realise that these things weren't respectable. So I changed to painting." As the author/illustrator later told Nicholas

Among Briggs's many self-illustrated children's books is his fairy-tale-inspired **Jim and the Beanstalk.** (Paperstar, 1997. Illustration © 1970 by Raymond Briggs. Used by permission of Coward-McCann, an imprint of Penguin Putnam Books for Young Readers, a division of Penguin Putnam Inc. All rights reserved.)

Wroe in the London *Guardian,* "when you're only fifteen and the big man with a beard tells you what to do, you generally do it."

In his painting courses Briggs did a great deal of figure drawing, which he recommends as "absolutely perfect training for an illustrator, in that you learn about tone and colour, and figure composition in general." It was a very traditional art education, similar to that of Renaissance painters: abstract art was not taught, and cartooning and illustration were scorned as too "commercial." Briggs continued to practice illustration in his spare time anyway. Ultimately, when he realized that painting was not really his strength and was unprofitable as well, he started accepting illustration assignments from publishers and advertising agencies.

"Out of all the work I did, I must have suited the children's book world best," Briggs remarked in *Designer,* "because that was the sort of work that increasingly came in. I didn't choose it; it chose me. I entered the field at a very good time, when there were some marvelous books being written and I was lucky enough to get some to illustrate." *The Mother Goose Treasury,* for which Briggs did nearly nine hundred pictures, was one example. Reviewers praised it for its completeness and for Briggs's exuberant illustrations, and in addition he received the Kate Greenaway Medal for his work. He found most other illustration projects "appalling," however, "and it was this that made me start writing," he maintained. "I could see simple grammatical faults even, and felt that if publishers were willing to publish tripe like that, I couldn't do worse. I wrote two or three little stories, and showed the first one to the editor just to get his advice—to see if he thought I might ever write anything. To my absolute amazement he said he'd publish it. To me, that just showed the standard. I thought it was staggering that someone who knew nothing about writing could make a first attempt and have it published, just like that." Although he has continued to write original stories, Briggs has also illustrated dozens of other story collections, as well as texts by writers such as Allan Ahlberg, Bruce Carter, and Elfrida Vipont.

Father Christmas was one of Briggs's first original books to become widely popular. Instead of the usual jolly or saintly image of Saint Nick, Briggs presents a grumbling but dutiful old fellow with very human foibles. Not fond of winter, Father Christmas dreams of a beach holiday and complains about "blooming chimneys" and "blooming soot." As Briggs observed in *Junior Bookshelf,* "I think the character of Father Christmas is very much based on my father," a man who delivered milk early each morning. "The jobs are similar and they both grumble a lot in a fairly humorous way." In the *Guardian,* Briggs described himself as a "miserable git," a fact that suggests that his depiction of

"Santa Claus as an over-worked curmudgeon," as Wroe characterized Saint Nick, also works the illustrator's own personality into the story. Briggs also drew on his own past for details of Father Christmas's house and other aspects of his life, sometimes unconsciously. Thirty years after *Father Christmas* was published, the characters were featured on stamps for the Royal Mail in the United Kingdom.

A few years after *Father Christmas* came *Fungus the Bogeyman,* Briggs's story about and descriptive guide to the mucky lives of bogeys, creatures that revel in filth and rise each night to frighten humans. Fungus is a happily married bogey who wonders about the meaning of his life and wistfully dreams of a day when bogeys and humans will get along with one other.

The Snowman, published the year after *Fungus the Bogeyman,* is a very different book, but like the earlier story it also draws on Briggs's life. The artist used his own house and garden as the setting for his gentle, loving tale. Unlike *Fungus the Bogeyman, The Snowman* is a wholesome, wordless story describing how a snowman comes to life and befriends the boy who made it. During a magical night, the snowman shares the human world and the world of snow people with the boy. In

Translated into numerous languages, Briggs's **The Snowman** *has become a childhood classic.* (Illustration © 1978 by Raymond Briggs. Used by permission of Random House Children's Books, a division of Random House, Inc.)

the morning the boy sadly discovers that his friend has mostly melted away. Briggs conveys his story without words, and decided to use colored pencil rather than pen and watercolor to illustrate the book. "I wanted to avoid the abrupt change that takes place when a brutal black pen line is scratched on top of a quiet pencil drawing," he explained of this decision during his acceptance speech for the *Boston Globe/Horn Book* Award. In addition to being a great success with readers, *The Snowman* has also been adapted for stage and screen. Images from the book have also made their way onto various products and memorabilia, as well as into Briggs's more recent books.

Like *The Snowman, The Bear* is a story of friendship and loss. Young Tilly becomes friends with an enormous polar bear who comes to stay with her at night and plays during the day. Her new friend's bear habits are frustrating to Tilly, however, and she realizes that bears and humans cannot share a house after all. The tale ends as Bear trudges into the Arctic wilderness where he belongs and dives into the water "whose chill one can almost feel—an indication of Briggs's power to draw readers into his pictorial storytelling," wrote a *Publishers Weekly* contributor. Noting the book's cartoon-strip feel, an *Economist* writer noted that *The Bear,* like many of Briggs's titles, "must be all the more enthralling to children for seeming like that." In *Booklist,* Annie Ayres dubbed the book a "magical winter escapade."

Briggs employs a different storytelling strategy with *The Man.* Instead of using very few words, as in *The Bear,* or no words at all, as in *The Snowman,* he emphasizes the dialogue between young John and the seven-inch-tall man the boy discovers in his room one night. The tiny man causes a lot of trouble between John and his parents, demands food but complains about everything John brings him, and generally makes a mess out of John's life. As John and the man begin to understand each other, however, themes such as self-image, religion, diversity, and philosophy are explored through their conversations. "Busy panel art drolly portrays the contentious rapport between John and Man," explained a *Publishers Weekly* contributor. Writing in *Booklist,* Susan Dove Lempke recommended the title for an audience older than the usual picture-book crowd, writing that they "will appreciate the passionate debate between the characters and the earthy humor Briggs works in." Noting that *The Man* addresses the most universal question "What does it mean to be a human?" Peter F. Neumeyer wrote in *Horn Book* that, rather than using a traditional narrative, Briggs combines sequential-paneled art and dialogue to relay his story. The author/illustrator "employs the limitations and advantages of this genre with astonishing virtuosity and to remarkable effect," Neumeyer added.

Ug: Boy Genius of the Stone Age is the tale of a search for soft trousers. Ug does not understand why he must wear stone pants or kick a stone ball in sports. He sees things in the world—trees being made of wood, for instance—that his peers and parents do not seem to understand. "Beneath the satiric barbs there's a touch of poignancy to this tale," wrote a *Kirkus Reviews* contributor. According to *School Library Journal* Shelley B. Sutherland, "it is a deceptively simple and wise look at some potentially weighty issues, done with a deft, sure, and amusingly light touch."

The idea for *The Puddleman* was inspired by Briggs's relationship with the grandchild of his partner, Liz. The little girl stated her belief that puddles are a substance of their own, and are not made from anything else. The main character of *The Puddleman,* Tom, puts on his rain boots to go out for a walk with his grandfather. Even though it has not rained lately, Tom insists that the puddles will be there. The boy is proven right when the invisible Puddleman places puddles carefully in Tom's path. "Briggs uses his signature comic-strip format to dramatize each bit of dialogue with panache," wrote Joanna Rudge Long in a review of *The Puddleman* for *Horn Book.* Kat Kan, writing in *Booklist,* dubbed the book a "a charmingly wacky tale."

Originally intended for adults, *When the Wind Blows* is Briggs's cartoon-style comment on how unprepared ordinary people are to deal with nuclear war. Its two characters are a retired couple living in rural Britain. They survived the bombing of England during World War II, and they ignorantly expect the next war to be much the same. They build a useless bomb shelter, following government guidelines, and cheerily go on with life after the bomb drops, wondering why the water is eventually shut off and nothing comes in on the radio. Briggs got the idea for the book when he saw a documentary on the effects of nuclear war. "I imagined what would actually happen if some ordinary people were told there would be war in three days' time," he told Bart Mills in a *Los Angeles Times* interview. Several critics judged *When the Wind Blows* too grim for young readers, and Briggs agreed. "We found it went into the children's bookshops and started selling there too, to my surprise," the author explained to *Times Educational Supplement* interview Richard North.

Like *When the Wind Blows, The Tin-Pot Foreign General and the Old Iron Woman* takes on serious issues through its focus on the Falklands war, and *Ethel and Ernest* depicts the working-class life of Briggs's parents. Because much of the first half of Briggs's life is recorded in the latter book, the work clearly shows the influences his childhood had on his work. Discussing the way Briggs's parents are depicted in *Ethel and Ernest,* a critic wrote on the British Council Contemporary Writers Web site that, "in their aspirations, stoicism, arguments and care for each other, we overhear typical British attitudes to class, sex, education and party politics." Gordon Flagg, writing for *Booklist,* noted that Briggs's drawings "well evoke period and milieu, and his spot-on dialogue nails the characters." A *Publishers*

Weekly also commented on the dialogue in *Ethel and Ernest,* calling it "heartbreakingly accurate," and "the pictures cinematic in their conveyance of delight and drama."

Briggs does not aim his books specifically at children or at adults. "Once children can read, I don't see this huge gulf between them and grown-ups," he commented in *Design Week.* "I just write and draw to please myself and feel it ought to please others," Briggs also noted in *Publishers Weekly.* His work appeals to all ages, in fact. His more adult-oriented books reach younger readers with their cartoon style, and the so-called children's books often discuss adult issues.

Despite his success as an illustrator, Briggs has expressed the wish that he were a "proper writer, having to do only the words," as he wrote in the *Guardian.* "Proper writers can start at the beginning, go on till they get to the end, then stop and hand it in," he explained. However, he added, there are advantages to the sequential art format he employs. Discussing *Ethel and Ernest,* he noted: "It is almost a mini-biography and even contains social history yet there is not a word of narration, only speech bubbles. It is the thing I am most pleased about in these books."

Biographical and Critical Sources

BOOKS

Children's Literature Review, Volume 10, Thomson Gale (Detroit, MI), 1986.

Hopkins, Lee Bennett, *Books Are by People,* Citation Press, 1969.

Jones, Nicolette, *Blooming Books,* J. Cape (London, England), 2003.

Kilborn, Richard, *The Multi-Media Melting Pot: Marketing "When the Wind Blows,"* Comedia, 1986.

Twentieth-Century Children's Writers, St. James Press (Detroit, MI), 1983.

PERIODICALS

Booklist, February 1, 1995, Annie Ayres, review of *The Bear,* p. 1008; February 1, 1996, Susan Dove Lempke, review of *The Man,* p. 931; September 15, 1999, Gordon Flagg, review of *Ethel and Ernest,* p. 212; September 1, 2001, Ilene Cooper, review of *The Adventures of Bert,* p. 112; November 1, 2002, Julie Cummins, review of *A Bit More Bert,* p. 502; November 15, 2002, Michael Cart, review of *Ug: Boy Genius of the Stone Age,* p. 600; November 1, 2006, Kat Kan, review of *The Puddleman,* p. 58; February 15, 2007, Hazel Rochman, review of *Collected Poems for Children,* p. 75.

Bookseller, October 18, 2002, "Illustration Show," p. 34; July 18, 2003, "Briggs's Blooming Books," p. 22.

Bulletin of the Center for Children's Books, March, 1995, review of *The Bear,* p. 229; February, 1996, review of *The Man,* p. 185; January, 2003, review of *Ug,* p. 190.

Designer, October, 1982, review of *The Snowman,* pp. 8-9.

Design Week, September 6, 2001, Nick Smurthwaite, "Set in Stone," p. 56; November 4, 2004, "After a Thirty-Year Hiatus, Cartoonist Raymond Briggs Has Resurrected His Father Christmas Character on a Series of Festive Stamps for Royal Mail," p. 5.

Economist, November 26, 1994, review of *The Bear,* p. 101.

Guardian (London, England), November 2, 2002, Raymond Briggs, "Why I'd Like to Be a Proper Author"; December 18, 2004, Nicholas Wroe, "Bloomin' Christmas."

Horn Book, February, 1980, Raymond Briggs, *Boston Globe/Horn Book* Award acceptance speech, p. 96; March-April, 1995, Maeve Visser Knoth, review of *The Bear,* p. 182; May-June, 1996, Peter F. Neumeyer, review of *The Man,* p. 315; September-October, 2002, Martha V. Parravano, review of *A Bit More Bert,* p. 548; November-December, 2002, Sarah Ellis, review of *Ug,* p. 734; January, 2003, review of *A Bit More Bert,* p. 12; November-December, 2006, Joanna Rudge Long, review of *The Puddleman,* p. 697.

Junior Bookshelf, August, 1974, Raymond Briggs, "That Blooming Book," pp. 195-196.

Kirkus Reviews, September 15, 2002, review of *Ug,* p. 1385; October 15, 2006, review of *The Puddleman,* p. 1066.

Library Journal, September 15, 1999, Stephen Weiner, review of *Ethel and Ernest,* p. 72.

Lion and the Unicorn, Volume 7-8, 1983-84, Suzanne Rahn, "Beneath the Surface with *Fungus the Bogeyman.*"

Los Angeles Times, November 10, 1982, Bart Mills, "Author! Author! Wind Blowing Raymond Briggs' Way," Part V, p. 12.

Publishers Weekly, November 5, 1973, Jean P. Mercier, interview with Briggs, p. 12; November 14, 1994, review of *The Bear,* p. 66; October 2, 1995, review of *The Man,* p. 73; March 15, 1999, review of *The Sand Children,* p. 56; August 9, 1999, review of *Ethel and Ernest,* p. 328; June 28, 1999, review of *All in a Day,* p. 81.

School Library Journal, October, 2002, Shelley B. Sutherland, review of *Ug,* p. 158; November, 2002, Teri Markson, review of *A Bit More Bert,* p. 110; March, 2007, Kirsten Cutler, review of *Collected Poems for Children,* p. 196.

Signal, January, 1979, Elaine Moss, "Raymond Briggs: On British Attitudes to the Strip Cartoon and Children's-Book Illustration," p. 28.

Sunday Mail (Glasgow, Scotland), December 3, 2006, "Snowman Writer Is Fizzing," p. 3.

Time, October 25, 1999, Steven Henry Madoff, review of *Ethel and Ernest,* p. 130.

Times Educational Supplement, June 11, 1982, Richard North, "Cartoon Apocalypse," p. 41; August 21, 1992, review of *The Man,* p. 20; October 8, 1998, Nicolette

Jones, review of *Under the Snow,* p. D10; October 31, 2003, Jane Doonan, "Portrait of a Comic Genius," p. 18.

ONLINE

The Snowman Web site, http://www.thesnowman.co.uk/ (November 19, 2007).

British Council Contemporary Writers Web site, http://www.contemporarywriters.com/ (November 19, 2007), "Raymond Briggs."

British Council Magic Pencil Web site, http://magicpencil.britishcouncil.org/ (November 19, 2007), "Raymond Briggs."*

*   *   *

BRIGGS, Raymond Redvers
See BRIGGS, Raymond

*   *   *

BUCKLEY, Susan
(Susan Washburn Buckley)

Personal
Born in LA.

Addresses
Home—New York, NY.

Career
Writer, editor, and curriculum developer. Project director in social studies programs for Holt, Prentice-Hall, and Scholastic; curriculum developer for National Geographic Society, National Endowment for the Humanities, and Oxford University Press; Gale Institute, senior program consultant for "Different Ways of Knowing" program. Editor of *AppleSeeds* (children's magazine).

Writings

(With Elspeth Leacock) *Journeys in Time: A New Atlas of American History,* illustrated by Rodica Prato, Houghton Mifflin (Boston, MA), 2001.

(With Elspeth Leacock) *Places in Time: A New Atlas of American History,* illustrated by Randy Jones, Houghton Mifflin (Boston, MA), 2001.

(As Susan Washburn Buckley) *The Industrial Revolution: 1790-1850,* National Geographic Society (Washington, DC), 2002.

(With Elspeth Leacock) *Journeys for Freedom: A New Look at America's Story,* illustrated by Rodica Prato, Houghton Mifflin (Boston, MA), 2006.

(With Elspeth Leacock) *Kids Make History: A New Look at America's Story,* illustrated by Randy Jones, Houghton Mifflin (Boston, MA), 2006.

Also author of professional resource books for teachers. General editor of "We the People" (social studies textbook series), Houghton Mifflin.

Sidelights
Susan Buckley is the coauthor of a number of critically acclaimed works of nonfiction for young readers, including *Journeys for Freedom: A New Look at America's Story.* A consultant in editorial and curriculum development, Buckley has worked in educational publishing for several decades. There, she has developed social-studies programs for such publishers as Holt, Prentice-Hall, and Scholastic, and she has served as a curriculum developer for the National Geographic Society and Oxford University Press, among others. In addition, Buckley acted as general editor of Houghton Mifflin's textbook series "We the People" and edits *AppleSeeds* magazine for children.

In 2001, Buckley joined frequent collaborator Elspeth Leacock in writing the companion volumes *Journeys in Time: A New Atlas of American History* and *Places in Time: A New Atlas of American History.* In the former, the coauthors use "story maps" to depict twenty journeys that helped shape the history of the United States, focusing on such well-known events as Christopher Columbus's voyage to the New World and the cross-continent expedition of Lewis and Clark, as well as the journeys of Venture Smith, an enslaved African prince, and Dame Shirley, a New Englander who traveled west to join the California gold rush. In *Journeys in Time,* according to *School Library Journal* contributor Pamela K. Bomboy, "a winning blend of facts, maps, and the drama of a well-written story results in an unusual and exciting view" of U.S. history.

Places in Time offers depictions of twenty historically significant locales, among them the ancient city of Cahokia, the battlefields of Saratoga and Gettysburg, Fort Laramie, and New York's Ellis Island. "The text is clear and interesting," observed *Kliatt* critic Daniel J. Levinson in a review of the two works, and John Peters stated in his review for *Booklist* that Buckley and Leacock "have drawn their information not just from published documents but from archives and their own interviews as well." *Journeys in Time* and *Places in Time* "will not turn geographically challenged youngsters into charting scholars, but they do hold potential for reinforcing location skills and relationship observations in a pleasant, nonthreatening format," remarked a *Horn Book* contributor.

Buckley and Elspeth also collaborated on *Journeys for Freedom,* which tells the stories of twenty individuals who escaped from persecution or enslavement. The coauthors profile such figures as Elizabeth Brasseux, an

Acadian exiled from Nova Scotia; Wetatonmi, a Nez Perce pursued by the U.S. Army; Peter McBride, a Mormon settler in Salt Lake City; Israel Veleris, a Jew who fled Nazi Germany, and Peter Malual, one of the "lost boys" of the Sudan. A critic in _Kirkus Reviews_ described the book as a "purposefully inspirational volume," and _Booklist_ contributor GraceAnne A. DeCandido called _Journeys for Freedom_ "as powerful as it is useful." In _Kids Make History: A New Look at America's Story,_ Buckley and Elspeth chronicle the experiences of twenty children and teens, including Nick Wilson, a rider for the Pony Express; Jane Sever, a visitor to the 1893 Chicago World's Fair; and Joan Zuber, a young girl who survived the attack on Pearl Harbor. In the words of a _Kirkus Reviews_ critic, "this useful resource will be a hit with teachers and students alike."

Biographical and Critical Sources

PERIODICALS

Booklist, June 1, 2001, John Peters, reviews of _Journeys in Time: A New Atlas of American History_ and _Places in Time: A New Atlas of American History,_ p. 1866; No-vember 15, 2006, GraceAnne A. DeCandido, review of _Journeys for Freedom: A New Look at America's Story,_ p. 44.

Horn Book, July 1, 2001, reviews of _Journeys in Time_ and _Places in Time,_ p. 471.

Kirkus Reviews, October 15, 2006, reviews of _Journeys for Freedom_ and _Kids Make History: A New Look at America's Story,_ p. 1067.

Kliatt, July, 2003, Daniel J. Levinson, reviews of _Journeys in Time_ and _Places in Time,_ p. 48.

School Library Journal, June, 2001, Pamela K. Bomboy, review of _Journeys in Time,_ p. 176; January, 2007, Grace Oliff, review of _Journeys for Freedom,_ p. 145, and Lisa Gangemi Kropp, review of _Kids Make History,_ p. 146.

ONLINE

Houghton Mifflin Web site, http://www.houghtonmifflin books.com/ (October 31, 2007), "Susan Buckley."*

* * *

BUCKLEY, Susan Washburn
See BUCKLEY, Susan

C

CARTER, Abby

Personal

Married; children: Samantha, Carter. *Hobbies and other interests:* Baking.

Addresses

Home and office—Hadlyme, CT.

Career

Illustrator and graphic artist. Fresh Samantha, Saco, ME, cofounder, 1992.

Illustrator

Marc Gave, *Tess and Tim,* Parents Magazine Press (New York, NY), 1988.

Marc Gave, *Travels with Tess and Tim,* Parents Magazine Press (New York, NY), 1990.

Gabrielle Charbonnet, *Snakes Are Nothing to Sneeze At,* Henry Holt (New York, NY), 1990.

Susan Beth Pfeffer, *Twin Surprises,* Henry Holt (New York, NY), 1991.

Michael Crowley, *New Kid on Spurwink Ave.,* Little, Brown (Boston, MA), 1992.

Kathryn Cristaldi, *Baseball Ballerina,* Random House (New York, NY), 1992.

Jayne Harvey, *Great-Uncle Dracula,* Random House (New York, NY), 1992.

Susan Beth Pfeffer, *Twin Troubles,* Henry Holt (New York, NY), 1992.

(Selected by Dorothy M. Kennedy), *I Thought I'd Take My Rat to School: Poems for September to June,* Little, Brown (Boston, MA), 1993.

Doug Johnson, *Never Babysit the Hippopotamuses!,* Henry Holt (New York, NY), 1993.

Jayne Harvey, *Great-Uncle Dracula and the Dirty Rat,* Random House (New York, NY), 1993.

Michael Crowley, *Shack and Back,* Little, Brown (Boston, MA), 1993.

Gabrielle Charbonnet, *Tutu Much Ballet,* Henry Holt (New York, NY), 1994.

Maryann Macdonald, *The Pink Party,* Hyperion Books for Children (New York, NY), 1994.

Suzanne Williams, *Edwin and Emily,* Hyperion Books for Children (New York, NY), 1995.

Anita Hakkinen, *Summer Legs,* Henry Holt (New York, NY), 1995.

Doug Johnson, *Never Ride Your Elephant to School,* Henry Holt (New York, NY), 1995.

Leah Komaiko, *Annie Bananie Moves to Barry Avenue,* Delacorte Press (New York, NY), 1996.

Suzanne Williams, *Emily at School,* Hyperion Books for Children (New York, NY), 1996.

Gibbs Davis, *Camp Sink or Swim,* Random House (New York, NY), 1997.

Marthe Jocelyn, *The Invisible Day,* Dutton Children's Books (New York, NY), 1997.

Judy Truesdell Mecca, *What a World!: Play Script,* Pleasant Co. (Middleton, WI), 1998.

Judy Truesdell Mecca, *Check under the Bed: A Mystery for You and Your Friends to Perform,* Pleasant Co. (Middleton, WI), 1998.

Marthe Jocelyn, *The Invisible Harry,* Dutton Children's Books (New York, NY), 1998.

Christina Hamlett, *Hairum-Scarum,* Pleasant Co. (Middleton, WI), 1998.

Leah Komaiko, *Annie Bananie and the People's Court,* Delacorte Press (New York, NY), 1998.

Bonnie Graves, *No Copycats Allowed!,* Hyperion Books for Children (New York, NY), 1998.

Leah Komaiko, *Annie Bananie and the Pain Sisters,* Delacorte Press (New York, NY), 1998.

Jeri Dayle, *Sock Crafts,* Random House (New York, NY), 1999.

Kathryn Cristaldi, *Baseball Ballerina Strikes Out,* Random House (New York, NY), 2000.

Marthe Jocelyn, *The Invisible Enemy,* Dutton Children's Books (New York, NY), 2002.

Reeve Lindbergh, *My Hippie Grandmother,* Candlewick Press (Cambridge, MA), 2003.

Rose-Marie Provencher, *Slithery Jake,* HarperCollins (New York, NY), 2004.

Suzanne Williams, *The Marvelous Mind of Matthew McGhee, Age 8: Master of Minds,* Aladdin (New York, NY), 2004.

Katharine Kenah, *The Best Seat in Second Grade,* Harper-Collins (New York, NY), 2005.

Jennifer Richard Jacobson, *Andy Shane and the Very Bossy Dolores Starbuckle,* Candlewick Press (Cambridge, MA), 2005.

Elise Broach, *What the No-Good Baby Is Good For,* Putnam's (New York, NY), 2005.

Katharine Kenah, *The Best Teacher in Second Grade,* HarperCollins (New York, NY), 2006.

Barbara M. Joose, *Dead Guys Talk: A Wild Willie Mystery,* Clarion Books (New York, NY), 2006.

Jennifer Richard Jacobson, *Andy Shane and the Pumpkin Trick,* Candlewick Press (Cambridge, MA), 2006.

Bonny Becker, *Holbrook: A Lizard's tale,* Clarion Books (New York, NY), 2006.

Dayle Ann Dodds, *Full House: An Invitation to Fractions,* Candlewick Press (Cambridge, MA), 2007.

Katharine Kenah, *The Best Chef in Second Grade,* Harper-Collins (New York, NY), 2007.

Also illustrator of graphics for Fresh Samantha.

Sidelights

Illustrating has always been a part of Abby Carter's life. Even as a young girl she created illustrations for a card company that she and her grandmother owned. Growing up to become a professional book illustrator, Carter has contributed art to over a dozen children's

Abby Carter's sprightly art and her engaging characters bring to life books such as **Camp Sink or Swim** *by Gibbs Davis.* (Illustration © 1997 by Abby Carter. Used by permission of Random House Children's Books, a division of Random House, Inc.)

books, such as *Slithery Jake,* by Rose-Marie Provencher, *My Hippie Grandmother,* by Reeve Lindbergh, and *The Best Teacher in Second Grade* by Katharine Kennah. In addition to her book illustration work, Carter created graphics for Fresh Samantha, a juice company that she and her husband founded in 1992 and named after their daughter. The company was sold in 2000.

Carter's illustrations have been recognized by critics for their cheerful, colorful, and exciting images. For instance, a *Kirkus Reviews* writer called Carter's work for *My Hippie Grandmother* "a wonder in electric Kool-Aid acid colors" and added that the artist possesses such a lively vision that "her watercolor and gouache figures fairly dance off the page." *Booklist* reviewer Carolyn Phelan characterized *My Hippie Grandmother* as a "sunny picture book" and commented that Carter's pictures "reflect the spirit of the verse" and capture the music in Lindberg's lighthearted story. Reviewing the picture book for *School Library Journal,* Judith Constantinides also noted the rhythm to be found in Carter's color illustrations and concluded that "colorful watercolor-and-gouache illustrations capture the happy mood of the verse."

Biographical and Critical Sources

PERIODICALS

Booklist, June 1, 2002, Gillian Engberg, review of *The Invisible Enemy,* p. 1723; March 1, 2003, Carolyn Phelan, review of *My Hippie Grandmother,* p. 1203; January 1, 2004, Hazel Rochman, review of *Slithery Jake,* p. 880; May 15, 2005, Hazel Rochman, review of *What the No-Good Baby Is Good For,* p. 1663; July, 2005, John Peters, review of *Andy Shane and the Very Bossy Dolores Starbuckle,* p. 1929; August, 2005, Kay Weisman, review of *The Best Seat in Second Grade,* p. 2039; May 1, 2006, Carolyn Phelan, review of *Dead Guys Talk: A Wild Willie Mystery,* p. 48; June 1, 2006, Hazel Rochman, review of *The Best Teacher in Second Grade,* p. 84; September 1, 2006, Julie Cummins, review of *Andy Shane and the Pumpkin Trick,* p. 137; January 1, 2007, Carolyn Phelan, review of *Holbrook: A Lizard's Tale,* p. 96.

Good Housekeeping, November, 1999, Caroline Sorgen, "A Juicy Tale," p. 26.

Horn Book, September-October, 2006, Betty Carter, review of *Andy Shane and the Pumpkin Trick,* p. 586.

Kirkus Reviews, January 1, 2003, review of *My Hippie Grandmother,* p. 63; June 15, 2005, Jennifer Jacobson, review of *Andy Shane and the Pumpkin Trick,* p. 684; June 15, 2005, Katharine Kenah, review of *The Best Seat in Second Grade,* p. 684; June 15, 2006, Katharine Kenah, review of *The Best Teacher in Second Grade,* p. 634; July 15, 2006, Jennifer Richard Jacobson, review of *Andy Shane and the Pumpkin Trick,* p. 724; October 15, 2006, review of *Holbrook,* p. 1065.

My Hippie Grandmother, *Reeve Lindbergh's intergenerational picture book, is brought to life in Carter's freewheeling watercolor art.* (Illustration © 2003 by Abby Carter. Reproduced by permission of Candlewick Press, Inc., Cambridge, MA.)

Publishers Weekly, October 27, 1997, review of *The Invisible Day,* p. 76; July 17, 2000, review of *School Zone,* p. 148; December 23, 2003, review of *My Hippie Grandmother,* p. 70; January 19, 2004, review of *Slithery Jake,* p. 75.

Resource Links, February, 1999, review of *Invisible Harry,* p. 9; April, 2002, Joanne de Groof, review of *The Invisible Enemy,* p. 23.

School Library Journal, September, 2000, Lisa Smith, review of *Baseball Ballerina Strikes Out!,* p. 193; May, 2002, Alison Grant, review of *The Invisible Enemy,* p. 154; April, 2003, Judith Constantinides, review of *My Hippie Grandmother,* p. 132; March, 2004, Edith Ching, review of *The Marvelous Mind of Matthew McGhee,* p. 187; March, 2004, Rosalyn Pierini, review of *Slithery Jake,* p. 180; July, 2004, Lisa G. Kropp, review of *I'd Thought I'd Take My Rat to School: Poems for September to June,* p. 45; June, 2005, Suzanne Myers Harold, review of *What the No-Good Baby Is Good For,* p. 105; August, 2005, Rachael Vilmar, review of *Andy Shane and the Very Bossy Dolores Starbuckle,* p. 97; October, 2005, Katharine Kenah, review of *The Best Seat in Second Grade,* p. S40; July, 2006, Gloria Koster, review of *The Best Teacher in Second Grade,* p. 80; September, 2006, Caitlin Augusta, review of *Dead Guys Talk,* p. 174; December, 2006, review of *Holbrook,* p. 94.

ONLINE

HarperCollins Web site, http://www.harpercollins.com/ (November 1, 2007), "Abby Carter."

HK Portfolio Web site, http://www.hkportfolio.com/ (November 1, 2007), "Abby Carter."

Houghton Mifflin Web site, http://www.houghtonmifflin books.com/ (November 1, 2007), "Abby Carter."*

*   *   *

CHRISTELOW, Eileen 1943-

Personal

Born April 22, 1943, in Washington, DC; daughter of Allan (an historian and business executive) and Dorothy (an economist) Christelow; married Albert B. Ahrenholz (a potter), December, 1965; children: Heather. *Education:* University of Pennsylvania, B.A. (architecture), 1965; graduate study, University of California, Berkeley.

Addresses

Home—East Dummerston, VT.

Career

Children's book author and illustrator. Freelance photographer in Philadelphia, PA, 1965-71; graphic designer and illustrator in Berkeley, CA, 1973-81; freelance writer and illustrator, beginning 1982.

Member

Society of Children's Book Writers and Illustrators.

Awards, Honors

Little Archer Award (WI), 1982, for *Henry and the Red Stripes;* Washington Irving Fiction Award, 1984, and Land of Enchantment Award, and Maud Hart Lovelace Award, both 1986, all for *Zucchini;* International Reading Association/Children's Book Council Children's Choice selection, 1987, for *The Robbery at the Diamond Dog Diner,* 1989, for *Five Little Monkeys Jumping on the Bed,* 1992, for *Five Little Monkeys Sitting in a Tree,* 1993, for *Five Little Monkeys with Nothing to Do,* 2001, for *Five Little Monkeys Wash the Car,* 2004, for *Vote!,* and 2007, for *Letters from a Desperate Dog; School Library Journal* Best Books list, 1995, for *What Do Authors Do?;* Notable Children's Book selection, American Library Association, 1999, for *What Do Illustrators Do?,* and *Vote!; Smithsonian* Notable Books for Children selection, 2002, and Oppenheim Toy Portfolio Gold Award, both for *Where's the Big Bad Wolf?*

Writings

SELF-ILLUSTRATED

Henry and the Red Stripes, Clarion (New York, NY), 1982.

Eileen Christelow (Reproduced by permission.)

Mr. Murphy's Marvelous Invention, Clarion (New York, NY), 1983.

Henry and the Dragon, Clarion (New York, NY), 1984.

Jerome the Babysitter, Houghton Mifflin (Boston, MA), 1987.

Olive and the Magic Hat, Houghton Mifflin (Boston, MA), 1987.

Jerome and the Witchcraft Kids, Clarion (New York, NY), 1988.

The Robbery at the Diamond Dog Diner, Houghton Mifflin (Boston, MA), 1988.

(Reteller) *Five Little Monkeys Jumping on the Bed,* Clarion (New York, NY), 1989.

Glenda Feathers Casts a Spell, Clarion (New York, NY), 1990.

Five Little Monkeys Sitting in a Tree, Clarion (New York, NY), 1991.

Don't Wake Up Mama: Another Five Little Monkey's Story, Clarion (New York, NY), 1992.

Gertrude, the Bulldog Detective, Clarion (New York, NY), 1992.

The Five-Dog Night, Clarion (New York, NY), 1993.

The Great Pig Escape, Clarion (New York, NY), 1994.

What Do Authors Do?, Clarion (New York, NY), 1995.

Five Little Monkeys with Nothing to Do, Clarion (New York, NY) 1996.

Not until Christmas, Walter!, Clarion (New York, NY) 1997.

Jerome Camps Out, Clarion (New York, NY) 1998.

What Do Illustrators Do?, Clarion (New York, NY) 1999.

Five Little Monkeys Wash the Car, Clarion (New York, NY) 2000.

The Great Pig Search, Clarion (New York, NY) 2001.

Where's the Big Bad Wolf?, Clarion (New York, NY) 2002.

Vote!, Clarion (New York, NY) 2003.

Five Little Monkeys Bake a Birthday Cake, Clarion (New York, NY) 2004.

Five Little Monkeys Play Hide-and-Seek, Clarion (New York, NY) 2004.

Letters from a Desperate Dog, Clarion (New York, NY) 2006.

Five Little Monkeys Go Shopping, Clarion (New York, NY) 2007.

Several of Christelow's works have been published in Spanish.

ILLUSTRATOR

(With others) Diane Downie, *Math for Girls, and Other Problem Solvers,* University of California Press (Berkeley, CA), 1981.

Barbara Dana, *Zucchini,* Harper (New York, NY), 1982.

Thomas Rockwell, *Oatmeal Is Not for Mustaches,* Holt (New York, NY), 1984.

Sue Alexander, *Dear Phoebe,* Little, Brown (New York, NY), 1984.

Barbara Steiner, *Oliver Dibbs and the Dinosaur Cause,* Simon & Schuster (New York, NY), 1986.

Jim Aylesworth, *Two Terrible Frights,* Simon & Schuster (New York, NY), 1987.

Joy Elizabeth Handcock, *The Loudest Little Lion,* Albert Whitman (Morton Grove, IL), 1988.

Barbara Steiner, *Oliver Dibbs to the Rescue!,* Avon Books (New York, NY), 1988.

Myra Cohn Livingston, selector, *Dilly Dilly Piccalilli: Poems for the Very Young,* Margaret K. McElderry Books (New York, NY), 1989.

Mary Elise Monsell, *The Mysterious Cases of Mr. Pin,* Atheneum (New York, NY), 1989.

Jim Aylesworth, *The Completed Hickory Dickory Dock,* Atheneum (New York, NY), 1990.

Mary Elise Monsell, *Mr. Pin: The Chocolate Files,* Atheneum (New York, NY), 1990.

Peggy Christian, *The Old Coot,* Atheneum (New York, NY), 1991.

Barbara Steiner, *Dolby and the Woof-Off,* Morrow (New York, NY), 1991.

Jan Wahl, *Mrs. Owl and Mr. Pig,* Lodestar (New York, NY), 1991.

Mary Elise Monsell, *Mr. Pin: The Spy Who Came North from the Pole,* Atheneum (New York, NY), 1993.

Jennifer Brutschy, *Celeste and Crabapple Sam,* Lodestar (New York, NY), 1994.

Maryann Macdonald, *Secondhand Star,* Hyperion (New York, NY), 1994.

Mary Elise Monsell, *Mr. Pin: A Fish Named Yum,* Atheneum (New York, NY), 1994.

Maryann Macdonald, *No Room for Francie,* Hyperion (New York, NY), 1995.

Eve Bunting, *The Pumpkin Fair,* Clarion (New York, NY), 1997.

(With Jo Ellen McAllister-Stammen and Walter Lyon Krudop) Jim Aylesworth, *The Pumpkin Fair,* Atheneum (New York, NY), 1998.

Darleen Bailey Beart, *The Flimflam Man,* Farrar, Straus & Giroux (New York, NY), 1998.

Christelow's photographs have appeared in *Progressive Architecture, Colloquy, Ford Foundation, Home, Media and Method, New York Times Book Review, Pennsylvania Gazette, Youth,* and *Teacher,* as well as in various textbooks. Creator of poster art for Children's Book Council.

Sidelights

Eileen Christelow is an award-winning author and illustrator who produces humorous, bright, and energetic picture books. Several of Christelow's tales, such as *The Great Pig Escape* and *Letters from a Desperate Dog,* are based on episodes from real life. Whether she is illustrating her own stories or those of other authors, Christelow's animal characters—from cats and dogs to alligators and penguins—are charming and expressive.

Christelow developed an early interest in the written word. "Books were a part of life in my family," she noted in an essay on her home page. "My parents read bedtime stories to me and my brother every night." Because her family did not own a television until she was a teenager, Christelow spent most of her spare time reading. "Much of my early childhood," she wrote, "was spent slouched in an armchair or up in a tree house with my nose in a book. . . . A good early education for a writer!" Christelow's interest in writing was stirred by her English teachers in middle school and high school, and she initially planned to major in English at college, although she lost her enthusiasm for the subject during her freshman year.

As Christelow once explained to *SATA,* her career as a picture-book creator developed from her interests in architecture and photography. "I majored in architecture at the University of Pennsylvania in Philadelphia," she stated. "While I was there, I discovered the darkroom in the graphics department. I spent more time there than I should have, taking photographs. After graduation, I earned my living as a freelance photographer, photographing buildings rather than designing them. I also photographed in the Philadelphia public school classrooms, skid row, and Chinatown. I took several trips with my cameras across the United States and one trip to Mexico. My photos appeared in various magazines and textbooks."

After a visit to Cornwall, England, and the birth of a daughter, Christelow and her family moved to Berkeley, California. There, as she recalled, "[I] found that I was tired of constantly looking at the world through a camera lens, so I began to learn about type, graphic design, and illustration. I eventually started freelancing as a designer producing ads, brochures, catalogues, and books. She decided to explore her possibilities as a children's book author and illustrator while raising her young daughter. "For several years my daughter and I researched the problem together," she later told *SATA,* "taking weekly trips to the library and reading at naptime and bedtime. I found the picture book format a fascinating and frustrating challenge. I learned about pacing and I learned to keep my text spare. I also found that the years I'd spent as a photographer, trying to cap-

In **What Do Authors Do?** *Christelow shares the challenges as well as the fun in being a children's book writer.* (Illustration © 1995 by Eileen Christelow. All rights reserved. Reproduced by permission of Houghton Mifflin Company.)

ture one photo that would tell an entire story, were invaluable to the process of creating stories with pens and pencils." One result of her efforts was the acquisition of a large collection of children's books, which helped her daughter to read and write. "And I wrote and illustrated several books—one of which is *Henry and the Red Stripes.*

"The idea for *Henry and the Red Stripes* first came to me when I was half asleep in a hot, steamy bath," Christelow explained. "It had been percolating in the back of my mind for months as I researched and illustrated a poster picturing twenty-six insects, reptiles, birds, and mammals camouflaged in a forest setting. That poster, combined with observing my daughter and her friends decorating themselves with paints and magic markers, led to the creation of Henry Rabbit."

Henry and the Dragon, the second "Henry" book, portrays the rabbit after a bedtime story. Henry thinks there must be a dragon about, and builds a trap to catch it. As Christelow noted in a *Junior Literary Guild* article, *Henry and the Dragon* "was inspired by memories" of her young daughter asking if any bears walked around the family house at night.

Another book by Christelow, *Jerome the Babysitter,* introduces a young alligator boy just as he begins his first

job babysitting. His twelve charges trick and mistreat him, and even trap him on the roof, but in the end Jerome proves he is a clever as well as competent caretaker. According to Lisa Redd in *School Library Journal,* the alligator characters are "delightful," and rendered with "expressive faces." In the words of a *Publishers Weekly* critic, the book presents a "side-splitting story" and "luridly colored cartoons." Christelow has published two other works about the energetic gator: *Jerome and the Witchcraft Kids* and *Jerome Camps Out,* the latter of which is based on a true story about a youngster who was forced to share a tent with the class bully while on a school trip. "The simple text is bolstered by Christelow's funny pen-and-watercolor artwork," remarked *Booklist* critic Ilene Cooper of the book.

The Robbery at the Diamond Dog Diner features a little hen who cannot keep her mouth shut. When she hides her dog friend's diamonds in her hollowed-out eggs, diamond thieves think she is a diamond-egg-laying hen, and kidnap the little hen. *The Five-Dog Night,* which a *Kirkus Reviews* critic called a "good-natured, entertaining yarn," surprises readers by demonstrating that a five-dog night is one so cold that five dogs in the bed make the best blanket. A young dog, intent on becoming a detective, spies on her neighbors in *Gertrude, the*

Bulldog Detective; although the neighbors provide her with some fake clues in an effort to discourage her, Gertrude manages to catch some real thieves by story's end.

Christelow has produced a number of works based on the popular children's song and finger play "Five Little Monkeys." She was inspired to write *Five Little Monkeys Jumping on the Bed,* the first title in the series, after hearing her young daughter recite the rhyme. "Whether sublimely happy or ridiculously goofy," wrote Corinne Camarata in *School Library Journal,* "Christelow's expressive monkeys pack a lot of appeal." While picnicking, the rambunctious crew fearlessly teases a crocodile in *Five Little Monkeys Sitting in a Tree.* According to *School Library Journal* reviewer Carey Ayres, young readers will "delight in the mischief-making—a humorous exaggeration of their own antics." In *Five Little Monkeys with Nothing to Do,* the bored quintet help their mother prepare for a visit from Grandma Bessie. "This is pure silliness—just the kind kids like," observed Cooper. When the family's old automobile goes up the sale, the gang decides it needs a good cleaning in *Five Little Monkeys Wash the Car.* "Christelow's watercolor-and-pencil illustrations show great energy and movement," noted Kathy Broderick in *Booklist.* A naive babysitter gets more than she bargained for in *Five Little Monkeys Play Hide-and-Seek,* a picture book in which Christelow's illustrations "convey a sharp sense of giddy, good-hearted fun," according to *Booklist* reviewer Carolyn Phelan.

Based on an incident involving an Iowa farmer, *The Great Pig Escape* concerns Bert and Ethel, a pair of vegetable farmers who decide to raise pigs. When it is time for the farmers to sell the pigs at the market, the porkers escape both the market and certain death by stealing clothes, disguising themselves as people, and blending in with the crowd. After safely reaching Florida, the pigs return the clothes, along with a postcard for their owners with the comment, "Oink!" *School Library Journal* contributor Cynthia K. Richey described Christelow's text as "lively" and "funny," noting that the book's pen and ink and watercolor illustrations are "filled with humor." A *Publishers Weekly* critic described the book as a "strategic endorsement of vegetarianism." In a follow-up, *The Great Pig Search,* Bert and Ethel head to the Sunshine State for a vacation, although Bert is determined to locate the missing swine. "The author gets a few more giggles out of a classic comedy plot," remarked a critic in *Publishers Weekly* in a review of *The Great Pig Search.*

Christelow provides her own take on a classic fairy story in *Where's the Big Bad Wolf?,* "a delicious parody" of The Three Little Pigs, according to *School Library Journal* reviewer Mary Elam. When the pigs' houses are huffed and puffed to bits, Detective Doggedly is called upon to investigate the case. A *Kirkus Reviews* contributor stated that Christelow's adaptation "is good clownish fun, and the rough-and-tumble art

keeps the farce bubbling." The somewhat testy relationship between Christelow's husband and their spirited pup, Emma, inspired *Letters from a Desperate Dog,* a story told in comic-strip format. Seemingly unable to please her owner, a frustrated Emma pens a letter to Queenie, the advice columnist at the *Weekly Bone,* whose words of wisdom encourage Emma to try her hand at acting. Cooper praised the story for its "heartfelt messages about friendship and the bond between animals and their human companions."

Fans of Christelow's work join aspiring young authors as the intended audience of her book *What Do Authors Do?* By following the efforts of two writers who have witnessed the same event, Christelow demonstrates how writers begin their books and prepare them for publication. According to *Horn Book* contributor Elizabeth S. Watson, "if ever there was a book to encourage youngsters to try their hand at writing, this is one." In a companion volume, *What Do Illustrators Do?,* Christelow examines another aspect of the creative process through the work of two artists. "By alighting on a subject with which her audience has some familiarity, Christelow instantly engages interest," concluded a reviewer in *Publishers Weekly.*

Biographical and Critical Sources

PERIODICALS

Booklist, September 1, 1996, Ilene Cooper, review of *Five Little Monkeys with Nothing to Do,* p. 140; April 15, 1998, Ilene Cooper, review of *Jerome Camps Out,* p. 1449; March 1, 1999, Stephanie Zvirin, review of *What Do Illustrators Do?,* p. 1204; May 1, 2000, Kathy Broderick, review of *Five Little Monkeys Wash the Car,* p. 1676; September 1, 2001, Michael Cart, review of *The Great Pig Search,* p. 113; October 15, 2002, Ilene Cooper, review of *Where's the Big Bad Wolf?,* p. 410; November 1, 2003, Ilene Cooper, review of *Vote!,* p. 492; August, 2004, Carolyn Phelan, review of *Five Little Monkeys Play Hide-and-Seek,* p. 1941; October 1, 2006, Ilene Cooper, review of *Letters from a Desperate Dog,* p. 57.
Horn Book, November-December, 1995, Elizabeth S. Watson, review of *What Do Authors Do?,* p. 754; March-April, 2002, Peter D. Sieruta, review of *The Great Pig Search,* p. 200.
Junior Literary Guild, March, 1984, review of *Henry and the Dragon.*
Kirkus Reviews, July 1, 1993, review of *The Five-Dog Night,* p. 857; July 15, 2002, review of *Where's the Big Bad Wolf?,* p. 1028; October 15, 2006, review of *Letters from a Desperate Dog,* p. 1067.
Publishers Weekly, February 22, 1985, review of *Jerome the Babysitter,* p. 158; June 27, 1994, review of *The Great Pig Escape,* p. 78; February 1, 1999, review of *What Do Illustrators Do?,* p. 84; September 3, 2001, review of *The Great Pig Search,* p. 87; August 25, 2003, review of *Vote!,* p. 64.

School Library Journal, March, 1986, Lisa Redd, review of *Jerome the Babysitter,* p. 145; July, 1989, Corinne Camarata, review of *Five Little Monkeys Jumping on the Bed,* p. 62; August, 1991, Carey Ayres, review of *Five Little Monkeys Sitting in a Tree,* p. 143; November, 1994, Cynthia K. Richey, review of *The Great Pig Escape,* p. 73; November, 1996, Meg Stackpole, review of *Five Little Monkeys with Nothing to Do,* p. 79; May, 2000, Denise Reitsma, review of *Five Little Monkeys Wash the Car,* p. 132; September, 2002, review of *Where's the Big Bad Wolf?,* p. 182; September, 2004, Roxanne Burg, review of *Five Little Monkeys Play Hide-and-Seek,* p. 156; November, 2006, Nancy Silverrod, review of *Letters from a Desperate Dog,* p. 86.

ONLINE

Eileen Christelow Home Page, http://www.christelow.com (November 10, 2007).*

*   *   *

COLEMAN, Janet Wyman

Personal

Married, 1972; children: two sons. *Education:* Wellesley College, graduated, 1988. *Hobbies and other interests:* Watercolor, designing needlepoint art.

Addresses

Home—Wayland, MA. *E-mail*—janet.coleman@gmail.com.

Career

Author, photographer, and multimedia producer. Professional photographer; Janet Wyman Coleman Productions (multimedia company), Wayland, MA, founder.

Member

Authors Guild.

Awards, Honors

Parents Choice Award, 2003, for *Baseball for Everyone;* Gold Award, National Parenting Publications, 2006, and Best Books for Young Adults selection, American Library Association, 2007, both for *Secrets, Lies, Gizmos, and Spies.*

Writings

Fast Eddie, illustrated by Alec Gillman, Four Winds Press (New York, NY), 1993.
Famous Bears & Friends: One Hundred Years of Teddy Bear Stories, Poems, Songs, and Heroics, Dutton (New York, NY), 2002.

Janet Wyman Coleman (Photograph by Virginia N. Durfee. Courtesy of Janet Wyman Coleman.)

(With Elizabeth V. Warren) *Baseball for Everyone: Stories from the Great Game,* Harry N. Abrams (New York, NY), 2003.
Secrets, Lies, Gizmos, and Spies: A History of Spies and Espionage, Harry N. Abrams (New York, NY), 2006.

Sidelights

In addition to her work creating educational multimedia productions, Janet Wyman Coleman is the author of fiction and nonfiction for young readers. In her debut novel, *Fast Eddie,* published in 1993, Coleman details the exploits of a mischievous raccoon and his frequent skirmishes with a suburban family. When Eddie notices the Plotkins cutting down trees, mowing a field, and adding chemicals to their lawn, he decides to retaliate by tipping over their garbage cans and artfully rearranging the spilled contents. An angry Mr. Plotkin attempts to trap the rascally raccoon, to little effect, and in response Eddie's actions become more destructive, despite warnings from the raccoon's best friend, the Plotkins' cat. Writing in *School Library Journal,* Maggie McEwen remarked that Coleman "does an excellent job of telling the story from the animals' point of view."

Coleman celebrates the 100th birthday of one of the world's favorite toys in *Famous Bears & Friends: One*

Hundred Years of Teddy Bear Stories, Poems, Songs, and Heroics. Here she traces the birth of the teddy bear to an incident involving President Theodore Roosevelt, an avid hunter who once refused to shoot an exhausted bear. Upon learning about Roosevelt's merciful act, a Brooklyn toymaker produced a stuffed animal in the president's honor. Coleman also examines the role German seamstress Margarete Steiff played in popularizing the teddy bear. In addition, she discusses the origins of the "mourning" teddy bears designed to commemorate the tragic sinking of the cruise ship *Titanic,* and relates the tale of Kumataro, the teddy bear that accompanied the crew of the space shuttle Discovery. Coleman also includes stories about fictional bears such as A.A. Milne's classic *Winnie-the-Pooh,* Michael Bond's *A Bear Called Paddington,* and Don Freeman's *Corduroy,* as well as bear-themed poems by Shel Silverstein and Judith Viorst. Writing in *Booklist,* Kathy Broderick described *Famous Bears & Friends* as "a beautifully designed collection of teddy bear history and story."

In 2003 Coleman published *Baseball for Everyone: Stories from the Great Game.* Illustrated with images from an exhibition at the American Folk Art Museum and drawing on *The Perfect Game* by Elizabeth V. Warren, *Baseball for Everyone* offers an anecdotal history of America's proverbial favorite pastime, complete with biographies of the game's most famous—and infamous—players. Many reviewers praised the color photographs, illustrated scorecards, and quilts that accompany the text. According to a *Publishers Weekly* critic, "The book's crisp design . . . hits a home run, making the most of a visual bounty that helps to underscore the sport's tremendous influence on the national psyche." *Baseball for Everyone* "merits attention for showing baseball's integral relationship to American culture," observed *Booklist* contributor John Peters, and a *Kirkus Reviews* critic called the work "a great addition to the literature of the great American game."

In *Secrets, Lies, Gizmos, and Spies: A History of Spies and Espionage* Coleman looks at intelligence-gathering methods through the ages. Heavily illustrated with images from the International Spy Museum, the work describes a variety of gadgets, weapons, and torture devices, discusses clandestine operations, and profiles both real and fictional spies. Coleman's "engrossing, readable text will hold the interest of even reluctant readers," predicted Lynn K. Vanca in *School Library Journal.* In the words of *Booklist* contributor Gillian Engberg, "the world of espionage is exposed in this captivating overview."

"I am often asked if I always knew I would be a writer," Coleman commented to *SATA.* "I answer, 'Absolutely not!' My strength in school was math and not English, so I wasn't encouraged at all. However, I love to tell stories. I think storytelling is a way of making sense out of what is happening as well as a way of entertaining, amusing and educating. When the cat crawls under the bed, I wonder what she's thinking and planning. What's

the story there? When I write nonfiction, I think about what is most surprising about a person or incident, and what's to be learned? Next to storytelling, learning is the most fun of all."

Biographical and Critical Sources

PERIODICALS

Booklist, February 15, 2003, Kathy Broderick, review of *Famous Bears & Friends: One Hundred Years of Teddy Bear Stories, Poems, Songs, and Heroics,* p. 1066; September 1, 2003, John Peters, review of *Baseball for Everyone: Stories from the Great Game,* p. 117; October 1, 2006, Gillian Engberg, review of *Secrets, Lies, Gizmos, and Spies: A History of Spies and Espionage,* p. 47.

Kirkus Reviews, August 1, 2003, review of *Baseball for Everyone,* p. 1014; October 1, 2006, review of *Secrets, Lies, Gizmos, and Spies,* p. 1012.

New York Sun, December 20, 2006, Otto Penzler, review of *Secrets, Lies, Gizmos, and Spies.*

Publishers Weekly, November 4, 2002, review of *Famous Bears & Friends,* p. 87; July 28, 2003, review of *Baseball for Everyone,* p. 97.

School Library Journal, June, 1993, Maggie McEwen, review of *Fast Eddie,* p. 104; February, 2003, Kathleen Kelly MacMillan, review of *Famous Bears & Friends,*

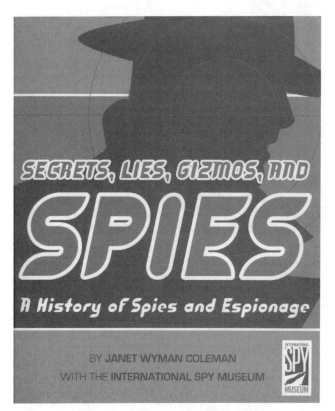

Cover of Coleman's **Secrets, Lies, Gizmos, and Spies,** *a fascinating and fully illustrated guide to espionage that is geared for young readers.*
(Abrams Books for Young Readers, 2006. Reproduced by permission.)

p. 184; October, 2003, Blair Christolon, review of *Baseball for Everyone,* p. 156; February, 2007, Lynn K. Vanca, review of *Secrets, Lies, Gizmos, and Spies,* p. 133.

ONLINE

Janet Wyman Coleman Home Page, http://janetcoleman.com (October 31, 2007).

*   *   *

COLLARD, Sneed B., III 1959-

Personal

Born November 7, 1959, in Phoenix, AZ; son of Sneed B. Collard, Jr. (a professor of biology) and Patricia Anne Case (a high school biology teacher). *Education:* Attended University of California—Davis, 1978-79, and University of Washington, Friday Harbor Marine Laboratories, 1982; University of California—Berkeley, B.A. (biology with marine emphasis; with honors), 1983; University of California—Santa Barbara, M.S. (scientific instrumentation), 1986. *Politics:* "Progressive." *Hobbies and other interests:* Swimming, bicycling, hiking, traveling, SCUBA diving, reading, going to movies, and planting oak trees.

Addresses

Home—Missoula, MT. *E-mail*—collard@bigsky.net.

Career

Freelance writer, 1984—. University of California—Berkeley, zoology department research assistant and research diving program assistant instructor, 1982-83; California Department of Fish and Game, wild trout program seasonal aide, 1983; Woodward-Clyde Consultants, environmental consultant, 1984; University of California—Santa Barbara, Neuroscience Research Institute, director of computer laboratory, 1986-92. California Department of Agriculture, Dutch elm disease project, agricultural aide, 1980; University of California—Santa Barbara, lab assistant, 1981.

Member

Society of Children's Book Writers and Illustrators, Planned Parenthood, "about fifteen environmental groups."

Awards, Honors

First prize, Area, District, and Division Tall-Tales contests, Toastmasters International, 1991; Competent Toastmaster Award, Toastmasters International, 1992; first prize, Area Evaluation Contest, Toastmasters International, 1993; Recommended Book for Reluctant Young Adult Readers selection, American Library Association, 1993, for *Sea Snakes;* Twenty Best Children's Books about the Earth selection, *1994 Information Please Environmental Almanac,* for *Do They Scare You? Creepy Creatures;* Best Book for the Teen Age designation, New York Public Library, 1997, for *Alien Invaders,* 1998, for *Monteverde,* 2001, for *Acting for Nature* and *Lizard Island;* Merit Award for Nonfiction, Society of Children's Book Writer's and Illustrators, 1997, 1998, for magazine articles; Outstanding Trade Science Book for Children designation, Children's Book Council/National Science Teachers Association (CBC/NSTA), 1998, for *Our Wet World,* 2002, for *Butterfly Count,* 2005, for *A Platypus, Probably;* Top-Ten Science Books for Children selection, *Booklist,* and Outstanding Trade Science Book for Children, CBC/NSTA, all 2000, and ASPCA Henry Bergh Award finalist, 2001, all for *The Forest in the Clouds;* Teacher's Choice selection, International Reading Association, for *Beaks;* ASPCA Henry Bergh Children's Book Award for illustration, 2003, for *Animals Asleep,* illustrated by Anik McGrory; CBC/NSTA Outstanding Trade Science Book for Children designation, and ASPCA Henry Bergh Children's Book Award, both 2005, both for *The Prairie Builders;* named *Washington Post*/Children's Book Guild Children's Nonfiction Writer of the Year, 2006; Western Spur Award for storytelling finalist, 2006, for *Shep;* Green Earth Book Award, and Bank Street College of Education Best Children's Book of the Year designation, both 2006, both for *Flash Point;* John Burroughs Award for nature writing, and CBC/NSTA Outstanding Trade Science Book for Children designation, both 2007, both for *One Night in the Coral Sea;* Flicker Tale Award, 2007, for *Dog Sense; Booklist* Editor's Choice, 2007, for *Pocket Babies and Other Amazing Marsupials.*

Writings

NONFICTION; FOR CHILDREN

Sea Snakes, illustrated by John Rice, Boyds Mills Press (Honesdale, NY), 1993.

Do They Scare You? Creepy Creatures, illustrated by Kristin Kest, Charlesbridge (Watertown, MA), 1993, revised as *Creepy Creatures,* Charlesbridge (Watertown, MA), 1997.

Where Do We Live?, Charlesbridge (Watertown, MA), 1996.

Where Do They Live?, Charlesbridge (Watertown, MA), 1996.

Alien Invaders: The Ongoing Problem of Exotic Species Invasions, Franklin Watts (New York, NY), 1996.

Animal Dads, illustrated by Steve Jenkins, Houghton Mifflin (Boston, MA), 1997.

(And photographer) *Monteverde: Science and Scientists in a Costa Rican Cloud Forest,* Franklin Watts (New York, NY), 1997.

Our Wet World: Discovering Earth's Aquatic Ecosystems, illustrated by James M. Needham, Charlesbridge (Watertown, MA), 1998.

Animal Dazzlers: The Role of Brilliant Colors in Nature, Franklin Watts (New York, NY), 1998.

Birds of Prey: A Look at Daytime Raptors, Franklin Watts (New York, NY), 1999.

One Thousand Years Ago on Planet Earth, illustrated by Jonathan Hun, Houghton Mifflin (Boston, MA), 1999.

Acting for Nature: What Young People around the World Have Done to Protect the Environment, illustrated by Carl Dennis Buell, HeyDay Books (Berkeley, CA), 2000.

Making Animal Babies, illustrated by Steven Jenkins, Houghton Mifflin (Boston, MA), 2000.

Forest in the Clouds, illustrated by Michael Rothman, Charlesbridge (Watertown, MA), 2000.

(With Anthony D. Fredericks) *Amazing Animals: Nature's Most Incredible Creatures,* NorthWord Press (Minnetonka, MN), 2000.

A Whale Biologist at Work, Franklin Watts (New York, NY), 2000.

Lizard Island: Science and Scientists on Australia's Great Barrier Reef, Franklin Watts (New York, NY), 2000.

A Firefly Biologist at Work, Franklin Watts (New York, NY), 2001.

Beaks!, illustrated by Robin Brickman, Charlesbridge (Watertown, MA), 2002.

Leaving Home, Houghton Mifflin (Boston, MA), 2002.

The Deep-Sea Floor, illustrated by Gregory Wenzel, Charlesbridge (Watertown, MA), 2003.

B Is for Big Sky Country: A Montana Alphabet, illustrated by Joanna Yardley, Sleeping Bear Press (Chelsea, MI), 2003.

Animals Asleep, illustrated by Anik McGrory, Houghton Mifflin (Boston, MA), 2004.

A Platypus, Probably, illustrated by Andrew Plant, Charlesbridge (Watertown, MA), 2005.

One Night in the Coral Sea, illustrated by Robin Brickman, Charlesbridge (Watertown, MA), 2005.

(And photographer) *The Prairie Builders: Reconstructing America's Lost Grasslands,* Houghton Mifflin (Boston, MA), 2006.

Shep: Our Most Loyal Dog, illustrated by Joanna Yardley, Sleeping Bear Press (Chelsea, MI), 2006.

Pocket Babies and Other Amazing Marsupials, Darby Creek Publishing, 2007.

Reign of the Sea Dragons, illustrated by Andrew Plant, Charlesbridge (Watertown, MA), 2008.

Teeth!, illustrated by Phyllis Saroff, Charlesbridge (Watertown, MA), 2008.

Wings, illustrated by Robin Brickman, Charlesbridge (Watertown, MA), 2008.

Science Warriors ("Scientists in the Field" series), Houghton Mifflin (Boston, MA), 2008.

"WORLD OF DISCOVERY" SERIES

Green Giants—Twelve of the Earth's Tallest Trees, illustrated by Doug Talalla, NorthWord Press (Minnetonka, MN), 1994.

Tough Terminators—Twelve of the Earth's Most Fascinating Predators, illustrated by Doug Talalla, NorthWord Press (Minnetonka, MN), 1994.

Smart Survivors—Twelve of the Earth's Most Remarkable Living Things, illustrated by Doug Talalla, NorthWord Press (Minnetonka, MN), 1994.

"SCIENCE ADVENTURES" SERIES; NONFICTION

In the Deep Sea, Marshall Cavendish (New York, NY), 2006.

On the Coral Reefs, Marshall Cavendish (New York, NY), 2006.

In the Wild, Marshall Cavendish (New York, NY), 2006.

In the Rain Forest Canopy, Marshall Cavendish (New York, NY), 2006.

"AMERICAN HEROES" SERIES; BIOGRAPHIES

Benjamin Franklin: The Man Who Could Do Just about Anything, Marshall Cavendish (New York, NY), 2007.

John Adams: Our Second President, Marshall Cavendish (New York, NY), 2007.

Rosa Parks: The Courage to Make a Difference, Marshall Cavendish (New York, NY), 2007.

Sacagawea: Brave Shoshone Girl, Marshall Cavendish (New York, NY), 2007.

David Crockett: Fearless Frontiersman, Marshall Cavendish (New York, NY), 2007.

Abraham Lincoln: A Courageous Leader, Marshall Cavendish (New York, NY), 2007.

Thomas Jefferson, Marshall Cavendish (New York, NY), 2008.

Eleanor Roosevelt, Marshall Cavendish (New York, NY), 2008.

John Glenn, Marshall Cavendish (New York, NY), 2008.

FICTION

California Fire, McGraw-Hill (New York, NY), 1999.

Butterfly Count (picture book), illustrated by Paul Kratter, Holiday House (New York, NY), 2002.

Dog Sense (middle-grade novel), Peachtree (Atlanta, GA), 2005.

Flash Point (middle-grade novel), Peachtree (Atlanta, GA), 2006.

OTHER

Contributor of articles and stories to periodicals, including *Highlights for Children, Cricket, Christian Science Monitor, Images—Health Literacy '95, Pennywhistle Press, Clubhouse, Children's Digest, Misha, Outdoor California, Western Outdoors, Islands, Earth Steward Journal, Environmental Action,* and *Humanist.*

Sidelights

Sneed B. Collard III gained his love of nature as a child, and he shares that love through his work as an award-winning children's author. Winner of numerous honors for his nonfiction picture books such as *One Night in the Coral Sea, The Forest in the Clouds, A*

Sneed B. Collard III introduces children to the natural world in entertaining picture books such as **Beaks!,** *featuring illustrations by Robin Brickman.*

Firefly Biologist at Work, A Platypus, Probably, and *Pocket Babies and Other Amazing Marsupials,* as well as for the novels *Dog Sense* and *Flash Point,* Collard was named *Washington Post*/Children's Book Guild Children's Nonfiction Writer of the Year in 2006. "I write about creepy creatures and other things because I want people to learn about things they don't know about," Collard once explained to *SATA,* "To me, getting to learn something new is the greatest gift in life. I also hope that when people read my books, they will care more about the plants and animals I care about, and make better decisions about how to live on Earth."

Because both Collard's parents were biologists, the future writer saw much of the world while growing up. As Collard once told *SATA:* "The way things turned out in my young life, I got to travel a lot. My parents were divorced when I was about eight and this made me very sad. The good thing about it, though, was that my dad moved to Florida and I got to go see him twice a year. I also traveled a lot with my mom and stepfather. With all of these experiences, I felt a growing need to share with other people the things I had seen, heard, tasted, and smelled (even if they didn't smell too good!)."

After graduating from high school, Collard took a break before beginning college. "I got a summer job working as a cook at Mount Rushmore in South Dakota," he explained. "With the money I earned, I flew to Israel and spent four and a half months living with a family and working on a kibbutz. From Israel I took a ferry to Europe and hitchhiked through Greece." In retrospect, he added, "taking a year off from school was one of the best decisions I ever made." In addition to preparing him for the rigors of academic study, his travels helped Collard broaden his understanding of the earth's ecosystems.

Collard majored in biology at the University of California—Berkeley, and then got a job counting trout in mountain streams for the California Department of Fish and Game. "I don't understand why *everyone* does not study biology," he later remarked. "If you know about biology, your life will never be dull. Every animal and plant that you see will be an entire world waiting to be explored." While working outdoors and living in a van, Collard also contemplated his future. "I was lying in my sleeping bag, thinking about my life—and trout, of course—and I suddenly said to myself, 'Sneed, if you are going to do something with your life, now is the time.' Right then, I decided to become a writer."

Embarking upon his chosen profession by writing articles for magazines such as *Outdoor California* and *Children's Digest,* Collard discovered that writing could be a difficult way to make a living. As a result, he returned to graduate school at the University of California—Santa Barbara and learned to design instruments using computers. He worked at the university for several years following graduation, managing a computer laboratory by day while devoting his off hours and weekends to writing. His break came in 1990, when children's book publisher Boyds Mills Press asked if he would be interested in submitting a book about reptiles. After consulting with his father to select an appropriate subject, Collard began researching his first book, *Sea Snakes.*

"I rushed off to the library to read everything I could find on sea snakes," Collard recalled to *SATA.* "This was easy, because almost *nothing* had been published on these unusual marine reptiles. I devoured what little information I could find, but I still didn't know enough, so I tracked down all of the sea snake scientists (say that real fast five times!) listed in the books I'd read and called them up one by one. Most of the scientists were very helpful. Once I had all of the information together, I sat down and wrote the first draft of the book in a single day. Of course, the first draft is not the hardest part of writing a book. The ten *other* drafts are what really take time! After a month, however, I was ready to submit the manuscript."

Published in 1993, *Sea Snakes,* which a *Kirkus Reviews* critic called "an intriguing first look at an unusual reptile," describes the appearance and behavior of the snakes that are found in tropical seas around the world. The book is intended to help children understand the complex adaptations snakes make to their environment, and it includes numerous photographs and drawings. As Karey Wehner wrote in *School Library Journal,* Collard's book "will help fill a gap" in library collections; her suggestion that the book would benefit from captions to accompany its photographs was adopted in the work's second printing, and *Sea Snakes* ultimately appeared on the finalist list for the American Library Association Recommended Books for Reluctant Readers.

Collard completed the text of *Do They Scare You? Creepy Creatures* in a month, helped by scientists he worked with at the University of California—Santa Barbara. The book includes information on twenty-two animals with scary reputations, such as vampire bats, sharks, scorpions, tarantulas, and piranhas. As the author told *SATA,* his intention was to "show people how wonderful creepy creatures are and how our fears of animals are blown all out of proportion." The last creature Collard profiles in the book is the imaginary "razor-toothed, slime-encrusted bone muncher," which he invented as a way to "poke fun at our fears."

Focusing on the development of animals, Collard has written several books that share with children how young animals are created, are cared for, and eventually survive on their own in nature. In *Animal Dads* he introduces young readers to the many different ways fathers take care of their young, from keeping them safe to building shelters to even birthing them, as is the case with seahorses. Illustrated with paper-collage art by Steve Jenkins, *Animal Dads* addresses both a younger and older audience through Collard's use of a simple text printed in large type across the page for small children as well as a paragraph explaining more difficult concepts for older children. He uses a similar split-text technique in *Making Animal Babies,* which explains how animal young come into the world and the different methods by which creatures reproduce. Discussing a wide variety of living things, including sea animals, insects, and mammals, Collard shares with young readers how babies come about, and also reveals some of the mating rituals animals perform, how embryos develop, and how babies are born. Describing *Making Animal Babies* as "an attractive, informative, approachable look at a delicate subject," *School Library Journal* contributor Patricia Manning also praised Collard for creating "a good [book] for young children about reproduction."

Collard follows his animal subjects as they become older and prepare to live on their own in *Leaving Home,* a work that also incorporates a two-tiered text. Through this method, according to Phelan, the author "explores the concept imaginatively, writing with admirable simplicity in the short text, [and] introducing children to more complex thoughts and vocabulary in the longer one." Different in format, *Animals Asleep* finds all manner of creatures, from orangutan to otters to butterflies to giant clams, curling up for a nap. Evoking a child's own situation, in *Leaving Home* Collard shares with readers the reasons why various animals leave their families as well as the many ways in which they depart. *Leaving Home* also demonstrates how far some animals travel from their birthplace, whether they leave alone or with others their same age, and how gender plays a factor in when, exactly, males and females begin life apart from their parents. Calling the book "handsome," *School Library Journal* contributor Louise L. Sherman found *Leaving Home* appropriate "both as a concept picture book ideal for a storytime and as an informational source."

Pocket Babies and Other Amazing Marsupials includes Collard's own account of caring for a baby opossum when he was a young teen. From there, the book traces the fascinating history of these unusual mammals, particularly the way they care for their young. Citing the author's focus on scientists' efforts to save many marsupial species living in endangered habitats, Carolyn Phelan wrote in *Booklist* that Collard's "hansomely designed" book "introduces marsupials with panache." In *Kirkus Reviews,* a critic praised the "logically organized" information in *Pocket Babies and Other Amaz-*

A picture book featuring illustrations by Michael Rothman,* The Forest in the Clouds *allows Collard to share his knowledge of a threatened ecosystem. (Illustration © 2000 by Michael Rothman. Used by permission of Charlesbridge Publishing, Inc. All rights reserved.)

ing Marsupials, adding that the book is "appealing enough for the casual browser but also useful for serious middle-school research."

Many of Collard's books are the result of his travels. In 1994, for example, he went to Costa Rica to interview scientists working in a unique ecosystem known as a tropical cloud forest. The resulting book, *Monteverde: Science and Scientists in a Costa Rican Cloud Forest,* "not only documents the remarkable biology of the cloud forest, but the scientists who work there and efforts to protect this fragile ecosystem," the author explained. 1998 found Collard visiting Australia's Lizard Island, where he interviewed scientists studying the Great Barrier Reef in preparation for other nonfiction titles. "These travels, as well as my background as a biologist, provide me with an endless supply of book ideas," Collard explained.

Both *Monteverde* and *The Forest in the Clouds,* introduce readers to the Monteverde Cloud Forest of Costa Rica and the important relationship plants and animals

share in this unusual tropical ecosystem. Like many of Collard's books, both volumes also emphasize the need to preserve such natural wonders and conserve endangered habitats. Reviewing *The Forest in the Clouds* for *Booklist,* Phelan noted that Collard "gives a clear sense of the diversity of life to be found in a cloud forest and the need to protect it," and Randy Meyer wrote in the same periodical that, "thanks to the impassioned pen of science writer Collard, the scientific Shangri-la comes to life" in the pages of *Monteverde.*

Collard's work with scientist in the field have led to his "Science Adventures" books, which include *In the Deep Sea, On the Coral Reefs, In the Wild,* and *In the Rain Forest Canopy. In the Deep Sea* describes the work of Dr. Edith Widder and other biologists studying marine bioluminescence: the way some undersea species make their own light. For Collard, profiling Widder and her research had an unforeseen but amazing outcome. As he noted on his home page, "With Dr. Widder and other scientists, I spent five days out at sea. Even better, I got to dive two times in the research submersible Johnson Sea-Link. Each time, we dove to the bottom of the ocean, 3,000 feet deep. I saw viper fish, tripod fish, comb jellies, squid, and many other animals. Most of these were bioluminescent. I took tons of photographs and had the time of my life." In *On the Coral Reefs* Collard joins biologist Alexander Grutter to explore the unique environment in a coral reef, while *In the Wild* finds Tara Stoinski, Thomas Butynski, and other zoo biologists working to save the planet's endangered species. Sharing a similar theme, *A Firefly Biologist at Work* follows Collard's stepfather, firefly expert Jim Case, in his work studying the synchronus firefly native to riverbanks of Southeast Asia. Praising Collard's scientist-oriented studies as "clear and engaging," Piehl wrote in *School Library Journal* that the volumes are "solid choices" for budding biologists.

Other interesting creatures are introduced to young children in books like *Beaks!, Teeth!,* and *Wings!, A Platypus, Probably,* and *One Night in the Coral Sea,* the last two which focus on creatures native to Australia. In *A Platypus, Probably,* which features detailed paintings by Andrew Plant, Collard profiles an unusual nocturnal mammal that can breathe air yet feeds underwater. Focusing on the history and behavior of the platypus, the book is "an interesting informational read," according to a *Kirkus Reviews* writer, and Patricia Manning concluded that the book contains enough "data to satisfy enquiring minds."

Cover of Collard's nonfiction title **In the Deep Sea,** *featuring photography by marine biologist Edith Widder.* (Marshall Cavendish, 2006. Illustration © 2006 by Sneed B. Collard, III. Reproduced by permission.)

Featuring illustrations by Robin Brickman, *One Night in the Coral Sea* takes readers down into the depths of a coral reef in Australia's Great Barrier Reef during the spring spawning: the single night when the many coral species in that unique ecosystem reproduce. Collard's "basic" text shares with children "an amazing event that scientists discovered little more than 20 years ago," wrote Kathy Piehl in her *School Library Journal* review of the 2005 book. In *Kirkus Reviews* a critic dubbed *One Night in the Coral Sea* a work that "stands out" due to its "special focus" as well as Brickman's "riveting illustrations."

Turning his hand to fiction, Collard has also authored *Butterfly Count,* a picture book that introduces children to the world of science through the story of Amy. Described as a "gentle family story with an environmental message" by *School Library Journal* critic Maryann H. Owen, *Butterfly Count* shares the tale of Amy as she celebrates the Fourth of July holiday by going with her mother on a butterfly hunt. Taking place on a stretch of land once belonging to her great-great-grandmother Nora Belle, the hunt features conservationists, young and old, gathering to count the number and variety of butterflies living on the property, which is now a part of a prairie restoration project. Hoping to find at least one regal fritillary, Nora Belle's favorite, Amy finally locates the rare insect among her ancestor's graves in a portion of meadow that was said to have never been mowed by the early settlers. According to Ellen Mandel in *Booklist,* the author's decision to make Amy an older child broadens the story's appeal, "making the book well suited to children who can read and enjoy the story on their own."

In Collard's first novel, *Dog Sense,* he tells a story about thirteen-year-old Guy Martinez. After his single mom moves the family from California to a small Montana town to live with her father, Guy has to put away his surf board, adapt to new surroundings, and make new friends in his new eighth-grade class. Problems with a school bully make the move less than pleasant, but they are ultimately resolved with the help of his friendly, Frisbee-catching border collie, Streak. "Collard shows in his first novel that he can construct a suspenseful plot and create believable characters," wrote a *Kirkus Reviews* writer in appraising the author's fiction debut. In Guy, Collard creates what *Booklist* critic Shelle Rosenfeld called "an appealing, sympathetic protagonist" in his "straightforward narrative." Reviewing *Dog Sense* for *Publishers Weekly* a contributor praised the book as an "affecting" coming-of-age story that features "a sensitive yet resilient" teen.

Also set in Collard's home state of Montana, *Flash Point* finds high-school sophomore Luther Wright working for Kay, a local veterinarian, after school. Kay rescues injured birds of prey such as falcons, owls, and hawks, caring for them and ultimately releasing them back into the wild. As Luther becomes familiar with the wildlife in the surrounding forest, he raises the ire of

Cover of Collard's **Dog Sense**, *a coming-of-age story in which a boy and his dog move to a new town and catch the attention of a local bully.* (Peachtree, 2006. Reproduced by permission.)

his father, who works for the local lumber company and has been having his job curtailed by environmental regulations. A fire that ravages the area and the tragedy and conflicts that result serve as the focus of a "solid story" that "should appeal to readers interested in ecological themes such as managing fires in forests and protecting raptors," according to *Kliatt* critic Claire Rosser. In *School Library Journal* Laurie Slagenwhite wrote that themes relating to "logging, forest fires, and birds of prey" are "skillfully integrated" into Collard's tale, and a *Kirkus Reviews* writer dubbed *Flash Point* "well-paced" and "interesting."

When he is not writing, Collard spends his time traveling and speaking to groups about writing, science, and the environment. Despite the fact that being a writer has been difficult for him, particularly financially, Collard has enjoyed the support of his family and remains pleased with his career choice. He offered this advice to young people: "If you want something in life, don't be afraid to go after it. Different people will always tell you how you *should* live your life. Many of these people mean well, but they cannot see inside you, so what they tell you may not be right for you. However, just because you decide to do or be something does not mean it will be easy. To achieve something important and valuable takes a lot of hard work and you have to stick to it, even when it is hard and painful."

Biographical and Critical Sources

PERIODICALS

Booklist, May 15, 1997, Carolyn Phelan, review of *Animal Dads,* p. 1577; September 1, 1997, Randy Meyer, review of *Monteverde: Science and Scientists in a Costa Rican Cloud Forest,* p. 116; August, 1999, Ilene Cooper, review of *One Thousand Years Ago on Planet Earth,* p. 2048; May 1, 2000, John Peters, review of *Making Animal Babies,* p. 1672; June 1, 2000, Carolyn Phelan, review of *The Forest in the Clouds,* p. 1900; February 1, 2001, John Peters, review of *Lizard Island: Science and Scientists on Australia's Great Barrier Reef,* p. 1047; February 15, 2001, Carolyn Phelan, review of *A Whale Biologist at Work,* p. 1132; December 1, 2001, Gillian Engberg, review of *A Firefly Biologist at Work,* p. 654; March 1, 2002, Carolyn Phelan, review of *Leaving Home,* p. 1137; April 1, 2002, Ellen Mandel, review of *Butterfly Count,* p. 1332; March 1, 2004, Carolyn Phelan, review of *Animals Asleep,* p. 1190; May 15, 2005, Gillian Engberg, review of *One Night in the Coral Sea,* p. 1654; June 1, 2005, Carolyn Phelan, review of *The Prairie Builders: Reconstructing America's Lost Grasslands,* p.

Cover of Collard's young-adult novel **Flash Point,** *featuring photography by Kari Greer.* (Peachtree, 2006. Photograph © 2006 by Kari Greer. Reproduced by permission.)

1796; September 15, 2005, Carolyn Phelan, review of *A Platypus, Probably,* p. 68; October 15, 2005, Shelle Rosenfeld, review of *Dog Sense,* p. 50; February 1, 2006, Gillian Engberg, review of *On the Coral Reefs,* p. 46; January 1, 2007, John Peters, review of *Sacagawea: Brave Shoshone Girl,* p. 107; September 15, 2007, Carolyn Phelan, review of *Animal Babies and Other Amazing Marsupials,* p. 62.

Bulletin of the Center for Children's Books, April, 2004, Timnah Card, review of *Animals Asleep,* p. 321.

Kirkus Reviews, February 15, 1993, review of *Sea Snakes,* pp. 224-225; March 1, 2004, review of *Animals Asleep,* p. 220; June 15, 2005, reviews of *One Night in the Coral Sea* and *A Platypus, Probably,* p. 680; September 1, 2005, review of *Dog Sense,* p. 970; October 1, 2006, review of *Flash Point,* p. 1012; August 15, 2007, review of *Pocket Babies and Other Amazing Marsupials.*

Kliatt, November, 2006, Claire Rosser, review of *Flash Point,* p. 6.

Publishers Weekly, March 31, 1997, review of *Animal Dads,* p. 73; October 18, 1999, review of *One Thousand Years Ago on Planet Earth,* p. 82; October 31, 2005, review of *Dog Sense,* p. 57.

School Library Journal, March, 1993, Karey Wehner, review of *Sea Snakes,* p. 205; July, 2000, Patricia Manning, review of *Making Animal Babies,* p. 93; August, 2000, Kathy Piehl, review of *The Forest in the Clouds,* p. 168; March, 2001, Frances E. Millhouser, review of *A Whale Biologist at Work,* p. 232; May, 2001, Laura Younkin, review of *Lizard Island,* p. 162; December, 2001, Arwen Marshall, review of *A Firefly Biologist at Work,* p. 154; April, 2002, Louise L. Sherman, review of *Leaving Home,* p. 129; June, 2002, Maryann H. Owen, review of *Butterfly Count,* p. 92; July, 2003, Diane Olivio-Posner, review of *The Deep-Sea Floor,* p. 112; August, 2005, Kathy Piehl, review of *One Night in the Coral Sea,* p. 142; September, 2005, Patricia Manning, review of *A Platypus, Probably,* p. 190; October, 2005, Patricia Manning, review of *A Firefly Biologist at Work,* p. 62; November, 2005, Kathryn Childs, review of *Dog Sense,* p. 130; May, 2006, Kathy Piehl, review of *In the Deep Sea,* p. 142; August, 2006, Linda Zeilstra Sawyer, review of *Shep: Our Most Loyal Dog,* p. 102; December, 2006, Laurie Slagenwhite, review of *Flash Point,* p. 134.

ONLINE

Sneed B. Collard III Home Page, http://www.sneedbcollard iii.com (November 10, 2007).

* * *

CÔTÉ, Geneviève 1964-

Personal

Born 1964, in Montréal, Québec, Canada. *Education:* Concordia University, 1987.

Addresses

Home and office—Montréal, Québec, Canada. *E-mail*—cotege@netaxis.ca.

Career

Illustrator and author of children's books. *Exhibitions:* Works included in exhibitions at Albums Canadiens illustrés Remarquables 2000-03, New York Society of Illustrators, Biennale de l'Illustration Québécoise, Bibliotheque Nationale, Montréal, Marché Bonsecours, Art Gallery of Ontario, CAPIC Awards show, Salons de l'Illustration Québécoise, and Maison de la culture Côte-des Neiges, Montréal.

Member

Writer's Union of Canada, Canadian Children's Books Council, Association des Illustrateurs du Québec (president, 1993-95).

Awards, Honors

Applied Arts magazine award, 1999, 2000; Grand Prix d'Illustration Jeunesse GL&V, 2000; gold medal, Society of Illustrators, 2001; Governor General Award nominations, Canada Council for the Arts, 2003, 2007, for *Le premier printemps du monde* and *La grande aven-*

Geneviève Côté's unique, energetic illustrations are the perfect match for Janet S. Wong's story in the picture book **Minn and Jake.** (Illustration © 2003 by Geneviève Côté. Reprinted by permission of Farrar, Straus & Giroux, LLC.)

ture d'un petit mouton noir; Elizabeth Mrazik-Cleaver Award, International Board on Books for Young People (Canadian section), 2006, for *The Lady of Shalott;* Governor General Award for illustration, 2007, for *La petite rapporteuse de mots.*

Writings

SELF-ILLUSTRATED

Quel Éléphant?, Éditions Scholastic (Toronto, Ontario, Canada), 2006, translated as *What Elephant?,* Kids Can Press (Toronto, Ontario, Canada), 2006.

With You Always, Little Monday, Harcourt (Orlando, FL), 2007.

ILLUSTRATOR

Marie-Andrée Mativat, *Le bulldozer amoureux,* Héritage (Saint-Lambert, Québec, Canada), 1988.

Henriette Major, *Les mémoires d'une bicyclette,* Héritage (Montréal, Québec, Canada), 1989.

Cécile Gagnon, *Mes premières fois,* Héritage (Saint-Lambert, Québec, Canada), 1989.

Marc Porret, *L'almanach ensorcelé,* Véronique Lord (La-Salle, Québec, Canada), 1991.

Évelyne Wilwerth, *Mannequin noir dans barque verte,* Hurtubise (LaSalle, Québec, Canada), 1991.

Doumbi Fakoli, *Aventure a Ottawa,* LaSalle (Montréal, Québec, Canada), 1991.

Francine Girard, *Tante-lo est partie,* Boréal (Montréal, Québec, Canada), 1991.

Charlotte Gingras, *Les chats d'Aurélie,* Amérique Jeunesse (Boucherville, Québec, Canada), 1994, reprinted, 2006.

Johanne Gaudet, *Un ticket pour le bout du monde,* Boréal (Montréal, Québec, Canada), 1994.

Jacques Savoie, *Toute la beauté du monde,* La Courte Échelle (Montréal, Québec, Canada), 1995.

Jacques Savoie, *Les fleurs du capitaine,* La Courte Échelle (Montréal, Québec, Canada), 1996.

Jacques Savoie, *Une ville imaginaire,* La Courte Échelle (Montréal, Québec, Canada), 1996.

Jacques Savoie, *Les cachotteries de ma soeur,* Courte Échelle (Montréal, Québec, Canada), 1997.

Jacques Savoie, *Le plus beau des voyages,* La Courte Échelle (Montréal, Québec, Canada), 1997.

Jacques Savoie, *La plus populaire du monde,* La Courte Échelle (Montréal, Québec, Canada), 1998.

Bertrand Gauthier, *Adrien n'est pas un Chameau,* La Courte Échelle (Montréal, Québec, Canada), 1999.

Marie-Danielle Croteau, *La grande aventure d'un petit mouton noir,* Dominique et cie. (Saint-Lambert, Québec, Canada), 1999, translation published as *The Amazing Story of the Little Black Sheep,* Dominique and Friends (Saint Lambert, Québec, Canada), 1999.

Michele Marineau, adaptor, *L'affreux: conte Amérindien,* 2000.

Nathalie Loignon, *Christophe au grand coeur,* Dominique et cie. (Saint-Lambert, Québec, Canada), 2000.

Maryse Choiniere and Kim Choiniere, *Plume, papier, oiseau,* Soulieres (Saint-Lambert, Québec, Canada), 2002.

Rémi Savard and Catherine Germain, *Le premier printemps du monde,* Les 400 Coups (Montréal, Québec, Canada), 2002, translated by Donald Kellough as *First Spring: An Innu Tale of North America,* Simply Read Books (Vancouver, British Columbia, Canada), 2006.

Nathalie Loignon, *Songes et Mensonges,* Dominique et cie. (Saint-Lambert, Québec, Canada), 2002.

Édith Bourget, *Autour de Gabrielle/Un recueil de poésie écrit,* Soulieres (Saint-Lambert, Québec, Canada), 2003.

Marthe Pelletier, *Léo à la mer,* La Courte Échelle (Montréal, Québec, Canada), 2003.

Nancy Montour, *Le coeur au vent,* Dominique et cie. (Saint-Lambert, Québec, Canada), 2003.

Janet Wong, *Minn and Jake,* Farrar, Straus (New York, NY), 2003.

François Barcelo, *Premier voyage pour Momo de Sinro,* Québec Amérique (Montréal, Québec, Canada), 2003.

Charlotte Gingras, *Les perdus magnifiques,* Dominique et cie. (Saint-Lambert, Québec, Canada), 2004.

Un royaume inventé, La Courte Échelle (Montréal, Québec, Canada), 2004.

Michèle Marineau, *L'affreux: conte Amérindien,* Les 400 Coups (Montréal, Québec, Canada), 2005.

Gilles Tibo, *La chambre vide,* Soulieres (Saint-Lambert, Québec, Canada), 2005.

Marthe Pelletier, *Des amours inventés,* La Courte Échelle (Montréal, Québec, Canada), 2005.

Lord Alfred Tennyson, *The Lady of Shalott,* Kids Can Press (Toronto, Ontario, Canada), 2005.

Édith Bourget, *Les saisons d'Henri: recueil de poésie,* Soulieres (Saint-Lambert, Québec, Canada), 2006.

Charlotte Gingras, *La fabrique de Citrouilles,* La Courte Échelle (Montréal, Québec, Canada), 2007.

Charlotte Gingras, *L'île au Géant,* La Courte Échelle (Montréal, Québec, Canada), 2007.

Susin Fernlund-Nielsen, *The Magic Beads,* Simply Read Books (Vancouver, British Columbia, Canada), 2007.

Danielle Simard, *La petite rapporteuse de mots,* Les 400 Coups (Montréal, Québec, Canada), 2007.

Charlotte Gingras, *Les nouveaux bonheurs,* La Courte Échelle (Montréal, Québec, Canada), 2007.

Anne Renaud, *Missuk's Snow Geese,* Simply Read Books (Vancouver, British Columbia, Canada), 2008.

Sidelights

Illustrator and author Geneviève Côté has been recognized for her work in children's literature and honored with numerous awards, including the Elizabeth Mrazik-Cleaver Award in 2006 for her work illustrating a new

Côté's first self-illustrated picture book, **What Elephant?,** *features a humorous story and energetic watercolor and crayon art.* (Illustration © 2006 by Geneviéve Côté. Used by permission of Kids Can Press Ltd., Toronto.)

edition of Sir Alfred Tennyson's poem *The Lady of Shalott.* Côté has also been nominated twice for Canada's Governor General's Award in illustration, once for her work for Rémi Savard's *Le premier printemps du monde* and a second time for the art she created for *La grande aventure d'un petit mouton noir,* a book by Marie-Danielle Croteau that has also been published in an English-language edition as *The Amazing Story of the Little Black Sheep.* In addition to illustrating children's books, Côté has also created editorial illustrations for the *New York Times* and *Wall Street Journal.*

Côté artwork has been recognized for its elegant simplicity. For instance, in her self-illustrated title *With*

You Always, Little Monday—a story about a little bunny who goes on a quest to find his parents—a *Kirkus Reviews* contributor summarized the book's mixed-media illustrations as "a wonder" and added that Côté's work, while "deceptively simple on its surface, . . . is expression-filled and elegant in light and line." Côté's use of color has also been considered one of her strengths as an artist. As a reviewer noted in *Publishers Weekly,* her illustrations for *With You Always, Little Monday* are "lyrical and expressive" and despite the limited use of color, she successfully evokes "the cozy greenness of the forest and the icy blue glow of moonlight."

Biographical and Critical Sources

PERIODICALS

Booklist, October 1, 2003, Gillian Engberg, review of *Minn and Jake,* p. 322; October 1, 2005, Hazel Rochman, review of *The Lady of Shalott,* p. 54.

Bulletin of the Center for Children's Books, May, 2006, Deborah Stevenson, review of *First Spring: An Innu Tale of North America,* p. 421; October, 2003, Betsy Hearne, review of *Minn and Jake,* p. 83.

Canadian Book Review Annual, 2005, review of *The Lady of Shalott,* p. 537.

Horn Book, May-June, 2007, Susan Dove Lempke, review of *With You Always, Little Monday,* p. 262.

Kirkus Reviews, July 15, 2003, review of *Minn and Jake,* p. 969; September 1, 2005, review of *The Lady of Shalott,* p. 984; October 1, 2006, review of *What Elephant?,* p. 1012.

Library Media Connection, April-May, 2006, Leslie Schoenherr, review of *The Lady of Shalott,* p. 83.

Publishers Weekly, August 18, 2003, review of *Minn and Jake,* p. 79; April 16, 2007, review of *With You Always, Little Monday,* p. 50

Resource Links, February, 2006, Myra, Junyk, review of *First Spring,* p. 52; June, 2006, Denise Parrott, review of *First Spring,* p. 4; February, 2007, Claire Hazzard, review of *What Elephant?,* p. 2; June, 2007, Mary Moroska, review of *What Elephant?,* p. 43.

School Library Journal, March, 2000, Judith Constantinides, review of *The Amazing Story of the Little Black Sheep,* p. 194; October, 2003, Lee Bock, review of *Minn and Jake,* p. 142; December, 2005, Teresa Pfeifer, review of *The Lady of Shalott,* p. 175; July, 2006, Maryann H. Owen, review of *First Spring,* p. 94; December, 2006, Martha Simpson, review of *What Elephant?,* p. 96; April, 2007, Susan Moorhead, review of *With You Always, Little Monday,* p. 96.

ONLINE

Communication-Jeunesse Web site, http://www.communication-jeunesse.qc.ca/ (October 28, 2007), "Geneviève Côté."

Geneviève Côté Home Page, http://www.Genevievecoteillustration.com (October 28, 2007).

Harcourt Web site, http://www.harcourtbooks.com/ (October 28, 2007), "Geneviève Côté."

*   *   *

COWLES, Kathleen
See KRULL, Kathleen

*   *   *

CRAIG, Kit
See REED, Kit

D

de GOURSAC, Olivier 1959-

Personal

Born 1959, in France; married; children: five children.

Addresses

Office—Planète Mars, 28 rue de la gaîté, 75014 Paris, France.

Career

Space imaging specialist. Jet Propulsion Laboratory, Pasadena, CA, served on Viking mission team, c. 1980s, outreach correspondent in France for Mars Pathfinder mission, 1993-98; Taurus International, Rouen, France, mapped RMS *Titanic* wreck site, 1991; Planète Mars (French chapter of Mars Society), Paris, France, outreach manager for Mars exploration missions, 1999—.

Writings

À la conquête de Mars, Larousse (Paris, France), 2000, translated by Lenora Ammon as *Visions of Mars,* foreword by Jim Garvin, Harry N. Abrams (New York, NY), 2005.
Space: Exploring the Moon, the Planets, and Beyond, illustrated by Pascal Laye, Harry N. Abrams (New York, NY), 2006.

Coauthor of *The Cambridge Encyclopedia of Space;* contributor to *Le Figaro.*

Sidelights

Olivier de Goursac, a space imaging specialist, is the author of *Visions of Mars* and *Space: Exploring the Moon, the Planets, and Beyond.* An outreach manager for the French chapter of the Mars Society, de Goursac began his career as an imaging technician at NASA's Jet Propulsion Laboratory during the 1980s. He helped process images from the Viking Mission, the first successful landing on Mars, and later served as a correspondent in France for the Mars Pathfinder mission, which delivered a free-ranging robotic rover to the surface of the Red Planet. De Goursac has also used his experience to map the *Titanic* wreck site for Taurus International, one of the sponsors of the recovery expedition sent out to explore the remains of the ill-fated ocean liner, and he developed a model based on his findings that is still on exhibit at the National Sea Museum in France.

De Goursac received considerable acclaim for his work on the images of Mars' Valles Marineris, a vast system of canyons nearly seven miles deep and more than 3,000 miles long, done in collaboration with Andrew Lark. Using satellite data from the Mars Orbiter Laser Altimeter, an instrument that measures Martian topography through the use of a laser beam, de Goursac and Lark produced an extremely accurate map of the region. "My goal was to obtain the most natural-looking views, as if an astronaut was standing on the surface of Mars, or as if we were flying above Valles Marineris," he told Robert Roy Britt in an interview on *Space.com.* "Also, the dust opacity of the Martian atmosphere is accurately rendered and all colors and luminosity were very carefully balanced to be as close as possible to reality." In an interview with Aude Lecrubier for *Popsci.com,* de Goursac proclaimed, "We have revealed this canyon like no one before us."

In *Visions of Mars,* a 2005 work, de Goursac offers a selection of photographs, many previously unpublished, that are drawn from NASA's robotic exploration missions of the planet. The images capture Mars's polar ice caps, vast windswept plains, and towering peaks, including Olympus Mons, the solar system's largest known volcano. In addition, he presents a panoramic view of the Mars Pathfinder landing site, a look at stratocumulus clouds billowing over the Chasma Australe valley, and a picture of Phobos, one of the planet's two moons. The volume also contains a summary of the data collected about the planet. "After de Goursac's towering achievement, visible on these pages," remarked a contributor in the London *Sunday Times*, "all that remains is for us to find life" on the Red Planet.

In *Space* de Goursac discusses such topics as space travel, the history of rocketry, and the practical applications of space exploration. He also examines celestial bodies, including the planets of the solar system, asteroids, and the Earth's moon. Some critics felt that color photos and artists' renditions were the strength of the book; a contributor in *Kirkus Reviews* stated that "content takes a back seat to production value in this glossy, oversized, superficial survey of space exploration." "Space fans will love poring over the graphics," observed *School Library Journal* critic Jeffrey A. French.

Biographical and Critical Sources

PERIODICALS

Kirkus Reviews, October 15, 2006, review of *Space: Exploring the Moon, the Planets, and Beyond*, p. 1068.
School Librarian, autumn, 2006, review of *Space*, p. 149.
School Library Journal, February, 2007, review of *Space*, p. 134.
Sunday Times (London, England), May 15, 2005, "Wonders of Another World," review of *Visions of Mars*, p. 40.

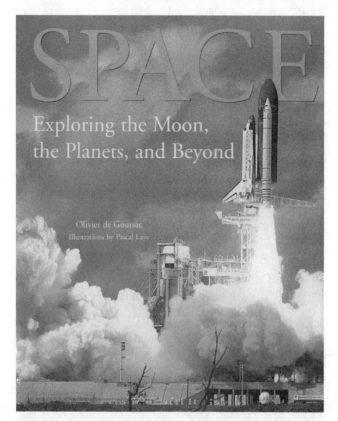

Cover of Olivier de Goursac's Space, *a history of space exploration featuring a cover photograph by Pascal Laye.* (Abrams Books for Young Readers, 2006. Cover photo © 2006 by NASA/Kennedy Space Center. Cover illustration © by Pascal Laye. Reproduced by permission.)

ONLINE

Discover Online, http://discovermagazine.com/ (December 3, 2004), Barry E. di Gregorio, "The Color of Mars."
French Mars Society Web site, http://www.planete-mars.com/ (October 31, 2007), "Olivier de Goursac."
Popsci.com, http://www.popsci.com/ (January, 2002), Aude Lecrubier, "A Postcard of Mars' Grandest Canyon."
Space.com, http://www.space.com/ (December, 2001), Robert Roy Britt, "Mars Rendered in New Light Using Spacecraft Data."*

* * *

DEWDNEY, Anna

Personal

Daughter of a doctor and Winifred Luhrmann (an author); children: two daughters. *Hobbies and other interests:* Running.

Addresses

Home—Putney, VT. *E-mail*—anna@annadewdney.com; dewdney@sover.net.

Career

Author, illustrator, and educator.

Member

Western Massachusetts Illustrators Guild.

Writings

SELF-ILLUSTRATED

Llama, Llama Red Pajama, Viking (New York, NY), 2005.
Grumpy Gloria, Viking (New York, NY), 2006.
Llama, Llama Mad at Mama, Viking (New York, NY), 2007.
Nobunny's Perfect, Viking (New York, NY), 2008.

ILLUSTRATOR

Dian Curtis Regan, *The Peppermint Race*, Holt (New York, NY), 1994.
Matt Christopher, *All-Star Fever: A Peach Street Mudders Story*, Little Brown (Boston, MA), 1995.
Matt Christopher, *Shadow over Second: A Peach Street Mudders Story*, Little Brown (Boston, MA), 1996.
Jake Wolf, *What You Do Is Easy, What I Do Is Hard*, Greenwillow (New York, NY), 1996.
Dorothy McKerns, *The Kid's Guide to Good Grammar: What You Need to Know about Punctuation, Sentence Structure, Spelling, and More*, Lowell House (Los Angeles, CA), 1998.

Anna Dewdney illustrates an original warmhearted bedtime tale in her picture book Llama Llama Red Pajama. (Illustration © 2005 by Anna Dewdney. Reproduced by permission of Viking, a division of Penguin Putnam Books for Young Readers.)

Harriet Heath, *Using Your Values to Raise Your Child to Be an Adult You Admire,* Parenting Press (Seattle, WA), 2000.

Sidelights

A teacher, artist, and author, Anna Dewdney began her career in children's literature by illustrating several chapter books. Her first picture-book project, *What You Do Is Easy, What I Do Is Hard,* written by Jake Wolf, features "watercolor, gouache and pencil pictures" that "favor the delicate and sweet," according to a *Publishers Weekly* contributor. April Judge, reviewing the work for *Booklist,* cited in particular Dewdney's "rollicking illustrations." Along with illustrating children's books, Dewdney has also created artwork for the parenting book *Using Your Values to Raise Your Child to Be an Adult You Admire.*

In her first self-illustrated picture book, *Llama, Llama Red Pajama,* Dewdney introduced loveable Baby Llama, who becomes agitated when his mother does not appear quickly with his drink of water. He worries and whimpers until finally she arrives to reassure him that she is always nearby. "Dewdney gives a wonderfully fresh twist to a familiar nighttime ritual with an adorable bug-eyed baby llama," wrote Julie Cummins in *Booklist.* In her *School Library Journal* review, Corrina Austin noted that the artist's "large, boldly colored pictures have a grand and sweeping quality," and a *Kirkus Reviews* contributor called the story "an uproariously funny tale" that "is bound to become a comical classic oft-requested at bedtime."

Baby Llama returns in *Llama, Llama Mad at Mama.* While Baby Llama and his mother are shopping, she pulls him away from all of the fun displays, making him try on clothing he does not like and not letting him play with toys. After he has a tantrum, Mama reassures her child that they will be done soon; she invites him to help push the cart so they can finish faster and then go get ice cream. "Snappy rhythm, pleasing rhyme and large-scale art . . . make this an involving read-aloud,"

A formerly fussed-over family dog worries that it has lost its special place in Dewdney's humorous **Grumpy Gloria.** (Illustration © 2006 by Anna Dewdney. Reproduced by permission of Viking, a division of Penguin Putnam Books for Young Readers.)

wrote a *Publishers Weekly* contributor. Jayne Damron, writing in *School Library Journal,* explained that "children will giggle at Dewdney's rhythmic rhymes," and a *Kirkus Reviews* critic deemed *Lllama, Llama Mad at Mama* "a perfect choice for preschool read-alouds."

Grumpy Gloria, Dewdney's second self-illustrated work, is the tale of a bulldog who worries that she has been replaced by her owner's new doll. "Large illustrations done in rich, bright colors are great for viewing at a distance," noted Kirsten Cutler in *School Library Journal.* According to a *Kirkus Reviews* contributor, "Gloria has personality to spare," while in *Publishers Weekly* a critic maintained that "humor . . . comes through not only in Gloria's facial expressions but also in the lilting descriptions of her feelings."

Discussing her drawing process on her home page, Dewdney explained: "People ask me how I come up with the faces that I draw. I answer that they are self-portraits. I make a lot of funny faces, anyway, just going about my day, but when I draw, I usually make the face of the character as I draw."

Biographical and Critical Sources

PERIODICALS

Booklist, November 15, 1994, Hazel Rochman, review of *The Peppermint Race,* p. 603; December 15, 1996, April Judge, review of *What You Do Is Easy, What I Do Is Hard,* p. 734; April 1, 2005, Julie Cummins, review of *Llama, Llama Red Pajama,* p. 1365.

Kirkus Reviews, May 1, 2005, review of *Llama, Llama Red Pajama,* p. 537; September 1, 2006, review of *Grumpy Gloria,* p. 902; August 1, 2007, review of *Llama, Llama Mad at Mama.*

Library Journal, December, 1999, Elizabeth Caulfield Felt, review of *Using Your Values to Raise Your Child to Be an Adult You Admire,* p. 174.

Publishers Weekly, October 21, 1996, review of *What You Do Is Easy, What I Do Is Hard,* p. 82; October 9, 2006, review of *Grumpy Gloria,* p. 54; July 16, 2007, review of *Llama, Llama Mad at Mama,* p. 162.

School Library Journal, April, 2005, Corrina Austin, review of *Llama, Llama Red Pajama,* p. 96; September, 2006, Kirsten Cutler, review of *Grumpy Gloria,* p. 165; September, 2007, Jayne Damron, review of *Llama, Llama Mad at Mama,* p. 162.

ONLINE

Anna Dewdney Home Page, http://www.annadewdney.com (October 8, 2007).

Western Massachusetts Illustrators Guild Web site, http://www.wmig.org/bios/ (October 22, 2007), "Anna Dewdney."*

*   *   *

DOUGLAS, Lola
See ZEISES, Lara M.

*   *   *

DOWNING, Johnette

Personal

Female. *Education:* Southeastern Louisiana University, B.A.

Addresses

Home and office—P.O. Box 13367, New Orleans, LA 70185-3367. *E-mail*—Info@JohnetteDowning.com.

Career

Singer, songwriter, and author. Worked at Isidore Newman School, New Orleans, LA, for fourteen years. Musical performer and recording artists.

Member

National Academy of Recording Arts and Sciences, Society of Children's Book Writers and Illustrators, Independent Children's Artist Network, Children's Music Network, Haiku Society of America, New Orleans Haiku Society.

Johnette Downing (Courtesy of Johnette Downing.)

Awards, Honors

Five Parents' Choice awards; two Parent's Guide to Children's Media awards; three National Parenting Publications awards; three iParenting Media awards; Family Choice award; Family Review Center award; Imagination Award.

Writings

A Squirrel Jumped out of a Tree, Colonial Press, 1990.
Today Is Monday in Louisiana, illustrated by Deborah Ousley Kadair, Pelican (Gretna, LA), 2006.
(Adapter) *Down in Louisiana: Traditional Song,* Pelican (Gretna, LA), 2007.

OTHER

Recordings include (with Dickie Knicks) *New Moon: Music for Little Folk,* 1990; *Music Time,* 1992, re-recorded 2005; *From the Gumbo Pot: Stirring up Tasty Tunes,* 1998; *Wild and Woolly Wiggle Songs,* 2001; *Silly Sing Along,* 2002; *The Second Line: Scarf Activity Songs,* 2003; and *Fins and Grins,* 2006.

Contributor of poetry to anthologies, including *Katrina-ku: Storm Poems,* New Orleans Haiku Society, 2006, and to periodicals such as *Frogpond, bottle rockets, World Haiku, Nisqually Delta Review,* and *YAWP.* Contributor of articles to *Pass It On!* and *Applause!*

Sidelights

Louisiana-based singer/songwriter Johnette Downing has performed her music all over the world, earning her the title "the Pied Piper of Louisiana music traditions," according to a reviewer for the *New Orleans Gambit Weekly.* Downing's songs are "consistently enjoyable and encouraging," wrote Paul Shackman in a review of her album *The Second Line: Scarf Activity Songs* for *Booklist.* In her music, as well as in her written work, Downing is dedicated to sharing her Louisiana musical and literary heritage with children. Her picture books *Today Is Monday in Louisiana* and *Down in Louisiana: Traditional Song* both focus on Downing's home state and the unique culture of that colorful region of America.

Today Is Monday in Louisiana, an adaptation of a popular song, introduces a new variety of Louisiana food for each day of the week. As the song moves on from day to day, each new verse repeats the previous meal, giving readers and listeners a chance to chime with the re-

Downing shares the beauty and uniqueness of her home state in her song book **Down in Louisiana,** *featuring collage art by Doborah Ousley Kadair.* (Pelican, 2007. Illustration © 2007 by Deborah Ousley Kadair.)

frain from memory. "Downing's rhythmic, repetitive text will appeal to children," wrote a *Kirkus Reviews* contributor, and Judith Constantinides wrote in *School Library Journal* that *Today Is Monday in Louisiana* would be "a pleasing addition to Louisiana lore and a fun, light note" for possible school projects on the state. As a *Publishers Weekly* critic maintained, "keeping with the spirit of the culture it celebrates," Downing's book includes a recipe and a full description of each dish, encouraging young readers to continue their discovery of the region's cuisine.

In *Down in Louisiana* Downing introduced young readers to another traditional Louisiana song, this time presenting a rhyming tour of the state's landscape. The book serves as both an introduction to the marshes, wetlands, and bayous of Louisiana and a counting game where young readers are encouraged to determine the number of native animals that appear on each page. A wide variety of unusual creatures—from pelicans and armadillos to crawfish and alligators—are pictured, each in their natural environment.

Biographical and Critical Sources

PERIODICALS

Booklist, November 1, 2003, Paul Shackman, review of *The Second Line: Scarf Activity Songs,* p. 524; February 1, 2006, Paul Shackman, review of *Music Time,* p. 77.

Children's Bookwatch, January, 2007, review of *Fins and Grins.*

Kirkus Reviews, October 15, 2006, review of *Today Is Monday in Louisiana,* p. 1069.

Publishers Weekly, February 2, 2004, "Sing, Play, Learn," p. 30; October 16, 2006, review of *Today Is Monday in Louisiana,* p. 52.

School Library Journal, February, 2004, Beverly Bixler, review of *The Second Line,* p. 77; December, 2005, Stephanie Bange, review of *Music Time,* p. 86; December, 2006, Judith Constantinides, review of *Today Is Monday in Louisiana,* p. 96; May, 2007, Kirsten Martindale, review of *Fins and Grins,* p. 75.

ONLINE

Johnette Downing Home Page, http://www.johnettedowning.com (October 8, 2007).

Pelican Publishing Web site, http://www.pelicanpub.com/ (October 22, 2007), "Johnette Downing."

*   *   *

DOWSWELL, Paul 1957-

Personal

Born 1957, in Chester, England; married; children: one daughter. *Education:* Goldsmiths College, degree (history), 1978.

Addresses

Home—Wolverhampton, England. *Agent*—Ivan Mulcahy and Charlie Viney, Mulcahy & Viney Ltd., 15 Canning Passage, Kensington, London W8 5AA, England. *E-mail*—paul@pauldowswell.co.uk; pauldowswell@hotmail.com.

Career

Writer, editor, and researcher. Usborne, Wolverhampton, England, senior editor, 1992-99; freelance writer, 1999—. Midlands Arts Centre, Birmingham, England, instructor in creative writing.

Awards, Honors

Geographical Association Highly Commended Award, 1992, for *The Usborne Geography Quizbook; Times Educational Supplement* Information Book Award shortlist, 1997, for *The Medieval Messenger;* Rhône-Poulenc Junior Prize for Science Books, 1999, for *The Complete Book of the Microscope;* Blue Peter Book Awards shortlist, 2002, for *True Stories of Heroes,* and 2003, for *True Polar Adventure Stories;* Warwickshire Book Award shortlist, 2008, for *Prison Ship.*

Writings

HISTORICAL FICTION

Powder Monkey: The Adventures of Sam Witchall, Bloomsbury (London, England), 2005, published as *Powder Monkey: Adventures of a Young Sailor,* Bloomsbury (New York, NY), 2005.

Prison Ship: The Adventures of Sam Witchall, Bloomsbury (London, England), 2006, published as *Prison Ship: Adventures of a Young Sailor,* Bloomsbury (New York, NY), 2007.

Battle Fleet: The Adventures of Sam Witchall, Bloomsbury (London, England), 2007.

NONFICTION

(With others) *The Enterprise of War,* Time-Life Books (New York, NY), 1991.

The Animal Quizbook, Usborne (London, England), 1992.

(Coauthor) *The Usborne Geography Quizbook,* Usborne (London, England), 1992.

(Coauthor) *The Usborne Science Quizbook,* Usborne (London, England), 1993.

(Coauthor) *Questions & Answers,* Usborne (London, England), 1994.

Tales of Real Escape, Usborne (London, England), 1994.

Tales of Real Survival, Usborne (London, England), 1995.

Tales of Real Heroism, Usborne (London, England), 1996.

Tales of Real Adventure, Usborne (London, England), 1996.

The Egyptian Echo, Usborne (London, England), 1996.

(Coauthor) *The Medieval Messenger,* Usborne (London, England), 1996.

The Roman Record, Usborne (London, England), 1997.

(Coauthor) *The Stone Age Sentinel,* Usborne (London, England), 1998.

(Coauthor) *Shock Horror History,* Usborne (London, England), 1998.

(Coauthor) *The Complete Book of the Microscope,* Usborne (London, England), 1999.

The Encyclopedia of Animal, Usborne (London, England), 1999.

Genetics: The Impact on Our Lives, Hodder (London, England), 2000, Steck-Vaughn (Austin, TX), 2001.

Extraordinary Wild Weather, illustrated by Stuart Harrison, Scholastic (New York, NY), 2001.

Victorians, Hodder (London, England), 2001.

The Usborne First Encyclopedia of Space, Usborne (London, England), 2001.

World of Witches and Wizards, Anness (London, England), 2001.

History through Poetry: World War I, Hodder (London, England), 2001.

Paul McCartney: An Unauthorized Biography, Heinemann Library (Chicago, IL), 2001.

John Lennon: An Unauthorized Biography, Heinemann Library (Chicago, IL), 2001.

Transportation, Heinemann Library (Chicago, IL), 2002.

Entertainment, Heinemann Library (Chicago, IL), 2002.

Everyday Life, Heinemann Library (Chicago, IL), 2002.

Medicine Heinemann Library (Chicago, IL), 2002.

Weapons and Technology of World War I, Heinemann Library (Chicago, IL), 2002.

The Vietnam War, World Almanac Library (Milwaukee, WI), 2002.

Hitler, Hodder (London, England), 2002.

Winston Churchill, Hodder (London, England), 2002.

(Coauthor) *True Ghost Stories,* Usborne (London, England), 2002.

True Stories of Heroes, Usborne (London, England), 2002.

True Survival Stories, Usborne (London, England), 2002.

True Escape Stories, Usborne (London, England), 2002.

(Coauthor) *True Spy Stories,* Usborne (London, England), 2002.

True Everest Stories, Usborne (London, England), 2002.

True Polar Adventure Stories, Usborne (London, England), 2002.

Sea and Shore, National Trust, 2002.

The Western Front in World War I, Hodder (London, England), 2002.

(With Gill Harvey) *True Adventure Stories,* Usborne (London, England), 2003.

Hair Decoration, Heinemann Library (Chicago, IL), 2003.

Investigating Murder Mysteries, Heinemann Library (Chicago, IL), 2003.

The Causes of World War II, Heinemann Library (Chicago, IL), 2003.

Pearl Harbor: December 7, 1941, Raintree Steck-Vaughn (Austin, TX), 2003.

True Stories of the First World War, Usborne (London, England), 2003, Scholastic (New York, NY), 2007.

True Stories of the Second World War, Usborne (London, England), 2003, Scholastic (New York, NY), 2005.

Paul Dowswell joined fellow author Gill Harvey in compiling **True Adventure Stories,** *a collection of tales in which heroes span the globe in their battle with nature and the elements.* (Usborne, 2003. Cover image © Getty Images. Reproduced by permission.)

The Russian Revolution: October 25, 1917, Raintree Steck-Vaughn (Austin, TX), 2004.

The Chernobyl Disaster: April 26, 1986, Raintree Steck-Vaughn (Austin, TX), 2004.

Sutton Hoo: The Anglo-Saxon Way of Life and Death, National Trust, 2004.

Genetic Engineering, World Almanac Library (New York, NY), 2005.

Military Aircraft, Raintree (Chicago, IL), 2005.

The Usborne Introduction to the Second World War, Usborne (London, England), 2005.

Dictatorship, Evans Brothers (London, England), 2005, World Almanac Library (Milwaukee, WI), 2006.

Usborne Book of War Stories, Usborne (London, England), 2006.

True Stories of the First World War, Scholastic (New York, NY), 2007.

Contributor to *The Illustrated Dictionary of Science,* Usborne (London, England), 1999.

Sidelights

British writer and editor Paul Dowswell is a prolific author of nonfiction for children and young adults, including such award-winning titles as *The Complete Book of the Microscope* and *True Polar Adventure Stories.* Dowswell has also published a number of critically acclaimed works of historical fiction, including *Powder Monkey: Adventures of a Young Sailor,* which is set during the Napoleonic Era. "I love history and am constantly reading it, and getting ideas from it," the author noted in an interview on the *Bloomsbury* Web site. "When you write fiction you can just take a snippet of something real, and turn it into something or someone who exists only in your story."

Born in Chester, England, Dowswell earned a degree in history from Goldsmiths College. He then began working as a researcher for museums and publishing houses, including BBC Books, the Science Museum, and the National Sound Archive. He started writing nonfiction works while at Time-Life Books in London, and he later moved to Usborne, where he edited and wrote nonfiction titles for children. In 1999, Dowswell became a freelance writer he and has since published

Cover of Dowswell's thrilling sea adventure Powder Monkey, *featuring artwork by Ian Butterworth.* (Bloomsbury, 2006. Reproduced by permission.)

more than sixty books. "History is my specialist subject, but I also enjoy writing about natural history, science, geography, in fact almost anything, apart from golf and mechanical engineering," he remarked on his home page. "I have a shamefully encyclopaedic knowledge of popular music, and seem to have picked up a strangely detailed understanding of the science and technology of warfare."

In 2005 Dowswell published his debut novel, *Powder Monkey,* which follows the adventures of Sam Witchall, a thirteen-year-old sailor aboard the British frigate HMS *Miranda.* In his *Bloomsbury* interview, the author discussed his inspiration for the work. "I was researching a piece on naval warfare and was struck by how young many of the sailors in [Horatio] Nelson's time were." He continued, "Boys whose voices had not yet broken were being sent to kill and be killed. I also thought it would be interesting to write the story from the point of view of a boy at the bottom of the ship's hierarchy rather than someone at the top."

Set in 1800, *Powder Monkey* follows Sam as he is abducted from a merchant ship and pressed into service as a powder monkey, a sailor who fetches gun powder from the ship's magazine below deck and delivers it to a cannon crew during battle. The job was extremely dangerous; as Dowswell noted on the *Powder Monkey* Web site, a boy like Sam "had just as much chance of being crushed by his own gun, or killed by flying splinters or an enemy cannon ball, as any other member of his gun crew." During his voyages, Sam also finds himself tested by fierce storms, thuggish bosun's mates, and the threat of severe punishments such as flogging. "Readers will be absorbed in the day-to-day life of young Sam," observed *School Library Journal* contributor Kimberly Monaghan, and a critic in *Kirkus Reviews* stated that "voracious fans of the nautical genre will happily sign on." Writing in the London *Independent,* Christina Hardyment described *Powder Monkey* as "more vivid than a Patrick O'Brian novel."

In Dowswell's follow-up, *Prison Ship: Adventures of a Young Sailor,* Sam and his friend Richard face death at the Battle of Copenhagen. Though they fight valiantly, the young men are falsely accused of cowardice by a corrupt midshipman and placed aboard a prison ship bound for Australia. "Historical details are seamlessly interwoven into the plot and the characters—which include Lord Nelson himself—are believable," Jayne Howarth commented in the *Birmingham Post.* According to a *Kirkus Reviews* contributor, "the violence of the naval action . . . is sharp and vivid," and Monaghan called *Prison Ship* a "historically accurate and vastly entertaining sequel."

Biographical and Critical Sources

PERIODICALS

Birmingham Post, November 4, 2006, Jayne Howarth, review of *Prison Ship: The Adventures of Sam Witchall,* p. 53.

Dowswell continues the adventures of his young nineteenth-century hero Sam Witchall in **Prison Ship,** *a novel featuring cover art by Ian Butterworth.* (Bloomsbury, 2006. Reproduced by permission.)

Booklist, November 15, 2002, Ilene Cooper, review of *The Vietnam War,* p. 599.

Book Report, November-December, 2002, Jo Clarke, review of *The Vietnam War,* p. 56.

Independent (London, England), October 21, 2005, Christina Hardyment, "Nautical Tales of Knights and Northern Lights," review of *Powder Monkey: The Adventures of Sam Witchall.*

Kirkus Reviews, October 1, 2005, review of *Powder Monkey: Adventures of a Young Sailor,* p. 1078; October 15, 2006, review of *Prison Ship: Adventures of a Young Sailor,* p. 1069.

Magpies, March, 2006, Lyn Linning, review of *Powder Monkey,* p. 32.

School Librarian, autumn, 2002, review of *The Vietnam War,* p. 161; spring, 2006, review of *Powder Monkey,* p. 42.

School Library Journal, February, 2002, Elizabeth Stumpf, review of *Medicine,* p. 142; July, 2002, Todd Morning, review of *The Vietnam War,* p. 132; October, 2004, Elizabeth Talbot, review of *The Russian Revolution: October 25, 1917,* p. 186; November, 2005, Kimberly Monaghan, review of *Powder Monkey,* p. 132; July, 2006, Jody Kopple, review of *Dictatorship,* p. 120; December, 2006, Kimberly Monaghan, review of *Prison Ship,* p. 136.

ONLINE

Bloomsbury Web site, http://www.bloomsbury.com/childrens/ (October 31, 2007), "Paul Dowswell."

Paul Dowswell Home Page, http://www.pauldowswell.co.uk (October 31, 2007).

Powder Monkey Web site, http://www.bloomsbury.com/powdermonkey/ (October 31, 2007), "Paul Dowswell."

E

EHRHARDT, Karen 1963-

Personal

Born 1963. *Education:* Vermont College, M.F.A. (writing for children and young adults).

Addresses

Home and office—La Honda, CA.

Career

Author. Palo Alto Library, Palo Alto, CA, former staff member.

Awards, Honors

Nick Jr. Award, *Nickelodeon* magazine, for *This Jazz Man.*

Writings

This Jazz Man, illustrated by R.G. Roth, Harcourt Children's Books (New York, NY), 2006.

Sidelights

In her first book for children, Karen Ehrhardt introduces young readers to the world of jazz by creating a read-along that mirrors the catchy children's song "This Old Man." *This Jazz Man* is written in verse form and correlates each number within the song to an array of famous jazz musicians, including Louis Armstrong, Charlie Parker, Dizzy Gillespie, and Charles Mingus. Ehrhardt includes a short biography on each artist in a useful appendix.

In reviewing Ehrhardt's book, several reviewers comment on the author's ability to educate young readers in a fun and engaging manner. In *Booklist* Gillian Engberg

remarked that *This Jazz Man* provides young readers with "a welcome introduction to the world of jazz" and noted that Ehrhardt's rhyming text "scans with a smooth, toe-tapping tempo." Judith Constantinides, writing in *School Library Journal,* also commented on the title's educational aspect and Ehrhardt's book as "fun for jazz aficionados and neophytes alike." Adrienne Wiley, reviewing the work for *American Music Teacher,* also commented on the title's broader appeal to adults

Karen Ehrhardt's picture book **This Jazz Man** *features a text as energetic as the accompanying artwork by R.G. Roth.* (Illustration © 2006 by Robert Roth. Reproduced by permission of Harcourt.)

and wrote of *This Jazz Man* that "adults will also enjoy the book not only for the appeal of the rhyme and artistic content, but the historical information as well."

Biographical and Critical Sources

PERIODICALS

American Music Teacher, April-May 2007, Adrienne Wiley, review of *This Jazz Man,* p. 87.

Booklist, November 15, 2006, Gillian Engberg, review of *This Jazz Man,* p. 53.

Bulletin of the Center for Children's Books, March, 2007, Elizabeth Bush, review of *This Jazz Man,* p. 289.

Kirkus Reviews, October 15, 2006, review of *This Jazz Man,* p. 1069.

Publishers Weekly, October 23, 2006, review of *This Jazz Man,* p. 48.

School Library Journal, December, 2006, Judith Constantinides, review of *This Jazz Man,* p. 98.

ONLINE

Harcourt Web site, http://www.harcourtbooks.com/ (October 28, 2007), "Karen Ehrhardt."

Katz Connects Web site, http://www.katzconnects.com/ (October 28, 2007), "Karen Ehrhardt."*

F

FERBER, Brenda A. 1967-

Personal

Born April 23, 1967; daughter of a doctor and an artist; married; husband's name Alan; children: Jacob, Faith, Sammy. *Education:* University of Michigan, earned degree. *Hobbies and other interests:* Spending time with family and friends, scrap booking, baking, yoga, karate.

Addresses

Home and office—Deerfield, IL. *E-mail*—brenda aferber@comcast.net.

Career

Author. Formerly worked for Leo Burnett advertising agency.

Awards, Honors

Sydney Taylor Award, Association of Jewish Libraries, Bank Street College of Education Best Children's Book of the Year designation, both 2007, both for *Julia's Kitchen.*

Brenda A. Ferber (Photograph by Suzanne Plunkett. Courtesy of Brenda A. Ferber.)

Writings

Julia's Kitchen, Farrar, Straus (New York, NY), 2006.
Jemma Hartman, Camper Extraordinaire, Farrar, Straus (New York, NY), 2009.

Sidelights

Brenda A. Ferber dreamed of becoming a writer as a young girl, inspired by reading books by Judy Blume. As she commented on her home page, "Judy captured my heart and soul in the pages of her books. I decided right then to become a children's book author, too."

Ferber's dreams of becoming a writer fell to the wayside as she got older, then reestablished themselves when she had children of her own. "Being around kids and books reignited my old writing fantasy," she recalled. She began her writing career by submitting stories to *Ladybug* magazine, and then approached publishing houses with her manuscripts. In 2004 Ferber won the Sydney Taylor Manuscript Competition for her draft of *Julia's Kitchen,* and the novel was published by Farrar, Straus & Giroux in 2006.

Julia's Kitchen centers on eleven-year-old Cara, whose world is turned upside down when she tragically loses her mother and sister in a house fire. Mourning the loss,

Cara begins to question her spirituality and her faith in God. The preteen learns to slowly regain her faith, however, when she re-establishes her mother's at-home catering business. A *Kirkus Reviews* critic noted that while *Julia's Kitchen* touches on the subject of faith, it is "more spiritual than religious in tone, . . . the emotions are real, the protagonist empathetic and the resolution [is] believeable." In a similar vein, Nanny Kim wrote in her *Booklist* review of *Julia's Kitchen* that the "major themes about grief and healing are beautifully addressed in [Ferber's] . . . strong debut novel."

Biographical and Critical Sources

PERIODICALS

Booklist, February 1, 2006, Nancy Kim, review of *Julia's Kitchen,* p. 47.
Bulletin of the Center for Children's Books, May, 2006, Deborah Stevenson, review of *Julia's Kitchen,* p. 399.
Kirkus Reviews, April 1, 2006, review of *Julia's Kitchen,* p. 346.

Cover of Ferber's middle-grade novel Julia's Kitchen, *featuring artwork by Pep Monsterrat.* (Illustration © 2006 by Pep Montserrat. Reprinted by permission of Farrar, Straus & Giroux, LLC.)

Library Media Connection, January, 2007, Michelle Glatt, review of *Julia's Kitchen,* p. 73.
School Library Journal, April, 2006, Susan Scheps, review of *Julia's Kitchen,* p. 138.
Voice of Youth Advocates, February, 2007, review of *Julia's Kitchen,* p. 487.
Washington Post Book World, July 9, 2006, Elizabeth Ward, review of *Julia's Kitchen,* p. 11.

ONLINE

Brenda A. Ferber Home Page, http://www.brendaferber. com (October 28, 2007).
Cynthia Leitich Smith Web site, http://cynthialeitichsmith. blogspot.com/ (October 28, 2007), "Brenda Ferber."

*   *   *

FOREMAN, Michael 1938-

Personal

Born March 21, 1938, in Pakefield, Suffolk, England; son of Walter Thomas (a crane operator) and Gladys Foreman; married Janet Charters, September 26, 1959 (divorced 1966); married Louise Phillips, December 22, 1980; children: (first marriage) Mark; (second marriage) Ben Shahn, Jack. *Education:* Lowestoft School of Art, national diploma in design (painting), 1958; Royal College of Art, A.R.C.A. (with first-class honours), 1963.

Addresses

Home and office—5 Church Gate, London SW6, England. *Agent*—John Locke, 15 E. 76th St., New York, NY 10021.

Career

Graphic artist and author of children's books. Lecturer in graphics at St. Martin's School of Art, London, England, 1963-66, London College of Printing, 1966-68, Royal College of Art, London, 1968-70, and Central School of Art, London, 1971-72. Art director of *Ambit,* beginning 1960, *Playboy,* 1965, and *King,* 1966-67. Elected Royal Designer to Industry, 1985. *Exhibitions:* Work exhibited in solo show at Royal Festival Hall, London, England, 1985, as well as in Europe, North America, and Japan.

Member

Chelsea Arts.

Awards, Honors

Festival International du Livre Silver Eagle Award, France, 1972; Francis Williams Memorial awards, Victoria and Albert Museum, 1972, and 1977, for *Monkey and the Three Wizards;* Kate Greenaway Commended Book designation, British Library Association (BLA),

Michael Foreman (Photograph by Mark Gerson. Reproduced by permission.)

1978, for *The Brothers Grimm: Popular Folk Tales;* Carnegie Medal, BLA, and Kate Greenaway Highly Commended Book designation, both 1980, and Graphics Prize, International Children's Book Fair (Bologna, Italy), 1982, all for *City of Gold, and Other Stories from the Old Testament;* Kate Greenaway Medal, and Kurt Maschler (Emil) Award, British Book Trust, both 1982, both for *Sleeping Beauty, and Other Favourite Fairy Tales;* Kate Greenaway Medal, 1982, for *Longneck and Thunderfoot;* Federation of Children's Book Groups award, England, 1983, for *The Saga of Erik the Viking;* Kate Greenaway Commended Book designation, and *New York Times* Notable Book designation, both 1985, both for *Seasons of Splendour;* Signal Poetry award, 1987, for *Early in the Morning;* named honorary fellow, Royal College of Arts, 1989; Kate Greenaway Medal, and W.H. Smith/Books in Canada Award, both 1990, both for *War Boy;* Nestlé Smarties Book Prize Gold Award, 1993, for *War Game,* and Silver Award, 1997, for *The Little Reindeer;* honorary degree from Plymouth University, 1998.

Writings

SELF-ILLUSTRATED

The Perfect Present, Coward (New York, NY), 1967.
The Two Giants, Pantheon (New York, NY), 1967.

The Great Sleigh Robbery, Hamish Hamilton (London, England), 1968, Pantheon (New York, NY), 1969.
Horatio, Hamish Hamilton (London, England), 1970, published as *The Travels of Horatio,* Pantheon (New York, NY), 1970.
Moose, Hamish Hamilton (London, England), 1971, Pantheon (New York, NY), 1972.
Dinosaurs and All That Rubbish, Hamish Hamilton (London, England), 1972, Crowell (New York, NY), 1973.
War and Peas, Crowell (New York, NY), 1974.
All the King's Horses, Hamish Hamilton (London, England), 1976, Bradbury Press (Scarsdale, NY), 1977.
Panda's Puzzle, and His Voyage of Discovery (also see below), Hamish Hamilton (London, England), 1977, Bradbury Press (Scarsdale, NY), 1978.
Panda and the Odd Lion (also see below), Hamish Hamilton (London, England), 1979.
Trick a Tracker, Philomel (New York, NY), 1981.
Land of Dreams, Holt (New York, NY), 1982.
Panda and the Bunyips, Hamish Hamilton (London, England), 1984, Schocken (New York, NY), 1988.
Cat and Canary, Andersen (London, England), 1984, Dial (New York, NY), 1985.
Panda and the Bushfire, Prentice-Hall (Englewood Cliffs, NJ), 1986.
Ben's Box (pop-up book), Hodder & Stoughton (London, England), 1986, Piggy Toes Press (Kansas City, MO), 1997.
Ben's Baby, Andersen (London, England), 1987, Harper (New York, NY), 1988.
The Angel and the Wild Animal, Andersen (London, England), 1988, Atheneum (New York, NY), 1989.
War Boy: A Country Childhood, Pavilion (London, England), 1989.
One World, Andersen (London, England), 1990.
(Editor) *Michael Foreman's World of Fairy Tales,* Pavilion (London, England), 1990, Arcade (New York, NY), 1991.
(Editor) *Michael Foreman's Mother Goose,* Harcourt (New York, NY), 1991.
(With Richard Seaver) *The Boy Who Sailed with Columbus,* Arcade (New York, NY), 1992.
Jack's Fantastic Voyage, Harcourt (San Diego, CA), 1992.
Grandfather's Pencil and the Room Full of Stories, Andersen (London, England), 1993, Harcourt (San Diego, CA), 1994.
War Game, Arcade (New York, NY), 1993.
Dad! I Can't Sleep!, Andersen (London, England), 1994, Harcourt (San Diego, CA), 1995.
After the War Was Over (sequel to *War Boy*), Pavilion (London, England), 1995, Arcade (New York, NY), 1996.
Surprise! Surprise!, Harcourt (San Diego, CA), 1995.
Seal Surfer, Andersen (London, England), 1996, Harcourt (San Diego, CA), 1997.
The Little Reindeer, Dial (New York, NY), 1996.
Look! Look!, Andersen (London, England), 1997.
Angel and the Box of Time, Andersen (London, England), 1997.
Jack's Big Race, Andersen (London, England), 1997.
Chicken Licken, Andersen (London, England), 1998.

Panda (includes *Panda's Puzzle* and *Panda and the Odd Lion*), Pavilion (London, England), 1999.

Little Red Hen, Andersen (London, England), 1999.

Rock-a-Doodle-Do!, Andersen (London, England), 2000.

Michael Foreman's Christmas Treasury, Pavilion (London, England), 2000.

Cat in the Manger, Andersen (London, England), 2000, Holt (New York, NY), 2001.

Saving Sinbad, Andersen (London, England), 2001, Kane/Miller (La Jolla, CA), 2002.

Michael Foreman's Playtime Rhymes, Candlewick Press (Cambridge, MA), 2002.

Wonder Goal, Andersen (London, England), 2002, Farrar, Straus & Giroux (New York, NY), 2003.

Evie and the Man Who Helped God, Andersen (London, England), 2002.

Dinosaur Time, Andersen (London, England), 2002, published as *A Trip to Dinosaur Time,* Candlewick Press (Cambridge, MA), 2003.

The Little Reindeer, Red Fox (London, England), 2003.

Hello, World, Candlewick (Cambridge, MA), 2003.

Cat on the Hill, Andersen (London, England), 2003.

Cat in the Manger, Red Fox (London, England), 2004.

Can't Catch Me!, Andersen (London, England), 2005.

(Reteller) *Classic Fairy Tales,* Sterling (New York, NY), 2005.

Mia's Story, Walker (London, England), 2006, published as *Mia's Story: A Sketchbook of Hopes and Dreams,* Candlewick (Cambridge, MA), 2006.

Noah's Ark, Tiger Tales (Wilton, CT), 2006.

ILLUSTRATOR

Janet Charters, *The General,* Dutton (New York, NY), 1961.

Cledwyn Hughes, *The King Who Lived on Jelly,* Routledge & Kegan Paul (London, England), 1963.

Eric Partridge, *Comic Alphabets,* Routledge & Kegan Paul (London, England), 1964.

Derek Cooper, *The Bad Food Guide,* Routledge & Kegan Paul (London, England), 1966.

Gwen Clemens, *Making Music,* 1966.

Leonore Klein, *Huit enfants et un bébé,* Abelard (London, England), 1966.

Mabel Watts, *I'm for You, You're for Me,* Abelard (London, England), 1967.

Sergei Vladimirovich Mikalkov, *Let's Fight!, and Other Russian Fables,* Pantheon (New York, NY), 1968.

Donald Davie, *Essex Poems,* 1969.

Jane Elliott, *The Birthday Unicorn,* 1970.

William Ivan Martin, *Adam's Balm,* Bowmar (Los Angeles, CA), 1970.

C.O. Alexander, *Fisher v. Spassky,* Penguin (London, England), 1972.

William Fagg, editor, *The Living Arts of Nigeria,* Studio Vista (Eastbourne, England), 1972.

Barbara Adachi, *The Living Treasures of Japan,* Wildwood House (Aldershot, England), 1973.

Janice Elliott, *Alexander in the Land of Mog,* Brockhampton Press (Leicester, England), 1973.

Janice Elliott, *The Birthday Unicorn,* Penguin (London, England), 1973.

Sheila Burnford, *Noah and the Second Flood,* Gollancz (London, England), 1973.

Jane H. Yolen, *Rainbow Rider,* Crowell (New York, NY), 1974.

Georgess McHargue, *Private Zoo,* Viking (New York, NY), 1975.

Barbara K. Walker, *Teeny-Tiny and the Witch-Woman,* Pantheon (New York, NY), 1975.

Cheng-en Wu, *Monkey and the Three Wizards,* translated by Peter Harris, Collins & World (London, England), 1976.

Jean Merrill, *The Pushcart War,* 1976.

Alan Garner, *The Stone Book,* Collins & World (London, England), 1976.

Alan Garner, *Tom Fobble's Day,* Collins & World (London, England), 1976.

Alan Garner, *Granny Reardun,* Collins & World (London, England), 1977.

Hans Christian Andersen, *Hans Christian Andersen: His Classic Fairy Tales,* translated by Erik Haugaard, Gollancz (London, England), 1977.

K. Bauman, *Kitchen Stories,* Nord Sud, 1977, published as *Mickey's Kitchen Contest,* Andersen (London, England), 1978.

Alan Garner, *The Aimer Gate,* Collins & World (London, England), 1978.

Bryna Stevens, reteller, *Borrowed Feathers, and Other Fables,* Random House (New York, NY), 1978.

Brian Alderson, translator, *The Brothers Grimm: Popular Folk Tales,* Gollancz (London, England), 1978.

Oscar Wilde, *The Selfish Giant,* Kaye & Ward (London, England), 1978.

Seven in One Blow, Random House (New York, NY), 1978.

Alan Garner, *Fairy Tales of Gold,* Volume 1: *The Golden Brothers,* Volume 2: *The Girl of the Golden Gate,* Volume 3: *The Three Golden Heads of the Well,* Volume 4: *The Princess and the Golden Mane,* Collins & World (London, England), 1979.

Bill Martin, *How to Catch a Ghost,* Holt (New York, NY), 1979.

Anthony Paul, *The Tiger Who Lost His Stripes,* Andersen (London, England), 1980, 2nd edition, Harcourt (San Diego, CA), 1995.

Ernest Hemingway, *The Faithful Bull,* Emme Italia, 1980.

Aldous Huxley, *After Many a Summer,* Folio Society (London, England), 1980.

Allen Andrews, *The Pig Plantagenet,* Hutchinson (London, England), 1980.

Peter Dickenson, *City of Gold, and Other Tales from the Old Testament,* Gollancz (London, England), 1980.

Terry Jones, *Terry Jones' Fairy Tales,* Pavilion (London, England), 1981, excerpts published separately as *The Beast with a Thousand Teeth, A Fisherman of the World, The Sea Tiger,* and *The Fly-by-Night,* P. Bedrick (New York, NY), 1994.

Oscar Wilde, *The Nightingale and the Rose,* 1981.

John Loveday, editor, *Over the Bridge,* Penguin (London, England), 1981.

Robert McCrum, *The Magic Mouse and the Millionaire,* Hamish Hamilton (London, England), 1981.

Rudyard Kipling, *The Crab That Played with the Sea: A Just So Story,* Macmillan (London, England), 1982.

Angela Carter, selector and translator, *Sleeping Beauty and Other Favourite Fairy Tales,* Gollancz (London, England), 1982, Schocken (New York, NY), 1984.

Helen Piers, *Longneck and Thunderfoot,* Kestrel (London, England), 1982.

Robert McCrum, *The Brontosaurus Birthday Cake,* Hamish Hamilton (London, England), 1982.

Terry Jones, *The Saga of Erik the Viking,* Pavilion (London, England), 1983.

Charles Dickens, *A Christmas Carol,* Dial (New York, NY), 1983.

Nanette Newman, *A Cat and Mouse Love Story,* Heinemann (London, England), 1983.

Robert Louis Stevenson, *Treasure Island,* Penguin (London, England), 1983.

Kit Wright, editor, *Poems for Nine-Year-Olds and Under,* Puffin (London, England), 1984.

Helen Nicoll, editor, *Poems for Seven-Year-Olds and Under,* Puffin (London, England), 1984.

Kit Wright, editor, *Poems for Ten-Year-Olds and Over,* Puffin (London, England), 1985.

Roald Dahl, *Charlie and the Chocolate Factory,* Puffin (London, England), 1985.

Madhur Jaffrey, *Seasons of Splendour: Tales, Myths, and Legends of India,* Pavilion (London, England), 1985.

Robert McCrum, *Brontosaurus Superstar,* Hamish Hamilton (London, England), 1985.

Leon Garfield, adaptor, *Shakespeare Stories,* Gollancz (London, England), 1985, Houghton (Boston, MA), 1991.

William McGonagall, *Poetic Gems,* Folio Society (London, England), 1985.

Robert Louis Stevenson, *A Child's Garden of Verses,* Delacorte (New York, NY), 1985.

Nigel Gray, *I'll Take You to Mrs. Cole!* (picture book), Bergh, 1986, Kane/Miller (New York, NY), 1992.

Edna O'Brien, *Tales for the Telling: Irish Folk and Fairy Tales,* Pavilion (London, England), 1986.

Eric Quayle, *The Magic Ointment, and Other Cornish Legends,* Andersen (London, England), 1986.

Terry Jones, *Nicobobinus,* Pavilion (London, England), 1986.

Michael Moorcock, *Letters from Hollywood,* Harrap (London, England), 1986.

Charles Causley, *Early in the Morning,* Kestrel (London, England), 1986, Viking (New York, NY), 1987.

Rudyard Kipling, *Just So Stories,* Kestrel (London, England), 1987.

Rudyard Kipling, *The Jungle Book,* Kestrel (London, England), 1987.

Jan Mark, *Fun,* Gollancz (London, England), 1987, Viking (New York, NY), 1988.

Daphne du Maurier, *Classics of the Macabre,* Gollancz (London, England), 1987.

Clement C. Moore, *The Night before Christmas,* Viking (New York, NY), 1988.

Terry Jones, *The Curse of the Vampire's Socks,* Pavilion (London, England), 1988.

J.M. Barrie, *Peter Pan and Wendy,* Pavilion (London, England), 1988.

Martin Bax, *Edmond Went Far Away,* Harcourt (New York, NY), 1989.

David Pelham, *Worms Wiggle,* Simon & Schuster (New York, NY), 1989.

Eric Quayle, editor, *The Shining Princess, and Other Japanese Legends,* Arcade (New York, NY), 1989.

Ann Turnbull, *The Sand Horse* (picture book), Macmillan (New York, NY), 1989.

Christina Martinez, *Once upon a Planet,* 1989.

Roald Dahl, *The Complete Adventures of Charlie and Mr. Willy Wonka,* Puffin (New York, NY), 1990.

Kiri Te Kanawa, *Land of the Long White Cloud,* Arcade (New York, NY), 1990.

Brian Alderson, reteller, *The Arabian Nights; or, Tales Told by Sheherezade during a Thousand and One Nights,* Gollancz (London, England), 1992, Morrow (New York, NY), 1995.

Stacie Strong, adaptor, *Over in the Meadow* (pop-up book), Simon & Schuster (New York, NY), 1992.

Mary Rayner, *The Echoing Green,* 1992.

Terry Jones, *Fantastic Stories,* Viking (New York, NY), 1993.

Roald Dahl, *Charlie and the Great Glass Elevator,* Puffin (New York, NY), 1993.

Troon Harrison, *The Long Weekend,* Andersen (London, England), 1993, Harcourt (San Diego, CA), 1994.

Kit Wright, *Funnybunch,* 1993.

Toby Forward, *Wyvern Spring,* 1993.

Nanette Newman, *Spider the Horrible Cat,* Harcourt (San Diego, CA), 1993.

Nanette Newman, *There's a Bear in the Bath!,* Pavilion (London, England), 1993, Harcourt (San Diego, CA), 1994.

Toby Forward, *Wyvern Summer,* 1994.

Toby Forward, *Wyvern Fall,* 1994.

Michael Morpurgo, *Arthur, High King of Britain,* Pavilion (London, England), 1994, Harcourt (San Diego, CA), 1995.

Andrew Baynes, *Sarah and the Sandhorse,* 1994.

Sally Grindley, *Peter's Place,* Andersen (London, England), 1995, Harcourt (San Diego, CA), 1996.

Leon Garfield, adaptor, *Shakespeare Stories II,* Houghton (Boston, MA), 1995.

Antoine de Saint-Exupéry, *The Little Prince,* 1995.

Michael Morpurgo, editor, *Beyond the Rainbow Warrior: A Collection of Stories to Celebrate Twenty-five Years of Greenpeace,* Pavilion (London, England), 1996.

Michael Morpurgo, *Robin of Sherwood,* Harcourt (San Diego, CA), 1996.

James Riordan, *The Songs My Paddle Sings,* 1996.

Michael Morpurgo, *Farm Boy,* Pavilion (London, England), 1997.

Louise Borden, *The Little Ships: The Heroic Rescue at Dunkirk in World War II,* Margaret McElderry Books (New York, NY), 1997.

Ann Pilling, reteller, *Creation: Read-aloud Stories from Many Lands,* Candlewick Press (Cambridge, MA), 1997.

Michael Morpurgo, *Joan of Arc of Domrémy,* Harcourt (San Diego, CA), 1999.

Terry Jones, *The Lady and the Squire,* Pavilion (London, England), 2001.

Kenneth Grahame, *The Wind in the Willows,* Harcourt (San Diego, CA), 2002.

Sophie Smiley, *Bobby, Charlton, and the Mountain,* Andersen (London, England), 2003.

Michael Morpurgo, *Sir Gawain and the Green Knight,* Candlewick Press (Cambridge, MA), 2004.

L. Frank Baum, *The Wonderful Wizard of Oz,* Sterling (New York, NY), 2005.

Michael Morpurgo, *Kensuke's Kingdom,* Egmont (London, England), 2005.

Michael Morpurgo, reteller, *Beowulf,* Candlewick Press (Cambridge, MA), 2006.

Nicola Davies, *White Owl, Barn Owl,* Candlewick Press (Cambridge, MA), 2007.

Also illustrator of *The Young Man of Cury* by Charles Causley, Macmillan.

OTHER

Winter's Tales, illustrated by Freire Wright, Doubleday (New York, NY), 1979.

Also creator of animated films for television in England and Scandinavia.

Sidelights

British children's author and graphic artist Michael Foreman draws upon his real-life experiences when writing and illustrating books. While best known for illustrating the works of such wide-ranging authors as Rudyard Kipling, Oscar Wilde, and Terry Jones, Foreman has produced a number of solo works, including *Seal Surfer, Jack's Fantastic Voyage, Michael Foreman's Mother Goose,* and the award-winning *War Boy: A Country Childhood.* His artwork, whether rendered in expressive watercolor or more detailed pen-and-ink, was described by *Booklist* contributor Shelley Townsend-Hudson as possessing "a special peaceful, cozy elegance." Calling Forman's writing "in turn serious, whimsical, and poetic," an essayist in the *St. James Guide to Children's Writers* also hailed the author/illustrator's art, dubbing it "outstanding." "He combines a distinctive style of flowing watercolour with a genius for conveying atmosphere," the essayist commented, "and the visual richness of his work is always a feast for the eye."

Foreman was born in a fishing village on England's east coast in 1938, "and grew up there during [World War II]," he once recalled. Foreman's village, Pakefield, is Britain's closest town to Germany, and as Foreman once wrote, "The memory of those who passed through our village on the way to war will remain forever with the ghosts of us children in the fields and woods of long ago." Foreman's 1989 book *War Boy,* as well as its sequel, *After the War Was Over,* is a memoir of growing up in England during the war years, as Nazi bombers flew over the Suffolk coast, goods were rationed, fathers and older brothers were called to arms, and chil-

dren played in the wreckage of bombed-out buildings. Commented reviewer Christopher Lehmann-Haupt in the *New York Times:* "Though his memories are haunted by enemy bombers and V1 and V2 rockets, the author recalls in delicate watercolors the many joys of being a shopkeeper's child under siege: the licorice comforts that left your teeth stained black, or the millions of flower seeds that were exploded out of gardens and showered around the district so that 'the following spring and summer, piles of rubble burst into bloom.'" As *School Library Journal* critic Phyllis G. Sidorsky wrote, "Foreman's recollections are sharp and graphic as he poignantly recalls the servicemen who crowded into his mother's shop, grateful for her welcoming cup of tea and a place to chat." Because his mother ran the village shop, he also grew up delivering newspapers. "I used to read all the comics," he admitted on the *British Council Magic Pencil Web site.*

After graduating from the Lowestoft School of Art in the late 1950s, Foreman got his first illustration job, providing pictures for Jane Charters's text in *The General.* The book, published in 1961, was set in his home town, "and the local people recognised the church, the ice cream hut, and other scenes in the pictures," he later explained. By the time *The General* reached bookstore shelves, however, Foreman had left Pakefield and was living in London, studying toward the advanced design degree he received from the Royal College of Art in 1963. *The Perfect Present,* his first self-illustrated title, contains many scenes from London, where he has continued to make his home.

Although he worked as an art director for several magazines, and also taught at several schools in Great Britain, Foreman has devoted most of his career as a graphic artist to book illustration. Well traveled, he has been inspired by the diversity of culture and surroundings he has seen; "the sketches I bring back become the backgrounds for new books," he explained. For example, a trip to New Mexico and the state of Arizona inspired his artwork for Jane Yolen's 1974 picture book *Rainbow Rider,* while Foreman's own *Panda and the Odd Lion* contains illustrations based on his travels throughout Africa and in the city of Venice, Italy. *Mia's Story: A Sketchbook of Hopes and Dreams,* written and illustrated by Foreman, is based on people he met near Santiago, Chile. The fictional Mia lives in a shanty town; when she discovers a beautiful white flower and starts to cultivate the species at her home, she begins to make money for her family by selling the blossoms. "Foreman already has a distinguished reputation as an illustrator, but this is his finest work to date," wrote Nicolette Jones in the London *Sunday Times.* A *Kirkus Reviews* contributor noted that the tale has an "underlying tone of respect rather than outrage or pity" for Mia's family.

"Occasionally, I get the idea for a story while traveling, but usually it takes a long time to get the right place, the right story, and the right character to meet," ex-

Foreman and author Michael Morpurgo have collaborated on many books, among them **Beowulf,** *a retelling of an ancient British tale.* (Illustration © 2006 by Michael Foreman. Reproduced by permission of Candlewick Press, Inc., Cambridge, MA.)

plained Foreman. "Much of my time I am illustrating the work of other writers, and the subject matter varies from the Bible to Shakespeare to stories set in contemporary Britain or the future. My own books are never really about a place or country, but about an idea which is hopefully common to the dreams of everyone, one which works best, however, against a particular background."

One of those common dreams appears in *Wonder Goal,* the story of a new boy on the soccer team who comes through for his team mates at the last moment. From that golden goal, the story follows the boy as he grows up to play in the World Cup. "Foreman's language is appealingly simple," Todd Morning noted in *Booklist.* The watercolor art "emphasizes dramatic sports action yet contains subtle touches," wrote Peter D. Sieruta in *Horn Book.* An earlier, more universal experience is the theme behind *Hello World*, wherein a young child wakes up and ventures out into the world, tugging his teddy bear along. As he depicts the child discovering frogs, puppies, rocks and trees, and wonders of the natural world. Foreman "taps into a child's sense of wonder and discovery," according to a *Publishers Weekly* contributor.

Many of Foreman's works as author/illustrator feature engaging animal characters. In *Dad, I Can't Sleep,* Little Panda's father helps him to fall asleep by counting other animals. *Can't Catch Me!* follows the adventures of a spunky monkey, and *Seal Surfer* focuses on a handicapped boy living in Cornwall, England, who bonds with the seal he has watched being born on the rocky coast. While building a dramatic storyline—in one scene the boy is almost drowned, while in another the coastal seals are threatened by a particularly harsh winter—Foreman "keeps the tension loose" in *Seal Surfer*, noted a *Publishers Weekly* contributor, "thereby emphasizing the preeminence of the life cycles that shape his story."

One of several Christmas stories written and illustrated by Foreman, *The Little Reindeer* is about what happens when a city boy is accidentally given a young reindeer for a present. "Foreman's touching tale sparkles like a Christmas ornament," noted a *Publishers Weekly* contributor, who also praised the book's "lyrical watercolors." Two dogs are the main characters of *Saving Sinbad,* in which an unnamed canine hero saves a little girl's terrier from drowning. The tale is set in a fishing village, much like the one where the author/illustrator grew up. "Foreman's watercolors give a dog's-eye view of both the heroics and of the aftermath," wrote Connie Fletcher in *Booklist.*

While many of Foreman's books are inspired by people and places he has seen, some have a more personal basis. Foreman's *War Game* is a picture-book tribute to four of his uncles who perished in World War I. In this unusual book he presents the many sides of war—the excitement, the daily grind, the horror—through a combination of original watercolors, archive material, and stark text. The main portion of *War Game* focuses a hopeful moment where English and German soldiers joined in a game of soccer on Christmas Day, 1914, before the realities of war intrude once again. As *Junior Bookshelf* reviewer Marcus Crouch noted, *War Game* "is a story to be retold to each generation, and it could hardly have been told to deeper effect." Writing in *Publishers Weekly,* a reviewer commented that Foreman "transmutes the personal experiences of his uncles into

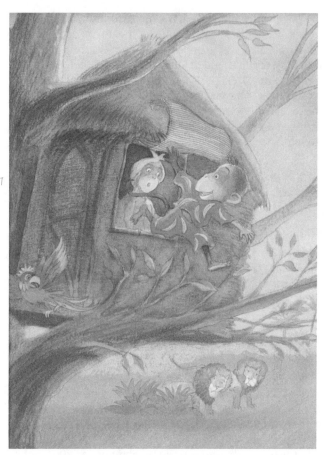

Foreman tells an original story about a mischevious monkey in his self-illustrated picture book **Can't Catch Me!** (Andersen Press, 2006. Illustration © 2005 by Michael Foreman. Reproduced by permission.)

a universal story. . . . History springs to life in this admirable work." Equally appreciative of the value of Foreman's book, *Bulletin of the Center for Children's Books* contributor Deborah Stevenson called *War Game* "an unusual war story [that] would certainly help to humanize a faraway but significant event for young readers."

A sequel to *War Game, After the War Was Over* begins during the summer of 1945, and focuses on Foreman's years growing up in the aftermath of World War II. The story features moments such as playing on the beach, now cleared of mines, and using wrecked landing crafts as pirate ships. Foreman was also able to use these memories of war in illustrations for books such as Michael Morpurgo's *Toro! Toro!*

Among his book projects, Foreman has also illustrated several anthologies of activities, rhymes, and stories, many of which he has also edited. About *Michael Foreman's Playtime Rhymes*, a *Kirkus Reviews* contributor wrote, "Foreman's legions of fans will turn to this one to prompt their memories of long-forgotten poems or to learn new ones."

"My books are not intended for any particular age group," Foreman once commented, "but the type is large and inviting for young readers who like to explore the pages after the story has been read to them. In addition I want the story to have some relevance for the adult reader. Less a question of age—more a state of mind." Foreman added on the *British Council Magic Pencil Web site,* "It's a question of creating another world, believable in its own right. . . . I keep trying to make things more real . . . in an emotional sense, telling a story by capturing the essence of the situation, giving it some meaning."

Biographical and Critical Sources

BOOKS

Children's Literature Review, Volume 32, Thomson Gale (Detroit, MI), 1994.

Something about the Author Autobiography Series, Volume 21, Thomson Gale (Detroit, MI), 1996.

St. James Guide to Children's Writers, 5th edition, St. James Press (Detroit, MI), 1999.

PERIODICALS

Booklist, March 15, 1998, Karen Hutt, review of *The Songs My Paddle Sings,* p. 1242; December 1, 2000, Shelley Townsend-Hudson, review of *Michael Foreman's Christmas Treasury,* p. 702; February 15, 2001, John Peters, review of *The Lady and the Squire,* p 1137; December 15, 2002, Connie Fletcher, review of *Saving Sinbad,* p. 766; April 15, 2003, Todd Morning, review of *Wonder Goal,* p. 1477; February 15, 2004, Todd Morning, review of *Toro! Toro!,* p. 1060, Julie Cummins, review of *Hello World,* p. 1062; April 15, 2004, Connie Fletcher, review of *Gentle Giant,* p. 1447; November 1, 2004, Carolyn Phelan, review of *Sir Gawain and the Green Knight,* p. 480; August 1, 2006, Carolyn Phelan, review of *Mia's Story,* p. 86; March 1, 2007, Linda Perkins, review of *Beowulf,* p. 74; May 15, 2007, Gillian Engberg, review of *White Owl, Barn Owl,* p. 53.

Bookseller, February 18, 2005, Caroline Horn, "Brand Status for Foreman," p. 27; May 12, 2006, "Tips for Time at the Top," p. 19.

Bulletin of the Center for Children's Books, October, 1994, Deborah Stevenson, review of *War Game,* p. 43; November, 2006, Karen Coats, review of *Mia's Story,* p. 122; March, 2007, Karen Coats, review of *Beowulf,* p. 303.

Horn Book, May-June, 1996, Elizabeth S. Watson, review of *Peter's Place,* p. 323; May-June, 1997, Ann A. Flowers, review of *The Little Ships: The Heroic Rescue at Dunkirk in World War II,* p. 302; March-April, 2003, Peter D. Sieruta, review of *Wonder Goal,* p. 202.

Junior Bookshelf, February, 1994, Marcus Crouch, review of *War Game,* p. 31.

Kirkus Reviews, September 1, 2002, review of *Michael Foreman's Playtime Rhymes,* p. 1308; October 1, 2002, review of *Saving Sinbad,* p. 1469; March 15,

2003, review of *Wonder Goal,* p. 466; October 15, 2003, review of *Hello World,* p. 1271; January 15, 2004, review of *Toro! Toro!,* p. 86; July 1, 2004, review of *Cat on the Hill,* p. 629; October 15, 2004, review of *Sir Gawain and the Green Knight,* p. 1011; January 1, 2005, review of *Dolphin Boy,* p. 55; July 1, 2006, review of *Mia's Story,* p. 677; October 15, 2006, review of *Beowulf,* p. 1075; December 1, 2006, review of *Can't Catch Me,* p. 1219.

New York Times, December 3, 1990, Christopher Lehmann-Haupt, "Presents of Words, Pictures, and Imagination."

Publishers Weekly, April 25, 1994, review of *War Game,* p. 78; August 12, 1996, review of *Robin of Sherwood,* p. 84; March 24, 1997, review of *Seal Surfer,* p. 83; October 6, 1997, review of *The Little Reindeer,* p. 55; February 22, 1999, review of *Joan of Arc of Domrémy,* p. 95; September 24, 2001, review of *Cat in the Manger,* p. 52; December 22, 2003, review of *Hello World,* p. 59; April 26, 2004, review of *Gentle Giant,* p. 64.

Resource Links, December, 2003, Kathryn McNaughton, review of *Evie's Garden,* p. 4.

School Librarian, winter, 2005, review of *Dolphin Boy,* p. 187; winter, 2006, Trevor Dickinson, review of *Mia's Story,* p. 187.

School Library Journal, May, 1990, Phyllis G. Sidorsky, review of *War Boy: A Country Childhood,* p. 116; October, 2000, review of *Michael Foreman's Christmas Treasury,* p. 59; March, 2001, Lisa Prolman, review of *The Lady and the Squire,* p. 250; April, 2003, Blair Christolon, review of *Wonder Goal,* p. 118; December, 2003, Kathleen Simonetta, review of *A Trip to Dinosaur Time,* p. 113; January, 2004, Judith Constantinides, review of *Hello World,* p. 97; May, 2004, Kathy Krasniewicz, review of *Gentle Giant,* p. 120, Shawn Brommer, review of *Toro! Toro!,* p. 154; October, 2004, Connie C. Rockman, review of *Sir Gawain and the Green Knight,* p. 172; April, 2006, Miriam Lang Budin, review of *Classic Fairy Tales,* p. 124; August, 2006, Marianne Saccardi, review of *Mia's Story,* p. 87; December, 2006, Susan Scheps, review of *Beowulf,* p. 166.

Sunday Times (London, England), June 18, 2006, Nicolette Jones, review of *Mia's Story,* p. 48.

Times Educational Supplement, November 5, 2004, Geraldine Brennan, "Dear Mr. Morpingo: Inside the World of Michael Morpurgo," p. 19.

ONLINE

Andersen Press Web site, http://www.andersenpress.co.uk/ (November 19, 2007), "Michael Foreman."

British Council Contemporary Writers Web site, http://www.contemporarywriters.com/ (November 19, 2007), "Michael Foreman."

British Council Magic Pencil Web site, http://magicpencil.britishcouncil.org/ (November 19, 2007), "Michael Foreman."

Eduplace Web site, http://www.eduplace.com/ (November 19, 2007), "Michael Foreman."

Walker Books Web site, http://www.walkerbooks.co.uk/ (November 19, 2007), "Michael Foreman."*

*   *   *

FRIEND, Natasha 1972-

Personal

Born April 28, 1972, in Norwich, NY; married; husband's name Erik; children: Jack, Ben. *Education:* Bates College, B.A., 1994; Clemson University, M.A.

Addresses

Home—CT.

Career

Writer and teacher. Former teacher at Brearley School, New York, NY, and École Bilingue, Cambridge, MA. Brimmer and May Summer Camp, Chestnut Hill, MA, former director.

Awards, Honors

Milkweed Prize for Children's Literature, and Golden Sower Award, both for *Perfect;* Quick Pick for Reluctant Readers citation, American Library Association, for *Lush.*

Writings

Perfect, Milkweed Editions (Minneapolis, MN), 2004.
Lush, Milkweed Editions (Minneapolis, MN), 2006.
Bounce, Scholastic (New York, NY), 2007.

Contributor to periodicals, including *Family Fun,* and to anthologies, including *Chicken Soup for the Volunteer's Soul.*

Sidelights

Natasha Friend worked as a teacher before she got her start writing novels for young adults. Her first book, *Perfect,* focuses on thirteen-year-old Isabelle and the young teen's battle with bulimia. "As a former competitive gymnast I was introduced to the concept of dieting and weight control at an early age," Friend explained on her home page while discussing the inspiration for her story. "I went on my first diet at the age of eleven." Isabelle's bulimia is less caused by athletics than by grief; her father died several years before and she is unable to cope except by binging on food and then throwing up. When Isabelle meets Ashley, a popular girl who also has an eating disorder, the two quickly become friends, and Isabelle learns that her new friend may not be as "perfect" as she seems. "Friend knows middle school kids and delivers beautifully," wrote Mary R. Hofmann in a *School Library Journal* review of *Perfect.*

The "graphic binging and purging scenes" in *Perfect* "help explain the disease to readers without seeming didactic," wrote a *Publishers Weekly* reviewer. "Friend combines believable characters and real-life situations into a fine novel," Denise Moore concluded in *School Library Journal,* and a *Kirkus Reviews* contributor deemed the book "clearly and simply written with a nice balance of humor and drama." Noting the prevalence of eating disorders among teens, Claire Rosser wrote in *Kliatt* that *Perfect* "addresses the fact that eating disorders are plaguing ever-younger adolescent girls." Through her careful attention to Isabelle's voice, "Friend elevates what could have been just another problem novel to a truly worthwhile read," Debbie Carton concluded in *Booklist.*

In Friend's second young-adult novel, *Lush,* Samantha and her family are hiding her father's alcoholism from the world. The teen is tired of pretending, however, and she is angry and frustrated at her father's inability to change. She releases some of her burden in an anonymous letter she leaves in a library book, and she soon begins corresponding with an unknown library pen pal. While the content of the novel is heavy, "the author avoids a maudlin tone by infusing the plot with details of typical teen life," wrote Rebecca M. Jones in *School Library Journal.* "Sam comes across as a savvy as well as naive teen who tells her own story with humor, honesty and hope," a *Kirkus Reviews* writer noted, while Carton called *Lush* "a believable, sensitive, character-driven story, with realistic dialogue."

Thirteen-year-old Evyn Linney has always wanted a mother, but her father's plan to marry a woman with six children is not exactly what she had in mind. As Friend tells Evyn's story in *Bounce,* she learns about living in a mixed family and grows accustomed to the changes happening in her life. "Friend offers no fairy-tale ending but presents, through hip conversations and humor, believable characters and a feel-good story," D. Maria LaRocco noted in her review for *School Library Journal.* As Rosser wrote, in *Bounce* Friend gives readers "a chance to spend time with smart, caring, funny people," and as she tells Evyn's story "the realistic and genuinely humorous details . . . set this text apart," according to a *Kirkus Reviews* contributor. In *Publishers Weekly* a reviewer also commended Friend for her "unmistakable gift for exploring family dynamics."

When asked on her home page where she gets her ideas, Friend explained that they come from "stories from my own life, or from the lives of my friends, or from articles and books I've read. Often I begin with a 'seed'— just the beginning of an idea, or a first sentence—and from there a plot begins to develop."

Biographical and Critical Sources

PERIODICALS

Booklist, January 1, 2005, Debbie Carton, review of *Perfect,* p. 844; March 15, 2006, Lolly Gepson, review of

Perfect, p. 73; November 1, 2006, Debbie Carton, review of *Lush,* p. 41.

Kliatt, November, 2004, Claire Rosser, review of *Perfect,* p. 8; July, 2006, Sunnie Grant, review of *Perfect,* p. 43; September, 2007, Claire Rosser, review of *Bounce,* p. 12.

Kirkus Reviews, October 15, 2004, review of *Perfect,* p. 1006; October 15, 2006, review of *Lush,* p. 1071; August 1, 2007, review of *Bounce.*

Publishers Weekly, November 8, 2004, review of *Perfect,* p. 57; July 30, 2007, review of *Lush,* p. 87; September 17, 2007, review of *Bounce,* p. 56.

School Library Journal, December, 2004, Denise Moore, review of *Perfect,* p. 146; November, 2005, Mary R. Hofmann, review of *Perfect,* p. 57; April, 2006, Stephanie A. Squicciarini, review of *Perfect,* p. 82; December, 2006, Rebecca M. Jones, review of *Lush,* p. 138; September, 2007, D. Maria LaRocco, review of *Bounce,* p. 196.

ONLINE

Kids Read Web site, http://www.kidsreads.com/authors/ (October 22, 2007), profile of Friend.

Natasha Friend Home Page, http://www.natashafriend. com (October 8, 2007).

Scholastic Web site, http://www.scholastic.com/ (October 22, 2007), "Natasha Friend."

Teen Reads Web site, http://www.teenreads.com/ (October 22, 2007), interview with Friend.*

G

GARZA, Xavier

Personal

Born in Rio Grande City, TX; married; wife's name Irma; children: Vincent. *Education:* University of Texas—Edinburg, B.F.A. (art), 1994; University of Texas—San Antonio, M.A. (art history), 2007.

Addresses

Home—San Antonio, TX. *E-mail*—xaviergarza@hotmail.com.

Career

Artist, storyteller, and writer. Storyteller, performing in Texas, Arizona, and eastern Washington. *Exhibitions:* Painting collections have been exhibited throughout Texas, including at Guadalupe Cultural Arts Center, Nuestra Palabra de Houston, various Mexican consulates, Gallista Gallery, and The Ice House, Dallas.

Writings

SELF-ILLUSTRATED

Creepy Creatures and Other Cucuys, Piñata Books (Houston, TX), 2004.

Lucha Libre: The Man in the Silver Mask (bilingual English/Spanish), Cinco Puntos Press (El Paso, TX), 2005.

Juan and the Chupacabras/Juan y el chupacabras, illustrated by April Ward, Piñata Books (Houston, TX), 2006.

The Legend of Charro Claus and the Tejas Kid (bilintual English/Spanish), Cinco Puntos Press (El Paso, TX), 2006.

Zulema and the Witch Owl, Piñata Books (Houston, TX), 2008.

Stories included in anthologies *Penn English: Chicano Writings,* Pennsylvania State Press, 2001; *Aztlanahuac Project: Cantos al sexto sol,* Wings Press, 2002; and *Once upon a Cuento,* Curbstone Press.

Xavier Garza (Photograph by Karen Arneson. Courtesy of Xavier Garza.)

OTHER

Contributor of short fiction to periodicals, including *Mañana, Monitor, Milwaukee Spanish Journal, TABE, Corpus Christi Caller Times, Mesquite Review,* and *San Antonio Current.* Illustrations included in anthologies, including *Contemporary Chicana/Chicano Art: Works, Culture, and Education,* University of Arizona Press.

Sidelights

An artist, storyteller, and writer, Xavier Garza has produced several collections of paintings that have been exhibited throughout Garza's home state of Texas. Much of Garza's art is inspired by his memories of growing up in a close-knit family in southern Texas, and he shares the stories from his childhood in picture books such as *Creepy Creatures and Other Cucuys, Lucha Libre: The Man in the Silver Mask,* and *Juan and the Chupacabras/Juan y el chupacabras.*

In *Creepy Creatures and Other Cucuys* Garza retells fifteen stories recalled from his childhood. In "The Vanishing Hitchhiker," "The Onion House," and "The Chupacabras," readers learn the ways "cucuys," or supernatural beings, invade and influence the lives of the living. The terrifying chupacabra, a wingéd creature with green skin and glowing red eyes, makes a second appearance in *Juan and the Chupacabras/Juan y el chupacabras,* a bilingual picture book that finds two young cousins sneaking out one night, determined to find out if their grandfather's story about his childhood battle with the sharp-toothed creature is truth or fiction. In *School Library Journal,* Maria Otero-Boisvert deemed *Juan and the Chupacabras/Juan y el chupacabras* "an excellent choice for storytime and classroom sharing," and a *Kirkus Reviews* writer wrote that Garza's texts "flow smoothly" and contain enough adventure "to keep younger readers involved."

Garza's self-illustrated picture book *Lucha Libre:* is inspired by a form of Mexican wrestling in which good and evil battle in the form of masked wrestlers or luchadors who wear colorful costumes. Transformed into saints, Aztec heroes, or other fantastic characters, wrestlers act out the traditional heroic drama, and good (los tecnicos) always wins out against evil (los rudos). In Garza's tale, which is set in the mid-twentieth century, a boy named Carlitos realizes that, despite his mask, his favorite luchador, the popular Man in the Silver Mask, has eyes that remind the young boy of someone he knows. Praising Garza's folk-art-styled illustrations for reflecting "the rowdy spirit of the stylized sport," a *Kirkus Reviews* contributor predicted that *Lucha Libre* will appeal to "every wrestling fan under the age of ten." In *School Library Journal* Ann Welton wrote that the book's "fluid" text and "grainy graphic-novel-style" illustrations combine to "create an oddly compelling and sophisticated package."

Describing the inspiration for his art on the Latinalo Art Community Web site, Garza wrote: "From the flour tortillas filled with rice and beans that I ate as a boy to the songs by Pedro Infante that my grandmother sang to me as she rocked me to sleep, I paint what I know and have experienced in my life. Going to Mexican wrestling in Reynosa and having a firm belief in God while enduring the tedious rituals of being a Roman Catholic, by birth if not practice, are all elements that make up the images and inspirations for all of my work as an artist."

Biographical and Critical Sources

PERIODICALS

Kirkus Reviews, July 1, 2005, review of *Lucha Libre: The Man in the Silver Mask,* p. 735; October 15, 2006, review of *Juan and the Chupacabras/Juan y el chupacabras,* p. 1071.
School Library Journal, October, 2005, Ann Welton, review of *Lucha Libre,* p. 148; October, 2006, Maria Otero-Boisvert, review of *Juan and the Chupacabras/ Juan y el chupacabras,* p. 144.

ONLINE

Arte Público Press Web site, http://www.arte.uh.edu/ (November 12, 2007), "Xavier Garza."
Gallista.com, http://www.gallista.com/ (November 12, 2007), "Xavier Garza."
Latinalo Art Community Web site, http://latinoartcommunity.org/ (November 12, 2007), "Xavier Garza."

Cover of Texas artist Garza's picture book Lucha Libre, *which focuses on a popular form of Mexican wrestling.* (Cinco Puntos Press, 2005. Illustration © by Xavier Garza. Reproduced by permission.)

*   *   *

GODWIN, Sam
See PIROTTA, Saviour

GORBACHEV, Valeri 1944-

Personal

Born June 10, 1944, in USSR (now Ukraine); immigrated to United States, 1991; son of Gregory and Polina Gorbachev; married, October, 1970; wife's name Victoria (a librarian); children: Konstantin, Shoshana Alexandra. *Education:* Attended Academy of Art, Kiev, USSR (now Ukraine).

Addresses

Home—Brooklyn, NY. *E-mail*—g-valeri@hotmail.com.

Career

Artist; author and illustrator of children's books. *Exhibitions:* Works included in exhibitions of children's book illustration in the former Soviet Union. Solo exhibitions in Moscow and St. Petersburg, Russia.

Awards, Honors

Parent's Guide Children's Media Award, and Kansas State Reading Recommended List inclusion, both 1998, both for *Nicky and the Big, Bad Wolves;* Missouri Building Block Picture Book Award nomination, 2003, for *One Rainy Day;* Oppenheim Toy Portfolio Gold Award, 2005, for *Big Little Elephant;* California Young Reader Medal nomination, 2005, for *The Giant Hug* written by Sandra Horning; Garden State Book Award nomination, 2008, for *Ms. Turtle the Babysitter.*

Writings

SELF-ILLUSTRATED; FOR CHILDREN

The Three Little Pigs: Full-Color Sturdy Book, Dover (New York, NY), 1995.
Arnie the Brave, Grosset & Dunlap (New York, NY), 1997.
(With Warren Longmire) *The Flying Ship,* Star Bright (New York, NY), 1997.
Fool of the World and the Flying Ship, Star Bright (New York, NY), 1998.
Nicky and the Big, Bad Wolves, North-South (New York, NY), 1998.
Where Is the Apple Pie?, Philomel (New York, NY), 1999.
Nicky and the Fantastic Birthday Gift, North-South (New York, NY), 2000.
Peter's Picture, North-South (New York, NY), 2000.
Chicken Chickens, North-South (New York, NY), 2001.
Goldilocks and the Three Bears, North-South (New York, NY), 2001.
Nicky and the Rainy Day, North-South (New York, NY), 2002.
One Rainy Day, Philomel (New York, NY), 2002.
Chicken Chickens Go to School, North-South (New York, NY), 2003.
The Big Trip, Philomel (New York, NY), 2004.

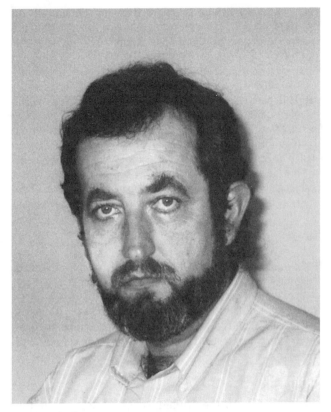

Valeri Gorbachev (Reproduced by permission.)

Whose Hat Is It?, HarperCollins (New York, NY), 2004.
Ms. Turtle the Babysitter, HarperCollins (New York, NY), 2005.
That's What Friends Are For, Philomel (New York, NY), 2005.
Big Little Elephant, Harcourt (Orlando, FL), 2005.
Heron and Turtle, Philomel (New York, NY), 2006.
Red Red Red, Philomel (New York, NY), 2007.
Christopher Counting, Philomel (New York, NY), 2008.
Dragon Is Coming!, Harcourt (Orlando, FL), 2008.
Turtle's Penguin Day, Knopf (New York, NY), 2008.

ILLUSTRATOR

Joy N. Hulme, *What If? Just Wondering Poems,* Boyds Mills Press (Honesdale, PA), 1993.
Laurie A. Jacobs, *So Much in Common,* Boyds Mills Press (Honesdale, PA), 1994.
Pamela J. Farris, *Young Mouse and Elephant: An East African Folktale,* Houghton Mifflin (Boston, MA), 1996.
Miriam Kosman, *Red, Blue, and Yellow Yarn: A Tale of Forgiveness,* Hachai Publications (Brooklyn, NY), 1996.
Patricia Blanchard and Joanne Suhr, *There Was a Mouse,* Richard C. Owens (Katonah, NY), 1997.
Carol Roth, *Little Bunny's Sleepless Night,* North-South (New York, NY), 1999.
Judy Sierra, *Silly and Sillier: Read Aloud Tales from around the World,* Knopf (New York, NY), 2002.
Carol Roth, *Who Will Tuck Me in Tonight?,* North-South (New York, NY), 2003.

Lesléa Newman, *Where Is Bear?,* Harcourt (Orlando, FL), 2004.

Sandra Horning, *The Giant Hug,* Knopf (New York, NY), 2005.

Michael J. Rosen, *Three Feet Small,* Harcourt (Orlando, FL), 2005.

Dee Lillegard, *Go!: Poetry in Motion,* Knopf (New York, NY), 2006.

David Martin, *All for Pie, Pie for All,* Candlewick Press (Cambridge, MA), 2006.

Lisa Moser, *Squirrel's World,* Candlewick Press (Cambridge, MA), 2007.

Lesléa Newman, *Skunk's Spring Surprise,* Harcourt (San Diego, CA), 2007.

OTHER

When Someone Is Afraid, illustrated by Kostya Gorbachev, Star Bright Books (New York, NY), 2005.

Author and illustrator of several dozen books published in Russian. Contributor to children's magazines, including *Highlights for Children, Highlights High Five,* and *Ladybug.*

Sidelights

Since arriving in the United States at the end of the cold war, Valeri Gorbachev has established himself as a popular author and illustrator of children's books, in-

cluding *Nicky and the Big, Bad Wolves* and *One Rainy Day.* Gorbachev, who was born in the Ukraine, also creates artwork for titles by other writers, such as David Martin's *All for Pie, Pie for All.* The artist/author's success is all the more remarkable in light of the fact that he did not know any English when he came to the United States.

Gorbachev likes to draw "animals endowed with bold personalities," according to a *Publishers Weekly* reviewer. This penchant was an established part of his repertoire while in the Soviet Union, where he created a bestselling picture-book series around a lively pig named Hrusha. In the United States, Gorbachev's characters have included the "chicken chickens," which must bolster their courage to try new things, and Pig and Goat, a pair who cannot quite trust each other's versions of events. Reviewing the books featuring these characters, *Booklist* reviewer Ellen Mandel noted that Gorbachev "etches humor and delight into each droll illustration."

Similarities and differences among people is the theme of Laurie A. Jacobs' *So Much in Common,* one of the first books Gorbachev illustrated after immigrating to the United States. In Jacobs' story, Philomena Midge, a hippo, and Horace Abercrombie, a goat, are two friends who share different interests. The pair, however, easily acknowledge what they enjoy about each other: Philo-

Gorbachev has created artwork for texts by many authors, including his work for Laurie A. Jacobs' So Much in Common. (Illustration © 1994 by Boyds Mills Press. All rights reserved. Reproduced by permission.)

mena enjoys Horace's sense of humor while Horace savors Philomena's cooking. Other friends tell the hippo and goat that they have nothing in common, but the duo only grow closer in a story that promotes acceptance and diversity. Gorbachev enhances the book's text with "cheerful pen-and-ink and watercolor drawings of the animal village," according to *School Library Journal* reviewer Janet M. Bair. A *Publishers Weekly* contributor noted that the illustrator's drawings "bring the characters playfully to life."

Young Mouse and Elephant: An East African Folktale, with a text by Pamela J. Farris, is another children's book that includes Gorbachev's drawings. In the humorous tale Young Mouse claims to be the strongest animal on the African plains. Young Mouse's grandfather bruises his ego when he disagrees and states that Elephant is the strongest. Young Mouse goes out looking to challenge Elephant, proclaiming that he will "break Elephant apart and stomp her to bits." According to *School Library Journal* reviewer Jennifer Fleming, Gorbachev perfectly pairs his drawings to the folktale by making them "full of mischief and fun" as well as a "delightful match for this clever retelling." In *Booklist* Annie Ayres wrote that the "sprightly ink-and-watercolor illustrations should amuse the small and swaggering."

The Giant Hug, featuring a text by Sandra Horning, concerns Owen, a young piglet who wants to send a long-distance greeting to his grandmother on her birthday. "Gorbachev's ink-and-watercolor artwork charms," observed a *Publishers Weekly* critic of the title. In *Go!: Poetry in Motion,* a collection by Dee Lillegard, the illustrator's "double-page scenes teem with a bright mix of busy, anthropomorphized animals," according to a *Kirkus Reviews* contributor. In Martin's *All in Pie, Pie for All* a read-aloud about a family's favorite treat, Gorbachev's "drawings create a series of charming domestic scenes," according to *Booklist* reviewer Carolyn Phelan. A skunk emerges from her winter sleep and begins searching for her friends in *Skunk's Spring Surprise,* a picture book by Lesléa Newman in which Gorbachev's "cheery animals . . . will be irresistible to the preschool set," in the opinion of a *Kirkus Reviews* critic.

Gorbachev is equally at home illustrating established folktales from other nations. His version of *Goldilocks and the Three Bears* was described by Sheilah Kosco in *School Library Journal* as "a perfect version for preschoolers," and a contributor to *Publishers Weekly* wrote that the "snug interiors" "conjure a cozy and comforting world." Another *Publishers Weekly* reviewer concluded that Gorbachev's illustrations for Judy Sierra's *Silly and Sillier: Read-Aloud Tales from around the World* "reflect the international settings and reinforce the playfulness of the tales."

Among Gorbachev's self-illustrated works, *Nicky and the Big, Bad Wolves* is a picture book about a small bunny named Nicky who awakens one night terrified by

Gorbachev's animal characters decide to expand their educational opportunities in his self-illustrated picture book Chicken Chickens Go to School. (Illustration © 2003 by Valeri Gorvachev. Used by permission of North-South Books, Inc., New York.)

a nightmare he has had. In describing how Nicky relates his dream to his rabbit mother and four rabbit siblings, Gorbachev "wrings every last ounce of humor from the action" with his "particularly droll" pen-and-ink and watercolor illustrations, according to a reviewer for *Publishers Weekly*. The same commentator concluded that *Nicky and the Big, Bad Wolves* has a "fresh, friendly sensibility" that will "keep little ones coming back for more."

In *Chicken Chickens* two baby chicks make their first trip to the playground, where they are terrified by the play equipment. With the help of a kindly beaver, the two overcome their fears and learn to master the slide. Judith Constantinides, writing in *School Library Journal*, commended Gorbachev for endowing his animal characters with human expressions, "all in a simple and lively style." A *Publishers Weekly* critic felt that the book "takes a familiar preschool scenario and spins it out with gusto." In a follow-up, *Chicken Chickens Go to School,* the timid chicks venture into the classroom for the first time. Their efforts to bond with the other students fall flat, however, until the chicks need help crossing a stream during a class hike. "Subtle messages about overcoming fear and finding friendship add depth," observed *Booklist* contributor Ilene Cooper.

Friendship is also the theme of *One Rainy Day,* a counting book featuring Pig and Goat, who made their first appearance in *Where Is the Apple Pie?* After rain-soaked Pig arrives at Goat's house carrying a bouquet of flowers, Goat helps his companion dry off and is treated to a tall tale involving a mouse, porcupines, buffaloes, leopards, and elephants. *Booklist* reviewer Helen Rosenburg praised the book's "bold pictures, humorous text, and opportunities for audience participation," and a contributor for *Kirkus Reviews* recommended the title for sharing, commenting that "the sweet, simple text and fold-out spread showing all the counted animals will help keep readers' and listeners' attention." In *The Big Trip,* Pig's announcement of his travel plans is greeted with skepticism by Goat, who suggests that every mode of transportation is fraught with danger. "An upbeat ending and the charming pen-and-ink and watercolor illustrations relieve some of the negative tension" of Gorbachev's narrative, Teri Markson wrote in *School Library Journal.* Goat expresses concern for an apparently despondent Pig in *That's What Friends Are For,* described as "a pleasing story showing the lengths one friend will go to ensure the comfort of another" by a *Kirkus Reviews* critic.

Gorbachev has published a number of books that feature a turtle as the main character. In *Ms. Turtle the Babysitter* three energetic frogs test the patience of their kindly guardian. According to *School Library Journal* reviewer Corrina Austin, "the pen-and-ink and watercolor cartoons seamlessly complement the text." A pair of mismatched pals find common ground in three stories collected as *Heron and Turtle,* a work described as "sweet but not cloying, tender but not sentimental" by *Booklist* critic Linda Perkins. In *Red Red Red* Turtle's neighbors become curious when they spot him rushing around town in search of something red, and the other animals soon join Turtle on his quest. "Gorbachev's pen-and-ink and watercolor illustrations reflect the colorful mystery's genial mood" of this story, noted Kitty Flynn in a *Horn Book* review of *Red Red Red.*

Gorbachev once told *SATA:* "I arrived in the United States in 1991 with my wife, my two children, my suitcases, and dozens of characters I had created. . . . In my native Ukraine, I illustrated forty children's books, half of which I also wrote. They have been translated into Finnish, German, and Spanish, and I have participated in many exhibitions of children's books in the former Soviet Union and abroad. I have also had solo exhibitions in Moscow and St. Petersburg. For many years government officials denied me the right to leave the country. The demise of communism at last cleared the way for me and my family to move to the United States.

"When I illustrate a book, the drawings and the text become one, and it is not really possible for me to separate the drawings from the text. I love to draw for children and to create books when I am both author and illustrator. I think that my work in children's magazines

Gorbachev's **Red Red Red** *features the engaging animal characters and detailed illustrations that have made his books popular with young children.* (Illustration © 2007 by Valeri Gorbachev. Reproduced by permission of Philomel Books, a division of Penguin Putnam Books for Young Readers.)

helped me to connect with the reading audience. Now I am enjoying my work with American magazines. I also love American children's books because they have strong visual appeal, and the connection between author and illustrator is close. Often the author and artist are the same person. That is how I understand children's literature. I hope that American children will love my books as much as Russian children do. My characters will take on nuances of American culture, but the basic qualities of the characters show the similarities among people all over the world."

Biographical and Critical Sources

PERIODICALS

Booklist, May 1, 1996, Annie Ayres, review of *Young Mouse and Elephant: An East African Folktale,* p. 1509; July, 2001, Gillian Engberg, review of *Goldilocks and the Three Bears,* p. 2013; September 1, 2001, John Peters, review of *Chicken Chickens,* p. 114; May 15, 2002, Helen Rosenburg, review of *One Rainy Day,* p. 1600; August, 2003, Ilene Cooper, review of *Chicken Chickens Go to School,* p. 1992; May 1, 2004, Carolyn Phelan, review of *The Big Trip,* p. 1563; January 1, 2005, Jennifer Mattson, review of

The Giant Hug, p. 869; May 15, 2005, Ilene Cooper, review of *That's What Friends Are For*, p. 1664; October 1, 2005, John Peters, review of *Big Little Elephant*, p. 62; June 1, 2006, Linda Perkins, review of *Heron and Turtle*, p. 82; September 1, 2006, review of *All for Pie, Pie for All*, p. 68; November 1, 2006, Hazel Rochman, review of *Go!: Poetry in Motion*, p. 57; February 15, 2007, Shelle Rosenfeld, review of *Skunk's Spring Surprise*, p. 84.

Childhood Education, winter, 2005, Patricia Crawford, review of *That's What Friends Are For*, p. 111.

Horn Book, March-April, 2007, Kitty Flynn, review of *Red Red Red*, p. 183.

Kirkus Reviews, April 1, 2002, review of *One Rainy Day*, p. 491; March 1, 2004, review of *The Big Trip*, p. 222; June 1, 2004, review of *Whose Hat Is It?*, p. 536; June 1, 2005, review of *That's What Friends Are For*, p. 636; October 15, 2006, review of *Go!*, p. 1073; December 1, 2006, review of *Skunk's Spring Surprise*, p. 1224; January 15, 2007, review of *Red Red Red*, p. 73.

Publishers Weekly, June 21, 1993, p. 104; June 13, 1994, review of *So Much in Common*, p. 63; April 13, 1998, review of *Nicky and the Big, Bad Wolves*, p. 74; June 1, 1999, Ellen Mandel, review of *Little Bunny's Sleepless Night*, p. 1844; February 15, 2000, Ilene Cooper, review of *Where Is the Apple Pie?*, p. 1117; April 15, 2000, Marta Segal, review of *Peter's Picture*, p. 1550; May 7, 2001, review of *Goldilocks and the Three Bears*, p. 245; June 25, 2001, review of *Chicken Chickens*, p. 71; September 30, 2002, review of *Silly and Sillier: Read-Aloud Tales from around the World*, p. 71; June 9, 2003, review of *Chicken Chickens Go to School*, p. 50; January 17, 2005, review of *The Giant Hug*, p. 55; September 11, 2006, review of *All for Pie, Pie for All*, p. 53.

School Library Journal, August, 1993, p. 158; December, 1994, Janet M. Bair, review of *So Much in Common*, p. 76.; April, 1996, Jennifer Fleming, review of *Young Mouse and Elephant*, p. 124; June, 2000, Sue Sherif, review of *Peter's Picture*, p. 112; June 2001, Sheilah Kosco, review of *Goldilocks and the Three Bears*, p. 116; August, 2002, Doris Losey, review of *One Rainy Day*, p. 156; September, 2001, Judith Constantinides, review of *Chicken Chickens*, p. 189; November, 2002, Carol L. MacKay, review of *Silly and Sillier*, p. 150; September, 2003, Julie Roach, review of *Chicken Chickens Go to School*, p. 179; March, 2004, Teri Markson, review of *The Big Trip*, p. 169; July, 2004, Mary Elam, review of *Whose Hat Is It?*, p. 76; May, 2005, Kathleen Kelly MacMillan, review of *Three Feet Small*, p. 95; July, 2005, Judith Constantinides, review of *That's What Friends Are For*, p. 73; August, 2005, Corrina Austin, review of *Ms. Turtle the Babysitter*, p. 95; September, 2005, Linda Staskus, review of *Big Little Elephant*, p. 170; January, 2006, Susan Weitz, review of *When Someone Is Afraid*, p. 97; September, 2006, Kathleen Whalin, review of *All for Pie, Pie for All*, p. 180; December, 2006, Susan Weitz, review of *Go!*, p. 125; March, 2007, Martha Simpson, review of *Red Red Red*, p. 162.

ONLINE

Carus Publishing Web site, http://www.cricketmag.com/ (November 10, 2007), "Meet the Illustrator: Valeri Gorbachev."

*   *   *

GRANDPRÉ, Mary 1954-

Personal

Born 1954, in SD; married Kevin Whaley (a designer; divorced); married Tom Casmer (an illustrator and designer); children: Julia. *Education:* Pomona College, B.A. (fine arts); Minneapolis College of Art and Design, degree.

Addresses

Home—Sarasota, FL.

Career

Illustrator and graphic designer. Film work includes environment/scenery development for DreamWorks' animated film *Antz* and character development for Disney's *Ice Age*.

Awards, Honors

Middle East Book Award, Middle East Outreach Council, 2001, for *The House of Wisdom*; awards from Society of Illustrators, *Communication Arts*, *Graphis*, *Print*, and *Art Direction*.

Writings

(And illustrator, with husband, Tom Casmer) *Henry and Pawl and the Round Yellow Ball*, Dial (New York, NY), 2005.

ILLUSTRATOR

Aleksandr Sergeevich Pushkin, *The Snow Storm*, Creative Education (Mankato, MN), 1983.

Jennifer Armstrong, *Chin Yu Min and the Ginger Cat*, Crown (New York, NY), 1993.

Christopher King, *The Vegetables Go to Bed*, Crown (New York, NY), 1994.

Domenico Vittorini, *The Thread of Life: Twelve Old Italian Tales*, new edition, Crown (New York, NY), 1995.

Marguerite W. Davol, *Batwings and the Curtain of Night*, Orchard (New York, NY), 1997.

Jennifer Armstrong, *Pockets*, Crown (New York, NY), 1998.

Florence Parry Heide and Judith Heide Gilliland, *The House of Wisdom*, Dorling Kindersley (New York, NY), 1999.

Rozanne Lanczak Williams, *The Purple Snerd,* Harcourt (San Diego, CA), 2000.

Deborah Blumenthal, *Aunt Claire's Yellow Beehive Hair,* Dial (New York, NY), 2001.

Toni Buzzeo, *The Sea Chest,* Dial (New York, NY), 2002.

Tony Mitton, *Plum: Poems,* Arthur A. Levine (New York, NY), 2003.

Nancy Willard, *Sweep Dreams,* Little, Brown (New York, NY), 2005.

Phyllis Root, *Lucia and the Light,* Candlewick (Cambridge, MA), 2006.

Contributor of illustrations to periodicals, including *Atlantic Monthly, Wall Street Journal,* and *Time.*

ILLUSTRATOR; "HARRY POTTER" NOVEL SERIES BY J.K. ROWLING

Harry Potter and the Sorcerer's Stone, Arthur A. Levine (New York, NY), 1998.

Harry Potter and the Chamber of Secrets, Arthur A. Levine (New York, NY), 1999.

Harry Potter and the Prisoner of Azkaban, Arthur A. Levine (New York, NY), 1999.

Harry Potter and the Goblet of Fire, Arthur A. Levine (New York, NY), 2000.

Harry Potter and the Order of the Phoenix, Arthur A. Levine (New York, NY), 2003.

Harry Potter and the Half Blood Prince, Arthur A. Levine (New York, NY), 2005.

In Mary GrandPré's artwork for Toni Buzzeo's **The Sea Chest** *she reflects the story's mystery and sense of adventure.* (Illustration © 2002 by Mary GrandPré. Reproduced by permission of Dial Books for Young Readers, a division of Penguin Putnam Books for Young Readers.)

Harry Potter and the Deathly Hallows, Arthur A. Levine (New York, NY), 2007.

GrandPré's illustrations also appear in the Hebrew translations of the series.

Sidelights

Illustrator Mary GrandPré has been drawing for most of her life. From early illustrations of Mickey Mouse when she was five, to mimicking Spanish surrealist Salavador Dali paintings at age ten, GrandPré loved making art, and she developed her unique style while attending college in her twenties. It was around that time that she started thinking about illustration as a career. "I'd always thought of illustration as kind of a boring, commercial thing. I was a fine arts major, so I approached illustration with that attitude. And it came to a point where it really worked for me because I started solving illustration ideas with the natural way that I draw," she explained to John Jarvis in *Communication Arts.* Along with work in full-length animated films such as the Dreamworks movie *Antz,* GrandPré has illustrated several children's books. Although she is probably best known for as the illustrator of the U.S. edition of the "Harry Potter" series by British writer J.K. Rowling, GrandPré's illustration projects ranging from bedtime stories to fairy tales.

GrandPré has collaborated with a number of authors in the course of her career as an illustrator. Reviewing the artist's work for Jennifer Armstrong's *Chin Yu Min and the Ginger Cat, Horn Book* contributor Nancy Vasilakis wrote that the "strong, almost exaggerated, characterizations" reveal both "humor and fine style." Writing about the same title, a *Publishers Weekly* contributor maintained that GrandPré's "sumptuous palette of golds, gingers, browns and maroons suffuses the illustrations with warmth, and . . . create an aura of mystery befitting the [book's] exotic locale." Another *Publishers Weekly* critic commented on the art in Christopher King's *The Vegetables Go to Bed,* writing that it "displays her flair for unusual perspectives and lighting." Kathy Broderick, writing in *Booklist,* commented on the "beautiful new illustrations" GrandPré contributed to a new edition of Domenico Vittorini's *The Thread of Life: Twelve Old Italian Tales,* while a *Publishers Weekly* critic commented that the "lush, dramatic pastel drawings" the artist pairs with Marguerite W. Davol's text in *Batwings and the Curtain of Night* "evoke motion so adroitly."

The House of Wisdom, set in ancient Baghdad and featuring a text by Florence Parry Heide and Judith Heide Gilliland, received a Middle East Book Award for its contribution to helping young readers gain an understanding of the Middle East. As Alicia Eames wrote in *School Library Journal,* GrandPré's "brilliantly hued, detailed pastels capture the grandeur and beauty" of the story's exotic setting. In Rozanne Lanczak Williams' *The Purple Snerd,* GrandPré creates a strange creature

with a curling purple tail; "The book has great visual appeal," wrote Melaine S. Wible in *School Library Journal.* Barbara Buckley, in a *School Library Journal* review of Toni Buzzeo's *The Sea Chest,* wrote that "GrandPré's oil paintings create the dramatic effects of the story." John Peters noted writing in his *Booklist* review noted of the same title that GrandPré's art "creates luminous New England scenes in rich, warm colors," while in *School Library Journal* Jane Barrer commented of Nancy Willard's *Sweep Dreams* that the artist's "oil-wash and colored-pencil artwork is as tender and expressive as the story." GrandPré's "evocative, dimly lit acrylics" for *Lucia and the Light* "capture the eerie mystery and shivery suspense" of Phyllis Root's story, according to *Booklist* contributor Gillian Engberg.

GrandPré and her husband, Tom Casmer, are the joint author-illustrators of *Henry and Pawl and the Round Yellow Ball.* Henry is a young artist who is frustrated because he cannot create "something important." When his dog Pawl loses a beloved yellow ball, Henry creates posters to help them locate it; when a man returns the ball and compliments Henry's posters, the boy realizes that his art has accomplished something. "Smoothly sculpted 3D figures and flat, childlike drawings co-exist harmoniously," wrote a *Kirkus Reviews* contributor in reviewing the work, and Joy Fleishhacker noted in

GrandPré illuminates her illustrations for Florence Parry Heide and Judith Heide Gilliland's **The House of Wisdom** *with a light characteristic of the story's desert setting.* (Illustration © 1999 by Mary GrandPré. Reproduced by permission of DK Publishing, a division of Penguin Putnam Books for Young Readers.)

School Library Journal that "Henry's frustrations over his abilities are realistically portrayed, as is the antidote to his problem." GrandPré discussed the husband-and-wife collaboration in an article for the *Sarasota Herald Tribune.* "Our challenge was for the two of us to blend our styles together," she wrote. "Tom's style is based in line, a strong sense of line work and structure. But it also has kind of a quirkiness and a funky edge to it, and really vibrant color. It's everything that I love in artwork, and it's not like mine; we're kind of opposites in our work, and that's where we had to find how to make those things blend. And we really did."

Biographical and Critical Sources

PERIODICALS

Booklist, November 1, 1995, Kathy Broderick, review of *The Thread of Life: Twelve Old Italian Tales,* p. 469; August, 1998, John Peters, review of *Pockets,* p. 2012; September 15, 2002, John Peters, review of *The Sea Chest,* p. 238; July, 2005, Hazel Rochman, review of *Sweep Dreams,* p. 1931; December 1, 2006, Gillian Engberg, review of *Lucia and the Light,* p. 45.

Communication Arts, January-February, 2000, John Jarvis, interview with GrandPré, p. 108.

Detroit Free Press, June 21, 2007, "Potter Artist Mary GrandPré Makes Magic."

Horn Book, May-June, 1993, Nancy Vasilakis, review of *Chin Yu Min and the Ginger Cat,* p. 326.

Interview, November, 2000, Steven Heller, "Talk Back," p. 40A.

Kirkus Reviews, January 15, 2005, review of *Henry and Pawl and the Round Yellow Ball,* p. 118; October 15, 2006, review of *Lucia and the Light,* p. 1079.

Publishers Weekly, March 15, 1993, review of *Chin Yu Min and the Ginger Cat,* p. 86; July 12, 1993, "Flying Starts," p. 24; April 11, 1994, review of *The Vegetables Go to Bed,* p. 63; March 3, 1997, review of *Batwings and the Curtain of Night,* p. 75; August 23, 1999, review of *The House of Wisdom,* p. 58; February 17, 2003, review of *Plum: Poems,* p. 75; November 27, 2006, review of *Lucia and the Light,* p. 50.

Sarasota, November, 2003, Kay Kipling, "Mary's Magic," p. 72.

Sarasota Herald Tribune (Sarasota, FL), April 2, 2006, Ruth Lando, "Illustrating Harry," p. L96.

School Library Journal, January, 2001, Melaine S. Wible, review of *The Purple Snerd,* p. 112; July, 2001, Jeanne Clancy Watkins, review of *Aunt Claire's Yellow Beehive Hair,* p. 72; August, 2002, Barbara Buckley, review of *The Sea Chest,* p. 147; January, 2003, Alicia Eames, review of *The House of Wisdom,* p. 83; May, 2003, Grace Oliff, review of *Plum,* p. 140; May, 2005, Joy Fleishhacker, review of *Henry and Pawl and the Round Yellow Ball,* p. 78; July, 2005, Jane Barrer, review of *Sweep Dreams,* p. 84.

ONLINE

Mary GrandPré Home Page, http://www.marygrandpre. com (October 8, 2007).

Scholastic Web site, http://www.scholastic.com/ (October 22, 2007), "Mary GrandPré."*

* * *

GRAY, Rita

Personal

Married; children: two. *Education:* Completed B.S. and M.S.W. at universities in New York.

Addresses

Home—New York, NY. *E-mail*—info@ritagraytoday. com.

Career

Writer. Formerly operated an after-school program.

Writings

PICTURE BOOKS

Nonna's Porch, illustrated by Terry Widener, Hyperion (New York, NY), 2004.

The wide-eyed, adventurous young colt who stars in Rita Gray's **The Wild Little Horse** *is brought to life in the paintings of artist Ashley Wolff.* (Illustration © 2005 by Ashley Wolff. Reproduced by permission of Dutton Children's Books, a division of Penguin Putnam Books for Young Readers.)

Cover of Gray's picture book **Easy Street,** ***featuring illustrations by Mary Bono.*** (Illustration © 2006 by Mary Bono. Reproduced by permission of Dutton Children's Books, a division of Penguin Putnam Books for Young Readers.)

The Wild Little Horse, illustrated by Ashley Wolff, Dutton (New York, NY), 2005.

Easy Street, illustrated by Mary Bono, Dutton (New York, NY), 2006.

Mama Mine, Mama Mine, illustrated by Ponder Goembel, Dutton (New York, NY), 2008.

Sidelights

Rita Gray has always loved young children. Whether running an after-school program, working in social service, writing, or playing with her own children, her focus has always been on young lives. When she decided to begin writing, Gray started with a story book, *Nonna's Porch,* which is based on her own experience. In-

terestingly enough, her first story about growing up was written on her own Nonna's porch.

Nonna's Porch is a quiet picture book that describes a day as viewed by a grandchild visiting his grandmother's house. The boy describes the porch and the sounds he can hear from it, the games he plays with the other children, and the sound of his grandmother's heartbeat at the end of the day. "Gray's poetic first effort is as satisfying as an ice-cold glass of lemonade and as comforting as a hug from Grandma," wrote a *Kirkus Reviews* contributor. Kathy Piehl, in her review for *School Library Journal,* wrote that "Gray captures the sights and sounds of an idyllic summer day in the country." According to a *Publishers Weekly* contributor, "even youngest readers will grasp that Nonna, in her serene stillness, animates everything and everyone in her vicinity."

Gray's *The Wild Little Horse* features a story of youthful curiosity and exploration. A young horse goes exploring and discovers a larger world around him before coming home to the comfort of the barn and his mother. "Little horse lovers will be besotted," predicted a *Kirkus Reviews* contributor. Carol Schene, writing for *School Library Journal,* noted that Gray's "rhyming verse reads easily and is interspersed with repeated sound."

Unlike the quiet of *Nonna's Porch, Easy Street* is full of noise as the characters build an asphalt roadway. Using "minimal rhyme," according to a *Kirkus Reviews* contributor, Gray offers children a step-by-step look at how a road is built. Older readers can gain additional insight into road construction in the book's afterword, which goes into greater depth about the process. Cassandra A. Lopez, reviewing *Easy Street* for *School Library Journal,* considered the picture book an "energetic read-aloud," while the *Kirkus Reviews* contributor maintained that the details in the afterword "compliment . . . the read-aloud bounce of the text."

Gray explores the relationship between children and their mothers in *Mama Mine, Mama Mine.* Featuring different animal mothers on the farm, she describes the chores each creature does while away from its young ones. In addition to being informative, *Mama Mine, Mama Mine* also reassures young readers that working mothers always return home.

Biographical and Critical Sources

PERIODICALS

Kirkus Reviews, October 15, 2004, review of *Nonna's Porch,* p. 1007; August 15, 2005, review of *The Wild Little Horse,* p. 914; May 1, 2006, review of *Easy Street,* p. 458.
Publishers Weekly, November 29, 2004, review of *Nonna's Porch,* p. 39.
School Library Journal, November, 2004, Kathy Piehl, review of *Nonna's Porch,* p. 104; September, 2005, Carol Schene, review of *The Little Wild Horse,* p. 171; June, 2006, Cassandra A. Lopez, review of *Easy Street,* p. 113.

ONLINE

Hyperion Web site, http://www.hyperionbooksforchildren. com/ (October 22, 2007), "Rita Gray."
Rita Gray Home Page, http://www.ritagraytoday.com (October 8, 2007).
TransAtlantic Literary Agency Web site, http://www.tla1. com/Talent/ (October 22, 2007), profile of Gray.*

GREGORICH, Barbara 1943-

Personal

Born December 10, 1943, in Sharon, PA; daughter of Joseph and Mary Gregorich; married Philip Passen (a musician and graphic artist). *Education:* Kent State University, B.A. (literature and history), 1964; University of Wisconsin—Madison, M.A. (literature), 1965; postgraduate studies at Harvard University, 1966-67.

Addresses

Home—Chicago, IL. *Agent*—Jane Jordan Browne, Multimedia Product Development, Inc., 410 S. Michigan Ave., Ste. 724, Chicago, IL 60605-1465. *E-mail*—barbara@barbaragregorich.com.

Career

Kent State University, Kent, OH, instructor in English, 1965-66; Cleveland State University, Cleveland, OH, instructor in English, 1966; Cuyahoga Community College, Cleveland, instructor in English, 1967-71; *Boston Globe,* Boston, MA, typesetter, 1971-73; *Post-Tribune,* Gary, IN, typesetter, 1973; *Chicago Tribune,* Chicago, IL, typesetter, 1973-76; U.S. Postal Service, Matton, IL, letter carrier, 1976-77; Society for Visual Education, Chicago, writer and producer, 1977-78; freelance writer, 1978-83, 1991—; School Zone Publishing Company, Grand Haven, MI, editor, 1983-91. Teacher at writing workshops.

Member

Authors Guild, Society for Children's Book Writers and Illustrators, Mystery Writers of America, Sisters in Crime, Private Eye Writers of America.

Awards, Honors

Chicago Women in Publishing Award for Children's Books, 1984, for *Sue Likes Blue;* SABR-MacMillan Baseball Research Award, Casey Award nomination, and Chicago Women in Publishing Award for Adult Nonfiction, all 1993, all for *Women at Play;* Cooperative Children's Book Center Choice designation, 2007, for *Waltur Buys a Pig in a Poke and Other Stories.*

Writings

FOR CHILDREN

Vocabulary Vampire, Learning Works, 1982.
The Comprehension Adventure, Learning Works, 1984.
D'Nealian Handwriting Activity Book, Scott, Foresman, 1985.
Logical Logic, Learning Works, 1986.
"*Lift Off Reproducible*" series, eighteen books, School Zone Publishing (Grand Haven, MI), 1990.

(With Christopher Jennison) *Racing Math: Checkered Flag Activities and Projects for Grades 4-8,* illustrated by Doug Klauba, Good Year Books (Tucson, AZ), 1998, 2nd edition, 2006.

Waltur Buys a Pig in a Poke, and Other Stories, illustrated by Kristin Sorra, Houghton Mifflin (Boston, MA), 2006.

Waltur Paints Himself into a Corner, and Other Stories, illustrated by Kristin Sorra, Houghton Mifflin (Boston, MA), 2007.

Also author of *Dramatic Literature* and *Fables and Legends,* published by McDonald Publishing, and of *Easy Manners for Every Day, Words of a Feather,* and *World Geography Skills,* published by J. Weston Walch.

"HORIZONS II" SERIES; NONFICTION

Adjectives and Adverbs, School Zone Publishing (Grand Haven, MI), 1980.

Apostrophe, Colon, Hyphen, School Zone Publishing (Grand Haven, MI), 1980.

Capital Letters, School Zone Publishing (Grand Haven, MI), 1980.

Comma, School Zone Publishing (Grand Haven, MI), 1980.

Context Clues, School Zone Publishing (Grand Haven, MI), 1980.

Dictionary Skills, School Zone Publishing (Grand Haven, MI), 1980.

Figures of Speech, School Zone Publishing (Grand Haven, MI), 1980.

Period, Question Mark, Exclamation Mark, School Zone Publishing (Grand Haven, MI), 1980.

Prefixes, Bases, and Suffixes, School Zone Publishing (Grand Haven, MI), 1980.

Prepositions and Conjunctions, School Zone Publishing (Grand Haven, MI), 1980.

"AN I KNOW IT!" SERIES; NONFICTION

Blends, School Zone Publishing (Grand Haven, MI), 1981.

Consonants, School Zone Publishing (Grand Haven, MI), 1981.

Long Vowels, School Zone Publishing (Grand Haven, MI), 1981.

Rhyming Families, School Zone Publishing (Grand Haven, MI), 1981.

Short Vowels, School Zone Publishing (Grand Haven, MI), 1981.

Word Problems: Grades 1-2, School Zone Publishing (Grand Haven, MI), 1981.

Word Problems: Grades 3-4, School Zone Publishing (Grand Haven, MI), 1981.

"GET READY!" SERIES; NONFICTION

Alphabet: Lowercase, School Zone Publishing (Grand Haven, MI), 1983.

Alphabet: Uppercase, School Zone Publishing (Grand Haven, MI), 1983.

Beginning Sounds, School Zone Publishing (Grand Haven, MI), 1983.

Colors, School Zone Publishing (Grand Haven, MI), 1983.

Connect the Dots, School Zone Publishing (Grand Haven, MI), 1983.

Counting One to Ten, School Zone Publishing (Grand Haven, MI), 1983.

Does It Belong?, School Zone Publishing (Grand Haven, MI), 1983.

Following Directions, School Zone Publishing (Grand Haven, MI), 1983.

Hidden Pictures, School Zone Publishing (Grand Haven, MI), 1983.

Mazes, School Zone Publishing (Grand Haven, MI), 1983.

Rhyming Pictures, School Zone Publishing (Grand Haven, MI), 1983.

Same or Different, School Zone Publishing (Grand Haven, MI), 1983.

School Time Fun, School Zone Publishing (Grand Haven, MI), 1983.

Shapes, School Zone Publishing (Grand Haven, MI), 1983.

What's Missing?, 1983.

"START TO READ" SERIES

The Gum on the Drum, School Zone Publishing (Grand Haven, MI), 1984.

My Friend Goes Left, School Zone Publishing (Grand Haven, MI), 1984.

Up Went the Goat, School Zone Publishing (Grand Haven, MI), 1984.

The Fox on the Box, School Zone Publishing (Grand Haven, MI), 1984.

Jog, Frog, Jog, School Zone Publishing (Grand Haven, MI), 1984.

Sue Likes Blue, School Zone Publishing (Grand Haven, MI), 1984.

Say Good Night, School Zone Publishing (Grand Haven, MI), 1984.

I Want a Pet, School Zone Publishing (Grand Haven, MI), 1984.

Beep, Beep, School Zone Publishing (Grand Haven, MI), 1984.

Nine Men Chase a Hen, School Zone Publishing (Grand Haven, MI), 1984.

Jace, Mace, and the Big Race, School Zone Publishing (Grand Haven, MI), 1985.

Elephant and Envelope, School Zone Publishing (Grand Haven, MI), 1985.

Noise in the Night, School Zone Publishing (Grand Haven, MI), 1991.

"BEGINNER GAMES" SERIES; NONFICTION

Alphabet Avalanche, School Zone Publishing (Grand Haven, MI), 1986.

Counting Caterpillars, School Zone Publishing (Grand Haven, MI), 1986.

Reading Railroad, School Zone Publishing (Grand Haven, MI), 1986.

Word Wagon, School Zone Publishing (Grand Haven, MI), 1986.

"READ AND THINK" SERIES

The Great Ape Trick, School Zone Publishing (Grand Haven, MI), 1987.

It's Magic, School Zone Publishing (Grand Haven, MI), 1987.

Nicole Digs a Hole, School Zone Publishing (Grand Haven, MI), 1987.

The Fox, the Goose, and the Corn, School Zone Publishing (Grand Haven, MI), 1988.

Trouble Again: Reading Workbook, School Zone Publishing (Grand Haven, MI), 1988.

FOR ADULTS

She's on First (novel), Contemporary Books (New York, NY), 1987.

Dirty Proof (novel), Pageant Books, 1988.

Writing for the Educational Market, J. Weston Walch, 1990.

Women at Play: The Story of Women in Baseball, Harcourt Brace (New York, NY), 1993.

Biographical and Critical Sources

PERIODICALS

Booklist, June 1, 2006, Hazel Rochman, review of *Waltur Buys a Pig in a Poke, and Other Stories,* p. 82.

Choice, June, 1995, review of *Women at Play: The Story of Women in Baseball,* p. 1553.

Kirkus Reviews, June 15, 2006, review of *Waltur Buys a Pig in a Poke, and Other Stories,* p. 633.

Library Journal, May 1, 1987, Joyce Smothers, review of *She's on First,* p. 80; May 15, 1993, Kathy Ruffle, review of *Women at Play,* p. 75.

Publishers Weekly, July 22, 1988, Penny Kaganoff, review of *Dirty Proof,* p. 52; June 19, 2006, review of *Waltur Buys a Pig in a Poke, and Other Stories,* p. 63.

School Library Journal, July, 2006, Carol L. KacKay, review of *Waltur Buys a Pig in a Poke, and Other Stories,* p. 78.

USA Today, June 11, 1987, review of *She's on First,* p. C2.

Voice of Youth Advocates, June, 1991, review of *She's on First,* p. 90.

ONLINE

Barbara Gregorich Home Page, http://www.barbara gregorich.com (November 12, 2007).*

H

HERBERT, Don 1917-2007
(Donald Jeffrey Herbert, Mr. Wizard)

OBITUARY NOTICE— See index for *SATA* sketch: Born July 10, 1917, in Waconia, MN; died of multiple myeloma, June 12, 2007, in Bell Canyon, CA. Actor, television and radio personality, producer, and writer. Almost every American child whose family owned a television in the 1950s knew Mr. Wizard. When those children had children of their own, many of the new generation were also entertained and educated by Mr. Wizard on the Nickelodeon cable television network. Interestingly, Don "Mr. Wizard" Herbert did not set out to become an icon of children's television. His career began modestly on stage in New York City, where he stayed until World War II interrupted his progress. After a stint in the Army Air Forces, he moved to Chicago and ventured into radio as a producer and actor for local children's programs and an on-air interviewer and announcer. He made his debut as Mr. Wizard on television in 1951 and never looked back. When his series went on hiatus in 1965, Herbert became a producer of radio science shows and videotape series for schools. *Mr. Wizard* resurfaced briefly throughout the 1970s, then moved to cable television in 1983. Herbert's method of operation was to combine the respectability of a white shirt and tie with the presentation skills of a magician, using common household objects to illustrate scientific facts and processes. His assistants were ordinary boys and girls, who helped to bridge the gap between the sound stage and the living room. Herbert's contributions to educational broadcasting were honored with many awards, including a George Foster Peabody Broadcasting Award from the Henry W. Grady School of Broadcasting and Mass Communications at the University of Georgia in 1953, two awards from the Manufacturing Chemists Association, and two National Mass Media Awards from the Thomas Alva Edison Foundation. Herbert's popular television series led to the creation of thousands of Mr. Wizard fan clubs around the world and, according to some commenta-

tors, steered many young men and women toward future careers in science. Herbert also published his television experiments in nearly a dozen books, including *Mr. Wizard's Science Secrets, Mr. Wizard's Experiments for Young Scientists, Mr. Wizard's 400 Experiments in Science, Secret in the White Cell: Case History of a Biological Search, Mr. Wizard's Supermarket Science,* and *Mr. Wizard's Mystery Garden.*

OBITUARIES AND OTHER SOURCES:

PERIODICALS

Chicago Tribune, June 13, 2007, sec. 2, p. 12.
Los Angeles Times, June 13, 2007, p. B10.
New York Times, June 13, 2007, p. C13.
Washington Post, June 13, 2007, p. B6.

* * *

HERBERT, Donald Jeffrey
See HERBERT, Don

* * *

HOSLER, Danamarie 1978-

Personal

Born 1978, in Miami, FL. *Education:* Maryland Institute College of Art, B.F.A. (illustration; summa cum laude), 2000.

Addresses

Home—Baltimore, MD. *E-mail*—greenstarstudio@ greenstarstudio.com.

Career

Illustrator, soft-sculpture artist, and muralist. Greenstarstudio, Baltimore, MD, designer of greeting cards, home goods, and Knitimals™. Walters Art Museum, Balti-

Danamarie Hosler (Photograph courtesy of Danamarie Hosler.)

more, member of part-time staff. *Exhibitions:* Mural installations at Baltimore, MD, Farmer's Market and Health Department Building; Everglades Elementary School, Miami, FL; Miami Shores Elementary School, Miami; Thomas Johnson Elementary School, Baltimore; and other locations.

Awards, Honors

Softie Awards finalist several times, for Knitimals™.

Illustrator

Bobbie Combs, *1, 2, 3: A Family Counting Book,* Two Lives Publishing (Ridley Park, PA), 2000.

Betty S. Evans, *The Case of the Stolen Scarab,* Two Lives Publishing (Ridley Park, PA), 2004.

Jennifer Bryan, *The Different Dragon,* Two Lives Publishing (Ridley Park, PA), 2006.

Contributor of illustrations to periodicals, including *Cricket, Progressive, Hopkins Undergraduate Research Journal,* and *Cats.*

Sidelights

A soft-sculpture artist, muralist, and knitter who is known for her whimsical approach, Danamarie Hosler has also contributed illustrations to several books published by Pennsylvania-based Two Lives Publishing, a firm dedicated to creating children's books for children growing up in same-sex parent and other non-traditional families. Her illustration projects for Two Lives include Jennifer Bryan's *The Different Dragon, 1, 2, 3: A Family Counting Book* by Bobbie Combs, and the elementary-grade chapter book *The Case of the Stolen Scarab* by Betty S. Evans. For Hosler, book illustration is only one of many artistic outlets. In addition to creating mural installations for schools and other public settings, under her Greenstarstudio label she also designs and markets greeting cards, painted objects, and her popular Knitimals™ soft-sculpture animals.

The Different Dragon deals with a controversial subject: children being raised by same-sex parents. In the story, a boy and one of his two mothers play their nighttime game of creating imaginative stories, this time about a dragon that decides that being fierce is not as fun as being friendly. Noting that Bryan's "freewheeling tale" is rendered less weighty by Hosler's use of "warm colors" and "comfortably cluttered" settings, a *Kirkus Reviews* writer concluded that *The Different Dragon* is "playful enough" to keep young readers amused. Calling the picture book "beautifully illustrated," a *Children's Bookwatch* contributor dubbed *The Different Dragon* "a soft-stated yet groundbreaking" work.

Biographical and Critical Sources

PERIODICALS

Children's Bookwatch, February, 2007, review of *The Different Dragon.*
Kirkus Reviews, October 15, 2006, review of *The Different Dragon,* p. 1066.
School Library Journal, March, 2005, Betty S. Evans, review of *The Case of the Stolen Scarab,* p. 211.

ONLINE

Baltimore Messenger Online, http://www.baltimore messenger.com/ (April 11, 2007), Cara Mattlin "The Art of Knitting."
Danamarie Hosler Home Page, http://www.greenstarstu dio.com (November 12, 2007).

*   *   *

HOWARD, Ellen 1943-

Personal

Born May 8, 1943, in New Bern, NC; daughter of Gerald Willis Phillips (a salesman) and Betty Jeane Chord (a banker); married Kermit W. Jensen, June 15, 1963 (divorced June 15, 1969); married Charles F. Howard, Jr. (a grant proposal writer), June 29, 1975; children:

Ellen Howard (Photograph © Rices Photography. Reproduced by permission.)

(first marriage) Anna Elizabeth; (stepchildren) Cynthia, Laurie, Shaley. *Education:* Attended University of Oregon, 1961-63; Portland State University, B.A. (with honors), 1979. *Politics:* "Liberal Democrat." *Religion:* Unitarian-Universalist.

Addresses

Home and office—980 Holiday Ct. South, Salem, OR 97302. *E-mail*—cfhjreh@comcast.net.

Career

Writer and educator. Worked in various libraries and offices, 1963-77; Collins Foundation, Portland, OR, secretary, 1980-88; Vermont College M.F.A. Program in Writing for Children and Young Adults, member of adjunct faculty, 1998—; volunteer for various social causes.

Member

Authors Guild, Society of Children's Book Writers and Illustrators (regional advisor, 1985-88, 1994-97; national board member, 2000-02).

Awards, Honors

Golden Kite Honor Book, Society of Children's Book Writers and Illustrators, 1984, for *Circle of Giving;* Notable Children's Trade Book in the Field of Social Stud-

ies, National Council for Social Studies/Children's Book Council, 1985, for *When Daylight Comes,* 1986, for *Gillyflower,* and 1988, for *Her Own Song;* Best Books designation, *School Library Journal,* 1987, for *Edith Herself;* Children's Middle Grade Award, International PEN USA Center West, 1989, for *Her Own Song;* Notable Children's Book selection, American Library Association, 1990, for *Sister;* Children's Crown Collection honor, National Christian Schools Association, 1993; Christopher Award, and Parents' Choice Gold Award, both 1996, both for *The Log Cabin Quilt;* SCBWI-Michigan Memorial Award, 1997; Child Study Children's Book Committee of Bank Street College Recommendation for Outstanding Merit, 1997, for *A Different Kind of Courage; Smithsonian* Notable Book designation, 1999, and Judy Lopez Memorial Award, and Leslie Bradshaw Award for Books for Young Readers (OR), both 2000, all for *The Gate in the Wall.*

Writings

Circle of Giving, Atheneum (New York, NY), 1984.
When Daylight Comes, Atheneum (New York, NY), 1985.
Gillyflower, Atheneum (New York, NY), 1986, reissued as *Gilly's Secret,* Aladdin, 1993.
Edith Herself, illustrated by Ronald Himler, Atheneum (New York, NY), 1987.
Her Own Song, Atheneum (New York, NY), 1988.
Sister, Atheneum (New York, NY), 1990.
The Chickenhouse House, illustrated by Nancy Oleksa, Atheneum (New York, NY), 1991.
The Cellar, illustrated by Patricia Mulvihill, Atheneum (New York, NY), 1992.
The Big Seed, illustrated by Lillian Hoban, Simon & Schuster (New York, NY), 1993.
The Tower Room, Atheneum (New York, NY), 1993.
Murphy and Kate, illustrated by Mark Graham, Simon & Schuster (New York, NY), 1995.
A Different Kind of Courage (also published as *The Children's War*), Atheneum (New York, NY), 1996.
The Log Cabin Quilt, illustrated by Ronald Himler, Holiday House (New York, NY), 1996.
The Gate in the Wall, Atheneum (New York, NY), 1999.
The Log Cabin Christmas, illustrated by Ronald Himler, Holiday House (New York, NY), 2000.
The Log Cabin Church, illustrated by Ronald Himler, Holiday House (New York, NY), 2002.
The Log Cabin Wedding, illustrated by Ronald Himler, Holiday House (New York, NY), 2006.

Contributor to periodicals, including *The Lion and the Unicorn.*

Sidelights

As a child growing up in Portland, Oregon, Ellen Howard dreamed of being a writer. Encouraged by her family to think in more practical terms, she abandoned the notion. She attended college for a few years without

Life on the prairie in the 1800s is brought to life in Howard's award-winning The Log Cabin Quilt, *featuring artwork by Ronald Himler.* (Illustration © 1996 by Ronald Himler. Reproduced by permission of Holiday House, Inc.)

earning a degree, and then married and began a family. Some years later, Howard returned to college and earned her bachelor's degree. She also took up writing. She explained in an interview with Cynthia Leitich Smith for *Cynsations* online that she thought of herself as a "late-bloomer. Although I told and wrote stories from childhood (and gained some familial notoriety for keeping my little brother and sister awake after bedtime with said stories), there was an eighteen-year hiatus between the last story I wrote in high school and the first story I wrote for a college creative writing class." The publication of one of Howard's stories in a magazine encouraged her and, after much hard work and many submissions, her first book, *Circle of Giving,* was published in 1984. Since the publication of *Circle of Giving,* Howard has produced a variety of works for young people, including historical novels, stories based on her own family experiences, and problem novels. She has been praised for presenting lively stories in well-researched settings and for her sensitive portrayal of characters facing difficult issues.

Circle of Giving is the story of two young girls who move to Los Angeles in the 1920s. Marguerite, once popular in Oregon, has the most difficulty making friends and adjusting to her new surroundings. Eventually she begins to develop a friendship with Francie, a neighbor with cerebral palsy, and slowly realizes that Francie has the potential to read and write. Marguerite and Francie are soon working together to surprise Francie's mother at a neighborhood Christmas party. According to Karen Stang Hanley in *Booklist, Circle of Giving* is a "tender, moving story" based on an actual occurrence related to Howard "by her mother and grandmother."

Howard's second book, *When Daylight Comes,* is historical fiction set in 1733 on one of the U.S. Virgin Islands. In the story, slaves revolt and the ruling Danish government is killed along with all of the white people, except the doctor and the daughter of the magistrate, who is held captive. Helena, the captive girl, narrates the story as she deals with her grief. Noting that the author added just three fictional characters to the story, Tom S. Hurlburt wrote in *School Library Journal* that "Howard strives to be historically accurate. . . . *When Daylight Comes* is good reading, has a solemn and realistic ending and deals with a significant occurrence in the quest for freedom by enslaved blacks."

Her Own Song is a story based on actual events and set in early twentieth-century Portland, Oregon. Mellie, the eleven-year-old protagonist, hesitantly joins her friends as they mock the Chinese man at the laundry, but when her adoptive father has an accident, and her aunt is away on vacation, the Chinese man Geem-Wah helps her. Gradually, from Geem-Wah and her own recovered memories, Mellie learns that she was once a part of the Chinese family's household. Her mother, desperate for money, had sold her to a Chinese couple: Geem Wah's brother and his wife. Mellie was once "Mei-Li" and much loved. It was only later that authorities took her away from them and settled her with her adoptive parents. Despite the prejudice that separates the Chinese community from the white community, Mellie attempts to maintain her new friendship. According to *Horn Book* critic Margaret A. Bush, Howard's "use of timeless themes to illuminate a particular historical situation is well conceived and executed." *Junior Bookshelf* commentator Marcus Crouch described *Her Own Song* as "a remarkable piece of writing," and added: "the intricate details which eventually fit into a kind of jig-saw are cleverly traced, and the feelings of Mellie—Mei-Li—are most sensitively described."

World War II is the setting for *A Different Kind of Courage,* which is based on efforts to save children during the war. In the story, two French children must escape from Adolph Hitler's Nazi troops. Bertrand leaves Paris with his mother, and Zina stays at a camp until her family is forced to move on. The children end up on the same train, bound to the coast and then to the United States. They do not understand, however, why they have been sent away, and feel abandoned as well as frightened. The work, according to Mary M. Burns in *Horn Book,* "evokes time and place, and the unusual subject is treated with the sensitivity and insight characteristic of Howard's writing." *School Library Journal* contributor Ann W. Moore maintained that the novel "gives an interesting and unusual look at World War II."

In the late 1980s, Howard began to publish stories based on her grandmother's experiences. The first, *Edith, Herself,* is set in the 1890s. Edith is going through a difficult period in her life. Her mother has died, and she must live with her older sister Alena, her sister's strict Christian husband John, their son Vernon, who is close in age to Edith, and John's mother. Adjusting to her new home is made even more difficult when the others discover that Edith has "fits," or epileptic seizures. Epilepsy was not well understood in the 1890s, and Edith's family must decide whether she can attend school given her condition. Roger Sutton, writing in the *Bulletin of the Center for Children's Books,* appreciated Howard's "complex characterizations," her "lyrical prose," as well as her "infusion of great drama into the quietest scenes."

After noting Edith's "inner toughness," Crouch predicted in *Junior Bookshelf* that "many small girls will respect and warm to the strength of this heroine."

Sister, published after *Edith, Herself,* is set in an earlier period, before Edith is born, when Alena is still living at home in Illinois in 1886. Since the father of the family is away, and Alena's mother has many children to care for, twelve-year-old Alena has a great deal of responsibility. There are meals to prepare and laundry to finish, in addition to caring for the children. Alena is also a good student and dreams of going to Normal School. When her mother gives birth, Alena, who knows nothing about her body or babies, must assist; although terrified by much of the process, she marvels at the result, and grieves when the baby dies days later. Depressed by the death of the child, Alena's mother cannot work, and Alena must give up school to run the household. "This is a slow paced, thoughtful treatment of a year of growth and change in one young woman's life," wrote Christine Prevetti in *Voice of Youth Advocates.* Ethel R. Twichell remarked in a *Horn Book* review of *Sister* that Howard provides "a convincing portrayal of a sturdy and appealing heroine." The novelist "manages to instill excitement and momentum into the drama of everyday life," concluded Zena Sutherland in her review for the *Bulletin of the Center for Children's Books.*

The Tower Room deals with grief and recovery, and also touches on the subject of abortion. The story centers on fifth-grader Mary, whose mother has died. The year is 1953, and Mary is living with her Aunt Olive in a Michigan town. Without the overt love of her aunt, or of her classmates at school, Mary takes solace in the tower room, a sealed-off room in Olive's house to which she has found another entrance. One day, a girl tells Mary that her mother died as the result of having an abortion; Mary runs from school and hides in the tower room. When she hears her aunt crying, Mary reveals herself and, as Donna Houser noted in the *Voice of Youth Advocates,* her aunt realizes that "both of them have some ghosts in their past that should be discussed." According to a *Kirkus Reviews* critic, *The Tower Room* is "unusually engaging" and has "a real heartwarmer of a conclusion."

When asked by Leitich Smith to explain what it is about historical fiction that sparked her imagination, Howard replied: "From the time when my grandparents, who lived with us, were telling about their childhoods and my mother was telling about hers, I have been imagining the past. Now, even my own childhood is historical! In 1993, I published *The Tower Room,* which was set in the year 1953, when I was ten years old. I was astonished when reviewers called it 'historical fiction!'"

The Gate in the Wall is set in early Victorian England in the world of the laborers who work on the shipping canals. Ten-year-old orphan Emma is forced to perform factory labor as a spinner of silk. Though the work is hard, she makes very little money. When Emma is locked out of work for being late, she begins looking for other options, and soon finds herself working for a boatwoman named Mrs. Minshull. Emma finds herself loading and unloading cargo and guiding Mrs. Minshull's boats through the locks and canals. "Howard has created a cast of characters who are fully dimensional and engaging," wrote a *Horn Book* critic, while Hazel Rochman commented in *Booklist* that "readers will be gripped by the social history."

Along with her historical fiction, Howard has written several novels on more contemporary issues. *Gillyflower* takes up the sensitive issue of sexual abuse. Gilly's life is difficult now that her father is out of work and her mother must work evenings at the hospital. Gilly must keep the house clean and care for her sister Honey, and also deal with the sexual predations of her father, which she does not completely understand. As a way of coping, she imagines the existence of a beautiful, good princess named Juliana. When another family moves in next door, Gilly develops a friendship with her new neighbor Mary Rose, and comes to realize that what her father is doing to her is wrong. When she perceives a threat to her sister Honey, she brings herself to tell her mother what has happened. She does not need Juliana any more. "Gilly's story is developed sensitively and crafted capably," commented Betsy Hearne in the *Bulletin of the Center for Children's Books*. A *Publishers Weekly* critic asserted that the strength of the book is that it "is no sugar-coated parable."

On a lighter note, Howard has also written picture books and chapter books for younger children. Two of these involve characters she first introduces in *Edith, Herself* and *Sister*. *The Chickenhouse House*, a chapter book for readers in grades two to four, features Alena as a young child. Alena's family leaves her grandfather's house for a new farm an hour away. As their house is not ready, the family must live in a small building which they intend to make into a chicken house. Although Alena is initially disturbed by these developments, by the time the new home is ready it too seems odd. According to Burns, Howard's "narrative . . . provides a sense of family solidarity" and "the joys of simple pleasures." *School Library Journal* contributor Virginia Golodetz similarly maintained that *The Chickenhouse House* is a "warm family story about a universal experience [that] is sure to please young and beginning readers."

The Cellar is also based on the childhood of Howard's grandmother. In this story, Faith (another of Alena and Edith's sisters) is teased by her brothers as she attempts to do what they do. She proves her bravery and competence by making her way into the dark root cellar to bring her family apples for a treat. Praising the portrayal of nineteenth-century farm life, a *Kirkus Reviews* critic described the story as "beautifully crafted." Similarly, a *Publishers Weekly* critic noted that in *The Cellar* Howard "evokes the simple pleasures of rural life of a century ago."

Murphy and Kate is another book for younger children that follows the growth of a baby named Kate and her puppy companion, Murphy. The two play together and learn together until Kate begins school. Even then, they remain the best of friends. One day, returning home from school, fourteen-year-old Kate finds that Murphy is not around, waiting for her as he usually does. Kate finds Murphy just in time to say good-bye. *Murphy and Kate* is "a sensitive, honest focus on coping with the loss of a beloved pet," concluded Ellen Mandel in *Booklist,* and *School Library Journal* contributor Marianne Saccardi recommended the book as "a comforting story for children experiencing a similar loss."

Beginning with *The Log Cabin Quilt,* Howard has written a series of books about a girl named Elvira who, after her mother's death, moves with her family in a covered wagon. Her new life in Michigan is not what Elvira expected, and she longs for her mother's presence. However, when the family is in danger of freezing, it is Elvira's idea of using their scrap cloth to caulk the cabin walls that saves the day. "This expressive picture book brings the past to life," wrote Carolyn Phelan in a *Booklist* review of *The Log Cabin Quilt.* Also featuring illustrations by Ronald Himler, *The Log Cabin Christmas* finds Elvira's family celebrating their first Christmas since the death of her mother, although there is not enough money for stockings or treats. Forbidden from talking about it, Elvira develops a plan to bring a little bit of Christmas to their new home. In *School Library Journal,* a reviewer called the story "an insightful glimpse of how simple comforts and family love can define Christmas."

Because they have not been to church in so long, Elvira has trouble remembering what church was like in *The Log Cabin Church,* a book set the spring following Elvira's Christmas. Though Granny longs for a church, planting the fields takes priority over building a new building. However, one Sunday, Elvira's father takes the day off and dresses in his Sunday clothes, their neighbors come to share worship, and Elvira remembers what church is really about. "Howard's use of old-fashioned vocabulary and dialect . . . adds to the authenticity," wrote Kay Weisman in a review for *Booklist.* In *The Log Cabin Wedding* Elvira's father and the neighboring Widow Aiken announce their intentions to marry. Elvira is furious, unwilling to accept Widow Aiken and her sons into her family. However, when Widow Aiken offers to teach the young girl to read, Elvira realizes that this new step-family might have something to offer. Young readers "will relate to Elvira's first-person narrative," wrote Pat Leach in *School Library Journal.*

When asked by Leitich Smith what advice she offered young writers, Howard replied that she could only offer advice most young writers had already heard. "The truth is, we learn to write by reading and writing," she said. She also encouraged budding writers to establish a career doing something that would leave energy for writing. "We can always make time to write, if we care enough to do so. But we need to leave ourselves the energy, the emotional stamina and the quiet that are the real necessities of the writing life."

Howard, who makes her home in Oregon, continues to write for children. She once wrote in a speech she shared with *SATA* that the joy of writing a book "goes on and on, as we watch our book go out into the world

The adventures of Howard's prairie family continues in **The Log Cabin Wedding,** *a book featuring Ronald Himler's detailed drawings.* (Illustration © 2006 by Ronald Himler. Reproduced by permission of Holiday House, Inc.)

in the same way we watch our children grow up. Sometimes we doubt that we have done as well as we could have. Sometimes we feel so proud! But always we know that we have done something important. That is the thing about writing. It is an important thing to do."

Biographical and Critical Sources

PERIODICALS

Booklist, May 15, 1984, Karen Stang Hanley, review of *Circle of Giving,* pp. 1343-44; May 1, 1995, Ellen Mandel, review of *Murphy and Kate,* p. 1580; December 15, 1996, p. 731; December 15, 1996, review of *The Log Cabin Quilt,* p. 731; February 15, 1999, Hazel Rochman, review of *The Gate in the Wall,* p. 1070; April 15, 2000, Barbara Baskin, review of *The Gate in the Wall,* p. 1561; November 15, 2000, Shelley Townsend-Hudson, review of *The Log Cabin Christmas,* p. 648; October 1, 2002, Kay Weisman, review of *The Log Cabin Church,* p. 345; September 15, 2006, Hazel Rochman, review of *The Log Cabin Wedding,* p. 71.

Bulletin of the Center for Children's Books, November, 1986, Betsy Hearne, review of *Gillyflower,* p. 51; May, 1987, Roger Sutton, review of *Edith, Herself,* p. 169; December, 1990, Zena Sutherland, review of *Sister,* p. 87; November, 1993, p. 85; May, 1999, review of *The Gate in the Wall,* p. 316; November, 2000, review of *The Log Cabin Christmas,* p. 106.

Horn Book, November-December, 1988, Margaret A. Bush, review of *Her Own Song,* p. 783; November-December, 1990, Ethel R. Twichell, review of *Sister,* pp. 749-50; July-August 1991, Mary M. Burns, review of *The Chickenhouse House,* p. 453; November-December, 1996, Mary M. Burns, review of *A Different Kind of Courage,* p. 736; March, 1999, review of *The Gate in the Wall,* p. 208; May, 2000, Kristi Beavin, review of *The Gate in the Wall,* p. 341.

Junior Bookshelf, February, 1989, Marcus Crouch, review of *Edith, Herself,* p. 29; December, 1989, review of *Her Own Song,* p. 296.

Kirkus Reviews, April 15, 1992, review of *The Cellar,* p. 538; September 1, 1993, review of *The Tower Room,* p. 1146; August 1, 2002, review of *The Log Cabin Church,* p. 1133; October 1, 2006, review of *The Log Cabin Wedding,* p. 1016.

Publishers Weekly, August 22, 1986, review of *Gillyflower,* pp. 99-100; April 6, 1992, review of *The Cellar,* p. 65; March 15, 1999, review of *The Gate in the Wall,* p. 59.

School Library Journal, November, 1985, Tom S. Hurlburt, review of *When Daylight Comes,* p. 86; July, 1991, Virginia Golodetz, review of *The Chickenhouse House,* p. 58; June, 1992, p. 115; June, 1995, Marianne Saccardi, review of *Murphy and Kate,* p. 87; November, 1996, Ann W. Moore, review of *A Different Kind of Courage,* pp. 106-107; March, 1999, Carol Fazioli, review of *The Gate in the Wall,* p. 210; October, 2000, review of *The Log Cabin Christmas,* p. 59; October, 2002, Margaret Bush, review of *The Log Cabin Church,* p. 112; December, 2006, Pat Leach, review of *The Log Cabin Wedding,* p. 101.

Voice of Youth Advocates, December, 1990, Christine Prevetti, review of *Sister,* p. 284; December, 1993, Donna Houser, review of *The Tower Room,* p. 293.

ONLINE

Cynsations Online, http://cynthialeitichsmith.blogspot.com/ (April 12, 2006), Cynthia Leitich Smith, interview with Howard.

Ellen Howard Home Page, http://usawrites4kids.drury.edu/ authors/howard/ (November 20, 2007).

*   *   *

HYDE, Shelley
See REED, Kit

J-K

JABLONSKI, Carla

Personal
Female. *Education:* Vassar College, B.S. (anthropology); New York University, M.A.

Addresses
E-mail—reader@carlajablonski.com.

Career
Writer, editor, actress, and trapeze artist. Consulting editor for publishers; freelance writer; editorial consultant and copywriter.

Writings

FOR CHILDREN

Home Sweet Homer (based on *Wishbone* television series), Big Red Chair Books (Allen, TX), 1998.

Legend of Sleepy Hollow (based on *Wishbone* television series), Lyrick Publishing (Allen, TX), 1998.

The Sorcerer's Apprentice (based on *Wishbone* television series), Little Red Chair Books (Allen, TX), 1999.

(With Anne Capeci and Brad Strickland) *The Wishbone Halloween Adventure* (based on *Wishbone* television series), Lyrick Publishing (Allen, TX), 2000.

The Gypsy Enchantment (based on *Charmed* television series), Pocket Pulse (New York, NY), 2001.

Esther Dyson: Web Guru (biography), Twenty-first Century Books (Brookfield, CT), 2002.

The Children's Crusade (based on "The Book of Magic" graphic-novel series by Neil Gaiman and John Bolton), Eos (New York, NY), 2003.

Bindings (based on "The Book of Magic" graphic-novel series by Neil Gaiman and John Bolton), Eos (New York, NY), 2003.

The Invitation (based on "The Book of Magic" graphic-novel series by Neil Gaiman and John Bolton), Eos (New York, NY), 2003.

Shadow of the Sphinx (based on *Charmed* television series), Simon Pulse (New York, NY), 2003.

Van Helsing: The Junior Novel (movie novelization), Harper Festival (New York, NY), 2004.

Lost Places (based on "The Book of Magic" graphic-novel series by Neil Gaiman and John Bolton), Eos (New York, NY), 2004.

Reckonings (based on "The Book of Magic" graphic-novel series by Neil Gaiman and John Bolton), Eos (New York, NY), 2004.

Consequences (based on "The Book of Magic" graphic-novel series by Neil Gaiman and John Bolton), Eos (New York, NY), 2004.

Thicker than Water, Razorbill (New York, NY), 2006.

Silent Echoes, Razorbill (New York, NY), 2007.

Author of script for children's musical, *My New York*.

Sidelights
Carla Jablonski did not realize that she wanted to be a writer until she found out that she already was one. "Actually, being a writer never occurred to me!," she admitted during an online interview for *Teens Read Too*. Jablonski grew up in New York City and studied anthropology in college. During graduate school, she worked part-time as an editor for the "Hardy Boys" novels, a job that led to freelance assignments writing tie-in novels based on popular television shows such as *Wishbone* and *Charmed*. In her twenties she also developed a more unusual skill: learning to be a trapeze artist.

In addition to her television tie-ins, Jablonski has also written several novels based on "The Book of Magic," a popular graphic-novel series by Neil Gaiman and John Bolton. Beginning with *The Invitation*, the series follows young Tim Hunter as he develops into a powerful magician in order to protect himself from those hunting him. Tim Wadham, reviewing the adaptation in *School Library Journal,* wrote that "kids hungry for fantasy" would enjoy the title.

In *Thicker than Water,* Jablonski's first original novel for teens, Kia is coping badly with her mother's failing health; meanwhile, the teen is unable to connect with her single dad. Giving into depression, Kia starts cutting herself, but this only makes her feel like more of an outcast. When she finds a group of teens who roleplay as vampires, Kia believes that she has found a place where she can fit in. However, as Kia spends more time with the group, especially the attractive Damon, she begins to wonder whether vampires might be real after all. "Jablonski deals with serious issues, including the search for reality," wrote a *Kirkus Reviews* contributor. Jennifer Mattson, reviewing *Thicker than Water* in *Booklist,* noted that while some of the story

Cover of Jablonski's young-adult novel **Silent Echoes,** *featuring a photograph by Shirley Green.* (Razorbill, 2007. Reproduced by permission of Razorbill, a division of Penguin Putnam Books for Young Readers.)

A freelance writer, Carla Jablonski has written the text for television tie-in novels such as **Charmed: Shadow of the Sphinx.** (Simon Spotlight Entertainment, 2004. Reproduced by permission of Simon Spotlight Entertainment, an imprint of Simon & Schuster Macmillan.)

seemed strained, Jablonski's "storytelling prompts intriguing contemplation of the allure of rituals and cults."

Jablonski takes readers back to the nineteenth century in *Silent Echoes.* The novel's heroine, Lucy, is a scam spiritualist whose father manages to cash in on her celebrity psychic act. When Lucy hears an actual voice during one of her sessions, she realizes that she has a real ability to connect with the spirits: in this case that of a modern teen named Lindsay. For her part, Lindsay fears she is going crazy, but even after she is diagnosed with schizophrenia, she continues to hear Lucy's voice. While Lucy uses the psychic connection to make a fortune, when she realizes that Lindsay needs her help she determines to do something to affect the future. Reviewing the novel, Kristin Anderson wrote in *School Library Journal* that *Silent Echoes* is "all good fun, and if readers leave more knowledgeable about the early women's movement in the United States, all the better." In her *Booklist* review, Ilene Cooper noted that Jablonski "cleverly twines the girls' lives and makes plausible not only how they have come into contact but also why."

Biographical and Critical Sources

PERIODICALS

Back Stage East, October 5, 2006, "My New York," p. 31.

Booklist, February 1, 2006, Jennifer Mattson, review of *Thicker than Water,* p. 44; March 1, 2007, Ilene Cooper, review of *Silent Echoes,* p. 74.

Book Report, November-December, 2002, Patricia Beddoe, "Techies," p. 53.

Kirkus Reviews, December 15, 2005, review of *Thicker than Water,* p. 1323.

Kliatt, January, 2007, Claire Rosser, review of *Silent Echoes,* p. 14.

Publishers Weekly, September 27, 1999, "PBS Puppy in New Book Series," p. 107; May 12, 2003, "More Fun for Fans," p. 69.

School Library Journal, August, 2003, Tim Wadham, review of *The Invitation,* p. 161; April, 2006, Karyn N. Silverman, review of *Thicker than Water,* p. 141; March, 2007, Kristin Anderson, review of *Silent Echoes,* p. 212.

ONLINE

Carla Jablonski Home Page, http://www.carlajablonski.com (October 9, 2007).

HarperCollins Web site, http://www.harpercollins.com/ (October 22, 2007), "Carla Jablonski."

Teens Read Too Web site, http://www.teensreadtoo.com/ (May 24, 2006), interview with Jablonski.*

*   *   *

KACER, Kathy 1954-

Personal

Born September 6, 1954, in Toronto, Ontario, Canada; daughter of Arthur and Gabriela Kacer; married Ian Epstein (a lawyer), December 19, 1981; children: Gabi Epstein, Jake Epstein. *Education:* University of Toronto, B.Sc., 1976; University of New Brunswick, M.A. (clinical psychology), 1978. *Religion:* Jewish.

Addresses

Home—Toronto, Ontario, Canada. *E-mail*—kathy_kacer@yahoo.com.

Career

The Griffin Centre (children's mental health center), Toronto, Ontario, Canada, clinical director, 1989-95; consultant in organizational development to social service agencies and Canadian government, 1995-99; writer, 1996—.

Kathy Kacer (Photograph by Nicki Kagan. Courtesy of Kathy Kacer.)

Member

International Board on Books for Young People (member of executive committee), Canadian Society of Children's Authors, Illustrators, and Performers (recording secretary, 2001-03; chair of programs, 2003-05), Writers Union of Canada.

Awards, Honors

Geoffrey Bilson Award for Historical Fiction for Young People shortlist, and Reader's Choice Award, Canadian Children's Book Center, both 1999, Silver Birch Award, Ontario Library Association, and Canadian Jewish Book Award in young-adult-fiction category, both 2000, Hackmatack Children's Choice Award, Maritime Library Association, 2001, and Red Cedar Book Award shortlist, Young Readers' Choice Association of British Columbia, 2002, all for *The Secret of Gabi's Dresser;* Sydney Taylor Book Award honorable mention, American Association of Jewish Libraries, 2001, Book of the Year shortlist, Canadian Library Association, and Red Maple Award, both 2002, all for *Clara's War;* Book of the Year shortlist, Canadian Library Association, 2004, and Red Cedar Book Award shortlist, 2006, both for *The*

Night Spies; Sydney Taylor Book Award honorable mention, and Norma Fleck Award shortlist for Canadian children's nonfiction, both 2005, both for *The Underground Reporters;* Norma Fleck Award for Canadian Children Nonfiction shortlist, 2006, Silver Birch Award shortlist, 2007, and Hackmatack Children's Choice Award nomination, Maritime Library Association, 2008, all for *Hiding Edith.*

Writings

NOVELS

The Secret of Gabi's Dresser (also see below), Second Story Press (Toronto, Ontario, Canada), 1999.
Clara's War, Second Story Press (Toronto, Ontario, Canada), 2001.
The Night Spies, Second Story Press (Toronto, Ontario, Canada), 2003.
The Underground Reporters, Second Story Press (Toronto, Ontario, Canada), 2003.
Hiding Edith: A True Story, Second Story Press (Toronto, Ontario, Canada), 2006.

"MARGIT: OUR CANADIAN GIRL" SERIES

Home Free, Penguin Canada (Toronto, Ontario, Canada), 2003.
A Bit of Love and a Bit of Luck, Penguin Canada (Toronto, Ontario, Canada), 2005.
Open Your Doors, Penguin Canada (Toronto, Ontario, Canada), 2006.
A Friend in Need, Penguin Canada (Toronto, Ontario, Canada), 2007.

OTHER

The Secret of Gabi's Dresser (play; based on the author's novel), first produced in Toronto, Ontario, Canada, 2004.

Sidelights

Kathy Kacer is an award-winning Canadian author of books for children and young adults. Kacer, whose European-born mother lived through World War II by hiding from Nazi soldiers and whose father survived the concentration camps, writes historical fiction and nonfiction about the Holocaust. "Their stories of survival were an inspiration to me as I was growing up," she remarked on her home page, reflecting on her parents' experiences. "As an adult, I was determined to write their stories down and pass them on to young readers."

Kacer's first book for children, *The Secret of Gabi's Dresser,* is a first-person fictionalized account of Kacer's mother's escape from the Nazis in Slovakia during

World War II. Starting in 1940, the story traces the encroaching Nazification of the country that would later become the Czech Republic, where ten-year-old Gabi and her family face increasing restrictions on their freedoms. In 1943, when the Nazis come to take her away, thirteen-year-old Gabi hides in a dresser while her mother manages to distract the soldiers from the hiding place, saving her daughter's life so that they both can go into hiding until the end of the war. Although Kacer's use of a child-narrator makes her rendering of some aspects of the story awkward, according to *Canadian Children's Literature* critic Marjorie Gann, the story itself is undeniably "gripping," the critic allowed. Writing in *Quill & Quire,* Patty Lawlor found more to like, writing that Kacer successfully renders "a reader-friendly, simply-told story about a Jewish girl during the Second World War." Lawlor also recommended the book for children not yet ready for Anne Frank's diary.

Kacer followed *The Secret of Gabi's Dresser* with *Clara's War,* offering readers another view of the Holocaust and the effect the Nazi plan for the Jews had on a family in Czechoslovakia. As before, Kacer draws upon historical events for the basis of her fictional story. In *Clara's War,* thirteen-year-old Clara is a less-fortunate girl than Gabi for she and her family have been captured by the Nazis and transported to Theresienstadt, a concentration camp that acts as a way-station before the final destination of Auschwitz. There, amazingly, a children's opera was secretly staged and performed fifty times between 1943 and liberation in 1945, according to Jeffrey Canton in *Quill & Quire.* Thus, along with the terror and suffering that are part of every day life for young Clara, there is also schoolwork, growing friendships, and participation in an artistic endeavor. While the novel is explicit about the horrors of camp life, Kacer's focus on this artistic venture transforms her novel into "a story of hope, courage, and humanity in the face of overwhelming suffering and adversity," Canton asserted. Lynne Remick also commented favorably on the novel in *Kliatt,* noting that Kacer's inclusion of historical photographs and information about child survivors of the death camp at the book's end. As a collection of experiences representing those of camp survivors, Clara's "story offers enlightenment and still allows the reader to grasp some hope for humanity and its future," Remick concluded.

In *The Night Spies,* a second work based on the wartime experiences of Kacer's mother, fourteen-year-old Gabi finds shelter in the barn of a kindly Czech farmer. Gabi is joined by her cousin, Max, whose parents were killed by Nazi soldiers and who has endured a long hike to locate the rest of his family. Tired of the cramped, dirty conditions in the barn and feeling isolated and restless, the youngsters sneak out after dark and assist a group of partisans by acting as scouts and spying on the Nazis. According to *School Library Journal* contributor Renee Steinberg, "there is appeal in Kacer's oft-exciting story and its focused depiction of the drudgery and risks faced by the Jews" and anyone who helped them. In *Booklist* Hazel Rochman noted that Kacer writes without sentiment, describing *The Night Spies* as "upbeat" and "realistic about the horror that haunts the survivors."

The Underground Reporters recounts the true story of a group of Jewish youngsters who rebelled against Nazi repression. Forced to adhere to strict laws that limited their freedoms, the children of Budejovice, Czechoslovakia, produced a community newspaper called *Klepy* (Czech for "gossip"), which contained stories, poems, jokes, and drawings. Much of the story is told through the reminiscences of John Freund, one of few survivors, who describes *Klepy*'s origins as well as life in Theresienstadt, the concentration camp to which the Jews of Budejovice were transported. "The writing . . . is captivating," observed *Booklist* reviewer Ilene Cooper. Kacer's biographical portraits "bring a sense of intrigue and thoughtful admiration for these brave, defiant teens," noted a critic in *Kirkus Reviews*. In the words of *Resource Links* contributor Maria Forte, *The Underground Reporters* "not only represents how the human spirit can triumph in adversity but also how human creativity is used time and time again to surmount what is cruel, inhumane and insupportable."

Kacer recounts the tale of Edith Schwalb, an Austrian teen fleeing the Nazis, in *Hiding Edith: A True Story*. During World War II the Jewish Scouts of France funded a safe house for Jewish refugee children in the French village of Moissac; the townspeople willingly cooperated with the effort, which saved hundreds of lives. Edith, who was separated from her parents and sister at age eleven, arrived in Moissac in 1943 and remained there for several months before being moves on to other safe hiding places. Writing in *Resource Links*, Julia Cox remarked that the author "paints a powerful picture of Edith's many losses—home, possessions, security, family life, and even her name when she is forced to pose as a Catholic orphan. But the book offers an equally strong impression of Edith's courage, strong will to survive and determination to remember who she is." Maureen Griffin, reviewing *Hiding Edith* in *Kliatt*, similarly noted that "the reader learns of her fear, loneliness, courage, resourcefulness and growing maturity."

Kacer is also the author of *Home Free*, the first of four titles she has written for Penguin Canada's "Margit: Our Canadian Girl" series. In her books, the author chronicles the experiences of Margit, a young Czech Jew who escapes to Canada while World War II is still raging in Europe. "Many of Margit's experiences of arriving in a strange country were taken from the experiences of my parents when they came here," Kacer stated in an online interview for the *Our Canadian Girl* Web site. She added, "I am . . . so grateful that they were

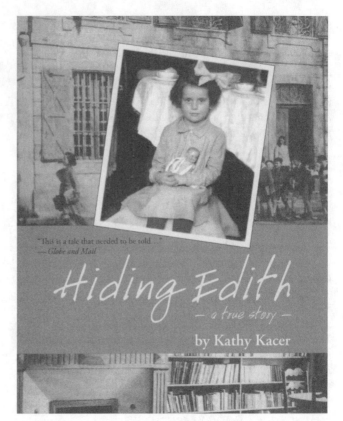

Cover of Kacer's Holocaust-era story Hiding Edith, *the true-life account of a child's experiences in wartime Austria.* (Second Story Press, 2006. Reproduced by permission.)

amongst the lucky ones who survived to pass their stories on to me."

Biographical and Critical Sources

PERIODICALS

Booklist, January 1, 2004, Hazel Rochman, review of *The Night Spies,* p. 857; February 15, 2005, Ilene Cooper, review of *The Underground Reporters,* p. 1076; December 1, 2006, Hazel Rochman, review of *Hiding Edith: A True Story,* p. 40.

Canadian Book Review Annual, 2004, Susan Merskey, review of *The Underground Reporters,* p. 552; 2005, Susan Merskey, review of *A Bit of Love and a Bit of Luck,* p. 497.

Canadian Children's Literature, fall, 1999, Marjorie Gann, review of *The Secret of Gabi's Dresser,* pp. 167-173.

Kirkus Reviews, January 15, 2005, review of *The Underground Reporters,* p. 122; October 15, 2006, review of *Hiding Edith,* p. 1073.

Kliatt, November, 2001, Lynne Remick, review of *Clara's War,* p. 16; November, 2006, Maureen Griffin, review of *Hiding Edith,* p. 36.

Quill & Quire, July, 1999, Patty Lawlor, review of *The Secret of Gabi's Dresser,* p. 49; May, 2001, Jeffrey Canton, review of *Clara's War,* p. 34.

Resource Links, April, 2005, Maria Forte, review of *The Underground Reporters,* p. 42; June, 2005, Victoria Pennell, review of *A Bit of Love and a Bit of Luck,* p. 15; October, 2006, Julia Cox, review of *Hiding Edith,* p. 24.

School Library Journal, February, 2002, Paula J. LaRue, review of *Clara's War,* p. 134; March, 2004, Renee Steinberg, review of *The Night Spies,* p. 214; August, 2005, Susan Scheps, review of *The Underground Reporters,* p. 145; December, 2006, Heidi Estrin, review of *Hiding Edith,* p. 164.

Voice of Youth Advocates, April, 2005, Sherry York, review of *The Underground Reporters,* p. 40.

ONLINE

Canadian Society of Children's Authors, Illustrators, and Performers Web site, http://www.canscaip.org/ (October 31, 2007), "Kathy Kacer."

Our Canadian Girl Web site, http://www.ourcanadiangirl. ca/ (October 31, 2007), interview with Kacer.

*   *   *

KADAIR, Deborah Ousley

Personal

Married; children: Gregory, Alex. *Education:* College of the Midland, associates degree; Louisiana State University, B.A.

Addresses

Home—Baton Rouge, LA.

Career

Illustrator. Formerly worked as an elementary school educator.

Member

Golden Key Honor Society, Phi Alpha Theta.

Writings

SELF-ILLUSTRATED

There Was an Ol' Cajun, Pelican (Gretna, LA), 2002.
Grandma's Gumbo, Pelican (Gretna, LA), 2003.

ILLUSTRATOR

Johnette Downing, *Today Is Monday in Louisiana,* Pelican (Gretna, LA), 2006.
Johnette Downing, *Down in Louisiana: Traditional Song,* Pelican (Gretna, LA), 2007.

Sidelights

Although Deborah Ousley Kadair has lived in Georgia, Texas, and Nebraska, it was the time she spent in Louisiana that inspired her career as a children's book author. The focus of the self-illustrated children's books *There Was an Ol' Cajun* and *Grandma's Gumbo,* Louisiana, also served as the inspiration for two books Kadair illustrated, both of which were written by Louisiana singer/songwriter Johnette Downing.

Kadair based her first self-illustrated title, *There Was an Ol' Cajun,* on the familiar rhyme "There Was an Old Woman Who Swallowed a Fly." The idea to give the story a Louisiana focus came when her Cajun husband swallowed, not a fly, but a gnat. The main character in Katair's tale swallows bayou animal after bayou animal until it finally faces off against an alligator with no intention of being swallowed. "Kadair offers up a story of wily humor that begs to be read—with a Cajun inflection, of course," wrote a *Publishers Weekly* contributor. Judith Constantinides, writing in *School Library Journal,* called *There Was an Ol' Cajun* a "fine, humorous version of an extremely popular tale."

The text of *Grandma's Gumbo* contains a rhyming description of the process of making a popular Louisiana meal. Told from the perspective of three grandchildren helping their grandmother create the dish, the story offers a catchy refrain that may encourage young readers to chant along. Sean George, writing in *School Library Journal,* cited in particular Kadair's "stylized, naïve collage illustrations."

Working as an illustrator, Kadair has contributed her signature cut-paper collages to Johnette Downing's *Today Is Monday in Louisiana.* Each of the images in this book shows a traditional Louisiana dish, and "Kadair's trademark collages illustrate close-ups of each new food," according to a *Kirkus Reviews* contributor. In *Publishers Weekly* a critic noted of the illustrations that

In her detailed collage art for **Today Is Monday in Louisiana***,, Deborah Ousley Kadair brings to life Johnette Downing's picture-book text.*
(Pelican, 2006. Illustration © 2006 by Deborah Ousley Kadair. Reproduced by permission.)

"they prove to be a tasty medium for conveying the mouthwatering flavors." According to *School Library Journal* reviewer Judith Constantinides, "the simplicity of Kadair's bold, bright collages fits the text perfectly." Kadair's second collaboration with Downing, *Down in Louisiana: Traditional Song,* features pictures of animals native to Louisiana. On her home page, Downing wrote of her collaborator's work that Kadair's "illustrations are just delightful."

Biographical and Critical Sources

PERIODICALS

Kirkus Reviews, October 15, 2006, review of *Today Is Monday in Louisiana,* p. 1069.
Publishers Weekly, March 4, 2002, review of *There Was an Old Cajun,* p. 79; October 16, 2006, review of *Today Is Monday in Louisiana,* p. 52.
School Library Journal, December, 2002, Judith Constantinides, review of *There Was an Old Cajun,* p. 98; February, 2004, Sean George, review of *Grandma's Gumbo,* p. 115; December, 2006, Judith Constantinides, review of *Today Is Monday in Louisiana,* p. 96.

ONLINE

Johnette Downing Home Page, http://www.johnettedowning.com/ (October 22, 2007), "Down in Louisiana."
Pelican Publishing Web site, http://www.pelicanpub.com/ (October 11, 2007), "Deborah Ousley Kadair."*

*   *   *

KENNY, Kathryn
See KRULL, Kathleen

*   *   *

KENNY, Kevin
See KRULL, Kathleen

*   *   *

KRULL, Kathleen 1952-
(Kathleen Cowles, Kathryn Kenny, Kevin Kenny)

Personal

Born July 29, 1952, in Fort Leonard Wood, MO; daughter of Kenneth (an artists' representative) and Helen (a counselor) Krull; married Paul W. Brewer (an artist and

Kathleen Krull (Photograph by Paul Brewer. Reproduced by permission of Kathleen Krull.)

writer), October 31, 1989; stepchildren: Jacqui, Melanie. *Education:* Lawrence University, B.A. (magna cum laude), 1974. *Hobbies and other interests:* Music, gardening, quilting, travel.

Addresses

Home—San Diego, CA. *E-mail*—kkrull1@san.rr.com.

Career

Author. Harper & Row Publishers, Evanston, IL, editorial assistant, 1973-74; Western Publishing, Racine, WI, associate editor, 1974-79; Raintree Publishers, Milwaukee, WI, managing editor, 1979-82; Harcourt Brace Jovanovich, San Diego, CA, senior editor, 1982-84; freelance writer, 1984—.

Member

Society of Children's Book Writers and Illustrators.

Awards, Honors

Notable Children's Trade Book in the Field of Social Studies designation, Children's Book Council (CBC)/ National Council for the Social Studies (NCSS), 1980, for *Sometimes My Mom Drinks Too Much;* Chicago Book Clinic Award, 1980, for *Beginning to Learn about Colors;* New York Art Directors Club Award, 1980, for *Beginning to Learn about Shapes;* Notable Book designation, American Library Association (ALA), for *I Hear America Singing;* ALA Best Books for Young Adults selection, for *The Book of Rock Stars;* Books for the Teen Age selection, New York Public Library, for *V Is for Victory;* Jane Addams Picture Book Award, Jane Addams Peace Association, ALA Notable Book designation, 100 Titles for Reading and Sharing selection, New York Public Library, and Parents' Choice Award, all for *Wilma Unlimited;* Golden Kite Honor Award, Society of Children's Book Writers and Illustrators, ALA Notable Book designation, PEN West Children's Literature Award, and *Boston Globe/Horn Book* Honor Award, 1993, all for *Lives of the Musicians;* ALA Best Books for Young Adults selection, Notable Children's Trade Books in the Language Arts designation, and International Reading Association (IRA) Teacher's Choice citation, all for *Lives of the Writers;* IRA Teacher's Choice citation, and 100 Titles for Reading and Sharing selection, New York Public Library, both for *Lives of the Artists;* IRA Teacher's Choice citation, 100 Titles for Reading and Sharing selection, New York Public Library, and Notable Children's Trade Book in the Field of Social Studies designation, CBC/NCSS, all for *Lives of the Athletes;* Books for the Teen Age selection, New York Public Library, 1998, for *Lives of the Presidents;* Jane Addams Picture Book Award, ALA Notable Book designation, Carter G. Woodson Honor Book Award, and Americas Award Honor designation, all 2003, and Christopher Award, 2004, all for *Harvesting Hope;* CBC/NCSS Notable Children's Trade Book in the Field of Social Studies designation, and 100 Titles for Reading and Sharing selection, New York Public Library, both for *A Woman for President;* ALA Notable Book designation, and CBC/NCSS Outstanding Science Book of the Year honor, both 2006, both for *Leonardo da Vinci;* ALA Notable Book designation, 2006, for *Isaac Newton;* ALA Notable Book designation, CBC/NCSS Outstanding Science Book of the Year designation, and Books for the Teen Age selection, New York Public Library, all 2006, all for *Sigmund Freud.*

Writings

FICTION; FOR CHILDREN

(Under house pseudonym Kathryn Kenny) *Trixie Belden and the Hudson River Mystery,* Western Publishing (Racine, WI), 1979.

(Under pseudonym Kevin Kenny; with mother, Helen Krull) *Sometimes My Mom Drinks Too Much,* illustrated by Helen Cogancherry, Raintree (Milwaukee, WI), 1980.

Alex Fitzgerald's Cure for Nightmares, illustrated by Irene Trivas, Little, Brown (Boston, MA), 1990, revised edition, illustrated by Wendy Edelson, Troll (Mahwah, NJ), 1998.

Alex Fitzgerald, TV Star, illustrated by Irene Trivas, Little, Brown (Boston, MA), 1991, revised edition, illustrated by Wendy Edelson, Troll (Mahwah, NJ), 1998.

Maria Molina and the Days of the Dead, illustrated by Enrique Sanchez, Macmillan (New York, NY), 1994.

Clip, Clip, Clip: Three Stories about Hair, illustrated by Paul Brewer, Holiday House (New York, NY), 2002.

(Compiler and adapter) *A Pot o' Gold: A Treasury of Irish Stories, Poetry, Folklore, and (of Course) Blarney,* illustrated by David McPhail, Hyperion Books (New York, NY), 2004.

How to Trick or Treat in Outer Space, illustrated by Paul Brewer, Holiday House (New York, NY), 2004.

"BEGINNING TO LEARN ABOUT" SERIES; WITH RICHARD L. ALLINGTON

Colors, illustrated by Noel Spangler, Raintree (Milwaukee, WI), 1979.

Shapes, illustrated by Lois Ehlert, Raintree (Milwaukee, WI), 1979.

Numbers, illustrated by Tom Garcia, Raintree (Milwaukee, WI), 1979.

Opposites, illustrated by Eulala Conner, Raintree (Milwaukee, WI), 1979.

Hearing, illustrated by Wayne Dober, Raintree (Milwaukee, WI), 1980.

Looking, illustrated by Bill Bober, Raintree (Milwaukee, WI), 1980.

Tasting, illustrated by Noel Spangler, Raintree (Milwaukee, WI), 1980.

Smelling, illustrated by Lee Gatzke, Raintree (Milwaukee, WI), 1980.

Feelings, illustrated by Brian Cody, Raintree (Milwaukee, WI), 1980.

Touching, illustrated by Yoshi Miyake, Raintree (Milwaukee, WI), 1980.

Thinking, illustrated by Tom Garcia, Raintree (Milwaukee, WI), 1980.

Writing, illustrated by Yoshi Miyake, Raintree (Milwaukee, WI), 1980.

Reading, illustrated by Joel Naprstek, Raintree (Milwaukee, WI), 1980.

Talking, illustrated by Rick Thrun, Raintree (Milwaukee, WI), 1980.

Spring, illustrated by Lynn Uhde, Raintree (Milwaukee, WI), 1981.

Summer, illustrated by Dennis Hockerman, Raintree (Milwaukee, WI), 1981.

Winter, illustrated by John Wallner, Raintree (Milwaukee, WI), 1981.

Autumn, illustrated by Bruce Bond, Raintree (Milwaukee, WI), 1981.

Letters, illustrated by Tom Garcia, Raintree (Milwaukee, WI), 1983.

Words, illustrated by Ray Cruz, Raintree (Milwaukee, WI), 1983.

Stories, illustrated by Helen Cogancherry, Raintree (Milwaukee, WI), 1983.

Science, illustrated by James Teason, Raintree (Milwaukee, WI), 1983.

Time, illustrated by Yoshi Miyake, Raintree (Milwaukee, WI), 1983.

Measuring, illustrated by Noel Spangler, Raintree (Milwaukee, WI), 1983.

NONFICTION; FOR CHILDREN

(Piano arranger) *The Christmas Carol Sampler,* illustrated by Margaret Cusack, Harcourt (San Diego, CA), 1983.

(Piano arranger and editor) *Songs of Praise,* illustrated by Kathryn Hewitt, Harcourt (San Diego, CA), 1989.

Gonna Sing My Head Off! American Folk Songs for Children, illustrated by Allen Garns, Knopf (New York, NY), 1992, published with compact disc as *I Hear America Singing: Folk Songs for American Families,* 2003.

It's My Earth, Too: How I Can Help the Earth Stay Alive, illustrated by Melanie Hope Greenberg, Doubleday (New York, NY), 1992.

Lives of the Musicians: Good Times, Bad Times (and What the Neighbors Thought), illustrated by Kathryn Hewitt, Harcourt (San Diego, CA), 1993.

Lives of the Writers: Comedies, Tragedies (and What the Neighbors Thought), illustrated by Kathryn Hewitt, Harcourt (San Diego, CA), 1994.

V Is for Victory: America Remembers World War II, Knopf (New York, NY), 1995.

Lives of the Artists: Masterpieces, Messes (and What the Neighbors Thought), illustrated by Kathryn Hewitt, Harcourt (San Diego, CA), 1995.

Wilma Unlimited: How Wilma Rudolph Became the World's Fastest Woman, illustrated by David Diaz, Harcourt (San Diego, CA), 1996.

Lives of the Athletes: Thrills, Spills (and What the Neighbors Thought), illustrated by Kathryn Hewitt, Harcourt (San Diego, CA), 1997.

Wish You Were Here: Emily's Guide to the Fifty States, illustrated by Amy Schwartz, Doubleday (New York, NY), 1997.

Lives of the Presidents: Fame, Shame (and What the Neighbors Thought), illustrated by Kathryn Hewitt, Harcourt (San Diego, CA), 1998.

They Saw the Future: Psychics, Oracles, Scientists, Inventors, and Pretty Good Guessers, illustrated by Kyrsten Brooker, Atheneum (New York, NY), 1999.

A Kid's Guide to America's Bill of Rights: Curfews, Censorship, and the 100-Pound Giant, illustrated by Anna DiVito, Avon Books (New York, NY), 1999.

Lives of Extraordinary Women: Rulers, Rebels (and What the Neighbors Thought), illustrated by Kathryn Hewitt, Harcourt (San Diego, CA), 2000.

Supermarket, illustrated by Melanie Hope Greenberg, Holiday House (New York, NY), 2001.

M Is for Music, illustrated by Stacy Innerst, Harcourt (Orlando, FL), 2003.

What Really Happened in Roswell?: Just the Facts (Plus the Rumors) about UFOs and Aliens, illustrated by Chris Santoro, HarperCollins (New York, NY), 2003.

Harvesting Hope: The Story of Cesar Chavez, illustrated by Yuyi Morales, Harcourt (San Diego, CA), 2003.

The Book of Rock Stars: Twenty-four Musical Icons That Shine through History, illustrated by Stephen Alcorn, Hyperion Books for Children (New York, NY), 2003.

The Night the Martians Landed: Just the Facts (Plus the Rumors) about Invaders from Mars, illustrated by Christopher Santoro, HarperCollins (New York, NY), 2003.

The Boy on Fairfield Street: How Ted Geisel Grew Up to Become Dr. Seuss, illustrated by Steve Johnson and Lou Fancher, Random House (New York, NY), 2004.

A Woman for President: The Story of Victoria Woodhull, illustrated by Jane Dyer, Walker (New York, NY), 2004.

(With Anne Elizabeth Rector) *Anne Elizabeth's Diary: A Young Artist's True Story,* illustrated by Anne Elizabeth Rector, Little, Brown (New York, NY), 2004.

Houdini: World's Greatest Mystery Man and Escape King, illustrated by Eric Velasquez, Walker (New York, NY), 2005.

Pocahontas: Princess of the New World, illustrated by David Diaz, Walker (New York, NY), 2007.

Contributor to *Open Your Eyes: Extraordinary Experiences in Far Away Places,* Viking (New York, NY), 2003.

"WORLD OF MY OWN" NONFICTION SERIES

City within a City: How Kids Live in New York's Chinatown, with photographs by David Hautzig, Lodestar (New York, NY), 1994.

The Other Side: How Kids Live in a California Latino Neighborhood, with photographs by David Hautzig, Lodestar (New York, NY), 1994.

Bridges to Change: How Kids Live on a South Carolina Sea Island, with photographs by David Hautzig, Lodestar (New York, NY), 1995.

One Nation, Many Tribes: How Kids Live in Milwaukee's Indian Community, with photographs by David Hautzig, Lodestar (New York, NY), 1995.

"GIANTS OF SCIENCE" SERIES

Leonardo da Vinci, illustrated by Boris Kulikov, Viking (New York, NY), 2005.

Isaac Newton, illustrated by Boris Kulikov, Viking (New York, NY), 2006.

Sigmund Freud, illustrated by Boris Kulikov, Viking (New York, NY), 2006.

Marie Curie, illustrated by Boris Kulikov, Viking (New York, NY), 2008.

FOR CHILDREN; UNDER PSEUDONYM KATHLEEN COWLES

The Bugs Bunny Book, Western Publishing (Racine, WI), 19751975.

The Seven Wishes, Western Publishing (Racine, WI), 19761976.

Golden Everything Workbook Series, Western Publishing (Racine, WI), 1979.

What Will I Be? A Wish Book, Western Publishing (Racine, WI), 1979.

OTHER

Twelve Keys to Writing Books That Sell (for adults), Writer's Digest (Cincinnati, OH), 1989.

Presenting Paula Danziger, Twayne (New York, NY), 1995.

Regular children's book reviewer for Dominion Parenting Media.

Sidelights

Kathleen Krull has made a career of educating and entertaining children and young adults. The author of critically acclaimed works of fiction and nonfiction, including the *Boston Globe/Horn Book* Honor title *Lives of the Musicians: Good Times, Bad Times (and What the Neighbors Thought),* Krull "is a fixture in the children's literature world," noted Deborah Stevenson in the *Bulletin of the Center for Children's Books Online.* Krull is perhaps best known for *Harvesting Hope: The Story of Cesar Chavez, Houdini: World's Greatest Mystery Man and Escape King,* and other biographies that combine "her signature blend of spicy gossip and intriguing information," according to Stevenson.

Krull was a self-proclaimed "book addict" from the time she could read; as she later told *SATA,* "reading a lot is the main job requirement for being a writer." Encouraged by several of the nuns who taught her in Catholic school, she quickly began writing. Her earliest works, as Krull recalled, included "*A Garden Book* (second grade) and *Hair-Dos and People I Know* (fifth)." By the time she graduated from college, she was certain she wanted to be a writer, but to make a living while

Krull takes a unique view of the life of classical musicians such as J.S. Bach in Lives of the Musicians, *featuring illustrations by Kathryn Hewitt.*

she developed her craft, she entered the publishing business. "It was a way to work with real writers, learn from them, participate in a highly creative world, and get a paycheck all at the same time," Krull explained to *SATA.* Over a decade, through a series of jobs with various publishers, she rose from editorial assistant to senior editor and moved from the Midwest to San Diego, California. Editing hundreds of books, she worked with such authors as Tomie dePaola, Eve Bunting, Patricia Hermes, Anne Lindbergh, Jane Yolen, Charles Mikolaycak, Arnold Adoff, Amy Schwartz, Judy Delton, and Lael Littke.

Krull's first published works were issued by companies that employed her. Then, in 1984, with her solid credentials in writing and publishing, she made the break to full-time writer. Since then she has produced books covering a wide range of interests and age groups, and she is especially well regarded by critics for her contributions to children's music appreciation. Krull's extensive background in music—she played several instruments as a child and minored in music during college—has made her "passionate about helping to ensure that music remains important in the lives of children."

Inspired by Krull's eight years serving as a church organist (which began at age twelve), *Songs of Praise* collects fifteen hymns accompanied by historical notes, alternative verses, piano scores, and guitar chords. Praised as a "stylish collection" by a *Publishers Weekly* contributor, *Songs of Praise* features hymns from England, Germany, Holland, and North America, among them "Amazing Grace," "Jesus Loves Me," and the Doxology. Phillis Wilson concluded in *Booklist* that Krull's work, which is paired with illustrations by Kathryn Hewitt, creates a "veritable feast for the ears, the eyes, and the heart."

Gonna Sing My Head Off! American Folk Songs for Children, a comprehensive collection of sixty-two American songs, grew out of a love for the folk music Krull learned from her parents, from her guitar study, and from her "fear that traditional music was losing its place in the lives of children." From "I've Been Working on the Railroad," "Take Me out to the Ball Game," and "Oh, Susanna" to "What Have They Done to the Rain?," this "superbly edited" collection, according to a *Publishers Weekly* contributor, provides readers with "an invigorating musical tour of American history and American regions." As Oscar Brand wrote in the *New York Times Book Review,* the keys of the arrangements "are eminently singable, the chords easily playable," making the collection "totally enjoyable." A *Kirkus Reviews* critic praised the "scrupulous" care Krull takes in relating the origins of the songs, and Hazel Rochman stated in *Booklist* that the headnotes "express the sense of connection with ordinary people's lives that is at the heart of this collection." *School Library Journal* reviewer Ann Stell concluded that *Gonna Sing My Head Off!* contains "so many outstanding selections that no one will be disappointed." Krull's book made a reappearance in 2003 under the title *I Hear America Singing: Folk Songs for American Families,* complete with a compact disc containing twenty-three of the sixty-two songs featured in the book.

Lives of the Musicians reveals Krull's passion for music and her use of research to unearth quirky facts. This work, which grew out of a lunchtime conversation, profiles the lives of twenty composers and provides information about them that, as Malcolm Jones wrote in *Newsweek,* "unstuffs a host of shirts and delivers wonderful musical trivia." Classical composers J.S. Bach, Beethoven, Brahms, Mozart, and Vivaldi, operetta composers Gilbert and Sullivan, ragtime composer Scott Joplin, and even folk singer Woody Guthrie are all featured here in humorous detail. A *Publishers Weekly* critic praised Krull's editorial work, writing that the author "masterfully distills the essentials of each musician's life into snappy prose." "Even those only remotely interested in music will be hooked," concluded the critic in a reaffirmation of Krull's intent. "If this book brings readers close (or closer) to the music, and to thinking about music as a career or hobby, that would be my ultimate goal," the author once noted; "But in the meantime, eccentric people make for fascinating reading."

Another musically inspired offering from Krull is *M Is for Music,* an eclectic, largely pictorial introduction to the world of song. "The range of words explored [in *M Is for Music*] is almost as vast as the world of music itself," commented *School Library Journal* contributor Jane Marino. For example, on the "B is for Beatles" page, three "bees" labeled with the names of classical composers—Bach, Beethoven, and Brahms—fly around the modern British rock band. Performers from jazz trumpeter Louis Armstrong to rock musician Frank Zappa, instruments from accordion to zither, and musical styles from *a cappella* to zydeco are also included. "I wanted to do *M Is for Music* as a unique, all-encompassing, eclectic tribute to the power of music in our lives," Krull told an interviewer on the Harcourt Books Web site. "It's meant as a springboard to musical activities and discussion of all kinds." The "Musical Notes from A to Z" appendix provides explanations for the terms listed in the text, but not for the numerous items that artist Stacy Innerst incorporates into the complex, collage-like illustrations she contributes to the book. "Best for those ready to explore an interest in music, *M Is for Music* . . . will also appeal to those just learning the alphabet," remarked a *Kirkus Reviews* critic.

It's My Earth, Too: How I Can Help the Earth Stay Alive provides a good example of Krull's contribution of other nonfiction subjects to children's literature. The volume received attention as the first children's book to be printed on recycled paper with environmentally friendly soybean inks and water-soluble glue, thus reinforcing the book's message. Throughout the book, author Krull reminds children that judicious use of tech-

nology is best, and provides twelve suggestions for children that generally emphasize changing habits, thinking about one's actions, and trying to avoid greediness. With its list of suggestions, the book "could be very useful as an idea starter or discussion book in classrooms," Tina Smith Entwistle remarked in a *School Library Journal* review, while Kay Weisman, writing in *Booklist,* found that the "simple, rhythmic text" would be "particularly appropriate for this age level."

Krull also investigates individual American communities such as New York City's Chinatown and California's Latino neighborhoods in her "World of My Own" series. The purpose of the series, as she once explained, "is to explore, from a child's point of view, various American communities that for one reason or another not many people know about. We may eat in the restaurants of these comparatively unassimilated neighborhoods or read about them when there are problems, but most people in fact know very little about life there." In conducting her research, Krull added, "interviews with actual children and families in these neighborhoods allowed me to do one of my favorite things, which is to ask nosy questions." Reviewing the first two books, *City within a City: How Kids Live in New York's Chinatown* and *The Other Side: How Kids Live in a California Latino Neighborhood,* Rochman noted in *Booklist* that Krull's "lively photo-essays" are written in "an informal, chatty style, weaving together information about family, friends, school, [and] religion," among other things. Krull uses quotations to allow her subjects to speak for themselves; as a result, as Roger Sutton remarked in the *Bulletin of the Center for Children's Books,* "in many ways, these books are a model for the genre." Reviewing all of the books in the series, Leigh Fenly similarly concluded in the *San Diego Union-Tribune* that while multicultural books have become a "hot market," Krull "refreshingly takes the genre into the reality zone."

Describing *Lives of the Writers: Comedies, Tragedies (and What the Neighbors Thought),* a *Kirkus Reviews* critic called Krull's work "another colorful, enthralling excursion into our cultural heritage." With entertaining details about authors from Hans Christian Andersen to Jack London, the author "knows exactly how to captivate her audience," combining historical particulars with "amusing anecdotes that put flesh and blood on dry literary bones," according to a *Publishers Weekly* critic. Nevertheless, "the glimpses she provides are respectful of their times and influences without being dull," *School Library Journal* contributor Sally Margolis noted, which should be "enough to whet readers' appetites for more biography and for the writers' actual works," as Mary Harris Veeder concluded in *Booklist.* Krull ventures into the world of painting, sculpture, and other fine arts in her intriguing companion volume, *Lives of the Artists: Masterpieces, Messes (and What the Neighbors Thought).*

As Krull once commented in *SATA,* her "what the neighbors thought" approach allowed her to create "warts

Artist David Diaz pairs his woodcut-inspired art with Krull's picture-book biography Wilma Unlimited, *the story of Olympic-class runner Wilma* **Rudolph.** (Illustration © 1996 by David Diaz. All rights reserved. Reproduced by permission of Harcourt, Inc. Reproduced in the UK by permission of Writer's House Ltd., on behalf of author.)

and all" portraits that are both "lively and humanizing." In her opinion, being a successful biographer requires not only "having good research skills," but "being a good listener" with a taste for gossip. "Gossip is underrated as a motive for studying history," Krull commented. "As JFK once said about or to J. Edgar Hoover, 'All history is gossip.'" For example, her book *Lives of the Presidents: Fame, Shame (and What the Neighbors Thought)* features both political and personal details about each U.S. chief executive, including hints of scandals such as President Bill Clinton's extramarital affairs. This, like the rest of the series, *Lives of the Presidents* displays Krull's "proven knack for delivering generous dollops of covert asides along with fun facts and pertinent information," commented a *Publishers Weekly* reviewer.

Outside the "Lives of" series but in a similar vein is *They Saw the Future: Psychics, Oracles, Scientists, Inventors, and Pretty Good Guessers,* which profiles a dozen people, including Nostradamus, Marshall McLuhan, and Jeane Dixon, who made detailed predictions about the world with varying degrees of success. This

volume has a "healthily skeptical" tone, encouraging readers to scrutinize even apparently accurate projections, while also providing extensive information about the times and cultures in which each subject lived, reported a *Publishers Weekly* contributor.

In her writing, Krull likes to show how famous people overcame adversity. Many of the men and women she has written about have had to surmount major obstacles, and she has found that reading about this appeals to children. An example comes from Wilma Rudolph, the subject of *Wilma Unlimited: How Wilma Rudolph Became the World's Fastest Woman.* After contracting polio as a child, Rudolph was told she was unlikely to regain the ability to walk. However, she managed not only to walk but to run, and she eventually became an Olympic champion. Krull originally set out to write about Rudolph in *Lives of the Athletes: Thrills, Spills (and What the Neighbors Thought),* but decided that the runner's story was so fascinating that it merited an entire book. "My interest in biography as a literary form comes from curiosity about the details of others' lives," Krull stated on her home page. "To put it in a simple

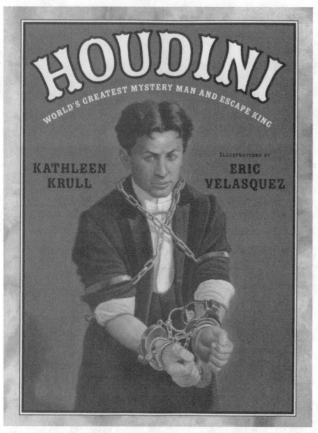

Cover of Krull's generously illustrated middle-grade biography Houdini, *featuring artwork by Eric Velasquez.* (Walker, 2005. Illustration © 2005 by Eric Velasquez. Reproduced by permission.)

way, I'm nosy." The author continued, "More intellectually, I'm intrigued by the shape and structure of a person's life—the arc, the story of it. As stories, biographies are some of the very best—people have definite beginnings, middles, and demises. I'm motivated by the challenge of trying to write about a life in a pithy, meaningful way—sculpting with words a portrait that conveys the essence of a person—accurately yet dramatically."

Cesar Chavez, another courageous American who battled against adversity, is profiled in *Harvesting Hope.* Although this biography, aimed at elementary school children, gives the details of the activist's childhood and discusses Chavez's early efforts to organize migrant farm workers in California, the majority of *Harvesting Hope* deals with the National Farm Workers Association's 1965 strike. "Focusing on one event makes the story appealing to younger readers," maintained *School Library Journal* contributor Sue Morgan. Because of that limited focus, Krull was able to provide gripping details of the strike and the accompanying three-hundred-mile protest march, including the fact that the marchers' feet blistered so badly that they bled. For readers who are interested in what happened to Chavez after 1965, Krull provides an author's note outlining the activists' later life. Overall, as Susan Dove Lempke

concluded in *Horn Book, Harvesting Hope* "is a powerfully moving tribute to an important person in U.S. history."

In *A Woman for President: The Story of Victoria Woodhull* Krull shares the little-known story of the first woman to run for the presidency of the United States. Woodhull, a fortune-teller, financial whiz, and suffragist, was the candidate of the Equal Rights Party in 1872. "Krull's writing style is lively and engaging," observed *School Library Journal* contributor Ann Welton in a review of *A Woman for President. Houdini,* a "perceptive and dramatic tribute," according to a critic in *Kirkus Reviews,* examines the life of famed escape artist Harry Houdini, who mesmerized audiences with his feats of derring-do in the early twentieth century. "The author's crisp narrative style and careful choice of detail are evident here," wrote Heide Piehler in a review of Krull's biography for *School Library Journal.* Krull looks at an important figure in America's colonial history in *Pocahontas: Princess of the New World,* "an accessible portrait of the Native American girl who helped maintain a fragile peace between her tribe and English colonists," according to a *Publishers Weekly* reviewer. A critic in *Kirkus Reviews* noted that Krull's "narrative economically continues the intertwined stories of Pocahontas's maturation and the travails of the white settlers," including John Smith, the English captain who owed his life to the Powhatan girl, and John Rolfe, the tobacco farmer who married her.

In 2005 Krull introduced her "Giants of Science" biography series, illustrated by Boris Kulikov. The works "show how scientific discovery is never a revelation arriving in a single, mind-blowing flash," Krull wrote in a *Book Links* essay. In *Leonardo da Vinci,* she focuses on the great artist's scientific achievements and describes life in the Middle Ages. "Readers will come away from this accessible volume with an understanding of who Leonardo was," remarked *School Library Journal* reviewer Laura Younkin, and *Booklist* critic Carolyn Phelan described the work as a "very readable, vivid portrait set against the backdrop of remarkable times." In *Isaac Newton,* Krull profiles the seventeenth-century British scientist who invented calculus and discerned the basic principles of physics. The author's "conversational tone . . . lends a lively voice to a biography chock-full of information," Betty Carter wrote in *Horn Book.* Krull looks at the father of psychoanalysis in *Sigmund Freud,* a "lucid and thoughtful examination of Freud's life, work and legacy," a contributor in *Kirkus Reviews* stated. *Booklist* reviewer GraceAnne A. DeCandido praised the author for her "breezy, forthright, and intelligent approach" to her subject.

Krull has also written fictional tales for children, some of which feature the character Alexandra Fitzgerald. In *Alex Fitzgerald's Cure for Nightmares,* the nine year old attempts to cope with the nightmares she has been having since she began to live with her father in

California. Alexandra is worried that the other children in school will find out about her nightmares, but when she finally tells a friend about her problem, she is given some worry dolls and the nightmares finally stop. Krull once commented, "The inspiration for this book combined my stepdaughter's insomnia (and her resulting obsession with worry dolls) with my own experiences as a California transplant." *Booklist* critic Wilson found the story "a sensitive and upbeat handling of a problem" that is "presented within an engaging school-activities plot."

Alexandra returns in *Alex Fitzgerald, TV Star,* which was inspired by an article about a girl "chosen to play the part of the young Madonna in a Pepsi commercial," as Krull once noted. "I got to wondering how sudden fame would affect an ordinary kid. Also, with hours of my childhood spent at the piano, I've had my own visions of fame and stardom." In this story, fourth grader Alex is invited to audition for a music video. Excited about the celebrity status she imagines, she forgets to buy her father a Christmas present, asks him to spend more money than he has, and annoys her friends. Krull's "pleasant, entertaining story," according to Stephanie Zvirin of *Booklist,* is "wrapped around an important lesson." A *Kirkus Reviews* writer praised the author's "good ear for dialogue," while *Bulletin of the Center for Children's Books* critic Ruth Ann Smith concluded that readers will "sympathize with Alex's dreams of stardom, especially since they don't materialize."

Explaining her eclectic writing credits, Krull once observed: "I seem to write several different kinds of books, and I hope to do even more in the future. My passions include music, humor, gardening, food, health, history, travel, and people—neighbors and others. I aim for making my books as fresh as I can—using ideas and combinations of words only I would use. I try to be clear and funny and relevant to what is going on in children's lives, as well as true to my own memories of childhood. My 'hidden agenda' is always to create books that will mean as much to readers as books have meant to me."

Biographical and Critical Sources

BOOKS

Graham, Paula, editor, *Speaking of Journals: Children's Book Writers Talk about Their Diaries,* Boyds Mills Press (Honesdale, PA), 1999.

Robb, Laura, *Nonfiction Writing from the Inside Out,* Scholastic (New York, NY), 2004.

PERIODICALS

Book Links, November, 2005, Kathleen Krull, "The 'Anti-Eureka' Series," p. 46.

Cover of Krull's picture book **Pocahontas, Princess of the New World,** *featuring nostalgic soft-toned art by David Diaz.* (Walker, 2007. Illustration © 2007 by David Diaz. Reproduced by permission.)

Booklist, November 15, 1988, Phillis Wilson, review of *Songs of Praise,* p. 586; June 15, 1990, Phillis Wilson, review of *Alex Fitzgerald's Cure for Nightmares,* p. 1986; March 1, 1991, Stephanie Zvirin, review of *Alex Fitzgerald, TV Star,* p. 1388; July, 1992, Kay Weisman, review of *It's My Earth, Too: How I Can Help the Earth Stay Alive,* p. 1941; October 15, 1992, Hazel Rochman, review of *Gonna Sing My Head Off! American Folk Songs for Children,* p. 424; April 15, 1994, Hazel Rochman, review of *City within a City: How Kids Live in New York's Chinatown* and *The Other Side: How Kids Live in a California Latino Neighborhood;* September 15, 1994, Mary Harris Veeder, review of *Lives of the Writers: Comedies, Tragedies (and What the Neighbors Thought);* March 1, 2002, Ilene Cooper, review of *Lives of Extraordinary Women: Rulers, Rebels (and What the Neighbors Thought),* p. 1147; June 1, 2003, Traci Todd, review of *Harvesting Hope: The Story of Cesar Chavez,* pp. 1795-1796; August 1, 2003, review of *M Is for Music,* p. 1019; March 1, 2005, Jennifer Mattson, review of *Houdini: World's Greatest Mystery Man and Escape King,* p. 1200; September 1, 2005, Carolyn Phelan, review of *Houdini,* p. 126; April 1, 2006, Kay Weisman, review of *Isaac Newton,* p. 38; December 1, 2006, GraceAnne A. DeCandido, review of *Sigmund Freud,* p. 36.

Bulletin of the Center for Children's Books, May, 1991, Ruth Ann Smith, review of *Alex Fitzgerald, TV Star,* pp. 221-222; May, 1994, Roger Sutton, review of *City within a City* and *The Other Side.*

Children's Digest, September-October, 2003, review of *I Hear America Singing!: Folk Songs for American Families,* p. 28.

Christian Science Monitor, August 23, 2001, review of *Lives of Extraordinary Women,* p. 21.

Constitutional Commentary, summer, 2002, Luke Paulsen, review of *A Kid's Guide to America's Bill of Rights,* pp. 291-295.

Horn Book, July-August, 2003, Susan Dove Lempke, review of *Harvesting Hope,* pp. 480-481; January-February, 2004, Joanna Rudge Long, review of *The Boy on Fairfield Street: How Ted Geisel Grew up to Become Dr. Seuss,* p. 103; September-October, 2005, Betty Carter, review of *Leonardo da Vinci,* p. 345; May-June, 2006, Betty Carter, review of *Isaac Newton,* p. 345; September-October, 2006, Betty Carter, review of *Sigmund Freud,* p. 607.

Instructor, October, 1997, Judy Freeman, review of *Lives of the Athletes: Thrills, Spills (and What the Neighbors Thought),* p. 24.

Kirkus Reviews, June 1, 1991, review of *Alex Fitzgerald, TV Star,* p. 730; October 1, 1992, review of *Gonna Sing My Head Off!,* p. 1257; September 15, 1994, review of *Lives of the Writers;* January 15, 2002, review of *Clip Clip Clip: Three Stories about Hair,* p. 106; May 15, 2003, review of *What Really Happened in Roswell?: Just the Facts (Plus the Rumors) about UFOs and Aliens,* p. 753; July 1, 2003, review of *Harvesting Hope,* p. 911; August 1, 2003, review of *M Is for Music,* p. 1019; September 15, 2003, review of *The Book of Rock Stars: Twenty-four Musical Icons That Shine through History,* p. 1177; March 1, 2005, review of *Houdini,* p. 289; June 15, 2005, review of *Leonardo da Vinci,* p. 685; March 1, 2006, review of *Isaac Newton,* p. 233; September 1, 2006, review of *Sigmund Freud,* p. 906; April 1, 2007, review of *Pocahontas: Princess of the New World.*

Newsweek, November 22, 1993, Malcolm Jones, review of *Lives of the Musicians: Good Times, Bad Times (and What the Neighbors Thought).*

New York Times Book Review, November 8, 1992, Oscar Brand, "These Songs Were Made for You and Me," review of *Gonna Sing My Head Off!,* p. 44; October 3, 1993, p. 31; October 23, 1994, p. 30; April 23, 1995, p. 27; September 10, 1995, p. 35; November 16, 2003, Paul O. Zelinsky, review of *M Is for Music,* p. 37.

Publishers Weekly, November 8, 1987; October 5, 1992, review of *Gonna Sing My Head Off!,* p. 72; January 25, 1993, review of *Songs of Praise,* p. 88; February 22, 1993, review of *Lives of the Musicians,* pp. 96-97; May 30, 1994, p. 58; August 1, 1994, review of *Lives of the Writers,* p. 79; May 15, 1995, review of *V Is for Victory: America Remembers World War II,* p. 75; April 29, 1996, review of *Wilma Unlimited: How Wilma Rudolph Became the World's Fastest Woman,*

p. 73; June 8, 1998, review of *Lives of the Presidents: Fame, Shame (and What the Neighbors Thought),* p. 60; June 7, 1999, review of *They Saw the Future: Psychics, Oracles, Scientists, Inventors, and Pretty Good Guessers,* p. 84; February 25, 2002, review of *Clip Clip Clip,* p. 66; June 3, 2002, review of *V Is for Victory,* p. 91; May 5, 2003, review of *Harvesting Hope,* p. 221; July 7, 2003, review of *What Really Happened in Roswell?,* p. 73; September 8, 2003, review of *M Is for Music,* p. 74; December 22, 2003, *The Book of Rock Stars,* p. 62; January 12, 2004, review of *The Boy on Fairfield Street,* p. 54; April 4, 2005, review of *Houdini,* p. 59; April 16, 2007, review of *Pocahontas,* p. 51.

San Diego Union-Tribune, August 7, 1994, Leigh Fenly, review of "World of My Own" series.

School Library Journal, July, 1992, Tina Smith Entwistle, review of *It's My Earth, Too,* p. 70; October, 1992, Ann Stell, review of *Gonna Sing My Head Off!,* p. 105; May, 1993, p. 117; July, 1994, p. 111; October, 1994, Sally Margolis, review of *Lives of the Writers,* pp. 134-135; December, 1994, p. 77; October, 1995, p. 164; June, 1996, p. 116; March, 2002, Jody McCoy, review of *Clip Clip Clip,* p. 192; February, 2003, Lee Bock, review of *Wilma Unlimited,* p. 97; June, 2003, Sue Morgan, review of *Harvesting Hope,* pp. 129-130; September, 2003, Jane Marino, review of *M Is for Music,* pp. 200-201; October, 2003, Jeffrey Hastings, review of *The Night the Martians Landed,* pp. 193-194, and Ann G. Brouse, review of *What Really Happened in Roswell?,* p. 194; January, 2004, Anne Chapman Callaghan, review of *The Boy on Fairfield Street,* p. 119; November, 2004, Catherine Threadgill, review of *How to Trick or Treat in Outer Space,* p. 110; September, 2004, Ann Welton, review of *A Woman for President: The Story of Victoria Woodhull,* p. 189; December, 2004, Ginny Gustin, review of *Lives of the Musicians,* p. 60; April, 2005, Heide Piehler, review of *Houdini,* p. 124; October, 2005, Laura Younkin, review of *Leonardo da Vinci,* p. 190; March, 2006, Rick Margolis, "Big Newton," p. 55, John Peters, review of *A Woman for President,* p. 90, and John Peters, review of *Isaac Newton,* p. 243; December, 2006, Nancy Silverrod, review of *Sigmund Freud,* p. 164; April, 2007, Lucinda Snyder Whitehurst, review of *Pocahontas,* p. 123.

Skipping Stones, March-April, 2003, review of *Harvesting Hope,* p. 32.

Teacher Librarian, September-October, 1998, Teri Lesesne, "The Many Lives of Kathleen Krull."

ONLINE

Bulletin of the Center for Children's Books Online, http://bccb.lis.uiuc.edu/ (April 1, 2007), Deborah Stevenson, "True Blue: Kathleen Krull."

Harcourt Books Web site, http://www.harcourtbooks.com/ (September 1, 2003), interview with Krull.

Kathleen Krull Home Page, http://www.kathleenkrull.com (November 10, 2007).

L

LILLEGARD, Dee

Personal

Married Wayne Stoker.

Addresses

Home and office—Castro Valley, CA.

Career

Poet and author of nonfiction books for children.

Writings

Where Is It?, illustrated by Gene Sharp, Children's Press (Chicago, IL), 1984.

(With husband, Wayne Stoker) *I Can Be an Electrician,* Children's Press (Chicago, IL), 1986.

(With Wayne Stoker) *I Can Be a Welder,* Children's Press (Chicago, IL), 1986.

I Can Be a Baker, Children's Press (Chicago, IL), 1986.

I Can Be a Carpenter, Children's Press (Chicago, IL), 1986.

My First Martin Luther King Book, illustrated by Helen Endres, Children's Press (Chicago, IL), 1987.

My First Columbus Day Book, illustrated by Helen Endres, Children's Press (Chicago, IL), 1987.

James A. Garfield: Twentieth President of the United States, Children's Press (Chicago, IL), 1987.

I Can Be a Secretary, Children's Press (Chicago, IL), 1987.

I Can Be a Plumber, Children's Press (Chicago, IL), 1987.

I Can Be a Beautician, Children's Press (Chicago, IL), 1987.

Percussion: An Introduction to Musical Instruments, Children's Press (Chicago, IL), 1987.

Woodwinds: An Introduction to Musical Instruments, Children's Press (Chicago, IL), 1987.

John Tyler: Tenth President of the United States, Children's Press (Chicago, IL), 1987.

Richard Nixon: Thirty-seventh President of the United States, Children's Press (Chicago, IL), 1988.

Strings: An Introduction to Musical Instruments, Children's Press (Chicago, IL), 1988.

Brass: An Introduction to Musical Instruments, Children's Press (Chicago, IL), 1988.

James K. Polk: Eleventh President of the United States, Children's Press (Chicago, IL), 1988.

Sitting in My Box, illustrated by Jon Agee, Dutton (New York, NY), 1989.

(With Wayne Stoker) *America the Beautiful: Nevada,* Children's Press (Chicago, IL), 1991.

My Yellow Ball, illustrated by Sarah Chamberlain, Dutton (New York, NY), 1993.

The Hee-Haw River, illustrated by Allan Eitzen, Holt (New York, NY), 1995.

The Day the Daisies Danced, illustrated by Rex Barron, Putnam's (New York, NY), 1996.

The Wild Bunch, illustrated by Rex Barron, Putnam's (New York, NY), 1997.

Tortoise Brings the Mail, illustrated by Jillian Lund, Dutton (New York, NY), 1997.

The Poombah of Badoombah, illustrated by Kevin Hawkes, Putnam's (New York, NY), 1998.

The Song of Celestine, illustrated by Dean Morrissey, Little, Brown (Boston, MA), 1998.

The Big Bug Ball, illustrated by Rex Barron, Putnam's (New York, NY), 1999.

Tiger, Tiger, illustrated by Susan Guevara, Putnam's (New York, NY), 2002.

Who Will Sing a Lullaby?, illustrated by Dan Yaccarino, Knopf (New York, NY), 2007.

Balloons, Balloons, Balloons, illustrated by Bernadette Pons, Dutton (New York, NY), 2007.

POETRY

September to September: Poems for All Year Round: A Collection of Original Poems Especially Designed for Classroom Use, Children's Press (Chicago, IL), 1986.

Do Not Feed the Table, illustrated by Keiko Narahashi, Doubleday (New York, NY), 1992.

Wake up House!: Rooms Full of Poems, illustrated by Don Carter, Knopf (New York, NY), 2000.

Hello School!: A Classroom of Poems, illustrated by Don Carter, Knopf (New York, NY), 2001.

Go!: Poetry in Motion, illustrated by Valeri Gorbachev, Knopf (New York, NY), 2006.

Sidelights

Dee Lillegard is a poet and the author of nonfiction titles for children. Many of her books are about careers, holidays, and musical instruments. She has also written several picture books for young readers. Working with New Age writer James Redfield, she adapted Redfield's *New York Times* bestselling novel *The Celestine Prophecy* into a book for younger readers, *The Song of Celestine.*

My Yellow Ball contains a story about a ball game as well as a journey into the imagination. In the book, Lillegard's young narrator imagines where her ball might travel should she throw it high enough. The author adapts Aesop's fable "The Tortoise and the Hare" as the humorous picture book *Tortoise Brings the Mail.* Here slow Tortoise is a mail carrier, but he hands his job over to Rabbit, Crow, and Fox, when they insist that they are much faster. Of course, the faster animals fail, and Tortoise must persevere to make his customers happy. Reviewing Lillegard's work, a *Publishers Weekly*

Cover of Lillegard's poetry collection Wake up House!, *featuring artwork by Don Carter.* (Illustration © 2000 by Don Carter. Used by permission of Alfred A. Knopf, an imprint of Random House Children's Books, a division of Random House, Inc.)

critic commented on the "simple, well-chosen language" in *My Yellow Ball.* "Youngsters will cheer for the underdog Tortoise and relish the ending," according to Lauren Peterson in a review of *Tortoise Brings the Mail* for *Booklist.* The "nicely paced tale offers a gentle lesson in appreciation," wrote a contributor to *Publishers Weekly.*

Lillegard draws on Middle-Eastern imagery for her tale *The Poombah of Badoombah,* a story about a prankster wizard. Though noting the inconclusive ending, a *Publishers Weekly* contributor commented of the picture book that "Lillegard's inventive verse and vocabulary . . . make for a peppy ride." In *Tiger, Tiger,* a young boy creates a tiger by waving a peacock feather on a hot day. Jody McCoy, writing in *School Library Journal,* considered the title "a perfect choice for reading aloud." In *Who Will Sing a Lullaby?* songbirds attempt to coax a young child to sleep. A *Kirkus Reviews* contributor considered the book "a sumptuous bedtime read."

Lillegard's poetry has been categorized in the Library of Congress "under both juvenile poetry and kitchen utensils," according to a *Publishers Weekly* contributor, who called her collection *Do Not Feed the Table* a "soufflé of a book." A collection of thirty-four poems about objects likely found at home, *Wake up House!:*

Dee Lillegard takes readers skyward in her book Balloons, Balloons, Balloons, *illustrated by Bernadette Pons.* (Illustration © 2007 by Bernadette Pons. Reproduced by permission of Dutton Children's Books, a division of Penguin Putnam Books for Young Readers.)

Rooms Full of Poems features "Lillegard's simple, cheerful rhymes [that] find poetry in the ordinary," according to Hazel Rochman in *Booklist*.

Moving from home to the classroom, Lillegard has also written *Hello School!: A Classroom Full of Poems.* "The brevity of the poems . . . makes the book ideal" for teaching young readers about the concepts behind poetry, according to Marta Segal in *Booklist*. Judy Freeman, writing in *Instructor*, felt that the entries in the collection "highlight the objects students take for granted." Rather than using every day objects for inspiration, Lillegard wrote about vehicles and things that move in *Go!: Poetry in Motion*. Along with trucks and airplanes, the poems "celebrate kid-powered contraptions" such as wagons and skateboards, according to a critic for *Kirkus Reviews*. In *Booklist*, Rochman noted that the collection "establishes books as a part of children's everyday play."

Biographical and Critical Sources

PERIODICALS

Booklist, February 1, 2000, Hazel Rochman, review of *Wake up House!: Rooms Full of Poems*, p. 1026; Au-

gust, 2001, Marta Segal, review of *Hello School!: A Classroom Full of Poems*, p. 2125; January 1, 2003, Lauren Peterson, review of *Tiger, Tiger*, p. 907; November 1, 2006, Hazel Rochman, review of *Go!: Poetry in Motion*, p. 57.

Detroit Free Press, April 6, 2007, Michele Siuda Jacques, "It's Never Too Early for a Little Poetry."

Horn Book, July-August, 1993, Lolly Robinson, review of *My Yellow Ball*, p. 445; May 15, 1997, Lauren Peterson, review of *Tortoise Brings the Mail*, p. 1580.

Instructor, August, 2002, Judy Freeman, review of *Hello School!*, p. 81.

Kirkus Reviews, October 1, 2002, review of *Tiger, Tiger*, p. 1474; October 15, 2006, review of *Go!*, p. 1073; August 15, 2007, review of *Who Will Sing a Lullaby?*

Publishers Weekly, May 24, 1993, review of *My Yellow Ball*, p. 87; July 5, 1993, review of *Do Not Feed the Table*, p. 73; March 31, 1997, review of *Tortoise Brings the Mail*, p. 73; April 20, 1998, review of *The Poombah of Badoombah*, p. 65; June 22, 1998, review of *The Song of Celestine*, p. 90; May 17, 1999, review of *The Big Bug Ball*, p. 78; February 14, 2000, review of *Wake up House!*, p. 196; August 13, 2001, "Schooltime Rhymes," p. 314; September 10, 2001, review of *Wake up House!*, p. 95.

School Library Journal, December, 2000, review of *Wake up House!*, p. 54; July, 2001, Sheryl L. Shipley, re-

Lillegard's poetry collection Go! Poetry in Motion *benefits from Valeri Gorbachev's detailed and action-filled art.* (Illustration © 2006 by Valeri Gorbachev. Used by permission of Alfred A. Knopf, an imprint of Random House Children's Books, a division of Random House, Inc.)

view of *Hello School!*, p. 95; December, 2002, Jody McCoy, review of *Tiger, Tiger,* p. 100; December, 2006, Susan Weitz, review of *Go!*, p. 125; February, 2007, Suzanne Myers Harold, review of *Balloons, Balloons, Balloons,* p. 90.

ONLINE

Penguin Web site, http://us.penguingroup.com/ (October 22, 2007), "Dee Lillegard."*

* * *

LOEHR, Mallory

Personal

Married; children: one.

Addresses

Home and office—Brooklyn, NY.

Career

Author. Random House, New York, NY, editor. Worked previously as a children's book-store manager.

Writings

Trucks, illustrated by Harry McNaught, Random House (New York, NY), 1992.

The Little Red Barn, illustrated by Richard Bernal, Random House (New York, NY), 1994.

The Little Country Book, illustrated by Edward Miller, Random House (New York, NY), 1994.

The Little Little Book, illustrated by Rosiland Solomon, Random House (New York, NY), 1995.

The Princess Book: Every Girl Can Be a Princess—with Princess Parties, Recipes, Costumes, and More!, illustrated by Jan Palmer, Random House (New York, NY), 1996.

The Little Dollhouse, illustrated by Jan Lebeyka, Random House (New York, NY), 1996.

The Little Pirate Ship, illustrated by Diane Dawson Hearn, Random House (New York, NY), 1997.

Earth Magic, Random House (New York, NY), 1999.

Babe: A Little Pig Goes a Long Way, illustrated by Christopher Moroney, Random House (New York, NY), 1999.

Water Wishes, Random House (New York, NY), 1999.

Wind Spell, Random House (New York, NY), 2000.

Fire Dreams, Random House (New York, NY), 2001.

Unicorn Wings, illustrated by Pamela Silin-Palmer, Random House (New York, NY), 2006.

Dragon Egg, illustrated by Hala Wittwer, Random House (New York, NY), 2007.

Sidelights

Mallory Loehr's children's books center on the magical worlds of fantasy and fiction. In *Unicorn Wings,* for example, she tells the story of a unicorn that has the power to heal with its mystical horn. However, more than anything, the unicorn wishes to have wings so that it may fly. Although the creature shares its wishes with everyone around it, its fails to materialize. One night the unicorn is visited by a white-winged mare that has broken its wing. The unicorn uses its magical healing horn to mend the mare's injury and in return the unicorn is given its own set of wings. A critic in *Kirkus Reviews* commented that Loehr's story, paired with dainty illustrations by Pamela Silin-Palmer, form a "confection" made "of what little girls are made of: rainbows, flowers, [and] twinkly stars."

Geared for elementary-grade readers, *Water Wishes* also falls within the fantasy genre. In this story, Loehr centers on three siblings who find a magical green bottle that can grant wishes. Polly and her brother Sam spot the gleaming green bottle in the ocean near where the two children are playing on the beach. At first the siblings are unable to retrieve the bottle, but in a twist of fate they find that their older brother, Joe, has gained possession of the same green bottle. After stealing the bottle from their brother, Polly and Sam encounter a series of adventures in which they are transformed into

Cover of Mallory Loehr's Unicorn Wings, *featuring artwork by Pamela Silin-Palmer.* (Illustration © 2006 by Pamela Silin-Palmer. Used by permission of Random House Children's Books, a division of Random House, Inc.)

mermaids and octopuses. Ellen Mandel, in her assessment for *Booklist,* dubbed *Water Wishes* "a fun, exciting, and promising" children's book.

Biographical and Critical Sources

PERIODICALS

Booklist, June 1, 1999, Ellen Mandel, review of *Water Wishes,* p. 1830.

Kirkus Reviews, October 15, 2006, review of *Unicorn Wings,* p. 1073.

Publishers Weekly, April 26, 1999, review of *Water Wishes,* p. 83.

School Library Journal, July, 1999, Carrie Schadle, review of *Water Wishes,* p. 76; September, 1999, Janie Schomberg, review of *Babe: A Little Pig Goes a Long Way,* p. 193; February, 2007, Susan Lissim, review of *Unicorn Wings,* p. 92.

ONLINE

Society of Children's Book Writers and Illustrators Web site, http://www.scbwi.org/ (October 28, 2007), "Mallory Loehr."*

* * *

LUNGE-LARSEN, Lise 1955-

Personal

Born October 15, 1955, in Oslo, Norway; daughter of Asbørn (an antiquarian book dealer) and Berit Lunge-Larsen; married Steven A. Kuross (an oncologist), August 19, 1978; children: Emily, Even, Erik. *Education:* Augsburg College, B.A., 1977; University of Minnesota, M.A. (applied linguistics), 1981. *Religion:* Lutheran.

Addresses

Home—2011 Lakeview Dr., Duluth, MN 55803. *E-mail*—LLL@chartermi.net.

Career

Children's book author and storyteller. College of St. Catherine, St. Paul, MN, instructor in English and director of English as a second language program, 1981-87; Hamline University, St. Paul, adjunct faculty member, 1982-90; University of Minnesota, Duluth, instructor in children's literature, 1990, 1994. Served on Board of Education, First Lutheran Church, Duluth.

Member

Society of Children's Book Writers and Illustrators, Children's Literature Network.

Lise Lunge-Larsen (Courtesy of Lise Lunge-Larsen.)

Awards, Honors

Minnesota Book Award, and American Library Association (ALA) Notable Book designation, both 2000, for *The Troll with No Heart in His Body, and Other Tales from Norway,* and 2002, for *Race of the Birkebeiners;* Great Lakes Book Award finalist, for *The Legend of the Lady Slipper;* Los Angeles Times Notable Book designation, and Bank Street College of Education Best Books designation, both 2002, both for *The Race of the Birkebeiners.*

Writings

(Reteller, with Margi Preus) *The Legend of the Lady Slipper: An Ojibwe Tale,* illustrated by Andrea Arroyo, Houghton Mifflin (Boston, MA), 1999.

(Reteller) *The Troll with No Heart in His Body, and Other Tales of Trolls from Norway,* illustrated by Betsy Bowen, Houghton Mifflin (Boston, MA), 1999.

The Race of the Birkebeiners, illustrated by Mary Azarian, Houghton Mifflin (Boston, MA), 2001.

Tales of the Hidden Folk: Stories of Fairies, Gnomes, Selkies, and Other Hidden Folk, illustrated by Beth Krommes, Houghton Mifflin (Boston, MA), 2004.

Noah's Mittens: The True Story of Felt, illustrated by Matthew Trueman, Houghton Mifflin (Boston, MA), 2006.

(Reteller) *The Adventures of Thor the Thunder God,* illustrated by Jim Madsen, Houghton Mifflin (Boston, MA), 2007.

Sidelights

In the environs of Duluth, Minnesota, where Lise Lunge-Larsen makes her home, she is known fondly as "The Troll Lady." The reason? As a storyteller and author of books such as *The Adventures of Thor the Thunder God* and *Tales of the Hidden Folk: Stories of Fairies, Gnomes, Selkies, and Other Hidden Folk,* she has focused on the tales of her native Norway, which are replete with trolls and other fantastic creatures. The daughter of an antiquarian bookseller, Lunge-Larsen grew up in Oslo, Norway literally immersed in literature because her family home doubled as a bookstore. Surprisingly, she did not envision becoming a storyteller or author when she grew up; as she later told *SATA,* "My parents' plan was that I should become a secretary then one day marry the boss!"

Life had different plans for Lunge-Larsen, however. Her receipt of the Crown Prince Harald Scholarship to Augsburg College in Minneapolis, Minnesota resulted in a move to the United States after high school. Although she intended to return to Norway after a year, she fell in love with Steve Kuross, a pre-med student, and the two made plans to marry. Lunge-Larsen worked toward her B.A. at Augsburg College and also found a job in a local children's library. "For the first time in my life, I was exposed to the writings of people like Dr. Seuss, A.A. Milne, Kenneth Graham, and C.S. Lewis," she later recalled. "Now I was in love not just with Steve but with children's books as well and spent nearly thirty-two hours a week (on the job!) reading every book in the children's library."

As Lunge-Larsen soon discovered, the library lacked some of her favorite stories, such as the Norse myths and sagas and the traditional tales collected by Norwegian folklorists Peter Christen Asbjørnsen and Jørgen Ingebretsen Moe. "I soon found myself telling anyone who would listen stories of trolls and other strange creatures from my own childhood, and in a short time found myself telling tales all over the state," she explained. As Sheryl Jensen wrote in an article on the writer for *Area Woman* magazine, Lunge-Larsen has become an expert storyteller: "From bellowing and roaring in the bass of a nasty troll hag to squealing and stammering like a terrified little boy, Lise uses her voice, her animated face, and her whirlwind of dynamic energy in a total body experience of storytelling."

After graduating with her B.A., Lunge-Larsen married Kuross. As a wedding gift, her father gave her a collection of troll stories in which he had written: "To Lise, with all my good wishes and the hope that even though she may forget her Norwegian, she will never forget her Norwegian trolls." While raising her three children, she continued her work as a storyteller and earned a graduate degree in teaching English as a second language, with a minor in children's literature, writing her thesis on storytelling as a teaching tool. "No matter what I did," she explained, "storytelling and children's literature soon was involved." In the early 1990s, with a quarter-century of storytelling experience behind her, Lunge-Larsen started committing her favorite Norwegian stories to paper.

"I find that much of my writing goes back to the world I experienced as a child—a world full of trolls, mysterious hidden creatures, heroes and heroines who have to battle evil among men, trolls, and other hidden forces," Lunge-Larsen explained to *SATA.* "I grew up in a landscape beautiful, haunting and alive and this very much shapes my experience of the world and now my writing. I am also interested in stories about that which is hidden from ordinary sight or knowledge, such as trolls or other hidden folk, or stories about how things got the way they are."

In *The Troll with No Heart in His Body, and Other Tales of Trolls from Norway* Lunge-Larsen shares eight folk tales retold from Asbjørnsen and Moe's *Samlede eventyr* (*Collected Stories*). Other eight traditional tales of magic are retold in *Tales of the Hidden Folk,* and here Lunge-Larsen introduces readers to hidden creatures such as flower fairies, dwarves, a water horse, and the seductive selkie, which lures humans into the sea. In *Booklist* John Peters made note of the stylized, "jewel-toned," folk-style art provided by Beth Krommes, while *School Library Journal* contributor Harriett Fargnoli praised Lunge-Larsen for retelling the stories in "an accessible manner that will captivate readers." A *Publishers Weekly* reviewer, appraising Lunge-Larsen's singular picture book *The Adventures of Thor the Thunder God,* concluded that the work presents readers with "an accessible and engaging doorway into the world of Norse mythology.

Lunge-Larsen's interest in the capacity of people to rise above their normal abilities and accomplish the extraordinary inspired her award-winning story *The Race of the Birkebeiners.* In this medieval Norwegian tale, based on a true story, the Birkebeiners—so named because they wear birch-bark leggings—save the infant Prince Hakon when they ski with the baby across the mountains during a blizzard in an effort to thwart assassins. Both *Booklist* contributor Gillian Engberg and *School Library Journal* critic Anne Chapman Callaghan praised the picture book for its compelling plot, unambiguous language, and detailed woodcut illustrations by Caldecott award-winning artist Mary Azarian. Noting Azarian's "stately art" and Lunge-Larsen's "direct and compelling prose," a *Publishers Weekly* contributor deemed *The Race of the Birkebeiners* an "engaging narrative" that brings to life a colorful incident from early Norwegian history.

Turning to the stories of her adopted country, Lunge-Larsen has also teamed up with writer Margi Preus to retell a Native American tale in *The Legend of the Lady Slipper: An Ojibwe Tale.* In the book, a young girl, the only well person among her people, battles through a snow storm to obtain medicinal herbs from a neighboring village. When her moccasins freeze to the ground

Lunge-Larsen's folk-tale collection **Tales of the Hidden Folk** *features intricate linocut illustrations by Beth Krommes.* (Illustration © 2004 by Beth Krommes.

on the return trip, the girl leaves them behind and walks the rest of the way leaving bloody footprints in the snow. Returning in the spring to retrieve her moccasins, she finds in their place the pink-and-white shoe-shaped flowers known as lady slippers: *ma-ki-sin waa-big-wann* in Ojibwe. In her review of *The Legend of the Lady*

Lunge-Larsen shares a story recalled from her own childhood in **The Adventures of Thor, the Thunder God,** *a large-format picture book illustrated by Jim Madsen.* (Illustration © 2007 by Jim Madsen. Reproduced by permission of Houghton Mifflin Company.)

Slipper for *Booklist*, GraceAnne A. DeCandido described the coauthors' retelling as "powerful"; and a *Publishers Weekly* critic praised the text and illustrations for their "unusual simplicity and fluidity." Writing in the *Bulletin of the Center for Children's Books*, Janice N. Harrington also praised the narrative style employed by Lunge-Larsen and Preus, particularly their use of nature metaphors and strong verbs. Harrington went on to point out how the tale "smoothly integrates Ojibwe words and phrases into an accessible narrative."

In *Noah's Mittens: The True Story of Felt* Lunge-Larsen uses the familiar story of Noah and the Ark to tell an amusing story about how felted wool was first devised. Among the many animals on Noah's ark are two sheep, and when the climate in the well-sealed boat reaches sauna status, the sheep's heavy coats start to tighten and shrink. Cutting off the felted wool to free the poor sheep, Noah is able to put the material to good use after the waters subside and his ark is deposited high on a snowy mountain peak. Given an extra dose of humor by Matthew Trueman's paintings, *Noah's Mittens* was described as "amusing" by Kathy Piehl, the critic adding in her *School Library Journal* review that the book would be a "good choice for storytime sharing before a romp in the snow." "Simple and wonderfully complex,"

according to *Booklist* writer Randall Enos, Lunge-Larsen's story combines with Trueman's art to "work well on many levels." Although a *Publishers Weekly* reviewer noted that the storyteller's "playful liberties . . . may not be for everyone," Lunge-Larsen's notes about the story's origins "are sure to spark curiosity and exploration."

Her work as a storyteller gave Lunge-Larsen an advantage when she turned to writing, providing her with "an intuitive sense of what kinds of stories children love," as she once commented. "When I work, I spend a lot of time telling the story out loud to myself to find the right rhythm and pacing. Sometimes I even record it. But whenever I am stuck, all I have to do is tell the story to groups of children. Somehow, with the kids there, I always find the words I am looking for, the section that needs to be tightened, or the part that needs to be played up." For Lunge-Larsen, a good story is more than entertaining: "My thoughts are perhaps best expressed by this old saying: 'When the bond between heaven and earth is broken, even prayer is not enough. Only a story can mend it.'"

Biographical and Critical Sources

PERIODICALS

Area Woman (Duluth, MN), December-January, 2002, Sheryl Jensen, "The Troll Lady: Lise Lunge-Larsen," pp. 26-27, 68-69.

Booklist, April 15, 1999, GraceAnne A. DeCandido, review of *The Legend of the Lady Slipper: An Ojibwe Tale*, p. 1533; March 15, 2000, review of *The Troll with No Heart in His Body, and Other Tales of Trolls from Norway*, p. 1360; July, 2001, Gillian Engberg, review of *The Race of the Birkebeiners*, p. 2014; September 1, 2004, John Peters, review of *The Hidden Folk: Stories of Fairies, Dwarves, Selkies, and Other Secret Beings*, p. 117; October 15, 2006, Randall Enos, review of *Noah's Mittens: The Story of Felt*, p. 54.

Bulletin of the Center for Children's Books, July, 1999, Janice N. Harrington, review of *The Legend of the Lady Slipper*, pp. 394-395; October, 2004, Timnah Card, review of *The Hidden Folk*, p. 87; November, 2006, Deborah Stevenson, review of *Noah's Mittens*, p. 134.

Horn Book, November, 1999, Roger Sutton, review of *The Troll with No Heart in His Body, and Other Tales of Trolls from Norway*, p. 748.

Kirkus Reviews, September 1, 2001, review of *The Race of the Birkebeiners*, p. 1295; September 1, 2006, review of *Noah's Mittens*, p. 907.

Publishers Weekly, April 12, 1999, review of *The Legend of the Lady Slipper*, p. 74; October 11, 1999, review of *The Troll with No Heart in His Body, and Other Tales of Trolls from Norway*, p. 76; September 3, 2001, review of *The Race of the Birkebeiners*, p. 88; July 31, 2006, review of *Noah's Mittens*, p. 77; June 11, 2007, review of *The Adventure of Thor the Thunder God*, p. 60.

School Library Journal, September, 2001, Anne Chapman Callaghan, review of *The Race of the Birkebeiners,* p. 217; December, 2004, Harriett Fargnoli, review of *The Hidden Folk,* p. 134; December, 2006, Kathy Piehl, review of *Noah's Mittens,* p. 107.

ONLINE

Minnesota Public Radio Web site, http://news.minnesota. publicradio.org/ (September 24, 2007), Stephanie Hemphill, review of *The Hidden Folk.*

M

MacLEOD, Elizabeth

Personal
Born October 21, in Thornhill, Ontario, Canada; married Paul Wilson. *Hobbies and other interests:* Reading, singing, swimming, tap dancing, theatre.

Addresses
Home—Toronto, Ontario, Canada. *E-mail*—emacleod@ writerinresidence.com.

Career
Author and editor of children's books. *OWL* magazine, editor; writer for a software company; freelance editor for publishers, including Kids Can Press.

Member
Canadian Society of Children's Authors, Illustrators, and Performers, Writers Union of Canada.

Awards, Honors
Silver Birch Award shortlist, for *The Phone Book, Lucy Maud Montgomery: A Writer's Life,* and *Albert Einstein;* Hackmatack Award shortlist, for *Get Started: Stamp Collecting for Canadian Kids, Albert Einstein, Lucy Maud Montgomery,* and *To the Top of Everest;* Hackmatack Award shortlist, Red Cedar Book Award shortlist, Silver Birch Award shortlist, and Notable Social Studies Trade Book for Young People selection, Children's Book Council (CBC), all for *Alexander Graham Bell: An Inventive Life;* National Science Teachers Association/CBC outstanding science trade book designation, for *Marie Curie;* Society of School Librarians International Honor Book designation, 2004, for *Helen Keller;* writing awards from Association of Educational Publishers.

Writings

Lions, Grolier (Toronto, Ontario, Canada), 1988.
Koalas, Grolier (Toronto, Ontario, Canada), 1989.
Puffins, Grolier (Toronto, Ontario, Canada), 1990.
Australia, Grolier (Toronto, Ontario, Canada), 1990.
(Editor) *The Games Book,* illustrated by Thach Bui, Greey de Pencier Books (Toronto, Ontario, Canada), 1990.
(Editor) *The Puzzlers Book,* illustrated by Gary Clement, Greey de Pencier Books (Toronto, Ontario, Canada), 1990.
The Recycling Book, illustrated by Jane Kurisu, Greey de Pencier Books (Toronto, Ontario, Canada), 1991.
Dinosaurs: The Fastest, the Fiercest, the Most Amazing, illustrated by Gordon Sauvé, Kids Can Press (Toronto, Ontario, Canada), 1994, Viking (New York, NY) 1995.
The Phone Book: Instant Communication from Smoke Signals to Satellites and Beyond, illustrated by Bill Slavin, Kids Can Press (Toronto, Ontario, Canada), 1995.
Get Started: Stamp Collecting for Canadian Kids, Kids Can Press (Toronto, Ontario, Canada), 1996.
I Heard a Little Baa, illustrated by Louise Phillips, Kids Can Press (Toronto, Ontario, Canada), 1998.
Bake It and Build It, illustrated by Tracy Walker, Kids Can Press (Toronto, Ontario, Canada), 1998.
Grow It Again, illustrated by Caroline Price, Kids Can Press (Toronto, Ontario, Canada), 1999.
Bake and Make Amazing Cakes, illustrated by June Bradford, Kids Can Press (Toronto, Ontario, Canada), 2001.
(With Laurie Skreslet) *To the Top of Everest,* Kids Can Press (Toronto, Ontario, Canada), 2001.
Gifts to Make and Eat, illustrated by June Bradford, Kids Can Press (Toronto, Ontario, Canada), 2001.
What Did Dinosaurs Eat? and Other Things You Want to Know about Dinosaurs, illustrated by Gordon Sauvé, Kids Can Press (Toronto, Ontario, Canada), 2001.
The Kids Book of Great Canadians, illustrated by John Mantha, Kids Can Press (Toronto, Ontario, Canada), 2004.
Bake and Make Amazing Cookies, illustrated by June Bradford, Kids Can Press (Toronto, Ontario, Canada), 2004.
Chock Full of Chocolate, illustrated by June Bradford, Kids Can Press (Toronto, Ontario, Canada), 2005.
The Kid's Book of Great Canadian Women, illustrated by John Mantha, Kids Can Press (Toronto, Ontario, Canada), 2006.

The Kid's Book of Canada at War, illustrated by John Mantha, Kids Can Press (Toronto, Ontario, Canada), 2007.

Contributor to educational anthologies.

Author's work has been translated into French.

"SNAPSHOTS: IMAGES OF PEOPLE AND PLACES IN HISTORY" SERIES

Alexander Graham Bell: An Inventive Life, Kids Can Press (Toronto, Ontario, Canada), 1999, revised edition, illustrated by Andrej Krystoforski, 2007.

Lucy Maud Montgomery: A Writer's Life, Kids Can Press (Toronto, Ontario, Canada), 2001, revised edition, illustrated by John Mantha, 2008.

The Wright Brothers: A Flying Start, Kids Can Press (Toronto, Ontario, Canada), 2002, revised edition, Illustrated by Andrej Krystoforski, 2008.

Alfred Einstein: A Life of Genius, Kids Can Press (Toronto, Ontario, Canada), 2003.

Helen Keller: A Determined Life, illustrated by Andrej Krystoforski, Kids Can Press (Toronto, Ontario, Canada), 2004.

Marie Curie: A Brilliant Life, Kids Can Press (Toronto, Ontario, Canada), 2004.

Harry Houdini: A Magical Life, Kids Can Press (Toronto, Ontario, Canada), 2005.

Eleanor Roosevelt: An Inspiring Life, Kids Can Press (Toronto, Ontario, Canada), 2006.

George Washington Carver: An Innovative Life, Kids Can Press (Toronto, Ontario, Canada), 2007.

Mark Twain: An American Star, Kids Can Press (Toronto, Ontario, Canada), 2008.

Sidelights

Elizabeth MacLeod is an author and editor of children's books. A native of Canada, she has written craft books, works of nonfiction, and picture books for young readers. MacLeod has also penned a number of critically acclaimed biographies, including *Alexander Graham Bell: An Inventive Life, Lucy Maud Montgomery: A Writer's Life,* and *George Washington Carver: An Innovative Life.*

One of MacLeod's first efforts, *Dinosaurs: The Fastest, the Fiercest, the Most Amazing,* appeared in 1994. In the work, she offers information on more than twenty species of the prehistoric creatures. According to a *Resource Links* contributor, the book will "whet the appetite of any fledgling dinosaur lover." A more recent volume, titled *What Did Dinosaurs Eat? and Other Things You Want to Know about Dinosaurs,* examines the size and weight, feeding habits, life span, intelligence, and personalities of several types of dinosaurs. A critic in *Kirkus Reviews* praised MacLeod's "vivid writing."

Grow It Again, Bake and Make Amazing Cakes, and *Bake and Make Amazing Cookies* are among the craft books published by MacLeod. Deemed "a promising source of worthwhile, inexpensive projects" by *Booklist*

critic Carolyn Phelan, *Grow It Again* gives instructions for growing plants from such things as pineapple tops and potato buds. *Bake and Make Amazing Cakes* provides directions for a variety of theme cakes, including creations shaped like a butterfly, a house, and a rainbow. In *School Library Journal* reviewer Carolyn Jenks remarked that the volume is "just the book for playful bakers." A companion work, *Bake and Make Amazing Cookies,* was described as a "dandy choice for beginning cooks" by Karen McKinnon in *Resource Links.*

The 1999 biography *Alexander Graham Bell* looks at the inventor of the telephone. MacLeod discusses several little-known aspects of Bell's life, including his experiments with flight and his fascination with the Mohawk Indian tribe. *Booklist* critic Carolyn Phelan noted that MacLeod's "text reads well, and the extended captions offer interesting facts." The author of the celebrated children's book *Anne of Green Gables* is the subject of MacLeod's 2001 biography *Lucy Maud Montgomery.* Readers will learn that Montgomery "had much in common with her fictitious heroine," observed a reviewer in *Publishers Weekly.*

MacLeod continues her series of biographical works with *The Wright Brothers: A Flying Start,* published in 2002. Using archival photographs and reproductions of historical documents, she presents an introduction to the men who made the first controlled, sustained flight. *School Library Journal* contributor Barbara Buckley

Cover of **Helen Keller: A Determined Life,** *a picture-book biography for middle-grade readers by Elizabeth MacLeod.* (Illustration © 2007 by Andrej Krystofoski. Used by permission of Kids Can Press, Ltd., Toronto.)

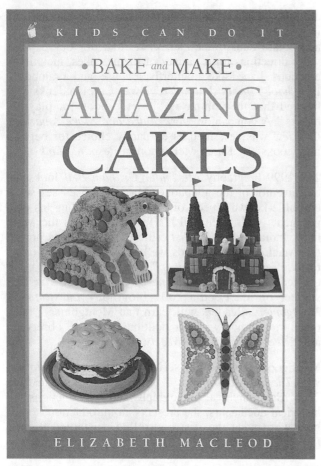

Cover of MacLeod's **Bake and Make Amazing Cakes,** *which provides young bakers with creative and yummy ways to spend an afternoon.* (Illustration © 2001 by June Bradford. Used by permission of Kids Can Press, Ltd., Toronto.)

stated that few books on the Wright Brothers "can rival this one for clarity of text and variety of illustration." *Alfred Einstein: A Life of Genius* surveys the life of the great physicist, touching on his early career as an assistant in a Swiss patent office, his landmark scientific discoveries, and his efforts for international peace following World War II. "The lively mix of text, sidebars, photographs, newspaper excerpts, equations, and Einstein's handwritten notes adds up to a format inviting browsing and offering much information to closer readers," wrote a critic in *Kirkus Reviews.*

One of the most fascinating characters of the turn of the twentieth century is the focus of *Harry Houdini: A Magical Life.* In a text that "manages to capture the human side of this master of escape," according to *Resource Links* reviewer Deb Nielsen, MacLeod follows the childhood of the acrobat and showman whose world-renown ability to escape from the grips of death captivated the world. Like each of MacLeod's biographies, *Harry Houdini* includes photographs, newspaper articles, and other reproductions that bring to life his live and times.

While his love of the public spotlight made him less well known than Houdini, agronomist and educator George Washington Carver led a life with an equally

lasting impact, as MacLeod shows in her 2007 biography. A man of wide-ranging talents, Carver dedicated himself to restoring the agriculture of the American south following the U.S. Civil War, and he advanced the fortunes of many of his fellow African Americans by encouraging the cultivation of peanuts, soybeans, and other crops that could flourish in a soil drained of nutrients through years of cotton farming. In addition to his work as a teacher at the Tuskegee Institute, he developed numerous industrial products that would assure peanut and soybean growers of a market for their crops. Citing the narrative's "richness of detail," *School Library Journal* contributor Anne L. Tormohlen concluded that "even reluctant readers will find something of interest about this exceptional individual" in MacLeod's well-illustrated biography.

MacLeod profiles several famous women in *Helen Keller: A Determined Life, Marie Curie: A Brilliant Life,* and *Eleanor Roosevelt: An Inspiring Life.* In her work about Keller, "America's First Lady of Courage," MacLeod includes both familiar and little-known events from her subject's life, "smoothly integrated to reveal the struggle, the sadness, and the success Keller experienced over the years," observed *Booklist* reviewer Stephanie Zvirin. In *Marie Curie* MacLeod focuses on the Nobel Prize winner who discovered the elements polonium and radium, while *Eleanor Roosevelt* profiles the life of a U.S. first lady who was known for her

In **Harry Houdini: A Magical Life** *MacLeod draws readers into the world of one of the most famous escape artists of all time.* (Kids Can Press, 2005. Used by permission.)

dedication to social issues. Carolyn Cutt, writing in *Resource Links,* dubbed MacLeod's biography of one of the world's most noted female scientists "excellent and informative," while Anne Chapman Callaghan deemed the text of *Eleanor Roosevelt* "clear, interesting, and affectionate toward its subject."

MacLeod once commented on her career to *SATA:* "There are two things that I really like about writing for kids. One is that I get to investigate lots of different topics. The other is that I think writing for kids is a challenge. They ask really interesting and difficult questions.

"The ideas for my books come from newspapers, Web sites, books, things friends say, the Internet, questions kids ask me when I visit their schools, the radio, TV, magazines—lots of places.

"I read books, magazines, newspapers, and the Internet to gather information. These are also all good ways to find experts who can answer any questions I have. I'm always amazed at how willing people are to spend time helping me understand a topic.

"If you think you might like to become a writer, it's a good idea to read a lot and write a lot. If you want to show someone your writing, then do it—but you don't have to. And if the person who reads your writing suggests changes, only make them if you want to. Try writing lots of different things—poems, stories, articles—to figure out what you like writing most."

Biographical and Critical Sources

PERIODICALS

Appleseeds, December, 2002, Sheila Wilensky, review of *The Wright Brothers: A Flying Start,* p. 29.

Booklist, December 1, 1998, Shelley Townsend-Hudson, review of *Bake It and Build It,* p. 665; June 1, 1999, Carolyn Phelan, review of *Grow It Again,* p. 1820; April 1, 2001, Carolyn Phelan, review of *Lucy Maud Montgomery: A Writer's Life,* p. 1462; September 15, 2001, Roger Leslie, review of *To the Top of Everest,* p. 215; November 1, 2001, Stephanie Zvirin, review of *Gifts to Make and Eat,* pp. 472-473; April 1, 2002, Carolyn Phelan, review of *The Wright Brothers,* p. 1338; March 1, 2003, Ilene Cooper, review of *Albert Einstein: A Life of Genius,* p. 1195; March 1, 2004, Stephanie Zvirin, review of *Helen Keller: A Determined Life,* pp. 1204-1205; October 15, 2005, Karen Hurt, review of *Harry Houdini: A Magical Life,* p. 45.

Children's Digest, July, 2000, review of *Alexander Graham Bell: An Inventive Life,* p. 28.

Kirkus Reviews, September 1, 2001, review of *What Did Dinosaurs Eat? and Other Things You Want to Know about Dinosaurs,* p. 1296; February 15, 2003, review of *Albert Einstein,* p. 311; August 1, 2004, review of *Marie Curie: A Brilliant Life,* p. 744; September 1, 2005, review of *Harry Houdini,* p. 977; September 1, 2006, review of *Eleanor Roosevelt: An Inspiring Life,* p. 907.

Cover of **Marie Curie: A Brilliant Life,** *in which MacLeod introduces readers to the physicist whose discovery of radium and polonium led to her own death.* (Kids Can Press, 2004. Used by permission of Kids Can Press Ltd., Toronto.)

Publishers Weekly, September 21, 1998, review of *I Heard a Little Baa,* p. 83; February 26, 2001, review of *Lucy Maud Montgomery,* p. 88.

Resource Links, June, 1998, review of *Dinosaurs: The Fastest, the Fiercest, the Most Amazing,* pp. 10-11; October, 1998, review of *I Heard a Little Baa,* p. 4; April, 1999, review of *Bake It and Build It,* p. 17; April, 2001, Victoria Pennell, review of *Lucy Maud Montgomery,* p. 18; June, 2001, Shannon Danylko, review of *Bake and Make Amazing Cakes,* p. 19; October, 2001, Shannon Danylko, review of *What Did Dinosaurs Eat?,* p. 27; April, 2002, Victoria Pennell, review of *The Wright Brothers,* pp. 36-37; April, 2003, Karen McKinnon, review of *Albert Einstein,* pp. 26-27; April, 2004, Laura Reilly, review of *Helen Keller,* p. 31, and Victoria Pennell, review of *The Kid's Book of Great Canadians,* pp. 31-32; October, 2004, Karen McKinnon, review of *Bake and Make Amazing Cookies,* pp. 25-26; December, 2004, Carolyn Cutt, review of *Madame Curie,* p. 28; February, 2006, Deb Nielsen, review of *Harry Houdini,* p. 36; April, 2007, John Dryden, review of *Eleanor Roosevelt,* p. 34.

School Library Journal, April, 2001, Kathleen Simonetta, review of *Lucy Maud Montgomery,* p. 164; June, 2001, Carolyn Jenks, review of *Bake and Make Amazing Cakes,* p. 139; September, 2001, Be Astengo, review of *To the Top of Everest,* p. 254; November, 2001, Patricia Manning, review of *What Did Dinosaurs Eat?,* p. 147; February, 2002, Augusta R. Malvagno, review of *Gifts to Make and Eat,* pp. 147-148; July, 2002, Barbara Buckley, review of *The Wright Brothers,* p. 138; May, 2003, Anne Chapman Callaghan, review of *Albert Einstein,* p. 174; May, 2004, Donna Cardon, review of *Helen Keller,* p. 134; November, 2004, Susan Lissim, review of *Marie Curie,* p. 169; February, 2005, Augusta R. Malvagno, review of *Bake and Make Amazing Cookies,* p. 150; April, 2006, Deanna Romriell, review of *Harry Houdini,* p. 158; November, 2006, Anne Chapman Callaghan, review of *Eleanor Roosevelt,* p. 162; June, 2007, Anne L. Tormohlen, review of *George Washington Carver: An Innovative Life,* p. 174.

ONLINE

Canadian Society of Children's Authors, Illustrators, and Performers Web site, http://www.canscaip.org/ (November 15, 2007), "Elizabeth MacLeod."*

* * *

McKY, Katie 1956-

Personal

Born August 28, 1956. *Education:* Harvard University, M.A. (education).

Addresses

Home and office—Eau Claire, WI. *E-mail*—katemcky@ post.harvard.edu.

Career

Writer and educator. Worked previously teaching emotionally disturbed and learning-disabled children.

Writings

It All Began with a Bean, Tanglewood Press (Terre Haute, IN), 2004.
Tough Kids, Tough Classrooms, Teaching Point Press (Jacksonville, FL), 2004.
Pumpkin Town!; or, Nothing Is Better and Worse than Pumpkins, illustrated by Pablo Bernasconi, Houghton Mifflin (Boston, MA), 2006.

Also contributor to periodicals.

Sidelights

As Katie McKy noted on her home page, two things have inspired her to write: "Adventures" and "playing with kids all those years." For over twenty years McKy taught learning-disabled children in various parts of the country, and her creative teaching method involved engaging with her students. Since her move from teacher to full-time author, McKy has produced several unique books for children, including *It All Began with a Bean* and *Pumpkin Town!; or, Nothing Is Better and Worse than Pumpkins.*

It All Began with a Bean was inspired by a question once posed by one of McKy's young students: What would happen if everyone in the world passed gas all at once? In her humorous picture book, McKy attempts to answer this provocative question. Piper L. Nyman, reviewing the book for *School Library Journal,* dubbed *It All Began with a Bean* "ridiculous to the extreme," adding that "the right audience is sure to get a laugh."

In *Pumpkin Town!* McKy takes on a milder topic: five brothers who throw pumpkin seeds into a field overlooking their town instead of selling the seeds as their father had instructed. The wind carries the pumpkin seeds throughout the town and what results is a small community over-populated with large, round pumpkins. A *Kirkus Reviews* critic described McKy's pumpkin tale as "a fun fable with Halloween overtones," while *School Library Journal* contributor Anne L. Tormohlen labeled the title "a good fall read-aloud, especially for those wanting to avoid Halloween-themed books."

Biographical and Critical Sources

PERIODICALS

Bulletin of the Center for Children's Books, October, 2006, Deborah Stevenson, review of *Pumpkin Town!; or, Nothing Is Better and Worse than Pumpkins,* p. 85.
Kirkus Reviews, September 1, 2006, review of *Pumpkin Town!,* p. 908.
School Library Journal, February, 2005, Piper L. Nyman, review of *It All Began with a Bean,* p. 107; November, 2006, Anne L. Tormohlen, review of *Pumpkin Town!,* p. 105.

ONLINE

Houghton Mifflin Web site, http://www.houghtonmifflin books.com/ (October 29, 2007), "Katie McKy."
Katie McKy Home Page, http://www.katiemcky.com (October 29, 2007).
Teaching Point Web site, http://www.teaching-point.net/ (October 29, 2007), "Tough Kids, Tough Classrooms."*

* * *

MEISEL, Paul

Personal

Married; children: three children. *Education:* Wesleyan University, B.A.; Yale University, M.F.A.

Addresses

Home and office—Newtown, CT. *E-mail*—paul@ paulmeisel.com.

Career

Illustrator and graphic artist. Has also worked in editorial and advertising illustration.

Writings

SELF-ILLUSTRATED

Zara's Hats, Dutton Children's Books (New York, NY), 2003.

ILLUSTRATOR

Patricia McKissack, *Monkey-Monkey's Trick: Based on an African Folktale,* Random House (New York, NY), 1988.

Jill A. Davidson, *And That's What Happened to Little Lucy,* Random House (New York, NY), 1989.

Billy Goodman, *A Kid's Guide to How to Save the Planet,* Avon Books (New York, NY), 1990.

William H. Hooks, *Mr. Monster,* Bantam Books (New York, NY), 1990.

Billy Goodman, *A Kid's Guide to How to Save the Animals,* Avon Books (New York, NY), 1991.

Ira Wolfman, *My World and Globe: From the Seven Continents to the Seven Seas, from Katmandu to Kalamazoo: An Interactive First Book of Geography,* Workman Publishing (New York, NY), 1991.

Joanna Cole, *Your Insides,* Putnam (New York, NY), 1992.

Christel Kleitsch, *Cousin Markie and Other Disasters,* Dutton Children's Books (New York, NY), 1992.

Alvin Schwartz, *Busy Buzzing Bumblebees, and Other Tongue Twisters,* HarperCollins (New York, NY), 1992.

Sarah Albee, *Halloween ABC,* Western Publishing Company (Racine, WI), 1993.

Carol Diggory Shields, *I Am Really a Princess,* Dutton Children's Books (New York, NY), 1993.

Andrea Zimmerman, *The Cow Buzzed,* HarperCollins (New York, NY), 1993.

William H. Hooks, *Mr. Dinosaur,* Bantam Books (New York, NY), 1994.

Barbara Ann Kipfer, *1,400 Things for Kids to Be Happy about: The Happy Book,* Workman Publishing (New York, NY), 1994.

Janice Lee Smith, *Wizard and Wart,* HarperCollins (New York, NY), 1994.

Games and Giggles Just for Girls!, Pleasant Company (Middleton, WI), 1995.

Carol Diggory Shields, *Lunch Money, and Other Poems about School,* Dutton Children's Books (New York, NY), 1995.

Janice Lee Smith, *Wizard and Wart at Sea,* HarperCollins (New York, NY), 1995.

Stephanie Calmenson, *Engine, Engine, Number Nine,* Hyperion Books for Children (New York, NY), 1996.

Janet Frank, *Daddies: All about the Work They Do,* Western Publishing Company (Racine, WI), 1996.

Kirby Puckett and Andre Gutelle, *Kirby Puckett's Baseball Games,* Workman Publishing (New York, NY), 1996.

William H. Hooks, *Mr. Dinosaur,* Gareth Stevens Publishing (Milwaukee, WI), 1997.

Margo Lundell, *Mommies: All about the Work They Do,* Golden Books (Racine, WI), 1997.

Joan L. Nodset, *Go Away, Dog,* HarperCollins (New York, NY), 1997.

Carol Diggory Shields, *I Wish My Brother Was a Dog,* Dutton Children's Books (New York, NY), 1997.

B.G. Hennessy, *Mr. Bubble Gum,* Gareth Stevens Publishing (Milwaukee, WI), 1997.

William H. Hooks, *Mr. Baseball,* Gareth Stevens Publishing (Milwaukee, WI), 1998.

Kathleen Weidner Zoehfeld, *What Is the World Made of?: All about Solids, Liquids, and, Gases,* HarperCollins (New York, NY), 1998.

Karen Magnuson Beil, *A Cake All for Me!,* Holiday House (New York, NY), 1998.

William H. Hooks, *Mr. Monster,* Gareth Stevens Publishing (Milwaukee, WI), 1998.

Cobi Jones and Andrew Gutelle, *Cobi Jones' Soccer Games,* Workman Publishing (New York, NY), 1998.

Anne Mazer, *The Fixits,* Hyperion Books for Children (New York, NY), 1998.

Betty Miles, *The Three Little Pigs,* Simon & Schuster Books for Young Readers (New York, NY), 1998.

Betty Miles, *The Tortoise and the Hare,* Simon & Schuster Books for Young Readers (New York, NY), 1998.

Janice Lee Smith, *Wizard and Wart in Trouble,* HarperCollins (New York, NY), 1998.

Jeanette Ryan Wall, *More Games and Giggles: Wild about Animals!,* Pleasant Company (Middleton, WI), 1998.

Spanish for Gringos: Shortcuts, Tips, and Secrets to Successful Learning, Barron's (Hauppauge, NY), 1999.

On beyond a Million: An Amazing Math Journey, Random House (New York, NY), 1999.

Melvin Berger, *Why I Sneeze, Shiver, Hiccup, and Yawn,* HarperCollins (New York, NY), 2000.

David Elliott, *The Cool Crazy Crickets,* Candlewick Press (Cambridge, MA), 2000.

Jean Craighead George, *How to Talk to Your Cat,* HarperCollins (New York, NY), 2000.

Kathleen Karr, *It Happened in the White House: Extraordinary Tales from America's Most Famous Home,* Hyperion Books for Children (New York, NY), 2000.

J. Philip Miller and Sheppard M. Greene, *We All Sing with the Same Voice,* HarperCollins (New York, NY), 2001.

Anne Rockwell, *Morgan Plays Soccer,* HarperCollins (New York, NY), 2001.

David Elliott, *The Cool Crazy Crickets to the Rescue!,* Candlewick Press (Cambridge, MA), 2001.

Michelle Edwards and Phyllis Root, *What's That Noise?,* Candlewick Press (Cambridge, MA), 2002.

Joan Holub, *Hooray for St. Patrick's Day!,* Puffin Books (New York, NY), 2002.

Bill Martin, Jr. and Michael Sampson, *Trick or Treat?,* Simon & Schuster Books for Young Readers (New York, NY), 2002.

Kimberly Brubaker Bradley, *Energy Makes Things Happen,* HarperCollins (New York, NY), 2003.

Anne Rockwell, *Katie Catz Makes a Splash,* HarperCollins (New York, NY), 2003.

Carol Diggory Shields, *Almost Late to School, and More School Poems,* Dutton Children's Books (New York, NY), 2003.

Judy Sierra, *Coco and Cavendish: Circus Dogs,* Random House (New York, NY), 2003.

Karen Magnuson Beil, *Mooove Oover!: A Book about Counting by Twos,* Holiday House (New York, NY), 2004.

Lynn Brunelle, *Pop Bottle Science,* Workman Publishing (New York, NY), 2004.

Judy Cox, *Go to Sleep, Groundhog,* Holiday House (New York, NY), 2004.

Anne Rockwell, *Chip and the Karate Kick,* HarperCollins (New York, NY), 2004.

Michael Elsohn, *What's the Matter in Mr. Whisker's Room?,* Candlewick Press (Cambridge, MA), 2004.

Judy Sierra, *Coco and Cavendish: Fire Dogs,* Random House (New York, NY), 2004.

Kimberly Brubaker Bradley, *Forces Make Things Move,* HarperCollins (New York, NY), 2005.

Kathy Duval, *The Three Bears' Christmas,* Holiday House (New York, NY), 2005.

Sheila Keenan, *Looking for Leprechauns,* Scholastic (New York, NY), 2005.

Anne Rockwell, *Brendan and Belinda and the Slam Dunk,* HarperCollins (New York, NY), 2005.

Sarah Sullivan, *Dear Baby: Letters from Your Big Brother,* Candlewick Press (Cambridge, MA), 2005.

B.G. Hennesey, *Mr. Ouchy's First Day,* Putnam's (New York, NY), 2006.

Anne Rockwell's *Why Are the Ice Caps Melting?: The Dangers of Global Warming,* Collins (New York, NY), 2006.

Shelley Moore Thomas, *Take Care, Good Knight,* Dutton Children's Books (New York, NY), 2006.

Kathy Duval, *The Three Bears' Halloween,* Holiday House (New York, NY), 2007.

Sidelights

Although he started his career in advertising, since the early 1990s Connecticut artist Paul Meisel has focused on illustrating picture books. Using a variety of techniques, including acrylics, gouache, watercolor, and mixed media, he has created artwork for over sixty children's books. In addition, with the 2003 picture book *Zara's Hats,* Meisel turns author as well, drawing inspiration from a family photograph. *Zara's Hats* tells a story about Selig the hat maker and his daughter Zara. When Selig runs out of the special feathers he uses to design his hats, he is forced to travel away from home to obtain more. While her father is away, daughter Zara begins crafting hats of her own, using materials found within her family's house. Before long, word spreads about the girl's unique hats, which become the newest fashion trend in town. As *School Library Journal* reviewer Martha Topol commented of Meisel's original picture book, in *Zara's Hats* "Meisel tells a fully fleshed out and engaging story," then brings it to life with his colorful illustrations.

In illustrating author Anne Rockwell's environmental-themed picture book *Why Are the Ice Caps Melting?: The Dangers of Global Warming,* Meisel contributes to the "Let's Read and Find Out Science" series. In the book, Rockwell offers a straightforward text while Meisel provides colorful and detailed illustrations that speak to the book's young audience. As Ilene Cooper commented in her review of *Why Are the Ice Caps Melting?* for *Booklist,* the illustrator's "ink-and-watercolor art, brimming with action, has a lightness the subject belies."

Other books featuring Meisel's art include one of his favorite projects: Judy Cox's humorous picture book *Go to Sleep, Groundhog!* The book finds a restless groundhog awaking sporadically in time to sample a winter's worth of other holidays. When he learns what he has been missing by hibernating, the animal is tempted to emerge from his hole earlier than the appointed Groundhog Day. Reviewing the book for *School Library Journal,* Kathleen Kelly MacMillan wrote that Meisel's "vibrant acrylic-and-gouache illustrations will help make this a favorite in storytimes." In *School Library Journal,* Grace Oliff and Ann Blanche Smith also praised Meisel's work for B.G. Hennessey's *Mr. Ouchy's First Day.* In addition to noting that the illustrator's "watercolor, gouache, and pen-and-ink" images inspire Hennessey's story with a "cozy feel," Oliff and Smith added that Meisel's images both "amplify humorous situations" in the text and "create them when the text does not." Discussing his illustrations for Sarah Sullivan's scrapbook-style picture book *Dear Baby: Letters from Your Big Brother,* a *Kirkus Reviews* writer concluded: "Meisel's mixed-media pictures are cheerful and engaging."

Biographical and Critical Sources

PERIODICALS

Audubon, May-June, 1997, review of *Why Are the Ice Caps Melting?: The Dangers of Global Warming,* p. 94.

Booklist, December 15, 1999, Ilene Cooper, review of *How to Talk to Your Cat,* p. 787; September 15, 2000, John Peters, review of *The Cool Crazy Crickets,* p. 240; September 1, 2001, Ellen Mandel, review of *The Cool Crazy Crickets to the Rescue,* p. 104; September 15, 2002, Stephanie Zvirin, review of *Trick or Treat?,* p. 246; February 1, 2003, review of *Energy Makes Things Happen,* p. 996; February 15, 2003, Gillian Engberg, review of *Zara's Hats,* p. 1075; August, 2003, review of *Almost Late to School!,* p. 1994; November 15, 2003, review of *Go to Sleep Groundhog!,* p. 599; May 1, 2004, Jennifer Mattson, review of *Chip and the Karate Kick,* p. 1564; September 1, 2005, Ilene Cooper, review of *The Three Bears' Christmas,* p. 124; September 15, 2005, Carolyn Phelan, review of *Forces Make Things Move,* p. 67; August 1, 2006, Hazel Rochman, review of *Mr. Ouchy's First Day,* p. 95; August 1, 2006, Hazel Rochman, review of *Letters from Your Big Brother,* p. 75; September 15, 2006, Carolyn Phelan, review of *Take Care, Good Knight,* p. 68; December 15, 2006, Ilene Cooper, review of *Why Are the Ice Caps Melting?,* p. 50.

Bulletin of the Center for Children's Books, January, 2004, Janice Del Negro, review of *Go to Sleep Groundhog!,* p. 186; December, 2006, Elizabeth Bush, review of *Why Are the Ice Caps Melting?,* p. 187; February, 2007, Elizabeth Bush, review of *Take Care, Good Knight,* p. 270.

Horn Book, November-December, 2005, review of *The Three Bears' Christmas,* p. 692.

Kirkus Reviews, July 1, 2002, review of *What's That Noise?,* p. 953; September 15, 2002, review of *Trick or Treat?,* p. 1395; February 1, 2003, review of *Zara's Hats,* p. 236; June 1, 2003, review of *Almost Late to*

School!, p. 811; December 15, 2003, review of *Go to Sleep Groundhog!,* p. 1449; May 1, 2004, review of *Chip and the Karate Kick,* p. 447; August 15, 2004, review of *What's the Matter in Mr. Whisker's Room?,* p. 812; September 15, 2004, review of *Mooove Oover!: A Book about Counting by Twos,* p. 910; July 1, 2005, review of *Forces Make Things Move,* p. 731; August 1, 2005, review of *Letters from Your Big Brother,* p. 859; November 1, 2005, review of *The Three Bears' Christmas,* p. 1192; June 1, 2006, review of *Mr. Ouchy's First Day,* p. 573; August 1, 2006, review of *Take Care, Good Knight,* p. 796; October 15, 2006, review of *Why Are the Ice Caps Melting?,* p. 1079.

Publishers Weekly, January 15, 2001, review of *We All Sing with the Same Voice,* p. 74; July 16, 2001, review of *Morgan Plays Soccer,* p. 179; September 23, 2002, review of *Trick or Treat?,* p. 23; December 16, 2002, review of *Zara's Hats,* p. 66; January 13, 2003, review of *How to Talk to Your Dog; How to Talk to Your Cat,* p. 63; May 5, 2003, review of *Katie Catz Makes a Splash,* p. 220; August 11, 2003, review of *Poetry for Teacher's Pets,* p. 282; January 12, 2004, review of *Go to Sleep Groundhog!,* p. 53; May 24, 2004, review of *True Companions,* p. 64; September 13, 2004, review of *Fun, by Nature,* p. 81; January 10, 2005, review of *We All Sing with the Same Voice,* p. 58; September 24, 2007, review of *The Three Bears,* p. 75; June 12, 2006, review of *Mr. Ouchy's First Day,* p. 52.

School Library Journal, August, 2000, Kate McLean, review of *The Cool Crazy Crickets,* p. 154; February, 2001, Genevieve Ceraldi, review of *We All Sing with the Same Voice,* p. 113; August, 2001, Blair Christolon, review of *Morgan Plays Soccer,* p. 158; December, 2002, Susan Marie Pitard, review of *What's That Noise?,* p. 94; Martha Topol, February, 2003, review of *Zara's Hats,* p. 116; August, 2003, Helen Foster James, review of *Almost Late to School!,* p. 152; February, 2004, Kathleen Kelly MacMillan, review of *Go to Sleep Groundhog!,* p. 104; October, 2004, Sandra Weizenback, review of *What's the Matter in Mr. Whisker's Room?,* p. 148; October, 2004, Laurie Edwards, review of *Mooove Oover!,* p. 109; September, 2005, Kara Schaff Dean, review of *Letters from Your Big Brother,* p. 187; July, 2006, Grac Oliff and Ann Blanche Smith, review of *Mr. Ouchy's First Day,* p. 79; August, 2007, Susan Moorhead, review of *The Three Bears' Halloween,* p. 80; June, 2004, Gay Lynn Van Vleck, review of *Chip and the Karate Kick,* p. 118.

ONLINE

Paul Meisel Home Page, http://paulmeisel.com (November 2, 2007).

Reading Is Fundamental Web site, http://www.rif.org/ (November 2, 2007), "Paul Meisel."

*   *   *

MONTGOMERY, Sy 1958-

Personal

Born February 7, 1958, in Frankfurt, Germany; daughter of Austin James (a U.S. Army general) and Willa

Sy Montgomery (Photograph by Dianne Taylor Snow. Reproduced by permission.)

Zane Montgomery; married Howard Mansfield (a writer), September, 1987. *Education:* Syracuse University, dual B.A.s (French and psychology; magazine journalism), 1979. *Politics:* "Town meeting." *Religion:* Christian.

Addresses

Home—Box 127, Hancock, NH 03449. *Agent*—Sarah Jane Freymann, 59 W. 71st St., No. 9B, New York, NY 10023. *E-mail*—sy@authorwire.com.

Career

Freelance journalist. Center for Tropical Ecology & Conservation, Antioch New England Graduate School, Keene, NH, associate. Lecturer on conservation topics at Smithsonian Institution, American Museum of Natural History, California Academy of Sciences, and other schools, universities, and conservation organizations.

Member

Society of Women Geographers, New England Environmental Educators.

Awards, Honors

Ray Bruner science writing fellow, American Public Health Association, 1982; Best New Nonfiction designation, New England Writers and Publishers Project, and finalist, *Los Angeles Times* science book award, both 1991, both for *Walking with the Great Apes;* Chris Award for Best Science Documentary, Columbus Film Festival, 1998, for *Mother Bear Man; Bulletin of the Center for Children's Books* Blue Ribbon Prize, 1999, International Reading Association Award for Excellence in Children's Books on Science, 2000, Orbis Pictus Honor Book designation, National Council of Teachers of English, 2000, John Burrough Nature Books for Young Readers listee, and Texas Bluebonnet Award nominee, Texas Library Association, all for *The Snake*

Scientist; Thomas Cook Travel Book Award nomination, 2001, for *Journey of the Pink Dolphins;* Oppenheim Toy Portfolio Gold Award, 2002, for *The Man-eating Tigers of Sundarbans;* Robert F. Silbert Informational Book Award Honor Book designation, 2005, for *The Tarantula Scientist;* Orbis Pictus Award, ALA Henry Bergh Children's Book Award, American Society for the Prevention of Cruelty to Animals, Sibert Honor Book, John Burroughs Young-Reader honor book, and Green Earth Honor Book, all 2007, all for *Quest for the Tree Kangaroo.*

Writings

NONFICTION FOR CHILDREN

The Snake Scientist ("Scientists in the Field" series), photographs by Nic Bishop, Houghton Mifflin (Boston, MA), 1999.

The Man-eating Tigers of Sundarbans, photographs by Eleanor Briggs, Houghton Mifflin (Boston, MA), 2001.

Encantado: Pink Dolphin of the Amazon, photographs by Dianne Taylor-Snow, Houghton Mifflin (Boston, MA), 2002.

Search for the Golden Moon Bear: Science and Adventure in the Asian Tropics ("Scientists in the Field" series), Houghton Mifflin (Boston, MA), 2004.

The Tarantula Scientist ("Scientists in the Field" series), photographs by Nic Bishop, Houghton Mifflin (Boston, MA), 2004.

Quest for the Tree Kangaroo: An Expedition to the Cloud Forest of New Guinea ("Scientists in the Field" series), photographs by Nic Bishop, Houghton Mifflin (Boston, MA), 2006.

Saving the Ghost of the Mountain ("Scientists in the Field" series), photographs by Nic Bishop, Houghton Mifflin (Boston, MA), 2008.

NONFICTION FOR ADULTS

Walking with the Great Apes: Jane Goodall, Dian Fossey, Birute Galdikas, Houghton Mifflin (Boston, MA), 1991.

Nature's Everyday Mysteries: A Field Guide to the World in Your Backyard (essays), foreword by Roger Tory Peterson, illustrated by Rodica Prato, Chapters (Shelburne, VT), 1993, also published as *The Curious Naturalist: Nature's Everyday Mysteries,* Down East Books (Camden, ME), 2000.

Spell of the Tiger: The Man-eaters of Sundarbans, Houghton Mifflin (Boston, MA), 1995.

Seasons of the Wild: A Year of Nature's Magic and Mysteries (essays), foreword by Elizabeth Marshall Thomas, illustrated by Rodica Prato, Chapters (Shelburne, VT), 1995.

Journey of the Pink Dolphins: An Amazon Quest, Simon & Schuster (New York, NY), 2000.

Search for the Golden Moon Bear: Science and Adventure in Pursuit of a New Species, Simon & Schuster (New York, NY), 2002.

The Wild out Your Window: Exploring Nature Near at Hand (essays), Down East Books (Camden, ME), 2002.

The Good Good Pig: The Extraordinary Life of Christopher Hogwood, Ballantine (New York, NY), 2006.

Contributor of essays and reviews to journals, including *International Wildlife, Discover, GEO, Nature, Animals, Orion,* and *Ranger Rick,* and to reference books such as *Encyclopedia Britannica.* Contributor to *The Nature of Nature: New Essays by America's Finest Writers on Nature,* Harcourt Brace, 1994. Author of monthly column "Nature's Journal" for *Boston Globe.* Contributor of radio commentaries to National Public Radio's *Living on Earth* program, and of documentary films to *National Geographic Explorer* television programs, including *Spell of the Tiger,* 1996, and *Mother Bear Man,* 1999.

Adaptations

A sound recording of *The Snake Scientist* was produced by Magnetix Corporation, 2000.

Sidelights

Writer, naturalist, and filmmaker Sy Montgomery swam with the pink dolphins of the Amazon, traveled through the mountain forests of New Guinea to catch sight of elusive tree kangaroos, and trailed man-eating tigers in the swamps of India. She shares these adventures with readers through such books as *Spell of the Tiger: The Man-eaters of Sundarbans, Quest for the Tree Kangaroo: An Expedition to the Cloud Forest of New Guinea, Journey of the Pink Dolphins: An Amazon Quest,* and *Search for the Golden Moon Bear: Science and Adventure in Pursuit of a New Species.* "To research my books and articles, I have been chased by an angry silverback gorilla in Zaire and bitten by a vampire bat in Costa Rica," the naturalist once revealed. "I have spent a week working in a pit with 18,000 snakes in Manitoba. I have been deftly undressed by an orangutan in Borneo, hunted by a tiger in India, and swum with piranhas, eels, and dolphins in the Amazon."

As companions to her books for adults, Montgomery has created junior versions of her adventure chronicles that are geared for younger readers. "I write for both adults and children in order to help us remember our duty to the earth," she once explained. "Children are a particularly important audience for they have an intuitive connection with plants and animals I hope to help honor and foster in my work. If our kind is to avert the poisonings and extinctions now in progress, today's children will do it."

In both *Spell of the Tiger* and its junior companion, *The Man-Eating Tigers of Sundarbans,* Montgomery transports readers to the Bay of Bengal, home to the world's largest mangrove swamp, and to the only population of tigers that seeks out human beings as prey rather than shying away from mankind, as most tigers do. "I avoided being eaten by my study subjects," she wryly reported, "while living in a mud hut among the most deadly man-eaters in the world." The people of the

Montgomery and photographer Nic Bishop share their around-the-world search for one of the most elusive mammals on earth in Quest for the Tree Kangaroo. (Houghton Mifflin, 2006. Photograph © by Nic Bishop. Reproduced by permission of Houghton Mifflin Company.)

Sundarbans worship the tiger as a god even as hundreds of them are hunted and killed annually by the creatures they call Daksin Ray. In addition to her books, Montgomery wrote and narrated a documentary film based on her work with the tigers for a *National Geographic Explorer* program that aired in 1996 to a worldwide audience.

"Montgomery writes lyrically of an alien land where outlines blur, tree roots reach for the sky, cyclones claim whole villages, and chanted mantras keep tigers from becoming angry," observed a *Kirkus Reviews* contributor of *Spell of the Tiger.* In *Publishers Weekly,* a contributor similarly focused on the author's ability to create a "vivid picture of the coastal forest and its people," and *Booklist* reviewer Donna Seaman wrote that Montgomery appears to "absorb the unique and surprisingly cosmic dynamic of the delta" as she pursues her elusive subject. "After all," Seaman noted, "there can be no revelation more humbling than the recognition that we, like other animals, are meat." Reviewing *The Man-Eating Tigers of Sundarbans* for *Booklist,* Ilene Cooper

wrote that the work has "clearly been written with young people in mind." Detailing tiger behavior from the viewpoint of both scientists and villagers, the work "immediately captures attention with fresh, engaging writing that turns a scientific study into a page-turning mystery," concluded the critic.

"*Journey of the Pink Dolphins* is the true story of my quest to follow an enigmatic, little-studied species of freshwater dolphin into the heart of the Amazon," Montgomery once explained. "My research required four separate expeditions, each a journey not only into some of the world's greatest jungles, but also a trip back into time, and a foray into a mythical, enchanted world where people say the dolphins can turn into people and seduce both men and women to live with them in a beautiful city beneath the water." In both *Journey of the Pink Dolphins* and the child-focused *Encantado: Pink Dolphins of the Amazon,* she introduces the world of the freshwater dolphins called *Encantados,* or "Enchanted," by the people of the Amazon and Orinoco rivers in South America. In *Encantado,* which features photographs by Dianne Taylor-Snow, Montgomery "writes with a contagious sense of wonder," according to a *Kirkus Reviews* writer.

Search for the Golden Moon Bear: Science and Adventure in Pursuit of a New Species finds Montgomery traveling with Gary Galbreath, an evolutionary biologist hoping to find a yet-undiscovered species of honey-colored bear reportedly seen in China and known as the golden moon bear. Traveling through Laos, Cambodia, and Thailand, Montgomery is a witness to the horrors of the black market for wildlife, the effects of the Khmer Rouge's terrorism, and the destruction of the traditional way of life of the region's hill tribes. Despite its tragedy, according to Seaman, Montgomery's "riveting chronicle" is nonetheless uplifting as it tells of "heroic wildlife specialists" and "bear lore sacred and scientific," in a prose containing both "humor . . . and a subtle but pervasive spirituality." "Making science exciting is Montgomery's talent, and she is in top form here," wrote *Library Journal* contributor Nancy Moeckel of the book. As a *Publishers Weekly* contributor predicted, "Readers who aren't conservationists to begin with will be by the end of this heady and haunting narrative."

Montgomery's adventures while on her search for the mythic species are recounted for younger readers in *Search for the Golden Moon Bear: Science and Adventure in the Asian Tropics.* "Though discussions of the region's bloody history have been toned down" in this volume, according to *Booklist* critic Jennifer Mattson the author nonetheless "frame[s] the adventure with thought-provoking context." In *Search for the Golden Moon Bear* Montgomery presents young readers with what *School Library Journal* contributor Patricia Manning called "an intelligent reportage of science as it happens . . . and lets readers see that the 'end' of an investigation holds within itself the nucleus of a new idea."

Award-winning wildlife photographer Nic Bishop and Montgomery team up on *Quest for the Tree Kangaroo,* part of her ongoing "Scientists in the Field" series. Here she accompanies biologist Lisa Dabek and her international research team on a trip to the dense mountain forests of Papua New Guinea in search of the Matschie's tree kangaroo. Fitting the animals with radio collars, the biologists hope to learn more about the unique animals and their interaction with their lush environment. The text presents what *Booklist* reviewer Gillian Engberg described as an "unusually strong, visceral sense of the work and cooperation fieldwork entails," while in *Audubon* Julie Liebach wrote that Bishop's colorful photographic images make "the forests of Papua New Guinea look like a Tolkien fantasy." Focusing on "both the hardships and exhilaration of the enterprise," according to *School Library Journal* critic Kathy Piehl, Montgomery provides "fascinating glimpses" into nature that "should encourage young scientists." *Quest for the Tree Kangaroo* features an "exemplary description of science field work," concluded a *Kirkus Reviews* writer, the critic adding that the author "connects the world of the young reader" to her book's exotic setting

through her well-paced narrative and references to the ways children are aiding the biologists' efforts. "Montgomery's friendliness and curiosity set the tone," asserted *Horn Book* contributor Danielle J. Ford, the critic explaining that the author "enthusiastically engages with the people, plants, and animals she encounters" throughout her fascinating journey.

The Snake Scientist and *The Tarantula Scientist* are specifically geared for a younger readership. The strength of Montgomery's approach in these books is that they exhibit "the excitement of science in action," according to Ruth S. Vose in her *School Library Journal* review of *The Snake Scientist.* Montgomery's profile of snake scientists centers on a zoologist who studies the red-sided garter snake in Canada, while the book's sidebars include information about aspects of the species that continue to mystify scientists and hints on how to visit snake dens. The book's "lively text" makes this an "outstanding" science book for young people, Vose averred. Featuring photographs by Bishop, *The Tarantula Scientist* transports readers to the rainforest of French Guiana, where Hiram College teacher and biologist Samuel Marshall collects the spiders he and his students will study in their Ohio laboratory. The tarantula species includes the largest spider on earth: the bird-eating Goliath tarantula. Praised by a *Kirkus Reviews* writer as "another [of Montgomery's] stellar excursion into the world of working scientists," the book contains numerous facts about spider biology and habits. "Montgomery has a gift for scene-setting," the *Kirkus Reviews* critic added, while in *School Library Journal* Patricia Manning deemed the work "a vivid look at an enthusiastic scientist energetically and happily at work."

Somewhat of a departure from much of her writing, *The Good Good Pig: The Extraordinary Life of Christopher Hogwood* shares with readers a journey of a different sort. Montgomery's book is set in a small town in rural New Hampshire, where Montgomery lives with her husband, writer Howard Mansfield. Given a sickly piglet that, as the runt of the litter, seemed unlikely to survive, the couple cared for the creature and nursed it to good health. Soon a part of the family, Christopher Hogwood eventually topped 750 pounds, and not only Montgomery and her husband, but also the entire community became dedicated to keeping the lovable pig fed. Due to his sociable nature, Christopher became a local celebrity, and through his presence not only the author but also many of his acquaintances benefited from his well-grounded perspective on life. At age fourteen, Christopher finally passes away, leaving a great void in many lives but also a legacy comprised of valuable life lessons, as Montgomery reveals in her loving tribute.

A national bestseller, *The Good Good Pig* also touched the hearts of readers around the world in its Portuguese, Dutch, German, Korean, and Japanese translation. In her memoir, Montgomery "writes with extraordinary lucidity, candor, and grace," noted Seaman, while *School Library Journal* reviewer Claudia C. Holland predicted that the author's "engaging writing style will captivate even the most uninspired teen readers." In *Library Jour-*

nal Wilda Williams commented that Montgomery studs her memoir with "fascinating tidbits of pig lore and natural history," and Holland noted that in *The Good Good Pig* she includes "delightful anecdotes about Christopher's personality, neighborhood wanderings, and haute skin care à la Pig Spa."

While she focuses on exotic adventures in many of her books, in her essays for the *Boston Globe* column "Nature's Journal" as well as her radio talks on NPR's *Living on Earth* program, Montgomery also inspires fascination with the typical suburban backyard. Her essay collection *Nature's Everyday Mysteries: A Field Guide to the World in Your Backyard* reveals many little-known facts about the natural world all around us, while the forty-nine essays in *The Wild out Your Window: Exploring Nature Near at Hand* are rife with "sex, violence, intrigue, and mystery," according to *Library Journal* writer Maureen J. Delaney-Lehman. Recommending *Nature's Everyday Mysteries* to "readers who know little about the natural world," *Booklist* reviewer Jon Kart-

man added that Montgomery's writing "will entertain and inform in equal proportions," and Delaney-Lehman dubbed her writings "delightful." Other essays by Montgomery are collected in *Seasons of the Wild: A Year of Nature's Magic and Mysteries.*

Discussing her ongoing adventures with *SATA,* Montgomery noted that research for the 2008 installment in her "Scientists in the Field" series with Bishop found her in the Altai Mountains of the Great Gobi in Mongolia, searching for snow leopards. "*Saving the Ghost of the Mountain* chronicles our expedition with Tom McCarthy and his colleagues at the Snow Leopard Trust to search for sign of the most elusive cat on Earth. It will feature gorgeous photos by Nic Bishop. And here, once again, Nic saved me from death, this time keeping me from falling off a cliff at 11,000 feet onto a rocky substrate of what looked like God's own Ginsu knives stuck blade-side-up in drying concrete.

"Besides once again failing to be killed, for me other highlights of the Gobi research included riding on Tom's

Cover of Montgomery's **The Snake Scientist,** *featuring photographs by noted nature photographer Nic Bishop.* (Houghton Mifflin, 1999. Photograph © 1999 by Nic Bishop. Reproduced by permission.)

Cover of **The Good Good Pig,** *Montgomery's touching memoir about the years of joy one large pig brought to her small New England hometown.* (Ballantine Books, 2006. Photograph © 2006 by Age Fotostock/SuperStock. Used by permission of Ballantine Books, a division of Random House, Inc.)

own personal camel, eating fresh yak butter with a nomad family in their traditional round felt tent, playing with an adorable wild sweet desert hedgehog, and sharing vodka made from goat's milk at a traditional Mongolian wedding.

"Work in progress includes a book on birds for adults, for which research will include a study of falconry and a trip to Australia to study the world's most dangerous bird, the cassowary. A new book for children will take Nic and me to New Zealand to document the nesting of the critically endangered kakapo, a giant, flightless, nocturnal parrot."

Biographical and Critical Sources

PERIODICALS

Audubon, Julie Leibach, review of *Quest for the Tree Kangaroo: An Expedition to the Cloud Forest of New Guinea,* p. 133.

Booklist, March 15, 1991, Sally Estes, review of *Walking with the Great Apes,* p. 1441; April 1, 1993, Jon Kartman, review of *Nature's Everyday Mysteries,* January 15, 1995, Donna Seaman, review of *Spell of the Tiger,* p. 878; February 15, 1999, Stephanie Zvirin, review of *The Snake Scientist,* p. 1064; February 15, 2000, Donna Seaman, review of *Journey of the Pink Dolphins: An Amazon Quest,* p. 1064; March 1, 2001, Ilene Cooper, review of *The Man-eating Tigers of Sundarbans,* p. 1277; September 15, 2002, Donna Seaman, review of *Search for the Golden Moon Bear: Science and Adventure in Pursuit of a New Species,* p. 187; December 1, 2004, Jennifer Mattson, review of *Search for the Golden Moon Bear,* p. 665; March 15, 2006, Donna Seaman, review of *The Good Good Pig: The Extraordinary Life of Christopher Hogwood,* p. 12; December 1, 2006, Gillian Engberg, review of *Quest for the Tree Kangaroo,* p. 58.

Bulletin of the Center for Children's Books, November, 2006, Deborah Stevenson, review of *Quest for the Tree Kangaroo,* p. 138.

Choice, March, 2001, A. Ewert, review of *The Curious Naturalist: Nature's Everyday Mysteries,* p. 1295; February, 2003, F.S. Szalay, review of *Search for the Golden Moon Bear,* p. 1009

Horn Book, July, 1999, Diana Lutz, review of *The Snake Scientist,* p. 485; March, 2001, review of *The Man-Eating Tigers of Sundarbans,* p. 232; July-August, 2004, Danielle J. Ford, review of *The Tarantula Scientist,* p. 469; January-February, 2007, Danielle J. Ford, review of *Quest for the Tree Kangaroo,* p. 85.

Kirkus Reviews, December 1, 1994, review of *Spell of the Tiger,* p. 1596; March 15, 2002, review of *Encantado: Pink Dolphin of the Amazon;* August 15, 2002, review of *Search for the Golden Moon Bear,* p. 1202; February 15, 2004, review of *The Tarantula Scientist,* p. 182; February 15, 2006, review of *The Good Good Pig,* p. 173; October 1, 2006, review of *Quest for the Tree Kangaroo,* p. 1020.

Library Journal, February 15, 2000, Nancy J. Moeckel, review of *Journey of the Pink Dolphins,* p. 193; October 15, 2002, Nancy J. Moeckel, review of *Search for the Golden Moon Bear: Science and Adventure in Pursuit of a New Species,* and Maureen J. Delaney-Lehman, review of *The Wild out Your Window: Nature Near at Hand,* both p. 92; May 15, 2006, Wilda Williams, review of *The Good Good Pig,* p. 121.

Publishers Weekly, January 11, 1991, review of *Walking with the Great Apes,* p. 85; January 9, 1995, review of *Spell of the Tiger,* p. 53; February 21, 2000, review of *Journey of the Pink Dolphins,* p. 79; August 19, 2002, review of *Search for the Golden Moon Bear,* p. 77; February 6, 2006, review of *The Good Good Pig,* p. 51.

School Library Journal, May, 1999, Ruth S. Vose, review of *The Snake Scientist,* p. 140; March, 2001, Margaret Bush, review of *The Man-eating Tigers of Sundarbans,* p. 274; May, 2004, Patricia Manning, review of *The Tarantula Scientist,* p. 172; December, 2004, Patricia Manning, review of *Search for the Golden Moon Bear,* p. 164; December, 2006, Kathy Piehl, review of *Quest for the Tree Kangaroo,* p. 166, and Claudia C. Holland, review of *The Good Good Pig,* p. 178.

ONLINE

Paula Gordon Show, http://www.paulagordon.com/shows/
   montgomery/ (January 15, 2001), "Spirit of Adventure" (includes audio excerpts from the show).
Sy Montgomery Home Page, http://www.authorwire.com
   (November 15, 2007).

*   *   *

MOORE, Patrick 1959-

Personal

Born 1959.

Addresses

Home and office—Brooklyn, NY.

Career

Author and illustrator.

Writings

(Self-illustrated) *The Mighty Street Sweeper,* Henry Holt
   (New York, NY), 2006.

Contributor of illustrations to periodicals, including
Esquire.

Patrick Moore mixes his humorous story with his unique cartoon art in his debut picture book **The Mighty Street Sweeper.** (Illustration © 2006 by Patrick
Moore. Reprinted by permission of Henry Holt & Company, LLC.)

Sidelights

The picture book *The Mighty Street Sweeper* marked the debut title of author and artist Patrick Moore. Moore, who has created editorial artwork for magazines such as *Esquire,* incorporates digital computer techniques into his vibrant images. In *The Mighty Street Sweeper* he centers his story on an outdated sweeper that pales in comparison to the newer models used to sweep the road. Jake, a squirrel who operates the machine, knows that the old street sweeper, though outdated, is still the best machine for the job. As a *Kirkus Reviews* critic remarked, Moore's tale of a humble street sweeper "honors the common, but far from average, making even the most ordinary seem extraordinary." A *Publishers Weekly* reviewer commented of *The Mighty Street Sweeper* that Moore "makes a winning children's book debut with this tribute to a distinctive truck."

In addition to commenting on his story, critics have also acknowledged Moore's bold designs for *The Mighty Street Sweeper.* Betty Carter in her review of the picture book for *Horn Book,* cited the author/illustrator for creating "bright, uncluttered illustrations" that "feature earnest animal drivers and create a humorous background." Linda Staskus, writing in *School Library Journal,* concluded that *The Mighty Street Sweeper* "will delight young truck lovers."

Biographical and Critical Sources

PERIODICALS

Booklist, October 15, 2006, Randall Enos, review of *The Mighty Street Sweeper,* p. 50.

Horn Book, January-February, 2007, Betty Carter, review of *The Mighty Street Sweeper,* p. 59.

Kirkus Reviews, September 1, 2006, review of *The Mighty Street Sweeper,* p. 909.

Publishers Weekly, October 23, 2006, review of *The Mighty Street Sweeper,* p. 49.

School Library Journal, October, 2006, Linda Staskus, review of *The Mighty Street Sweeper,* p. 142.*

*   *   *

MORPURGO, Michael 1943-

Personal

Born October 5, 1943, in St. Albans, England; son of Tony Valentine Bridge and Catherine Noel Kippe; stepson of Jake Eric Morpurgo; married Clare Allen, 1963; children: three children. *Education:* King's College London, B.A., 1967.

Addresses

Home—Langlands, Iddesleigh, Winkleigh, Devon EX19 8SN, England. *Agent*—David Higham Associates, 5-8 Lower John St., Golden Square, London W1R 4HA, England.

Michael Morpurgo (Photograph by James Ravilious. Reproduced by permission of the Estate of James Ravilious.)

Career

Writer and educator. Primary school teacher, 1967-75. Joint founder and director, Farms for City Children, 1976—; opened Nethercourt House farm, 1976, Treginnis Isaf, 1989, and Wick Court, 1998.

Awards, Honors

Whitbread Award runner up, 1982, for *War Horse;* Carnegie Medal runner up, 1988, for *King of the Cloud Forests;* London *Guardian* Children's Fiction Prize runner up, 1991, for *Waiting for Anya;* Silver Pencil Award (Holland); Best Books selection, *School Library Journal,* 1995, and Top of the List selection for Youth Fiction, *Booklist,* 1995, both for *The War of Jenkins' Ear;* Whitbread Award, 1995, for *The Wreck of the Zanzibar;* Nestlé Smarties Gold Medal, 1997, for *The Butterfly Lion;* Editor's Choice, *Books for Keeps,* 1999, for *Cockadoodle-Doo, Mr. Sultana!;* named member, Order of the British Empire, 1999, for creating Farms for City Children; named children's laureate of Scotland, c. 2004; Carnegie Medal shortlist, and *Guardian* Children's Fiction Prize longlist, both 2004, and Blue Peter Book Award, 2005, all for *Private Peaceful;* Blue Peter Award shortlist, 2006, for *The Amazing Story of Adolphus Tips.*

Writings

FICTION; FOR CHILDREN

It Never Rained: Five Stories, illustrated by Isabelle Hutchins, Macmillan (London, England), 1974.

Thatcher Jones, illustrated by Trevor Ridley, Macmillan (London, England), 1975.

Long Way Home, Macmillan (London, England), 1975.

(Compiler with Graham Barrett) *The Story-Teller,* Ward Lock (London, England), 1976.

Friend or Foe, illustrated by Trevor Stubley, Macmillan (London, England), 1977.

What Shall We Do with It?, illustrated by Priscilla Lamont, Ward Lock (London, England), 1978.

Do All You Dare, photographs by Bob Cathmoir, Ward Lock (London, England), 1978.

(Editor) *All around the Year,* photographs by James Ravilious, drawings by Robin Ravilious, new poems by Ted Hughes, J. Murray (London, England), 1979.

The Day I Took the Bull by the Horn, Ward Lock (London, England), 1979.

The Ghost-Fish, Ward Lock (London, England), 1979.

Love at First Sight, Ward Lock (London, England), 1979.

That's How, Ward Lock (London, England), 1979.

The Marble Crusher, and Other Stories, illustrated by Trevor Stubley, Macmillan (London, England), 1980.

The Nine Lives of Montezuma, illustrated by Margery Gill, Kaye & Ward (Kingswood, England), 1980.

Miss Wirtle's Revenge, illustrated by Graham Clarke, Kaye & Ward (Kingswood, England), 1981.

The White Horse of Zennor, and Other Stories from below the Eagle's Nest, Kaye & Ward (Kingswood, England), 1982.

The War Horse, Kaye & Ward (Kingswood, England), 1982, Greenwillow (New York, NY), 1983, reprinted, Scholastic (New York, NY), 2007.

Twist of Gold, Kaye & Ward (Kingswood, England), 1983, Viking (New York, NY), 1993, reprinted, Egmont (London, England), 2007.

Little Foxes, illustrated by Gareth Floyd, Kaye & Ward (Kingswood, England), 1984.

Why the Whales Came, Scholastic (New York, NY), 1985.

Tom's Sausage Lion, illustrated by Robina Green, A. & C. Black (London, England), 1986, reprinted, BBC Consumer Publishing (London, England), 2003.

Jo-Jo, the Melon Donkey, illustrated by Chris Molan, Simon & Schuster (New York, NY), 1987, illustrated by Tony Kerins, Heinemann (London, England), 1995.

King of the Cloud Forests, Viking (New York, NY), 1988.

My Friend Walter, Heinemann (London, England), 1988.

(With Shoo Rayner) *Mossop's Last Chance,* A. & C. Black (London, England), 1988.

Mr. Nobody's Eyes, Heinemann (London, England), 1989, Viking (New York, NY), 1990, reprinted, Egmont (London, England), 2007.

Conker (also see below), Heinemann (London, England), 1989.

(With Shoo Rayner) *Albertine, Goose Queen,* A. & C. Black (London, England), 1989.

(With Shoo Rayner) *Jigger's Day Off* (also see below), A. & C. Black (London, England), 1990.

Waiting for Anya, Heinemann (London, England), 1990, Viking (New York, NY), 1991, reprinted, Egmont (London, England), 2007.

Colly's Barn, illustrated by Alasdair Bright, Heinemann (London, England), 1991.

(With Shoo Rayner) *And Pigs Might Fly!* (also see below), A. & C. Black (London, England), 1991.

The Sandman and the Turtles, Heinemann (London, England), 1991, Philomel (New York, NY), 1994.

(With Shoo Rayner) *Martians at Mudpuddle Farm* (also see below), A. & C. Black (London, England), 1992.

The War of Jenkins' Ear, Heinemann (London, England), 1993, Philomel (New York, NY), 1995, reprinted, Egmont (London, England), 2007.

Snakes and Ladders, Heinemann (London, England), 1994.

(Editor) *Ghostly Haunts,* illustrated by Nilesh Mistry, Pavilion (London, England), 1994.

Arthur, High King of Britain, illustrated by Michael Foreman, Pavilion (London, England), 1994, Harcourt (San Diego, CA), 1995.

The Dancing Bear, illustrated by Christian Birmingham, Young Lion (London, England), 1994, Houghton (Boston, MA), 1996.

(With Shoo Rayner) *Stories from Mudpuddle Farm* (includes *And Pigs Might Fly!, Martians at Mudpuddle Farm,* and *Jigger's Day Off*), A. & C. Black (London, England), 1995.

(With Shoo Rayner) *Mum's the Word,* A. & C. Black (London, England), 1995.

(Editor) *Muck and Magic: Tales from the Countryside,* forward by HRH the Princess Royal, Heinemann (London, England), 1995.

The Wreck of the Zanzibar, illustrated by Christian Birmingham, Viking (New York, NY), 1995.

Blodin the Beast, illustrated by Christina Balit, Fulcrum (Golden, CO), 1995.

Sam's Duck, illustrated by Keith Bowen, Collins (London, England), 1996.

The King in the Forest, illustrated by T. Kerins, Simon & Schuster (New York, NY), 1996.

The Butterfly Lion, illustrated by Christian Birmingham, Collins (London, England), 1996.

The Ghost of Grania O'Malley, Heinemann (London, England), 1996, Viking (New York, NY), 1996.

Robin of Sherwood, illustrated by Michael Foreman, Harcourt (San Diego, CA), 1996.

(Editor) *Beyond the Rainbow Warrior,* Pavilion (London, England), 1996.

The Marble Crusher (includes *The Marble Crusher, Colly's Barn,* and *Conker*), Mammoth (London, England), 1997.

Farm Boy, illustrated by Michael Foreman, Pavilion (London, England), 1997.

Red Eyes at Night, illustrated by Tony Ross, Hodder (London, England), 1997.

Wartman, illustrated by Joanna Carey, Barrington Stoke (Edinburgh, Scotland), 1998.

Escape from Shangri-La, Philomel Books (New York, NY), 1998.

Cockadoodle-Doo, Mr. Santana!, illustrated by Michael Foreman, Scholastic (New York, NY), 1998, published as *Cockadoodle-Doo, Mr Sultana!,* illustrated by Holly Swain, Scholastic (London, England), 1998.

(Reteller) *Joan of Arc of Domremy,* illustrated by Michael Foreman, Harcourt Brace (San Diego, CA), 1999.

(Compiler) *Animal Stories,* illustrated by Andrew Davidson, Kingfisher (New York, NY), 1999.

Kensuke's Kingdom, illustrated by Michael Foreman, Heinemann (London, England), 1999, Scholastic (New York, NY), 2003.

The Rainbow Bear, illustrated by Michael Foreman, Doubleday (London, England), 1999.

Billy the Kid, illustrated by Michael Foreman, Pavilion (London, England), 2000.

Black Queen, Corgi Juvenile (London, England), 2000.

(Compiler) *The Kingfisher Book of Great Boy Stories: A Treasury of Classics from Children's Literature,* Kingfisher (New York, NY), 2000.

Wombat Goes Walkabout, illustrated by Christian Birmingham, Candlewick Press (Cambridge, MA), 2000.

The Silver Swan, illustrated by Christian Birmingham, Phyllis Fogelman Books (New York, NY), 2000.

From Hereabout Hill, Mammoth (London, England), 2000.

Who's a Big Bully Then?, illustrated by Joanna Carey, Barrington Stoke (Edinburgh, Scotland), 2000.

Mister Skip, Roaring Good Reads, 2000.

The King in the Forest, Hodder (London England), 2001.

Toro! Toro!, illustrated by Michael Foreman, Collins (London, England), 2002.

Out of the Ashes, illustrated by Michael Foreman, Macmillan (London, England), 2002.

Cool!, illustrated by Michael Foreman, Collins (London, England), 2002.

Because a Fire Was in My Head, Faber & Faber (London, England), 2002.

Beastman of Ballyloch, HarperCollins Canada (Toronto, Ontario, Canada), 2002.

Jim Davis: A High-Sea Adventure, Scholastic (New York, NY), 2002.

The Last Wolf, illustrated by Michael Foreman, Doubleday (London, England), 2002.

Sleeping Sword, Egmont (London, England), 2003.

Gentle Giant, illustrated by Michael Foreman, Collins (London, England), 2003.

Mairi's Mermaid, illustrated by Lucy Richards, Crabtree Publishing (New York, NY), 2003.

Cool as a Cucumber, illustrated by Tor Freeman, Walker (London, England), 2003.

Private Peaceful, Walker (London, England), 2003, Scholastic (New York, NY), 2006.

(Reteller) *Sir Gawain and the Green Knight,* illustrated by Michael Foreman, Candlewick Press (Cambridge, MA), 2004.

Little Albatross, illustrated by Michael Foreman, Doubleday (London, England), 2004.

Dolphin Boy, illustrated by Michael Forman, Anderson (London, England), 2004.

(Reteller) *The Orchard Book of Aesop's Fables,* illustrated by Emma Chichester Clark, Orchard (London, England), 2004, published as *The McElderry Book of Aesop's Fables,* Margaret K. McElderry Books (New York, NY), 2005.

I Believe in Unicorns, illustrated by Gary Blythe, Walker (London, England), 2005, Candlewick Press (Cambridge, MA), 2006.

(Reteller) *Beowulf,* illustrated by Michael Foreman, Candlewick Press (Cambridge, MA), 2006.

The Amazing Story of Adolphus Tips, Scholastic (New York, NY), 2006.

Alone on a Wide Sea, HarperCollins (London, England), 2006.

On Angel Wings, illustrated by Quentin Blake, Egmont (London, England), 2006, Candlewick Press (Cambridge, MA), 2007.

It's a Dog's Life, illustrated by Judith Allibone, Farrar, Straus & Giroux (New York, NY), 2007.

OTHER

(Compiler with Clifford Simmons) *Living Poets,* J. Murray (London, England), 1974.

(Librettist) *Words of Songs,* music by Phyllis Tate, Oxford University Press (Oxford, England), 1985.

Some of Morpurgo's books have been translated into Gaelic and Welsh.

Adaptations

Why the Whales Came was adapted as a film titled *When the Whales Came,* 1989, by Golden Swan Films; *My Friend Walter* was adapted as a television film by Portobello Films for Thames Television/WonderWorks, 1993; *Out of the Ashes* was adapted as a television film; *Billy the Kid* was adapted as a play, produced in Southwark, England, 2007. Several of Morpurgo's books have been adapted as audiobooks, including *Kensuke's Kingdom,* 2001; and *Private Peaceful,* read by Jeff Woodman, Recorded Books, 2005.

Sidelights

British author Michael Morpurgo has, over the years, contributed original children's literature in the genres of historical fiction, animal stories, fantasies, picture books, easy readers, and retellings of legend and myth. Often employing the rural setting he knows so well, Morpurgo places his young protagonists in challenging situations that ultimately test their character. Often praised for the simple elegance of his prose, Morpurgo is frequently lauded for creating books that are "heartwarming and sensitive," according to Jennifer Taylor in *St. James Guide to Young Adult Writers.*

Since leaving childhood himself, Morpurgo has hardly spent a day out of the company of children. A father by age twenty, he was a grandfather at age forty-three; a teacher in primary schools for a decade, he has also helped to run Farms for City Children—a venture that brings urban children to the countryside—since 1976. Although his books are generally uplifting and teach ethical lessons, Morpurgo is never preachy; his ability to spin an engaging tale is what has made books such

Cover of Morpurgo's young-adult novel The War of Jenkins' Ear, *featuring artwork by Toby Gowing.* (Illustration © 1995 by Toby Gowing. Reproduced by permission of Philomel, a division of Penguin Putnam Books for Young Readers.)

as *Why the Whales Came, The War of Jenkins' Ear, Waiting for Anya,The Wreck of the Zanzibar, Escape from Shangri-La, Out of the Ashes,* and *The Amazing Story of Adolphus Tips* so popular.

Morpurgo was born on October 5, 1943, in St. Albans, England, into a country that had been at war with Nazi Germany for over four years. At the age of seven he went away to a grammar school in Sussex where he was introduced to "class war," as he recalled to *Booklist* contributor Ilene Cooper. "The schoolboys and the village boys had fights and difficulties; walking along cow paths, we'd hurl insults at each other. It was an indication that there were people out there who didn't like you because of the way you spoke, and we didn't like them either. And while things have changed since the 1950s, class still seems to me to be a cancer that riddles our society." As a young schoolboy Morpurgo was viewed by his friends as "good at rugby and a bit stupid," as he admitted in his *Young Writer* interview. It was not until years later that he gained his love of reading, especially the novels of Robert Louis Stevenson, Paul Gallico, and Ernest Hemingway and the poetry of

Ted Hughes, a poet laureate of England and a close friend of Morpurgo's.

At age fourteen Morpurgo entered Kings School in Canterbury, graduating in 1962. The following year he married Clare Allen, daughter of the publisher of Penguin books, and the couple eventually raised two sons and one daughter. Meanwhile, he completed his degree at King's College London in 1967. Working as a teacher, he also completed his compulsory service in the British Army. Teaching turned his interest to writing. "I had a notion I could tell a tale when the children I was teaching really seemed to want to listen to the tales I told them," Morpurgo noted in *Young Writer.* "An acid test." Reading Hughes's *Poetry in the Making* influenced the young man to think that he too could string words together rhythmically, and the book literally got him writing. "No better invitation to write was ever written and I accepted," Morpurgo remarked in *Young Writer.* "I love the sound of words, the rhythm of a sentence."

Living in the countryside, Morpurgo wanted to introduce city-born-and-bred kids to the wonders of nature. To that end, he and his wife started Farms for City Children in the 1970s. Under this program, kids come to stay at the farm and work and take care of animals for several weeks. The program became so popular that the Morpurgos soon operated three farms where more than 2,000 children per year could the opportunity to get in touch with nature and themselves. In 1999, Morpurgo and his wife were honored in the Queen's Birthday List with the MBE for their work with Farms for City Children.

Morpurgo's early work includes both short novels for ten-to twelve-year-olds and picture books for younger readers. With books such as *Miss Wirtle's Revenge,* a tale about a little girl who competes successfully against a class full of boys, Morpurgo was noted for establishing a writing career "successfully outside the mainstream," in the opinion of *Times Literary Supplement* reviewer Josephine Karavasil. His short novel *Nine Lives of Montezuma,* published in 1980, details nine narrow-escape adventures of a farmyard cat named Montezuma. Told from the cat's point of view, the book also follows the farming year as a background story. When Montezuma dies, the cat knows that there is a descendant to take its place in the scheme of things on the farm. In *Junior Bookshelf* D.A. Young noted that the story "is told without sentimentality, though not without sentiment," and recommended *Nine Lives of Montezuma* "with confidence to cat-lovers of any age."

Animals play a starring role in Morpurgo's first book to be published in the United States. Based on a true story, *War Horse* describes World War I as seen through the eyes of Joey, a farm horse commandeered by the British Cavalry in 1914. At that time, mounted troops stood little chance against the mechanized horrors of modern warfare, and Joey endures bombardment and capture by the Germans. He is set to work pulling ambulances and

Cover of Morpurgo's 1990 novel Why the Whales Came, *featuring artwork by Walter Rane.* (Illustration © 1990 by Scholastic, Inc. Reproduced by permission of Walter Rane.)

guns, worked by different masters but never forgetting young Albert, the kind son of his original owner back in England. In the end, persistence and courage pay off as Joey and Albert are reunited. Kate M. Flanagan, writing in *Horn Book,* noted that "the courage of the horse and his undying devotion to the boy" permeate this book, which she maintained is written with "elegant, old-fashioned grace." In *Voice of Youth Advocates* Diane G. Yates commented that Morpurgo's "message about the futility and carnage of war comes across loud and clear." Highlighting similarities between *War Horse* and Anna Sewell's classic *Black Beauty,* Margery Fisher concluded in *Growing Point* that Morpurgo's book "is a most accomplished piece of story-telling, full of sympathy for an animal manipulated by man but preserving its dignity." Warmly received on both sides of the Atlantic, *War Horse* helped win an international audience for Morpurgo.

Morpurgo's novel *Twist of Gold* begins in 1840s Ireland. When famine hits, Sean and Annie O'Brien set off for North America to find their father, an adventurous journey that takes them across the ocean and then across a continent via wagon train and river boat. A story of a childhood test, *Twist of Gold* was described by Fisher as a "touching and inventive adventure story." More attention came Morpurgo's way with the 1985 publication of *Why the Whales Came,* a novel that was subsequently adapted for film. Set in 1914 on Bryher in the Scilly Islands off England's southwest coast, *Why the Whales Came* introduces siblings Gracie and Daniel. Forbidden to associate with the Birdman, a strange old man who lives on the far side of the island the children realize that the deaf old man is actually lonely, not evil. The three become fast friends as World War II hovers ominously in the background. On Bryher there is another, parallel war: one between the islanders and the ceaseless barrage of sea and weather. When a whale washes ashore, Gracie, Daniel, and the Birdman must convince residents to return the creature to the sea rather than butcher it and risk calling forth an ancient curse. "The success of Morpurgo's novel comes . . . from its portrait of the two children and from its exploration of the blend of superstition and communal spirit existing in an isolated settlement," noted Crouch. Cindy Darling Codell, writing in *School Library Journal,* commented that Morpurgo's language "is lean, yet lyrical," and that his descriptive paragraphs "let readers taste the salt of the sea and feel the grit of the islander's lives." In *Growing Point* Fisher dubbed *Why the Whales Came* "a forceful and exciting narrative."

The Scilly Islands also provide a setting for Morpurgo's Whitbread Award-winning novel *Wreck of the Zanzibar,* the story of a childhood on Bryher Island as told through the diary of Laura, whose secret treasure is Zanzibar, a carved wooden tortoise. Laura's narrative is the record of a harsh life, of adversity and the will to overcome. Crouch commented that *The Wreck of the Zanzibar,* while a short book, is "by no means a slight one," and praised the "beautiful timing throughout." A further tale with an island setting is recounted in *Ghost of Grania O'Malley,* a story set off the coast of Ireland and involving young Jessie, her American cousin Jack, and the ghost of the female pirate Grania O'Malley as they battle to prevent the ecological destruction of the island.

Morpurgo tells another animal-centered story in *Jo-Jo, the Melon Donkey,* a picture book for older children that is set in sixteenth-century Venice. Jo-Jo, a bedraggled old donkey owned by a melon farmer, is laughed at when he stands in the town's main square. The Doge's (chief magistrate's) daughter decides to be his friend, however, and when offered any horse in the kingdom, she opts for Jo-Jo, to her father's disgust. Ultimately, Jo-Jo helps to save the city from a flood and becomes a hero, whereupon the Doge allows the girl her wish. Amy Spaulding, writing in *School Library Journal,* noted that the "writing style follows that of the literary fairy tale, being at once simple and elegant." A *Kirkus Reviews* critic commented that, "with a nice blend of humor and sadness, Morpurgo brings to life the vibrancy of 16th-century Venice."

Illustrated by Christian Birmingham, *The Dancing Bear* features another animal in its picture-book story about young singer Roxanne and the orphaned bear cub she has raised. When a film crew comes to her remote village to make a video, Roxanne is lured by bright lights, and decides ultimately to leave with the group, pursuing fame and fortune as an entertainer. Her bear dies the following day. Although enjoying the poignant story, *School Library Journal* contributor Kathy East felt that Morpurgo's lesson is "likely to appeal more to adults, who will relate to the elderly narrator and his style, than to children."

In his picture books, Morpurgo often teams with illustrator Michael Foreman. In *The Rainbow Bear,* for example, the collaborators bring to life a story about a polar bear that decides to hunt rainbows rather than seals. The book is "a fable about the folly of trying to become something that you naturally are not," according to London *Observer* critic Kate Kellaway. As the reviewer further noted, Morpurgo's story is "gracefully told and elegantly concluded." Other picture-book collaborations between Morpurgo and Foreman include *Cockadoodle-Doo, Mr. Sultana!, Gentle Giant, Little Albatross,* and *Dolphin Boy.* A retelling of a traditional story about a rooster that refuses to be cheated out of a button it finds, *Cockadoodle-Doo, Mr. Sultana!* was praised by *School Librarian* critic Mary Medlicott as "rumbustiously full of life," with language "as rich as a plum pudding." *Dolphin Boy,* in which an impoverished seaside town is entertained by a group of dolphins, was praised by a *Kirkus Reviews* critic as "a happy tale" that "celebrates a collective act of kindness." Other illustrators noted for their collaboration with Morpurgo include Gary Blythe, Tony Ross, and Christian Birmingham.

As it does in his picture books, Morpurgo's love of animals also finds its way into his writing for young adults. In *Little Foxes,* for example, young Billy feels attracted to the wildlife living near a ruined church; the mythic Yeti save a lost boy in *King of the Cloud Forests;* Ocky the chimpanzee becomes a boy's companion in *Mr. Nobody's Eyes,* and giant turtles populate a child's dreams in *The Sandman and the Turtles, Farm Boy* details the memories of four generations of an English farming family, and in *Toro! Toro!* a man recalls his love for a bull in his native Spain. Reviewing *King of the Cloud Forests,* Jacqueline Simms wrote in the *Times Literary Supplement* that Morpurgo's "marvelous adventure story . . . will surely become a perennial favourite," and *Bulletin of the Center for Children's Books* contributor Roger Sutton predicted the "brief and dramatic novel . . . may woo reluctant readers back to the fold." "Morpurgo's storytelling style is unhurried," noted *School Library Journal* critic Lee Bock in a review of *Farm Boy,* while a *Kirkus Reviews* contributor called the book "a small gem" and an "expertly crafted reminder that stories can link generations." In *School Library Journal,* Shawn Brommer described *Toro! Toro!* as "ideal

for reluctant readers" in its focus "on the loss and grief that grows out of times of war."

Like *Toro! Toro!,* many of Morpurgo's novels are set during wartime and focus on the repercussions of political aggression. *Waiting for Anya* addresses the plight of Jewish children in France during World War II, while in *Escape from Shangri-La* an old man's memories of rescuing British forces from Dunkirk are rekindled by a granddaughter's affection. Another old man reflects on his life from boyhood to his years of soccer-playing as a youth, and then his capture by enemy troops during World War II in *Billy the Kid.* Returning to World War I, *Private Peaceful* follows the recollections of a young boy who, by lying about his age, followed his older brother from the family's farm into the British Army and, ultimately, into the trenches at the war's front lines.

Waiting for Anya is set in the Pyrenees just after the surrender of the French forces. Jo, a young shepherd, becomes involved in a scheme to save the local children when he discovers that a man named Benjamin is hiding them at a farm near the village of Lescun. Benjamin smuggles groups of these children across the border into Spain; he is also waiting for his own daughter, Anya, to make her way to his safe house from Paris. Jo begins delivering supplies to the farm, a job that becomes far riskier after the Nazis occupy Lescun and threaten to kill anyone aiding fugitives. Soon, however, the entire town is aiding the effort to smuggle the children across the border. Although Benjamin is captured and sent to Auschwitz, Anya's fate is more heartening, in Morpurgo's "gripping, clearly written story," as Ellen Fader described it in *Horn Book.* Crouch, reviewing the novel in *Junior Bookshelf,* called *Waiting for Anya* "an intensely exciting story guaranteed to keep a sensitive reader on the edge of his chair." Morpurgo's story is "rich in the qualities which make for critical approval," Crouch added, concluding that while "there have been many Second World War stories for the young, none . . . deals more convincingly with its perils and dilemmas."

In *Escape from Shangri-La* an old tramp named Popsicle turns out to be Cessie's long-lost grandfather. When the old man has a stroke, he is admitted to the Shangri-La nursing home, but his heath quickly declines. Finally Cessie finds her grandfather's real home: an old lifeboat that was used to help in the evacuation of British forces from Dunkirk during World War II. From a photograph and news clippings, Cessie learns that her grandfather took part in this heroic effort. After a faded photo of the Frenchwoman who hid him from the Germans after he fell overboard during the rescue effort makes Popsicle recall the past, Cessie helps her grandfather and other unhappy residents of the home make a break for it. Together they head to France to track down this woman, only to discover that she never returned from German arrest in 1940. "Readers will enjoy the climactic adventure and respond on a deeper

Cover of Morpurgo's award-winning novel Private Peaceful, *in which readers follow a young teen into battle during World War II.* (Scholastic, 2006. Reproduced by permission of Scholastic, Inc.)

level to the friendship between a spirited child and a lifelong loner," wrote John Peters in a *Booklist* review of *Escape from Shangri-La.*

Fourteen-year-old Thomas Peaceful is the narrator of Morpurgo's highly lauded novel *Private Peaceful,* in which "exquisitely written vignettes explore bonds of brotherhood that cannot be broken by the physical and psychological horrors" of World War I, according to *Horn Book* contributor Peter D. Sieruta. After Thomas's older brother Charlie enlists in the British Army and ships out for France, the younger teen lies about his age and signs up as well. In what *Booklist* critic Hazel Rochman described as a "terse and beautiful narrative," Thomas recalls his life from the cold depth of a trench, realizing that he will likely not survive the battle to be waged the following day. "Using first-person narration, Morpurgo draws readers into this young man's life, relating memories that are idyllic, sobering, and poignant," wrote *School Library Journal* contributor Delia

Fritz. The plot builds through the tragedy of a brother's mental illness, a frustrated love, the indignities of poverty, and a father's death. In praise of the novel, Rochman added that Morpurgo's suspenseful ending is "shocking, honest, and unforgettable."

Taking a lighter tone than he does in many of his stories focusing on war, Morpurgo introduces a spirited preteen girl through the pages of a decades-old diary in *The Amazing Story of Adolphus Tips.* The diary is given by Lily Tregenza to her grandson, Boowie, and through it Boowie gets to know a new side of the older woman he knows only as Grandma. Lily, a spirited young girl, watches her father leave to fight in World War II when she is twelve. When the family is forced to leave their Devon farmhouse on the English coast, so that the area can be used by U.S. Army troops rehearsing for the invasion of the French coast at Normandy, Lily's beloved cat Tips becomes missing. Worried about her cat, as well as about her father's safety, Lily learns to deal with both through her friendship with an African-American soldier named Adolphus. Lily's "personal story of anger and love is as gripping as the war drama"

Cover of Morpurgo's quirky middle-grade novel The Amazing Story of Adolphus Tips, *which finds a cat using up its nine lives during wartime.* (Scholastic Press, 2005. Photographs: cat © Corbis; background © The Imperial War Museum. Reproduced by permission of Scholastic, Inc.)

within her tale is set, according to Rochman, while in *Kirkus Reviews* a critic praised the girl's narration as "clear and believable."

Turning to his memories of his school years, Morpurgo sets *The War of Jenkins' Ear* in an English boarding school. Here young Toby Jenkins meets a remarkable boy named Christopher who claims to be the reincarnation of Jesus Christ. Although Christopher begins to develop a following among the students, he is betrayed by one of his friends and expelled from the school for blasphemy. *Quill and Quire* contributor Joanne Schott commented of the novel that "a strict school of 40 years ago makes a credible setting and gives scope for the complex relationships Morpurgo uses to examine questions of belief and credulity, deception and self-deception, loyalty and the pressure of doubt." Tim Rausch, writing in *School Library Journal,* called *The War of Jenkins' Ear* a book that "tackles provocative themes, dealing with the issues of hate, revenge, prejudice, and especially faith in an intelligent and fresh manner."

In *Kensuke's Kingdom* Morpurgo transports readers to an exotic setting. Here a young boy, who fell overboard from his family's boat, makes his way to a remote island. On his own except for a dog he befriends, the boy meets a mysterious old Japanese man, the Kensuke of the title, who slowly allows the boy into his heart. From an island, readers are transported into the past in *The Last Wolf,* which finds an old man researching his family tree on a computer his granddaughter has let him use. While doing his research, the man stumbles across an account taking place during the Jacobite rebellion in Scotland in 1745, when a young boy whose parents had been killed found a similarly orphaned wolf pup. Together the two managed to escape to Canada and a new life. *Kensuke's Kingdom* "must be ranked alongside Morpurgo's best," declared Linda Newbery in a *School Librarian* review, the critic adding that, "like several of his most successful stories, [the novel] has the feel of a fable."

Taking place in 2001, *Out of the Ashes* finds thirteen-year-old Becky Morley keeping a diary of the disastrous outbreak of hoof-and-mouth disease that has broken out in England. Becky, a farmer's daughter, is proud of her dad and loves her country life and her horse. All this changes as the epidemic reaches their Devon farm, as it did all three of the author's own farms in his Farms for City Children program. Within a matter of months the work of a lifetime has been destroyed for the Morleys and other farmers like them, although Morpurgo ends his novel on a positive note. George Hunt, writing in *Books for Keeps,* dubbed *Out of the Ashes* a "short novel powerfully told," and a *Times Educational Supplement* critic described the book as a "hard-hitting" and "heartfelt account" of a contemporary tragedy.

In addition to his original stories, Morpurgo has also breathed new life into old legends, from the stories of King Arthur to Aesop's Fables, Beowulf, a new version of the legend of Robin Hood, and a version of *Sir Gawain and the Green Knight* featuring Foreman's illustrations. *Arthur, High King of Britain,* which Morpurgo reshapes as a time-travel adventure, was dubbed "the real thing—darkness and all," by Heather McCammond-Watts in her *Bulletin of the Center for Children's Books* review. With *Robin of Sherwood* added twists such as an albino Marion create an "outstanding new version of the Robin Hood legend," according to Nancy Zachary in *Voice of Youth Advocates.* Morpurgo's version of *Sir Gawain and the Green Knight* is introduced to new generations through what Connie C. Rockman described in *School Library Journal* as "the vibrant and compelling voice of a storyteller," and a *Kirkus Reviews* writer praised it as a "handsomely packaged" and "fluid translation of the 14th-century tale."

Biographical and Critical Sources

BOOKS

Children's Literature Review, Volume 51, Thomson Gale (Detroit, MI), 1999, pp. 116-151.

Hobson, Margaret, Jennifer Madden, and Ray Pryterch, *Children's Fiction Sourcebook: A Survey of Children's Books for 6-13 Year Olds,* Ashgate Publishing (Aldershot, Hampshire, England), 1992, pp. 154-155.

St. James Guide to Young-Adult Writers, 2nd edition, edited by Tom Pendergast and Sara Pendergast, St. James Press (Detroit, MI), 1999, pp. 603-605.

PERIODICALS

Booklist, January 1, 1996, Ilene Cooper, interview with Morpurgo, p. 816; October 1, 1996, Carolyn Phelan, review of *Robin of Sherwood,* p. 350; June 1, 1997, Kathleen Squires, review of *The Butterfly Lion,* p. 1704; September 15, 1998, John Peters, review of *Escape from Shangri-La,* p. 231; February 15, 2004, Todd Morning, review of *Toro! Toro!,* p. 1060; April 15, 2004, Connie Fletcher, review of *Gentle Giant,* p. 1447; October 1, 2004, Hazel Rochman, review of *Private Peaceful,* p. 326; November 1, 2004, Carolyn Phelan, review of *Sir Gawain and the Green Knight,* p. 480; May 1, 2005, Hazel Rochman, review of *The McElderry Book of Aesop's Fables,* p. 1588; April 15, 2006, Hazel Rochman, review of *The Amazing Story of Adolphus Tips,* p. 59; March 1, 2007, Linda Perkins, review of *Beowulf,* p. 74.

Books for Keeps, September, 1997, Clive Barnes, review of *Sam's Duck,* p. 23; May, 1998, Gwynneth Bailey, review of *Red Eyes at Night,* p. 24; March, 1999, Rosemary Stores, review of *Cockadoodle-Doo, Mr.*

Sultana!, p. 21; May, 1999, review of *The Rainbow Bear*, p. 6; January, 2002, George Hunt, review of *Out of the Ashes*, p. 23; March, 2002, George Hunt, review of *Toro! Toro!*, p. 22.

Bulletin of the Center for Children's Books, July-August, 1988, Roger Sutton, review of *King of the Cloud Forests*, pp. 234-235; May, 1995, Heather McCammond-Watts, review of *Arthur, High King of Britain*, p. 317; December, 2004, Deborah Stevenson, review of *Private Peaceful*, p. 177.

Growing Point, November, 1980, Margery Fisher, review of *The Nine Lives of Montezuma*, p. 3776; November, 1982, Margery Fisher, review of *War Horse*, p. 3989; January, 1984, Margery Fisher, review of *Twist of Gold*, pp. 4183-4184; January, 1987, Margery Fisher, review of *Why the Whales Came*, p. 4749; November, 1989, pp. 5240-5245.

Horn Book, December, 1983, Kate M. Flanagan, review of *War Horse*, pp. 711-712; July-August, 1991, Ellen Fader, review of *Waiting for Anya*, p. 458; March-April, 1996, Elizabeth S. Watson, review of *The Wreck of the Zanzibar*, p. 198; November-December, 2004, Peter D. Sieruta, review of *Private Peaceful*, p. 713.

Junior Bookshelf, December, 1980, D.A. Young, review of *The Nine Lives of Montezuma*, p. 294; December, 1985, Marcus Crouch, review of *Why the Whales Came*, p. 279; August, 1988, pp. 179-80; December, 1989, pp. 298-299; February, 1991, Marcus Crouch, review of *Waiting for Anya*, pp. 35-36; June, 1992, pp. 113-114; August, 1995, Marcus Crouch, review of *The Wreck of the Zanzibar*, p. 148.

Kirkus Reviews, December 1, 1987, review of *Jo-Jo, the Melon Donkey*, p. 1677; April 15, 1997, review of *The Butterfly Lion*, p. 645; December 15, 1998, review of *Farm Boy;* September 15, 2004, review of *Private Peaceful*, p. 916; October 15, 2004, review of *Sir Gawain and the Green Knight*, p. 1011; January 1, 2005, review of *Dolphin Boy*, p. 55; June 1, 2005, review of *The McElderry Book of Aesop's Fables*, p. 641; April 1, 2006, review of *The Amazing Story of Adolphus Tips*, p. 352; October 15, 2006, reviews of *I Believe in Unicorns* and *Beowulf*, p. 1075.

Magpies, November, 1999, Catherine McClellan, review of *Wombat Goes Walkabout*, p. 6.

Observer (London, England), October 24, 1999, review of *Wombat Goes Walkabout*, p. 13, Kate Kellaway, review of *The Rainbow Bear*, p. 13.

Publishers Weekly, May 12, 1997, pp. 76-77; February 12, 1999, review of *Joan of Arc of Domremy*, p. 95; December 6, 2004, review of *Private Peaceful*, p. 60.

Quill and Quire, July, 1993, Joanne Schott, review of *The War of Jenkins' Ear*, p. 59.

School Librarian, autumn, 1998, Norton Hodges, review of *Escape from Shangri-La*, p. 147; spring, 1999, Jam Cooper, review of *Joan of Arc of Domremy*, pp. 40-41; summer, 1999, Mary Medlicott, review of *Cockadoodle-Doo, Mr. Sultana!*, p. 79; winter, 1999, Linda Newbery, review of *Kensuke's Kingdom*, p. 192; spring, 2001, Chris Brown, review of *Billy the Kid*, pp. 47-48; summer, 2001, Nikki Gamble, review of *The Silver Swan*, p. 90; autumn, 2001, Chris Brown, review of *Out of the Ashes*, pp. 158-159.

School Library Journal, February, 1987, Cindy Darling Codell, review of *Why the Whales Came*, p. 82; April, 1988, Amy Spaulding, review of *Jo-Jo, the Melon Donkey*, p. 87; July, 1995, Helen Gregory, review of *Arthur, High King of Britain*, p. 89; September, 1995, Tim Rausch, review of *The War of Jenkins' Ear*, p. 219; May, 1996, Kathy East, review of *The Dancing Bear*, p. 114; August, 1997, Gebregeorgis Yohannes, review of *The Butterfly Lion*, p. 158; March, 1999, Lee Bock, review of *Farm Boy*, p. 212; May, 1999, Shirley Wilton, review of *Joan of Arc of Domremy*, p. 128; April, 2001, Edith Ching, review of *The Kingfisher Book of Great Boy Stories: A Treasury of Classics from Children's Literature*, p. 146; March, 2004, Kathy Krasniewicz, review of *Gentle Giant*, p. 120; May, 2004, Shawn Brommer, review of *Toro! Toro!*, p. 154; October, 2004, Connie C. Rockman, review of *Sir Gawain and the Green Knight*, p. 172; November, 2004, Delia Fritz, review of *Private Peaceful*, p. 150; June, 2005, review of *The McElderry Book of Aesop's Fables*, p. 140; August, 2006, Jane G. Connor, review of *The Amazing Story of Adolphus Tips*, p. 126; December, 2006, Susan Helper, review of *I Believe in Unicorns*, p. 110.

Times Educational Supplement, February 8, 2002, review of *The Last Wolf, Toro! Toro!*, and *Out of the Ashes*, pp. 20-21; November 5, 2004, Geraldine Brennan, "Dear Mr. Morpingo: Inside the World of Michael Morpurgo," p. 19.

Times Literary Supplement, March 26, 1982, Josephine Karavasil, "Matters of Rhythm and Register," p. 347; February 19, 1988, Jacqueline Simms, "Magic Man," p. 200.

Voice of Youth Advocates, April, 1984, Diane G. Yates, review of *War Horse*, p. 32; February, 1997, Nancy Zachary, review of *Robin of Sherwood*, p. 330; June, 1998, Kathleen Beck, review of *The War of Jenkins' Ear*, pp. 103-104.

ONLINE

Achuka, http://www.achuka.com/ (April 20, 2003), "Michael Morpurgo."

Michael Morpurgo Home Page, http://www.michaelmorpurgo.org (November 15, 2007).

Young Writer Online, http://www.mystworld.com/youngwriter/ (February 12, 2003), "Michael Morpurgo."*

*   *   *

MR. WIZARD
See HERBERT, Don

*   *   *

MUNRO, Roxie 1945-

Personal

Born September 5, 1945, in Mineral Wells, TX; daughter of Robert Enoch (an automotive shop owner and boat builder) and Margaret (a librarian) Munro; married Bo Zaunders (a writer and photographer), May 17, 1986. *Education:* Attended University of Maryland, 1963-65, Maryland Institute College of Art, 1965-66, and Ohio University, 1969-70; University of Hawaii, B.F.A., 1969, graduate work, 1970-71. *Hobbies and other interests:* Travel, reading.

Addresses

Home—New York, NY. *Office*—43-01 21st St., Studio No. 340, Long Island City, NY 11101. *E-mail*—roxie@ roxiemunro.com.

Career

Roxie (dress company), Washington, DC, dress designer and manufacturer, 1972-76; television courtroom artist in Washington, DC, 1976-81; freelance artist, beginning 1976. *Exhibitions:* Work included in group shows staged at New York Public Library, New York, NY; Detroit Institute of Arts, Detroit, MI; High Museum, Atlanta, GA; Boston Atheneum, Boston, MA; Corcoran Gallery of Art, Washington, DC; Victoria and Albert Museum, London, England; Art Gallery of Ontario, Toronto, Ontario, Canada; Fine Arts Museum of San Francisco, San Francisco, CA, and others. Solo shows staged at Foundry Gallery, Washington, DC; Delaware Museum of Art; Zimmerli Museum, Rutgers University, Rutgers, NJ; Gotham Book Mart, New York, NY; Marin-Price Gallery, Chevy Chase, MD; Simie Maryles Gallery, Provincetown, MA; and Michael Ingbar Gallery of Architectural Art, New York, NY. Works included in many private and public collections.

Member

New York Artists' Equity, Society of Children's Book Writers and Illustrators.

Awards, Honors

Yaddo painting fellowship, 1980; Best Illustrated Children's Books citation, *New York Times,* and Best Children's Books citation, *Time,* both 1985, both for *The Inside-Outside Book of New York City;* Best Book selection, *School Library Journal,* 1996, for *The Inside-Outside Book of Libraries,* 2001, for *Feathers, Flaps, and Flops;* Bank Street College of Education Best Books designation, for *Gargoyles, Girders, and Glass Houses, Crocodiles, Camels, and Dugout Canoes,* and *The Inside-Outside Book of Washington, DC;* Notable Children's Trade Book in the Field of Social Studies designation, National Council on the Social Studies/ Children's Book Council; other awards.

Writings

SELF-ILLUSTRATED

Color New York, Arbor House (New York, NY), 1985.

The Inside-Outside Book of New York City, Dodd (New York, NY), 1985, revised edition, SeaStar Books (New York, NY), 2001.

The Inside-Outside Book of Washington, DC, Dutton (New York, NY), 1987.

Christmastime in New York City, Dodd (New York, NY), 1987.

Blimps, Dutton (New York, NY), 1989.

The Inside-Outside Book of London, Dutton (New York, NY), 1989.

The Inside-Outside Book of Paris, Dutton (New York, NY), 1992.

The Inside-Outside Book of Texas, SeaStar Books (New York, NY), 2001.

Mazescapes, SeaStar Books (New York, NY), 2001.

Doors, SeaStar Books (New York, NY), 2003.

Amazement Park, Chronicle Books (San Francisco, CA), 2005.

The Wild West Trail Ride Maze, Bright Sky Press (Albany, TX), 2006.

Circus, Chronicle Books (San Francisco, CA), 2006.

Mazeways: A to Z, Sterling Publishing (New York, NY), 2007.

Rodeo, Bright Sky Press (Albany, TX), 2007.

ILLUSTRATOR

Kay D. Weeks, *The Great American Landmark Adventure,* National Park Service and American Architectural Foundation (Washington, DC), 1982.

Diane Maddex, *Architects Make Zigzags: Looking at Architecture from A to Z,* Preservation Press (Washington, DC), 1986.

Kay D. Weeks, *American Defenders of Land, Sea, and Sky,* National Park Service (Washington, DC), 1996.

Julie Cummins, *The Inside-Outside Book of Libraries,* Dutton (New York, NY), 1996.

Bo Zaunders, *Crocodiles, Camels, and Dugout Canoes: Eight Adventurous Episodes,* Dutton (New York, NY), 1998.

Bo Zaunders, *Feathers, Flaps, and Flops: Fabulous Early Fliers,* Dutton (New York, NY), 2001.

Raymond D. Keene, *Learn Chess Fast: The Fun Way to Start Smart and Master the Game,* Bright Sky Press (Albany, TX), 2001.

Joseph Siano, editor, *The New York Times What's Doing around the World,* Lebhar-Friedman (New York, NY), 2001.

Bo Zaunders, *Gargoyles, Girders, and Glass Houses: Magnificent Master Builders,* Dutton (New York, NY), 2003.

Bo Zaunders, *The Great Bridge Building Contest,* Harry N. Abrams (New York, NY), 2004.

Michael P. Spradlin, *Texas Rangers: Legendary Lawmen,* Walker & Co. (New York, NY), 2008.

Contributor of illustrations to periodicals, including *New Yorker, Washington Post, U.S. News & World Report, Gourmet, Historic Preservation,* and *New Republic.*

Sidelights

Author and illustrator of the popular "Inside-Out" series, which focus on a selection of well-known cityscapes, Roxie Munro is an inveterate city watcher. She is also an artist with a unique visual sensibility, making her illustrations for her "Inside-Outside" series, as well as titles such as *Amazement Park, Rodeo,* and *Circus,* unique interactive experiences for young readers. "There's a wonderfully obsessive quality to her views," wrote Sam Swope in a review of *The Inside-Outside Book of New York City,* "as if she can't stop herself from capturing each water tower and skylight, each arch and colonnade."

Born in Mineral Wells, Texas, in 1945, Munro once told *SATA,* "Unlike many children's book creators, I don't have a lot of specific memories of my childhood. I remember mainly sensuous impressions: water running across rocks in a ditch, the dried fall leaves, the splash of waves across a boat's bow." Growing up in a small, rural town, much of Munro's spare time was spent "reading and daydreaming." Her parents encouraged their children to engage in independent, creative activities: drawing, making their own toys, and reading. The family also traveled a good deal together, and in annual vacations to the Northeast, South, and West Munro gained a familiarity with urban as well as rural America.

Munro's love of art inspired many early successes. In first grade she won a county art competition; in high school she was editor of the school yearbook and was also named "most talented" in her class. After studying art at the University of Maryland, the Maryland Institute College of Art, the University of Hawaii, and Ohio State University, Munro established a business as a dress designer, marketing her fashions to small boutiques in Washington, DC. She then freelanced for several years as a courtroom artist, working for newspapers and television. In 1981, Munro moved to New York City and continued her career as a freelance illustrator. Among her successes, she created cover art for fourteen issues of the prestigious *New Yorker* magazine, a periodical known for its distinctive covers.

Approaching book publishers, Munro was asked to come up with ideas for children's books, and *The Inside-Outside Book of New York City* was born. In this witty pictorial, Munro tells the story of the city visually, taking unique vantage points on well-known sites. For the Statue of Liberty, for instance, she looks not only at its exterior, but also from the inside out at the city. There are views of the inside of the New York Stock Exchange and of busy traffic. Other landmarks, viewed from both outside and inside, include St. Patrick's Cathedral and the animal cages at the Bronx Zoo. Munro looks through windows, behind bars, and even across theater footlights to get an intimate view of the city.

Winner of a *New York Times* Best Illustrated Children's Book Award in 1985, *The Inside-Outside Book of New York City* inaugurated a series of similar books, spanning the globe from London to Paris and also broadening its focus to depict Munro's home state of Texas. *The Inside-Outside Book of Texas* features pictures "ranging from the dramatic . . . to the mundane," according to a *Publishers Weekly* critic. Among the various sites and topics covered are a skyline of Dallas, ranch hands at chow time, the Texas Stadium (home of the Dallas Cowboys football team), the Lyndon B. Johnson Space Center in Houston, and various wildlife scenes. "Bright, cheerful colors invite the eye," noted *School Library Journal* contributor Ruth Semrau, and a *Horn Book* reviewer wrote that Munro not only introduces young readers to landmarks of the state, "but also cleverly stretches the definitional boundaries of inside and outside."

Extending her view skyward, Munro's *Mazescapes* invites readers to find their way through interconnected aerial mazes of cities and the countryside using any of six punch-out cars provided with the book. Alison Kastner, writing in *School Library Journal,* predicted that older fans of the "Where's Waldo" books who are looking for "something a little more challenging will find it in Munro's brightly colored and intricate paintings." The challenge the illustrator poses here is to find the way to the zoo and back home again through maze-like renderings of towns, cities, and countryside. Peter D. Sieruta observed in a *Horn Book* review that *Mazescapes* contains "the kind of dizzyingly detailed artwork that sends adults running for the Dramamine yet almost always entrances kids."

Dirigibles also get the Munro treatment in *Blimps,* a book done with "accurate and complete detail," according to a reviewer in *New Advocate.* "The fun thing here was the research," Munro noted in *Children's Book Illustration and Design.* "I got a three-hour ride in a blimp over Manhattan, and in England visited the biggest blimp-making factory in the world." A group of clowns guide readers through the hide-and-seek and lift-the-flap challenges in *Circus,* and other amusements await readers in *Ranch, Rodeo,* and *Amazement Park.* A collection of twelve mazes depicted in "cartoon art [that] is eye-catching and colorful," according to *School Library Journal* critic Julie Roach, *Amazement Park* features "intricate, colored-ink illustrations [that] beguile the eye with their exquisite attention to detail," in the opinion of a *Kirkus Reviews* contributor.

As an illustrator, Munro has also worked with a variety of writers, including her husband, Swedish photographer, artist, and writer Bo Zaunders. Illustrating his *Crocodiles, Camels, and Dugout Canoes: Eight Adventurous Episodes,* her illustrations add "even more liveliness" to the text, according to *Booklist* contributor Susan Dove Lempke. A reviewer for *Publishers Weekly* also commended the book-sized gathering of travelers and explorers, noting that the couple's enthusiasm "shine[s] through the pages of this absorbing picture book." A second husband-and-wife collaboration, *Feathers, Flaps, and Flops: Fabulous Early Fliers,* depicts

In Amazement Park *Roxie Munro treats readers to an assortment of mazes guaranteed to challenge even the most experienced maze afficionado.*
(Chronicle Books, 2005. Illustration © 2005 by Roxie Munro. Reproduced by permission.)

the exploits of some early aviators in seven sketches, while *Gargoyles, Girders, and Glass Houses: Magnificent Master Builders* focuses on seven architects who tackled building projects in which "enormous obstacles . . . would have daunted less courageous, less obsessive geniuses," according to *Horn Book* critic Sally P. Bloom. In *School Library Journal,* Louise L. Sherman praised Munro's "fine illustrations" in *Feathers, Flaps, and Flops,* and a *Horn Book* reviewer wrote that "playful perspective is a Roxie Munro hallmark." Munro's "captivating" illustrations for *Gargoyles, Girders, and Glass Houses,* in introducing readers to the works of

Mimar Koca Sinan, Antoni Gaudi, and others, "provides clear visual reference" and reflect the "grandeur and the subtle details" included in Zaunders' text. Citing the illustrator's "use of unusual perspectives" and "well-chosen details," Carolyn Phelan concluded in her *Booklist* review that Munro's art depicts monumental works of architecture as "within the scale of human use and understanding."

Characterizing her illustration work as "developing from perception," Munro once explained to *SATA* that it is also "very visual, spatial. Ideas develop from a kind of active seeing. When I walk down a street, ride a bus, or

Cover of Circus, *which features Munro's unique interactive mix of text and art.* (Illustration © 2006 by Roxie Munro. Used by permission of Chronicle Books, LLC, San Francisco. Visit ChronicleBooks.com.)

go up an escalator, I FEEL the changing space. I see patterns, paintings everywhere. My mind organizes reality. I'll notice two gray cars, a red car, a black car, and two more red cars—aha!—a pattern."

Biographical and Critical Sources

BOOKS

Children's Book Illustration and Design, edited by Julie Cummins, Library of Applied Design (New York, NY), 1992.

Children's Books and Their Creators, edited by Anita Silvey, Houghton Mifflin (New York, NY), 1995.

PERIODICALS

Booklist, October 15, 1996, Carolyn Phelan, review of *The Inside-Outside Book of Libraries,* p. 426; October 15, 1998, Susan Dove Lempke, review of *Crocodiles, Camels, and Dugout Canoes: Eight Adventurous Episodes,* p. 420; April 1, 2001, Gillian Engberg, review of *The Inside-Outside Book of Texas,* p. 1475; November 1, 2004, Carolyn Phelan, review of *Gargoyles, Girders, and Glass Houses: Magnificent Master Builders,* p. 498; December 1, 2004, Carolyn Phelan, review of *The Great Bridge-Building Contest,* p. 672.

Bulletin of the Center for Children's Books, October, 1996, Elizabeth Bush, review of *The Inside-Outside Book of Libraries,* p. 53; January, 2005, Elizabeth Bush, review of *Gargoyles, Girders, and Glass Houses,* p. 233.

Horn Book, March-April, 1992, Ellen Fader, review of *The Inside-Outside Book of Paris,* p. 221; September-October, 1996, Roger Sutton, review of *The Inside-Outside Book of Libraries,* p. 611; January-February, 1999, review of *Crocodiles, Camels, and Dugout Canoes,* p. 85; May-June, 2001, review of *The Inside-Outside Book of Texas,* p. 350; July-August, 2001, review of *Feathers, Flaps, and Flops: Fabulous Early Fliers,* p. 480; September-October, 2001, Peter D. Sieruta, review of *Mazescapes,* p. 577; November-December, 2004, Susan P. Bloom, review of *Gargoyles, Girders, and Glass Houses,* p. 732; May-June, 2005, Peter D. Sieruta, review of *Amazement Park,* p. 311.

Kirkus Reviews, November 15, 2004, review of *Gargoyles, Girders, and Glass Houses,* p. 1095; April 1, 2005, review of *Amazement Park,* p. 422; October 15, 2006, review of *Circus,* p. 1076.

New Advocate, winter, 1990, review of *Blimps,* p. 69.

New York Times Book Review, May 20, 2001, Sam Swope, "Oz on the Hudson," p. 30.

Publishers Weekly, November 29, 1991, review of *The Inside-Outside Book of Paris,* p. 50; August 19, 1996, review of *The Inside-Outside Book of Libraries,* p. 65; August 31, 1998, review of *Crocodiles, Camels, and Dugout Canoes,* p. 76; February 26, 2001, review of *The Inside-Outside Book of Texas,* p. 88; July 30, 2001, review of *Mazescapes,* p. 86.

School Library Journal, August, 1996, Nancy Menaldi-Scanlan, review of *The Inside-Outside Book of Libraries,* p. 134; November, 1998, Patricia Manning, review of *Crocodiles, Camels, and Dugout Canoes,* p. 144; June, 2001, Ruth Semrau, review of *The Inside-Outside Book of Texas,* p. 140; July, 2001, Louise L. Sherman, review of *Feathers, Flaps, and Flops,* p. 101; August, 2001, Alison Kastner, review of *Mazescapes,* p. 171; September, 2004, John Sigwald, review of *Ranch,* p. 190; December, 2004, Steven Engelfried, review of *Gargoyles, Girders, and Glass Houses,* p. 172; March, 2005, Edith Ching, review of *The Great Bridge-Building Contest,* p. 205; May, 2005, Julie Roach, review of *Amazement Park,* p. 112; December, 2006, Maryann H. Owen, review of *Circus,* p. 110.

Time, December 23, 1985, Stefan Kanfer, review of *The Inside-Outside Book of New York City,* p. 62.

ONLINE

Roxie Munro Home Page, http://www.roxiemunro.com (November 15, 2007).

N

NELSON, Suzanne 1976-

Personal
Born 1976; married. *Hobbies and other interests:* Travel.

Addresses
Home—Morristown, NJ.

Career
Novelist and editor.

Writings

"STUDENTS ACROSS THE SEVEN SEAS" SERIES; YOUNG-ADULT NOVELS

The Sound of Munich, Speak (New York, NY), 2006.
Heart and Salsa, Speak (New York, NY), 2006.

Biographical and Critical Sources

PERIODICALS

School Library Journal, June, 2006, review of *The Sound of Munich,* p. 164; July, 2006, Emily Garrett, review of *Heart and Salsa,* p. 109.

ONLINE

Penguin Group Web site, http://us.penguingroup/com/ (November 15, 2007), interview with Nelson.*

*   *   *

NEWBERY, Linda 1952-

Personal
Born August 12, 1952, in Romford, Essex, England; married. *Hobbies and other interests:* Reading, gardening, swimming, going to the cinema and theatre, walking, wildlife.

Addresses
Home—Northamptonshire, England. *Agent*—Patrick Janson-Smith, Christopher Little Literary Agency Ltd., 125 Moore Park Rd., London SW6 4PS, England. *E-mail*—L.newbery@btinternet.com.

Career
Writer and reviewer. Taught English in an Oxfordshire comprehensive school until 2000; tutor for Arvon Foundation. Worked variously as a secretary, riding instructor, and camp counselor.

Member
Scattered Authors' Society, Society of Authors (UK), Royal Society of Arts.

Awards, Honors
Writers' Guild Award nomination, for *The Wearing of the Green;* Carnegie Medal nomination, Birmingham Book Award shortlist, and Pick of the Year selection, Federation of Children's Book Groups, all 1995, all for *The Shouting Wind;* Carnegie Medal nomination, for *From E to You, Sisterland,* and *At the Firefly Gate;* Carnegie Medal nomination, and London *Guardian* Children's Fiction Prize shortlist, both for *The Shell House;* Calderdale Book of the Year shortlist, for *Polly's March;* Nestlé Children's Book Prize shortlist, for *Catcall;* Costa Children's Book of the Year, 2006, for *Set in Stone.*

Writings

YOUNG-ADULT NOVELS

Run with the Hare, Armada (London, England), 1988.
Hard and Fast, Armada (London, England), 1989.
Some Other War, Armada (London, England), 1990.

The Kind Ghosts, Lions (London, England), 1991.
The Wearing of the Green, Lions (London, England), 1992.
Riddle Me This, Lions (London, England), 1993.
The Shouting Wind, Collins (London, England), 1995.
The Cliff Path, Collins (London, England), 1995.
A Fear of Heights, Collins (London, England), 1996.
The Nowhere Girl, Adlib (London, England), 1997.
Flightsend, Scholastic (London, England), 1999.
(With Chris d'Lacey) *From E to You,* Scholastic (London, England), 2000.
The Damage Done, Scholastic (London, England), 2001.
No Way Back, Orchard (London, England), 2001.
Break Time, Orchard (London, England), 2001.
The Shell House, David Fickling Books (New York, NY), 2002.
Windfall, Orchard (London, England), 2002.
Sisterland, David Fickling Books (New York, NY), 2004.
Lost Boy, Orion (London, England), 2005, David Fickling Books (New York, NY), 2008.
Set in Stone, David Fickling Books (New York, NY), 2006.
Nevermore, Orion (London, England), 2008.

FOR CHILDREN

The Marmalade Pony, Hippo (London, England), 1994, published in *The Big Animal Magic Book,* Hippo (London, England), 1998.
Smoke Cat, illustrated by Anne Sharp, Hippo (London, England), 1995, published in *The Big Animal Ghost Book,* Scholastic (London, England), 1999.
Ice Cat, illustrated by Peter Kavanaugh, Scholastic (London, England), 1997.
Whistling Jack, illustrated by Anthony Lewis, Collins (London, England), 1997.
Star's Turn, Corgi Pups (London, England), 1999.
The Cat with Two Names, Hippo (London, England), 2000.
Blitz Boys, A. & C. Black (London, England), 2000.
(Reteller) Hans Christian Andersen, *The Little Mermaid,* illustrated by Bee Willey, Scholastic (London, England), 2001.
Mr. Darwin and the Ape Boy, illustrated by Dave Hopkins, Pearson Longman (Harlow, England), 2004.
Polly's March, Usborne (London, England), 2004.
At the Firefly Gate, Orion (London, England), 2004, David Fickling Books (New York, NY), 2007.
Catcall, Orion (London, England), 2006.
A Dog Called Whatnot, illustrated by Georgie Ripper, Crabtree (New York, NY), 2006.
Andie's Moon, Usborne (London, England), 2007.
Posy, illustrated by Catherine Rayner, Orchard (London, England), 2008.

OTHER

Contributor to short story and poetry anthologies. Reviewer for *School Librarian, Armadillo,* London *Guardian,* and *Times Educational Supplement.*

Sidelights

Linda Newbery is an award-winning British author of fiction for children and young adults. A former educator, she published her debut work, *Run with the Hare,* in 1988. Since then, her young-adult titles have earned five Carnegie Medal nominations, and her 2006 novel *Set in Stone* earned the prestigious Costa Children's Book of the Year award.

Newbery's road to becoming a published author was a circuitous one. As she once told *SATA:* "When I started at secondary school, the strict headmistress took my form for a weekly lesson. One week, she asked us all what we wanted to be when we grew up. My answer, without hesitation, was: 'I want to be a writer, and have lots of cats.' Everyone laughed at this, and the headmistress looked rather disapproving. Not a real job, evidently." Newbery was determined to pursue her dream, however, and began keeping a journal of stories and, later, poems. "I didn't discover teenage fiction until I was in my twenties and training to be a teacher," she added. "As soon as I came across marvelous writers like Robert Cormier, Jill Paton Walsh, K.M. Peyton, and Aidan Cambers, the urge to write fiction returned."

Newbery first gained critical attention for novels such as *Some Other War* and *The Nowhere Girl,* which explore connections between Britain's past—especially during World War I and II—and its present. "Both wars interest me because they were a time of tremendous social change and upheaval, the First World War in particular," the author noted in an interview on the *Achuka* Web site. "That's why I began *Some Other War* with a very traditional set-up—the Essex village, the large country house and the twin brother and sister who are employed there as groom and maidservant. That very English way of life, for which we have a kind of collective nostalgia in spite of its blatant social inequalities, was about to disappear." In other works, Newbery added, "I wanted to show how the past brushes against the present; in *The Nowhere Girl,* it's the impact of the German occupation on a village in rural Normandy, rather than actual combat."

Newbery has also written a number of picture books for young readers, including *Ice Cat* and *Mr. Darwin and the Ape Boy.* "I've written for younger children, but I keep returning to young adult fiction because I love the scope it offers," Newbery once explained to *SATA.* "I always enjoy learning or doing something new while I write; besides a great deal of background reading, I've traveled for research purposes to Dublin, Normandy, Berlin, and the First World War battlefields in France and Belgium."

A novel with a contemporary setting, *From E to You,* coauthored by Chris d'Lacey, tells the story of the friendship that grows between Guy and Annabelle through their frequent e-mails. In the beginning, both teens closely guard their feelings, as they have been thrown together by their fathers, but as they gradually reveal painful events of the present and recent past, the two build trust in each other and the friendship blossoms. A contributor to *Publishers Weekly,* who noted that the male coauthor contributed the female character's missives while Newbery created the voice of the character Guy, concluded that the authors "shape . . . two very distinct and likable characters and a cleverly composite tale."

Newbery's first book to be widely reviewed in the United States was *The Shell House,* an intertwining novel in which two storylines center on Graveney Hall. In 1917, the time-setting for one of the stories, the Hall was a beautiful English country home, but by the early twenty-first century, wherein the second story is set, it has become the burned-out shell of the title. Both stories center on a young man's quest for identity. Greg, at the center of the contemporary plot, is a seventeen-year-old student whose attraction to one of his fellow students, a handsome young athlete named Jordan, has him confused. Greg meets Faith, a young Christian teenager, on the grounds of the burned-out estate, and the two challenge each other on spiritual matters. Romantically, Greg eventually connects with Jordan, who is more comfortable with his homosexuality, and Greg ultimately reveals his sexual preferences to his parents. Greg's story is intertwined with scenes from an earlier era that center on Edmund. Destined to inherit Graveney Hall, Edmund is a soldier in World War I when he meets Alex, another soldier, and falls in love. The feeling is mutual, and the two form a relationship that ends with Alex's death on the battlefield. Edmund returns home to Graveney Hall utterly changed by the war, and his attempts to return to normality, by becoming engaged or seeking solace from the church vicar, ultimately end in disaster.

While Newbery has frequently been praised for her sensitive yet evocative handling of the quest for sexual identity among young men past and present, a few aspects of *The Shell House* were not universally admired. A contributor to *Publishers Weekly,* for example, dubbed Greg's story "a pitch perfect tale of contemporary teenage life," but faulted the parallel story of Edmund in 1917 as "overly dramatic if occasionally moving." For a contributor to *Kirkus Reviews,* on the other hand, "the parallel stories play off each other perfectly." The occasionally awkward rendering of the issues at hand, especially faith in God and sexual orientation, are easily overlooked in relation to the book's overall accomplishment, the critic added: "flaws aside, it stands as an ambitious, multilayered, and above all literary contribution to a literature that all too often seeks to dodge complexity." In her *Booklist* review, Michelle Kaske offered a similar opinion of Newbery's two narratives, claiming that, "woven together, the strands coalesce into a dramatic, if not complex, combination of both contemporary and historical fiction."

Sisterland, dubbed a "long, powerful story of love, anger, racism, loss, and guilt across generations" by *Booklist* critic Hazel Rochman, centers on a contemporary British family. Seventeen-year-old Hilly, whose life is already complicated by her father's infidelity and her sister's skinhead boyfriend, faces even more changes

Cover of Linda Newbery's middle-grade novel **At the Firefly Gate,** *featuring artwork by Jess Meserve.* (Jacket design and artwork © 2004 by Jess Meserve. Reproduced by permission of Orion Children's Books, an imprint of the Orion Publishing Group Ltd.)

when Heidigran, her senile grandmother, moves into the family home. One day, as Hilly plays the piano for her grandmother, the music triggers the elderly woman's long-suppressed memories of a lost sister and a secret past. "The sheer abundance of plots and subplots keeps the pages turning," noted a contributor in *Publishers Weekly,* and Miriam Budin Lang stated in *School Library Journal* that the "combination of complex issues is undeniably ambitious." According to a critic in *Kirkus Reviews,* "Newbery smoothly weaves together past and present in two distinct, gripping storylines that eventually merge."

Newbery's supernatural tale *At the Firefly Gate* concerns Henry, a timid young boy who has moved with his family from London to a quiet English village. Henry strikes up an unlikely friendship with Dottie, an elderly neighbor, who regales the youngster with tales of her fiancée, a Royal Air Force navigator (also named Henry) who disappeared during a World War II mission. Soon young Henry notices a spectral figure waiting at the orchard gate during the evenings, and he also begins having strange dreams of himself as a wartime pilot. The author "writes well, drawing readers into

Henry's shifting reality slowly and letting his puzzlement work itself out," noted *Booklist* reviewer Carolyn Phelan. "An abundance of small satisfactions await readers attuned to this novel's gentle cadences," commented a *Publishers Weekly* contributor.

In the gothic tradition, *Set in Stone* follows Samuel Godwin, an aspiring artist who is hired to tutor Juliana and Marianne Farrow, the daughters of wealthy widower and landowner Ernest Farrow. Samuel soon learns that the despondent Juliana and the unpredictable Marianne are harboring a terrible secret, one that appears to be shared by their governess, Charlotte Agnew. "Newbery's touch is graceful as she unveils layers of the mystery to Samuel, Charlotte and readers," a critic observed in a *Kirkus Reviews* appraisal, and *School Library Journal* reviewer Carolyn Lehman wrote that Newbery's conclusion offers "a look back on the compromises and losses throughout the characters' lives." "Evocatively written and carefully crafted," *Set in Stone* "will tantalize readers," remarked Ilene Cooper in *Booklist.*

"One of the delights of writing for young people is that you can range widely in terms of subject matter and age group," Newbery explained to *SATA.* "I enjoy the freedom of working on a long and complex novel one month, a picture book or a poem the next."

Biographical and Critical Sources

PERIODICALS

Booklist, August, 2002, Michelle Kaske, review of *The Shell House,* p. 1946; March 1, 2004, Hazel Rochman, review of *Sisterland,* p. 1202; September 1, 2006, Ilene Cooper, review of *Set in Stone,* p. 111; February 15, 2007, Carolyn Phelan, review of *At the Firefly Gate,* p. 78.

Bookseller, February 17, 2006, review of *Set in Stone,* p. 34.

Bulletin of the Center for Children's Books, November, 2002, review of *The Shell House,* p. 119; June, 2004, Karen Coats, review of *Sisterland,* p. 431; December, 2006, Elizabeth Bush, review of *Set in Stone,* p. 183; April, 2007, Elizabeth Bush, review of *At the Firefly Gate,* p. 341.

Horn Book, March-April, 2004, Susan P. Bloom, review of *Sisterland,* p. 185; March-April, 2007, Joanna Rudge Long, review of *At the Firefly Gate,* p. 199.

Kirkus Reviews, July 1, 2002, review of *The Shell House,* p. 960; March 15, 2004, review of *Sisterland,* p. 275; October 15, 2006, review of *Set in Stone,* p. 1076; February 1, 2007, review of *At the Firefly Gate,* p. 127.

Kliatt, March, 2004, Claire Rosser, review of *Sisterland,* p. 15; September, 2004, Myra Marler, review of *The Shell House,* p. 24; November, 2006, Claire Rosser, review of *Set in Stone,* p. 14.

New York Times Book Review, June 17, 2007, Julie Just, review of *At the Firefly Gate,* p. 15.

Publishers Weekly, June 25, 2001, review of *From E to You,* p. 73; June 24, 2002, review of *The Shell House,* p. 59; March 29, 2004, review of *Sisterland,* p. 64; February 19, 2007, review of *At the Firefly Gate,* p. 170.

School Librarian, summer, 2001, Chris Brown, review of *The Cat with Two Names,* p. 90.

School Library Journal, August, 2002, Joanne K. Cecere, review of *The Shell House,* p. 196; April, 2004, Miriam Lang Budin, review of *Sisterland,* p. 160; February, 2007, Carolyn Lehman, review of *Set in Stone,* p. 124; March, 2007, Connie Tyrell Burns, review of *At the Firefly Gate,* p. 216.

Voice of Youth Advocates, December, 2006, Chris Carlson, review of *Set in Stone,* p. 430.

ONLINE

Achuka Web site, http://www.achuka.co.uk/ (June, 1999), "Achuka Interview: Linda Newbery."

Linda Newbery Home Page, http://www.lindanewbery.co.uk/ (October 31, 2007).

Orion Books Web site, http://www.orionbooks.co.uk/ (October 31, 2007), interview with Newbery.

*   *   *

NOONAN, Brandon 1979-

Personal

Born May 8, 1979, in Yuba City, CA. *Education:* University of Southern California B.F.A. (film).

Addresses

Home—Berkeley, CA.

Career

Screenwriter and novelist.

Writings

Plenty Porter (young-adult novel), Amulet (New York, NY), 2006.

Author of screenplays, including *Dem,* produced by Pretty Pictures, 2006, and *Arrow,* produced by Warner Bros. Contributor to periodicals, including *Swink* online.

Sidelights

Twelve-year-old Plenty Porter, the narrator of Brandon Noonan's coming-of-age novel, is the youngest of eleven children raised by her sharecropper father in rural Galesburg, Illinois. Set in the early 1950s, *Plenty*

Porter recreates the stifled relationships within the girl's disconnected family, where civilized human interactions take a back seat to survival amid economic hardship. For Plenty, a sensitive and perceptive preteen who stands out because of her height, a friendship with Ed Prindergast, the son of the local landowner, provides the perspective needed to strive for more in her own life and recognize that her outsider role in both her own family and society at large does not limit her future.

Noonan, a graduate of the film program at the University of Southern California, wrote his highly praised young-adult novel while working as a Hollywood screenwriter. Among the films he has contributed screenplays to are *Dem,* which Noonan adapted from the 1967 novel by William Melvin Kelley, and the martial-arts movie *Arrow.*

In reviewing Noonan's first work of fiction, a *Kirkus Reviews* writer praised *Plenty Porter* as "smooth and compelling reading," while Cindy Dobrez compared the novel to Harper Lee's classic *To Kill a Mockingbird.* While noting that the book features an ending that readers cannot predict, the *Kirkus Reviews* critic added that Noonan's first novel "occasionally has the feel of a writing exercise." "Plenty has a distinctive voice," wrote *Kliatt* contributor Janis Flint-Ferguson in an enthusiastic review of the book, "and her account of the year is poignant in its innocent retelling" of alcoholism, abuse, and an attempted suicide driven by an older sister's despair. Faith Brautigam, discussing *Plenty Porter* in *School Library Journal,* cited the novel's "stylistically innovative" opening and concluded that the book's "beautifully written sentences, . . . well-shaped plot," and independent-minded young heroine make Noonan "a writer to watch."

Biographical and Critical Sources

PERIODICALS

Booklist, April 15, 2006, Cindy Dobrez, review of *Plenty Porter,* p. 57.
Bulletin of the Center for Children's Books, September, 2006, Karen Coats, review of *Plenty Porter,* p. 26.

Cover of Brandon Noonan's young-adult novel **Plenty Porter,** *which attracted critical praise when it was published in 2006.* (Amulet Books, 2006. Photograph © 2006 by Corbis. Reproduced by permission.)

Kirkus Reviews, April 15, 2006, review of *Plenty Porter,* p. 413.
Kliatt, May, 2006, Janis Flint-Ferguson, review of *Plenty Porter,* p. 12.
School Library Journal, August, 2006, Faith Brautigam, review of *Plenty Porter,* p. 126.

ONLINE

Harry N. Abrams Web site, http://www.hnabooks.com/ (November 15, 2007), "Brandon Noonan."*

P

PAUL, Dominique 1973-

Personal

Born 1973. *Education:* University of Maryland, College Park, B.A., 1998.

Addresses

Home and office—North Hollywood, CA.

Career

Writer, screenwriter, and storyteller. Director of film *The Possibility of Fireflies,* 2008.

Writings

The Possibility of Fireflies (also see below), Simon & Schuster (New York, NY), 2006.
(And director) *The Possibility of Fireflies* (screenplay; adapted from her novel), produced 2008.

Sidelights

Though Dominique Paul hoped to be a writer, it was not something she seriously considered as a way to make a living. After completing her novel *The Possibility of Fireflies* in 2002, the manuscript languished in a drawer until Paul signed on with an agent two years later. "In the two years it took me to find an agent for my book, I met a TV agent who recommended I turn the novel into a screenplay so he could get me work as a screenwriter," Paul explained to *YA Fresh Blog.* In the same week her novel sold, Paul heard back from a producer who loved her screenplay. By the time the novel was published in 2006, Paul was in the midst of casting and directing her own screenplay version of her story.

The Possibility of Fireflies, a coming-of-age novel set in the 1980s, finds fourteen-year-old Ellie learning that no one can save her from her situation but herself. Ellie

and her sister Gwen are pretty much on their own; their mother is irresponsible and their father has left the family. Ellie spends much of her time alone, thinking, and then she meets Leo, a night-owl neighbor who is determined to make it in Hollywood. Leo and Ellie connect, but although Ellie has a huge crush on Leo, he convinces her that to fully grow up must face life on her own terms. According to *Kliatt* contributor Claire Rosser, Ellie's mother is truly monstrous, and many of the novel's scenes are filled with the woman's hateful actions. Still, the critic added, "in the midst of ugliness are the tiny lights of fireflies, which Ellie sees."

Paul's "sensitively written story . . . is immediately gripping and emotionally intense," wrote a *Kirkus Reviews* contributor in an appraisal of *The Possibility of Fireflies.* Stephanie Zvirin, in her *Booklist* review, noted that Ellie has a "strong, distinctive voice—smart and sweet." Throughout the apparently bleak situation, Paul's young heroine "convincingly manages to convey her determination to be happy and find support," concluded Carol A. Edwards in her *School Library Journal* review.

Asked what advice she would give to aspiring writers, Paul told the *YA Fresh Blog* interviewer: "I would have to say that when searching for subject matter, it is always best to write what you know. That doesn't mean it has to be factually accurate. Just emotionally true."

Biographical and Critical Sources

PERIODICALS

Booklist, November 15, 2006, Stephanie Zvirin, review of *The Possibility of Fireflies,* p. 59.
Kirkus Reviews, October 1, 2006, review of *The Possibility of Fireflies,* p. 1022.
Kliatt, September, 2006, Claire Rosser, review of *The Possibility of Fireflies,* p. 17.

School Library Journal, November, 2006, Carol A. Edwards, review of *The Possibility of Fireflies,* p. 145.

ONLINE

Media Bistro Galley Cat, http://www.mediabistro.com/ (October 25, 2007), "From Author to Auteur."
Simon & Schuster Web site, http://www.simonsays.com/ (October 22, 2007), "Danielle Paul."
YA Fresh Blog, http://yafresh.blogspot.com/ (February 26, 2007), interview with Paul.*

*   *   *

PIROTTA, Saviour
(Sam Godwin)

Personal

Born in Malta.

Addresses

Home—England.

Career

Playwright, storyteller, and author of books for children. Professional storyteller at Commonwealth Institute for eight years.

Awards, Honors

Best Nonfiction Picture Book designation, English Association, 1998, for *A Seed in Need.*

Writings

CHILDREN'S FICTION

The Idiot King: A Play, Samuel French (London, England), 1985.
Let the Shadows Fly, Hamish Hamilton (London, England), 1986.
Great Siege Day, Hamish Hamilton (London, England), 1986.
(With Sarah-Jane Stewart) *The Flower from Outer Space,* Blackie (London, England), 1988.
Once inside a Circle, Oxford University Press (Oxford, England), 1988.
Jasper Joe and the Best Trick in the World, Blackie (London, England), 1988.
The Pirates of Pudding Beach, Macmillan (London, England), 1989.
(With Nancy Hellen) *Hey Riddle Riddle!,* Blackie (New York, NY), 1989.
Solomon's Secret, illustrated by Helen Cooper, Dial (New York, NY), 1989.

Do You Believe in Magic?, Dent (London, England), 1990.
A Giant Stepped on Joey's Toe, Hodder & Stoughton (London, England), 1990.
Dragonbusters, Blackie (London, England), 1990.
Pineapple Crush, Hodder & Stoughton (London, England), 1991.
The Vampire Trees, Blackie (London, England), 1991.
Little Bird, illustrated by Stephen Butler, Tambourine (New York, NY), 1992.
Chloe on the Climbing Frame, Dent (London, England), 1992, published as *Chloe on the Jungle Gym,* illustrated by Rhian Nest-James, Barron's (Hauppauge, NY), 1992.
Operation Carrot, Blackie (London, England), 1992.
But No Cheese!, Hodder & Stoughton (London, England), 1992.
Supper with the Spooks, Piper (London, England), 1992.
Fangerella, Dent (London, England), 1992.
Patch Learns to Bark, Brimax (Newmarket, England), 1993.
Follow That Cat!, illustrated by Peter Melnyczuk, Dutton (New York, NY), 1993.
Summer, Wayland (Hove, England), 1998.
Spring, Wayland (Hove, England), 1998.
Winter, Wayland (Hove, England), 1998.
Autumn, Wayland (Hove, England), 1998.
Pirates!, Wayland (Hove, England), 1998.
Angel, illustrated by Bettina Paterson, Little Simon (New York, NY), 2001.
The Treasure of Santa Cruz, Hodder Wayland (London, England), 2002.
The Best Prize of All, Hodder Wayland (London, England), 2002.
Santa, illustrated by Bettina Paterson, Little, Simon (New York, NY) 2003.
Patrick Paints a Picture, illustrated by Linzi West, Frances Lincoln (London, England), Simon (New York, NY) 2007.

ADAPTOR

Tales from around the World, Blackie (London, England), 1988.
Joy to the World: Christmas Stories from around the Globe, illustrated by Sheila Moxley, HarperCollins (New York, NY), 1998.
Native American Tales, Wayland (Hove, England), 1998.
African Tales, Wayland (Hove, England), 1998.
Stories from the Amazon, illustrated by Becky Gryspeerdt, Raintree Steck-Vaughn (Austin, TX), 2000.
Stories from China, illustrated by Tim Clarey, Raintree Steck-Vaughn (Austin, TX), 2000.
Jewish Festival Tales, illustrated by Anne Marie Kelly, Raintree Steck-Vaughn (Austin, TX), 2001.
Christian Festival Tales, illustrated by Helen Cann, Raintree Steck-Vaughn (Austin, TX), 2001.
The Sleeping Princess, and Other Fairy Tales from Grimm, Orchard (London, England), 2002, Margaret K. McElderry (New York, NY), 2006.
The Orchard Book of First Greek Myths, Orchard (London, England), 2003.

(With Alan Marks) *Guess My Name: A Celtic Fairy Tale and also Rumplestiltskin*, Franklin Watts (London, England), 2004, published as *Guess My Name*, Sea to Sea (North Mankato, MN), 2007.

(With Alan Marks) *The Golden Slipper: An Ancient Egyptian Fairy Tale and also Cinderella*, Franklin Watts (London, England), 2004, published as *The Golden Slipper*, Sea to Sea (North Mankato, MN), 2007.

(With Alan Marks) *The Glass Palace: An Arabian Fairy Tale and also Sleeping Beauty*, Franklin Watts (London, England), 2004, published as *The Glass Palace*, Sea to Sea (North Mankato, MN), 2007.

(With Alan Marks) *The Enchanted Gazelle: An African Fairy Tale and also Puss in Boots*, Franklin Watts (London, England), 2004, published as *The Enchanted Gazelle*, Sea to Sea (North Mankato, MN), 2007.

(With Alan Marks) *The Lonely Princess: An Indian Fairy Tale and also Rapunzel*, Franklin Watts (London, England), 2005, published as *The Lonely Princess*, Sea to Sea (North Mankato, MN), 2007.

(With Alan Marks) *The Giant Oak Tree: A Russian Fairy Tale and also Jack and the Beanstalk*, Franklin Watts (London, England), 2005, published as *The Giant Oak Tree*, Sea to Sea (North Mankato, MN), 2007.

Aesop's Fables, Kingfish (Boston, MA), 2005.

Icarus, the Boy Who Could Fly, Orchard (London, England), 2005.

The Secret of Pandora's Box, Orchard (London, England), 2005.

King Midas's Goldfingers, Orchard (London, England), 2005.

Perseus and the Monstrous Medusa, Orchard (London, England), 2005.

Arachne, the Spider Woman, Orchard (London, England), 2005.

Odysseus and the Wooden Horse, Orchard (London, England), 2005.

Traditional Stories from China, Hodder Wayland (London, England), 2006.

CHILDREN'S NONFICTION

Jerusalem, Dillon (New York, NY), 1993.

Rome, Dillon (New York, NY), 1993.

Pirates and Treasure (part of the "Remarkable World" series), Thomson Learning (New York, NY), 1995.

Monsters of the Deep (part of the "Remarkable World" series), Thomson Learning (New York, NY), 1995.

The Wild, Wild West (part of the "Remarkable World" series), Thomson Learning (New York, NY), 1996.

Fossils and Bones (part of the "Remarkable World" series), Raintree Steck-Vaughn (Austin, TX), 1997.

Turtle Bay, illustrated by Nilesh Mistry, Farrar, Straus (New York, NY), 1997.

People in the Rain Forest, Raintree Steck-Vaughn (Austin, TX), 1999.

Rivers in the Rain Forest, Raintree Steck-Vaughn (Austin, TX), 1999.

Predators in the Rain Forest, Raintree Steck-Vaughn (Austin, TX), 1999.

Trees and Plants in the Rain Forest, Raintree Steck-Vaughn (Austin, TX), 1999.

Italy, Raintree Steck-Vaughn (Austin, TX), 1999.

Christian Festivals Cookbook, with photography by Zul Mukhida, Raintree Steck-Vaughn (Austin, TX), 2001.

Buried Treasure, Raintree Steck-Vaughn (Austin, TX), 2002.

Albert Einstein, Raintree Steck-Vaughn (Austin, TX), 2002.

Chocolate, Smart Apple (North Mankato, MN), 2003.

Teeth, Smart Apple (North Mankato, MN), 2003.

Bread, Smart Apple (North Mankato, MN), 2004.

Health and Medicine, Smart Apple (North Mankato, MN), 2004.

We Love Passover, Wayland (Hove, England), 2006, published as *Passover*, PowerKids Press (New York, NY), 2007.

We Love Easter, Wayland (Hove, England), 2006, published as *Easter*, PowerKids Press (New York, NY), 2007.

We Love Divali, Wayland (Hove, England), 2006, published as *Divali*, PowerKids Press (New York, NY), 2007.

We Love Christmas, Wayland (Hove, England), 2006, published as *Christmas*, PowerKids Press (New York, NY), 2007.

We Love Chinese New Year, Wayland (Hove, England), 2006, published as *Chinese New Year*, PowerKids Press (New York, NY), 2007.

We Love Id-ul-Fitr, Wayland (Hove, England), 2006, published as *Id-ul-Fitr*, PowerKids Press (New York, NY), 2007.

Author's books have been translated into fifteen languages.

UNDER NAME SAM GODWIN

Burning Secret, Henderson (Woodbridge, England), 1996.

Pocahontas, Runaway Princess, Macdonald Young (Hove, England), 1998.

A Seed in Need: A First Look at the Plant Cycle, Macdonald Young (Hove, England), 1998.

The Drop Goes Plop: A First Look at the Water Cycle, Macdonald Young (Hove, England), 1998.

The Trouble with Tadpoles: A First Look at the Life Cycle of a Frog, Macdonald Young (Hove, England), 1999.

A Sword for Joan of Arc, Macdonald Young (Hove, England), 1999.

Oscar's Opposites: An Introduction to Opposites, Wayland (Hove, England), 1999.

Clockwise, Macdonald Young (Hove, England), 1999.

Charlie's Colours: An Introduction to Colour, Wayland (Hove, England), 1999.

The Case of the Missing Caterpillar: A First Look at the Life Cycle of a Butterfly, Macdonald Young (Hove, England), 1999.

Sister on the Street: The Story of Mother Teresa, Hodder Wayland (London, England), 2000.

The Hen Can't Help It: A First Look at the Life Cycle of a Chicken, Hodder Wayland (London, England), 2001.

Mary Seacole: A Story from the Crimean War, Hodder Wayland (London, England), 2001.

From Little Acorns: A First Look at the Life Cycle of a Tree, Hodder Wayland (London, England), 2001.

The Prince in the Crystal Palace, Hodder Wayland (London, England), 2001.

"TREMORS" SERIES; UNDER NAME SAM GODWIN

Picture of Evil, Hodder Wayland (London, England), 2000.

The Headmaster's Ghost, Hodder Wayland (London, England), 2000.

Welcome to the Waxworks, Hodder Wayland (London, England), 2001.

Tunnel of Fear, Hodder Wayland (London, England), 2001.

Sidelights

Although Saviour Pirotta had little access to books while growing up on the island of Malta, he benefited by being surrounded by storytellers. Introduced to the pirate lore of the Maltese islands as a child, Pirotta learned many of these native stories by heart. He drew on his love of pirate stories and other oral legends from Malta in his first drama, *The Idiot King: A Play,* which retells a Maltese folk tale. In the years since, he has moved from plays to books for children, creating original stories, adapting myths and folk tales from around the world, and authoring numerous nonfiction titles about nature-based topics, both under his own name and under the pen name Sam Goodwin.

Pirotta's original picture books, which include *Operation Carrot, Patch Learns to Bark,* and *Little Bird,* tell simple stories geared for very young readers. Another book, *Patrick Paints a Picture,* tells a simple story about a boy and his aunt as they plan to paint pictures and weaves it into a concept book that teaches toddlers about basic colors. A *Kirkus Reviews* contributor called *Patrick Paints a Picture* "a non-didactic, festive introduction" to both primary and secondary colors. Other picture books feature Pirotta's retelling of stories from around the world, including the fables of Aesop, Greek myths, British fairy stories such as Rapunzel and Snow White, and less-familiar tales from Russia, China, and Africa. According to *Book Report* contributor Tami Little, the stories in Pirotta's *Christian Festival Tales* "convey accurate information" about the included Christian holidays.

The Sleeping Princess and Other Fairy Tales from Grimm finds Pirotta retelling fairy tales "delightfully," according to a critic from *Bookseller.* "Pirotta writes like a story-teller, with great imagery and description," Robin L. Gibson wrote in her review of the book for *School Library Journal,* and a *Kirkus Reviews* contributor called the same title "a lovely new collection." Julie Cummins, writing for *Booklist,* noted that "Pirotta's down-to-earth language will read well aloud." In his retelling of Aesop's fables, Pirotta expands on the original tales; "Each telling contains descriptions of the setting, extensive dialogue, and rounded-out motivation," wrote Susan Hepler in a review of *Aesop's Fables* for *School Library Journal.*

Some of Pirotta's books combine a folk-tale-style story with environmental themes. *Turtle Bay* introduces two children who are curious about the elderly man who sweeps their local beach. When the old man explains that he is making clearing space for the turtles, his activity makes much more sense. Other titles, which offer a more straightforward nonfiction approach, include Pirotta's "Deep in the Rainforest" series, which includes *People in the Rain Forest* and other titles. The series offers factual information about rainforest topics, including a discussion of threats to the rainforest environment, and provides rainforest related crafts for readers. Helen Rosenberg, reviewing *People in the Rainforest* for *Booklist,* praised Pirotta's "accessible text" in the volume.

Pirotta's books published under his Sam Godwin pseudonym include the award-winning *A Seed in Need: A First Look at the Plant Cycle,* which introduces five-to-seven-year-old readers to basic science concepts. As Godwin, he is also the author of the "Tremors" series of middle-grade novels, concept books such as *Oscar's Opposites: An Introduction to Opposites,* and biographies of women such as Pocahontas, Joan of Arc, and Mother Teresa.

Despite his writings on numerous other topics, Pirotta has maintained his childhood love of pirates. His book *Buried Treasure* features lost pirate hoards, as well as mummies and burial mounds. As Cynthia M. Sturgis wrote in her review of the book for *School Library Journal,* although *Buried Treasure* offers only a basic introduction to its subject, the book "will attract browsers." During his visits to schools in his native England, Pirotta encourages his young audiences to follow their own interests in their own writing. As he explained to a contributor for the *Jubilee Books* Web site, Pirotta continues to focus at least some of his writing on "the dastardliest pirates ever committed to paper."

Biographical and Critical Sources

PERIODICALS

Booklist, January 1, 1999, Helen Rosenberg, review of *People in the Rain Forest* and *Rivers in the Rain Forest,* p. 869; November 1, 2006, Julie Cummins, "The Fairy Tales," p. 56.

Book Report, November-December, 2001, Tami Little, review of *Christian Festivals Cookbook,* p. 82.

Bookseller, June 21, 2002, review of *The Sleeping Princess and Other Fairy Tales from Grimm,* p. 35.

Kirkus Reviews, October 1, 2006, review of *The Sleeping Princess and Other Fairy Tales from Grimm,* p. 1022; October 15, 2007, review of *Patrick Paints a Picture.*

Natural History, December-January, 1997, Jean Craighead George, review of *Turtle Bay,* p. 8.

Publishers Weekly, June, 1992, review of *Little Bird,* p. 101.

School Library Journal, April, 2000, Wendy Lukehart, review of *Italy,* p. 124; September, 2001, Ann W. Moore,
review of *Jewish Festival Tales,* p. 218; February,
2002, Cynthia M. Sturgis, review of *Buried Treasure,*
p. 120; July, 2002, Edith Ching, review of *Albert Einstein,* p. 135; November, 2005, Susan Hepler, review
of *Aesop's Fables,* p. 119; November, 2006, Robin L.
Gibson, review of *The Sleeping Princess and Other
Fairy Tales from Grimm,* p. 123.

ONLINE

Franklin Watts Publisher Web site, http://www.wattspub.
co.uk/ (October 22, 2007), "Saviour Pirotta."
Houghton Mifflin Web site, http://www.houghtonmifflin
books.com/ (October 22, 2007), "Saviour Pirotta."
Jubilee Books Web site, http://www.jubileebooks.co.uk/
(October 11, 2007), interview with Pirotta.*

*   *   *

PLUM-UCCI, Carol 1957-

Personal

Born 1957, in NJ; married (marriage ended); children:
two. *Education:* Purdue University, B.S. (communications); graduate study at Rutgers University.

Addresses

Home—Southern NJ.

Career

Novelist. Miss America Organization, Atlantic City, NJ,
former staff writer; Rutgers University, Camden, NJ,
teaching assistant; Atlantic Cape Community College,
Mays Landing, NJ, instructor in English composition, c.
2004.

Awards, Honors

Kneale Award in Journalism for excellence in feature
writing, Purdue University, 1979; International Association of Business Communications Award of Excellence,
1992, for Miss America program book; Dalton Penn
Award for special publications, 1996; Evergreen Award
for Young-Adult Literature, Washington State Library
Association, and Rhode Island Educational Media Association, and Rhode Island Teen Book Award, Michael
L. Printz Honor Book silver medal, American Library
Association (ALA), and One-Book New Jersey Young-
Adult selection, all 2001, and Edgar Allan Poe Award
finalist in young-adult mystery division, 2002, all for
The Body of Christopher Creed; Michael L. Printz
Award nomination, and ALA Best Book for Young
Adults nomination, both 2002, both for *What Happened
to Lani Garver;* ALA Best Book for Young Adults
nomination, 2004, for *The She;* Edgar Allen Poe Award
finalist, 2007, for *The Night My Sister Went Missing.*

Carol Plum-Ucci (Reproduced by permission.)

Writings

YOUNG-ADULT NOVELS

The Body of Christopher Creed, Harcourt (San Diego,
CA), 2000.
What Happened to Lani Garver, Harcourt (San Diego,
CA), 2002.
The She, Harcourt (San Diego, CA), 2003.
The Night My Sister Went Missing, Harcourt (Orlando,
FL), 2006.

OTHER

Super Sports Star: Stephon Marbury, Enslow Publishers
(Berkeley Heights, NJ), 2002.
Celebrate Diwali, Enslow Publishers (Berkeley Heights,
NJ), 2007.

Adaptations

Plum-Ucci's novels adapted for audiobook include *The
Body of Christopher Creed,* read by Scott Shina, Recorded Books, 2002. *The Body of Christopher Creed*
was optioned for film by Dreamworks, 2001.

Sidelights

Award-winning young-adult novelist Carol Plum-Ucci
was working as a teaching assistant at Rutgers University when she wrote her first novel, *The Body of Chris-*

topher Creed. In this, as well as more recent books such as *What Happened to Lani Garver, The She,* and *The Night My Sister Went Missing,* she introduces teen protagonists who, when tragedy strikes, are forced to revisit their past from an altered perspective. In Plum-Ucci's novels, supernatural elements often figure in the mystery, providing another reason for the author's popularity among adolescent readers. According to *School Library Journal* contributor Kim Harris, Plum-Ucci "knows her audience and provides her readers with enough twists, turns, and suspense to keep them absorbed."

Born in New Jersey in 1957, and raised in an apartment above her family business—a funeral parlor—Plum-Ucci grew up in an area full of history. In addition to the stories from her family's own multi-generational saga, she became familiar with several local legends, including one about the monstrous Jersey Devil, a half-man, half-beast creature that was said to roam the state's nearby Pine Barrens region.

After graduating from high school, Plum-Ucci earned a communications degree at Purdue University, then worked at several writing jobs, including as a staff writer for the Miss America Organization, headquartered in Atlantic City. She eventually enrolled at Rutgers University, where she has worked as a teaching assistant instructing freshman in basic composition while earning her master's degree in English.

Plum-Ucci decided to sit down and write her first novel after her marriage began disintegrating and her employment situation began to tarnish. Stress from her personal life may have fueled her writing, because within eighteen weeks she completed the manuscript for a complete novel. Her story was geared toward teen readers, a group that appeared far less daunting to her than an adult audience. Unlike many adults, Plum-Ucci had happy memories of her adolescent years. "I had been an awesome teen-ager," she recalled to *Rutgers Focus* contributor Caroline Yount. "It was a great time, and I figured I would rather converse with people of that carefree mind-set."

Published as *The Body of Christopher Creed,* Plum-Ucci's award-winning debut novel is set in the author's native South Jersey and is narrated by sixteen-year-old Smithville High School junior Torey Adams. Popular with the right crowd, and a star of the school football team, Torey begins to have doubts about what the "right crowd" is all about after a geeky classmate named Christopher Creed suddenly disappears. While Torey's fellow students quickly transform the unpopular young man's disappearance into fodder for jokes and gossip, the event causes Torey to question his responsibility for the unhappiness that caused his classmate to leave without a trace. The class scapegoat, Chris had served as the brunt of jokes from Torey and his friends for years. An e-mail sent by Creed to the school's principal that mentions Torey and some of his cliquish friends by

name provides the curious teen with the only clue to Creed's disappearance. Fearing that Chris might be dead, Torey sets to work to solve the mystery of the teen's disappearance, joined by fellow teens Ali and Ali's boyfriend Bo. When their sleuthing brings on charges of trespassing, the three teens soon find suspicion falling on them while the mystery of Chris's disappearance remains unsolved.

The Body of Christopher Creed resonated with many readers and critics, as well as with its own author, who had based her book on a boy she knew as a child, as well as the teasing he received. Teased throughout elementary school, that boy eventually injured himself and was pulled out of high school; nobody ever heard from him again. Years later, Plum-Ucci was still haunted by memories of this boy, and wondered at the effects of his torment at the hands of his fellow students. Reviewing *The Body of Christopher Creed* for *Publishers Weekly,* a critic praised the book as a "well-crafted" novel that focuses on a timely topic: "the effect teenage intolerance can have on misfits."*School Library Journal* reviewer Jane P. Fenn also enjoyed the novel, citing Plum-Ucci's "fine feel for teen speech and thought."

In *What Happened to Lani Garver* readers are introduced to sixteen-year-old Clair McKenzie, a popular

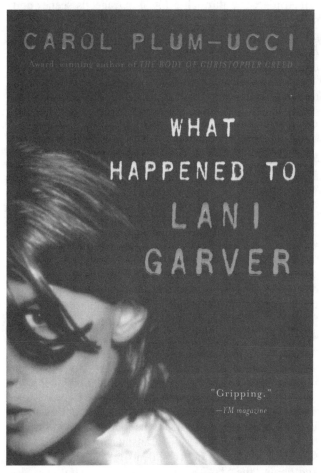

Cover of Plum-Ucci's popular mystery **What Happened to Lani Garver,** *which focuses on a troubled teen.* (Harcourt, Inc., 2004. Reproduced by permission of Harcourt.)

high-school cheerleader living in the tightly knit fishing community of Hackett Island. Clair's friendly demeanor hides a host of worries, among which are concern over her alcoholic mother, her own eating disorder, and nagging concerns that her fainting spells might signal that her leukemia has returned, Enter Lani Garver, an androgynous new student who causes a stir among the students at Coastal Regional High School. The streetwise Lani, who turns out to be a boy, sparks a blaze of gossip in school over the possibility that he is gay. Within the greater island community, he attracts attention because his pale, effeminate appearance stands out alongside most of the burly, hardworking fishermen's sons who live on the island. Encouraged by Lani to seek needed medical attention and deal with her bulimia, Claire also begins to wonder if Lani is in fact an angelic spirit sent by God to help her. Meanwhile her shallow friends decide that the newcomer's artsy tolerance is a threat to their way of life and they decide to break Lani's influence by breaking his spirit.

While many critics enjoyed the author's second fictional outing, some critics commented that *What Happened to Lani Garver* contains magical and New-Age elements that nudge the novel into fantasy. In *Booklist,* for example, Ilene Cooper wrote that while certain of Plum-Ucci's plot elements are "intriguing," readers are forced to "wade through a lot of extraneous scenes and situations to get at the good stuff." Calling *What Happened to Lani Garver* a "taut, provocative" novel, a *Publishers Weekly* contributor enjoyed the book far more, noting that the author fashions an ending that "crackles with suspense." *What Happened to Lani Garver* "is an involving, dramatic tale that will quickly draw readers in," maintained *Kliatt* contributor Paula Rohrlick, the critic adding that Plum-Ucci's "message about tolerance" adds intrigue. Reviewing the novel for *School Library Journal,* Lynn Bryant had particular praise for the author's ability to blend "outstanding writing, strong characterization, and riveting plot development."

The supernatural takes center stage in Plum-Ucci's third work of YA fiction, *The She.* In this story, eight-year-old Evan Barrett and his older brother, Emmett, are left orphaned after both their parents mysteriously disappear during a storm at sea. Although the boys decide to leave their home town to escape the sad memories, Evan is forced to return years later when a similar tragedy occurs and questions link it to his parents' fate. Now seventeen, he is able to review the facts regarding his parents' dissappearance from a more mature perspective: Despite the frantic Mayday sent by their father on the ship-to-shore radio, no wreckage was ever found, and no bodies were ever recovered. Pondering the mystery, Evan also wonders who made the loud, inhuman shrieks he heard on the final radio transmission. The circumstances surrounding both incidents rekindle a local legend about "the She," a deep-sea monster who, in a bitter, jealous rage, was said to drag entire ships down into the watery depths. Could the She have been re-

Cover of Plum-Ucci's **The She,** *which draws readers into the mysterious legend of a small coastal community.* (Harcourt, Inc., 2003. Reproduced by permission of Getty Images.)

sponsible for Evan's parents' death? As Evan begins to delve into his family's past, he also helps Gray Shailey, a troubled but horribly spoiled teen suffering from psychiatric trauma, to cope with a similar tragic loss. When Gray shares with Evan that she also heard horrible shrieks prior to her friends' drowning, the pair team up to uncover the mysteries that threaten to overshadow both their lives.

While noting that *The She* is a slower-paced read than Plum-Ucci's first books, a *Publishers Weekly* contributor wrote that the award-winning novel nonetheless "succeeds largely by shape-shifting, one moment resembling a mournful dirge, the next a supernatural thriller, the next a tightly woven mystery." Also commenting on the novel's diverse elements, a *Kirkus Reviews* contributor noted that Plum-Ucci "manages to keep readers balanced on a see-saw between rationality and the powers of the dark" in her "seagoing thriller." In *Booklist,* Cooper maintained that the novel's "many plot elements" are successfully woven together into a "serpentine story . . . [that] will grip readers." Citing Plum-Ucci's characteristic blurring of the boundaries between reality and fiction, Hillias J. Martin praised

The She in a review for *School Library Journal,* writing that "plot, character development, and action sequences all seamlessly gel into an intriguing and structurally sound mystery novel."

Taking place during the course of a single night, *The Night My Sister Went Missing* is characteristic Plum-Ucci with its focus on the power of peer pressure and a missing teen. The novel transports readers to the barrier islands off the New Jersey coast, where seventeen-year-old Kurt Carmody joins a nighttime gathering of local teens on an abandoned dock near his home. One of the teens, spoiled and wealthy Stacy Kearney, has brought a pistol, and when a single shot rings out, Kurt's younger sister Casey disappears. Kurt soon finds himself down at the local police station with the rest of his friends, as police begin the search for Casey's body and perhaps her murderer. Waiting there while his parents fly back from their West coast visit, the distraught teen overhears the interrogation of his friends, as rumors fly, secrets are exposed, and hidden animosities are revealed. "There's no doubt Plum-Ucci can tell a heck of a story," Cooper stated in her *Booklist* review of *The Night My Sister Went Missing,* the critic going on to add that readers will "race to the ending and won't guess it until they get there." While praising the author's ability to create suspense in "classic crime-fiction style," *School Library Journal* contributor Riva Pollard maintained that "it is Kurt's emotional growth that forms the heart of the story." Teen readers "will identify with the . . . harsh peer criticism," concluded Daniel Cockrell in *Journal of Adolescent and Adult Literacy,* and will "feel compassion for Kurt, who might be the primary suspect" in his sister's disappearance.

Pleased with her fiction-writing successes, Plum-Ucci plans to continue with her writing for young adults. As she noted to Braun, her advice to young writers is to "Keep it fun. If it's not fun, why are we doing it?"

Biographical and Critical Sources

PERIODICALS

Booklist, August, 2002, Ilene Cooper, review of *What Happened to Lani Garver,* p. 1947; September 15, 2003, Ilene Cooper, review of *The She,* p. 239; October 15, 2006, Ilene Cooper, review of *The Night My Sister Went Missing,* p. 41.

Bulletin of the Center for Children's Books, November, 2003, Elizabeth Bush, review of *The She,* p. 121; January, 2007, Karen Coats, review of *The Night My Sister Went Missing,* p. 225.

Journal of Adolescent and Adult Literacy, October, 2004, Daren Crovitz, review of *What Happened to Lani Garver,* p. 193; November, 2006, Daniel Cockrell, review of *The Night My Sister Went Missing,* p. 244.

Kirkus Reviews, September 1, 2002, review of *What Happened to Lani Garver,* p. 1318; September 15, 2003, review of *The She,* p. 1180; October 15, 2006, review of *The Night My Sister Went Missing,* p. 1077.

Cover of Plum-Ucci's **The Night My Sister Went Missing,** *a mystery that involves a missing teen, a group of friends, and a town's hidden secrets.* (Harcourt, 2006. Photograph © Diaphor Agency/IndexStock Imagery. Reproduced by permission of Harcourt.)

Kliatt, September, 2002, Paula Rohrlick, review of *What Happened to Lani Garver,* p. 13; September, 2003, Michele Winship, review of *The She,* p. 10.

Publishers Weekly, May 22, 2000, review of *The Body of Christopher Creed,* p. 94; August 19, 2002, review of *What Happened to Lani Garver,* p. 91; November 17, 2003, review of *The She,* p. 66.

School Library Journal, July, 2000, Kim Harris, review of *The Body of Christopher Creed,* p. 109; October, 2002, Lynn Bryant, review of *What Happened to Lani Garver,* p. 170; October, 2003, Hillias J. Martin, review of *The She,* p. 175; November, 2006, Riva Pollard, review of *The Night My Sister Went Missing,* p. 148.

Voice of Youth Advocates, May, 2002, Teri S. Lesesne, review of *What Happened to Lani Garver,* p. 391.

ONLINE

Carol Plum-Ucci Home Page, http://carolplumucci.com (November 15, 2007).

Rutgers Focus Online, http://www.rutgers.edu/focus/ (April 6, 2001), Caroline Yount, "Writing Her Way to the Top."*

PRATO, Rodica

Personal

Born in Bucharest, Romania; immigrated to France, then United States. *Education:* Studied architecture in France.

Addresses

Home—Studio 123, 154 W. 57th St., New York, NY 10019. *E-mail*—rodicaprato@mac.com.

Career

Illustrator and graphic artist. *Exhibitions:* Work exhibited by Le Club des Directeurs Artistiques, Paris, France; French Embassy Cultural Services, New York, NY; and other venues.

Awards, Honors

Society of Illustrators Award of Excellence; Visual Club award.

Illustrator

FOR CHILDREN

Eric Metaxas, *King Midas and the Golden Touch,* Rabbit Ears Books (Saxonville, MA), 1992.

Miles Chapin, *88 Keys: The Making of a Steinway Piano,* Clarkson Potter (New York, NY), 1997.

Eric Metaxas, adaptor, *The Gardener's Apprentice,* Creative Editions (Mankato, MN), 1998.

(With others) Karen Hesse, *Stowaway,* Margaret K. McElderry (New York, NY), 2000.

Elspeth Leacock and Susan Buckley, *Journeys in Time: A New Atlas of American History,* Houghton Mifflin (Boston, MA), 2001.

Elspeth Leacock and Susan Buckley, *Journeys for Freedom: A New Look at America's Story,* Houghton Mifflin (Boston, MA), 2006.

Illustrator of maps and other images for educational books, including "Hands on History" series, "Great Explorations" series, "Rulers and Their Times" series, "Early American Family" series, "Great Journeys" series, "How We Lived" series, and "Lifeways" series, all for Benchmark Books.

OTHER

Bernard Nominé, *Sifflets, flûtes et percussions,* Galliamard, (Paris, France), 1975.

Sy Montgomery, *Nature's Everyday Mysteries: A Field Guide to the World in Your Backyard* (essays), foreword by Roger Tory Peterson, Chapters (Shelburne, VT), 1993, published as *The Curious Naturalist: Nature's Everyday Mysteries,* Down East Books (Camden, ME), 2000.

The Brontë Way, privately published, 1994.

Sy Montgomery, *Seasons of the Wild: A Year of Nature's Magic and Mysteries,* Chapters Publishing, 1996.

Carole Walter, *Great Pies and Tarts,* Clarkson Potter (New York, NY), 1998.

Illustrator of numerous other books, including *The Martha Stewart Cookbook, Martha Stewart's New Old House, Martha Stewart's Gardening Month by Month,* and other volumes by Martha Stewart; *Biltmore Estates Activity Book; Water Magic,* by Mary Muryn; *Food for the Soul: Delicious Thought to Nourish Mind and Heart* by Barbara Milo Ohrbach; and *The Power of Attraction.* Illustrator of maps. Contributor of illustrations to numerous periodicals, including *American Heritage, Colonial Homes, Smart Money, Vanity Fair, Harper's, Garden Design, Book, Fortune, Victoria, Via, Country Living Gardener, McCalls, Worth, Holiday Craft, Reader's Digest, Food and Wine, Golf, Wall Street Journal, New York Times, Women's Day, Scientific American, Family Circle, Home,* and *Town and Country.*

Biographical and Critical Sources

PERIODICALS

Booklist, June 1, 2002, John Peter, review of *Journeys in Time: A New Atlas of American History,* p. 1866.

Horn Book, July, 2001, review of *Journeys in Time,* p. 471.

Kirkus Reviews, October 15, 2006, review of *Journeys for Freedom: A New Look at America's Story,* p. 1066.

Library Journal, Eric C. Shoaf, review of *88 Keys,* p. 76.

School Library Journal, June, 2001, Pamela K. Bomboy, review of *Journeys in Time,* p. 176; January, 2007, Grace Oliff, review of *Journeys for Freedom,* p. 145.

ONLINE

Rodica Prato Home Page, http://www.rodicaprato.com (November 12, 2007).*

R

RAVEN, Margot Theis

Personal

Married. *Education:* Rosemont College, B.A. (English); attended Villanova University and Kent State University; studied painting at De Cordova Museum.

Addresses

Home—Charleston, SC.

Career

Author, journalist, storyteller, and artist.

Member

Charleston Artist Guild.

Awards, Honors

Storytelling World Honor Award; Martin Luther King, Jr., Living the Dream Award; Fielder Freedom Award; Children's Crown Honor Book Award; James Madison Book Award nomination; Teacher's Choice Award, International Reading Association, for *Angels in the Dust;* Texas Bluebonnet Award finalist, 2004, for *Mercedes and the Chocolate Pilot;* Children's Africana Book Awards honor book, African Studies Association, 2005, for *Circle Unbroken;* Eric Hoffer Award Notable Book designation, 2006, for *America's White Table;* Carter G. Woodson Award Book, 2006, for *Let Them Play;* Jane Addams Children's Book Award, Books for Younger Children Category, 2007, for *Night Boat to Freedom.*

Writings

Angels in the Dust, illustrated by Roger Essley, BridgeWater Books (Mahwah, NJ), 1997.

M Is for Mayflower: A Massachusetts Alphabet, illustrated by Jeannie Brett, Sleeping Bear Press (Chelsea, MI), 2002.

Mercedes and the Chocolate Pilot: A True Story of the Berlin Airlift and the Candy That Dropped from the Sky, illustrated by Gijsbert van Frankenhuyzen, Sleeping Bear Press (Chelsea, MI), 2002.

Circle Unbroken: The Story of a Basket and Its People, illustrated by E.B. Lewis, Farrar, Straus & Giroux (New York, NY), 2004.

America's White Table, illustrated by Mike Benny, Sleeping Bear Press (Chelsea, MI), 2005.

Challenger: America's Favorite Eagle, illustrated by Gijsbert van Frankenhuyzen, Sleeping Bear Press (Chelsea, MI), 2005.

Let Them Play, illustrated by Chris Ellison, Sleeping Bear Press (Chelsea, MI), 2005.

Night Boat to Freedom, illustrated by E.B. Lewis, Farrar, Straus & Giroux (New York, NY), 2006.

Contributor to newspapers and magazines.

Adaptations

Circle Unbroken was adapted for orchestra by composer William Grant Still; *America's White Table,* was adapted for orchestra by Chamber Music Charleston.

Sidelights

Margot Theis Raven is the author of several award-winning picture books for children, among them *Circle Unbroken: The Story of a Basket and Its People* and *Night Boat to Freedom.* Raven, who has written for radio, television, and newspapers over the course of her career, often bases her works on events from U.S. history.

Raven published her debut title, *Angels in the Dust,* in 1997. Inspired by a *National Geographic* article the author once read, the work concerns an Oklahoma family struggling to maintain their farm during the Dust Bowl era of the 1930s. Narrated by Annie, an elderly woman recalling her childhood, the tale depicts the family's strength in the face of adversity. A critic in *Publishers Weekly* praised *Angels in the Dust,* citing the work's

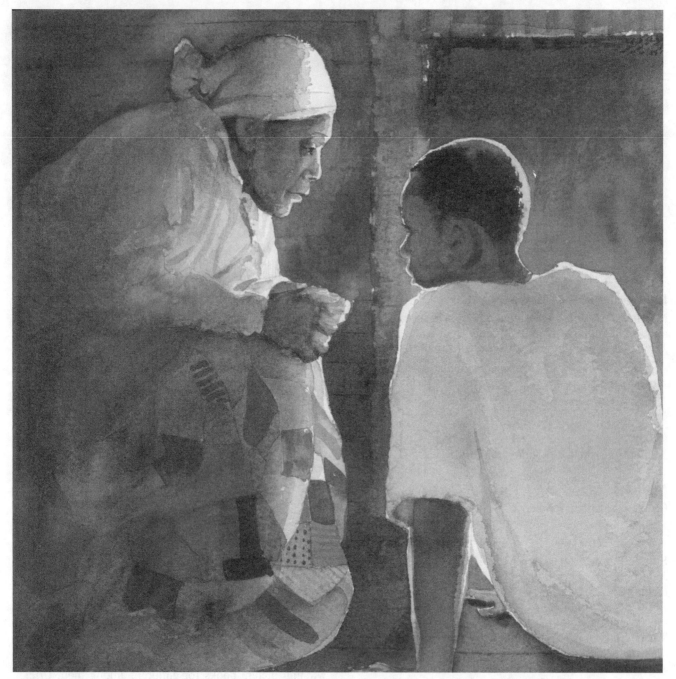

Margot Theis Raven introduces readers to the Underground Railroad in* Night Boat to Freedom, *a picture book featuring E.B. Lewis's evocative art.
(Illustration © 2006 by E.B. Lewis. Reprinted by permission of Farrar, Straus & Giroux, LLC.)

"heartland setting, simile-laden prose and uplifting message about weathering hard times," and Hazel Rochman wrote in *Booklist* that Raven's novel may encourage young readers "to ask about their own family histories of hardship and community."

A seven-year-old German girl and an American lieutenant form an unlikely relationship in *Mercedes and the Chocolate Pilot: A True Story of the Berlin Airlift and the Candy That Dropped from the Sky.* In the work, Raven chronicles the tale of young Mercedes, a West Berliner trapped behind the Soviet blockade of the German city in 1948, and Lt. Gail Halvorsen, a pilot who

dropped chocolate bars to the children as he delivered supplies to those trapped by the communists. "Raven's uplifting account imparts a positive humanitarian message," noted a *Kirkus Reviews* critic. According to a *Publishers Weekly* reviewer, in *Mercedes and the Chocolate Pilot* "a sketch of an uncommonly giving man and a rare friendship emerges."

In *Circle Unbroken* Raven examines the ties that bind successive generations. As an elderly woman teaches her grandchild how to fashion a sweetgrass Gullah basket, she recounts their family history, beginning with the youngster's "old-timey grandfather," an African villager who was captured and sold into slavery. "Raven's text masterfully frames several hundred years of African-American history within the picture-book format," observed Mary N. Oluonye in *School Library Journal.* A reviewer in *Publishers Weekly* called *Circle Unbroken* a "gracefully constructed tale, as intricate as the baskets and the history to which it pays tribute."

Challenger: America's Favorite Eagle tells the story of an abandoned eaglet that was rescued by humans and retrained as a free-flying bird. Challenger ultimately performed at the opening ceremonies of the 1996 Para-Olympics. Patricia Manning, writing in *School Library Journal,* described the work as "a fervent plea for the continued protection of the American bald eagle." *Let Them Play* centers on an all-black Little League baseball team that faced discrimination in 1955. "The poignant message of this tale rings true even today," noted *School Library Journal* critic Marilyn Taniguchi. In *America's White Table,* Raven describes a little-known military tradition. In the work, a young girl prepares a white table, a remembrance of prisoners of war and missing service members, to honor her uncle, a Vietnam War veteran. A white table is "the most important image we can ever have, and it's not political," Raven explained to Bruce Smith in the *Boston Globe.* "Even the flag can get politicized. This has no party and no agenda except that a person said 'yes' to duty, and that is always to be honored."

Drawn from accounts found in the Slave Narrative Collection, *Night Boat to Freedom* follows the efforts of Christmas John, a twelve-year-old Kentucky slave, and John's mentor, Granny Judith, an elderly plantation woman who creates dyed quilts, to help other escaped slaves cross the river to the free state of Ohio. "Raven both highlights the historical import of fabric arts in slave life and incorporates them metaphorically," remarked a *Kirkus Reviews* contributor while Nina Lindsay stated in *School Library Journal* that the author's "moving story is full of particulars that lend it authenticity."

Biographical and Critical Sources

PERIODICALS

Booklist, April 15, 1997, Hazel Rochman, review of *Angels in the Dust,* p. 1430; July, 2002, GraceAnne A. DeCandido, review of *Mercedes and the Chocolate Pilot: A True Story of the Berlin Airlift and the Candy That Dropped from the Sky,* p. 1841; February 15, 2004, Hazel Rochman, review of *Circle Unbroken: The Story of a Basket and Its People,* p. 1078; October 15, 2006, Hazel Rochman, review of *Night Boat to Freedom,* p. 47.

Raven relates a true story in Challenger: America's Favorite Eagle, *a large-format picture book featuring paintings by Gijsbert van Frankenhuyzen.* (Sleeping Bear Press, 2005. Illustration © 2005 by Gijsbert van Frankenhuyzen. Reproduced by permission.)

Boston Globe, May 30, 2005, Bruce Smith, "Dinner Table Tradition Memorializes Wars' Missing."

Kirkus Reviews, June 1, 2002, review of *Mercedes and the Chocolate Pilot,* p. 810; February 1, 2004, review of *Circle Unbroken,* p. 137; October 15, 2006, review of *Night Boat to Freedom,* p. 1077.

Publishers Weekly, January 20, 1997, review of *Angels in the Dust,* p. 401; April 15, 2002, review of *Mercedes and the Chocolate Pilot,* p. 64; December 22, 2003, review of *Circle Unbroken,* p. 60.

School Library Journal, August, 2002, Robyn Ryan Vandenbroek, review of *Mercedes and the Chocolate Pilot,* p. 179; April, 2004, Mary N. Oluonye, review of *Circle Unbroken,* p. 122; November, 2005, Marilyn Taniguchi, review of *Let Them Play,* p. 120; July, 2006, Patricia Manning, review of *Challenger: America's Favorite Eagle,* p. 92; November, 2006, Nina Lindsay, review of *Night Boat to Freedom,* p. 109.

ONLINE

Sleeping Bear Press Web site, http://www.sleepingbear press.com/ (October 31, 2007), "Margot Theis Raven."

Stories for Life Web site, http://www.stories4life.org/ (October 31, 2007), "Margot Theis Raven."*

REDSAND, Anna 1948-

Personal

Born 1948, in Grand Rapids, MI; children: one daughter.

Addresses

Home—Albuquerque, NM. *E-mail*—aredsand@yahoo.com.

Career

High school guidance counselor and writer. Also worked as an elementary, high-school, and college writing teacher.

Member

Authors Guild, Society for Children's Book Writers and Illustrators.

Photograph of Viktor Frankl consulting with a patient, from **Viktor Frankl: A Life Worth Living** *by Anna S. Redsand.* (Clarion Books, 2006. Illustration © IMAGNO/Franz Hubmann. Reproduced by permission.)

Awards, Honors

Notable Social Studies Trade Book for Young People designation, National Council for the Social Studies/Children's Book Council, Best Children's Books of the Year designation, Bank Street College of Education, and Books for the Teen Age designation, New York Public Library, all 2007, all for *Viktor Frankl: A Life Worth Living.*

Writings

Viktor Frankl: A Life Worth Living, Clarion Books (New York, NY), 2006.

Also author of short stories and poetry.

Sidelights

As a child, Anna Redsand always wanted to become a writer. At age eight she carried around a pocket-sized journal, the contents of which she read to her family. "Reading and writing have always been my favorite things to do" Redsand explained on her home page. In her work as a high school guidance counselor, Redsand often utilizes the principles of logotherapy, and this motivational philosophy inspired her first published book. Logotherapy is a type of psychotherapy that relies on the belief that a human's primary goal is to find meaning in his or her life. The founder of logotherapy, noted psychiatrist Viktor Frankl, is the topic of Redsand's award-winning biography *Viktor Frankl: A Life Worth Living.* Redsand was introduced to Frankl's logotherapy principle during college, and when she learned about his life and theories, the man became her hero: "For the first time, I read something hopeful that came out of a person's direct experience of the horrors of the Holocaust," Redsand explained on her home page.

Born in Austria in 1905 to Jewish parents, Frankl ultimately lost his parents at Auschwitz and his wife at Bergen-Belsen. Sent to the concentration camp at Türkheim, Frankl survived Nazi brutality and went on to translate his experiences into theory in *Man's Search for Meaning,* one of the most influential books to address the Holocaust. In *Viktor Frankl* Redsand details Frankl's childhood years, his life as a psychiatrist, and his contributions as a Holocaust survivor up until his death in 1997. Acknowledging Redsand for detailing the life of one of the most respected psychiatrists of the twentieth century, Rita Soltan wrote in *School Library Journal* that the author "successfully illuminates how the Holocaust deeply affected Frankl's life and career." An online reviewer for *Internet Bookwatch* called *Viktor Frankl* "a powerful blend of Holocaust images, history, and facts."

Discussing her own life purpose, Redsand told *SATA:* "Vicktor Frankl found meaning in his life through helping others find meaning in theirs. Like him, I find some of my greatest satisfaction in helping people, especially young people, discover their life purpose. I want more than anything to do that through my writing, as well as in my counseling and through author visits to schools.

"For anyone considering the writing life, I would say, don't wait for big blocks of time, because you may never find them. I wrote *Viktor Frankl* in twenty-minute segments every morning before I left for school and in two-hour blocks on weekends. I'm lucky now to work at an afternoon and evening high school, because morning is my best writing time, and I do have more time in the mornings now."

Biographical and Critical Sources

PERIODICALS

Booklist, October 15, 2006, Hazel Rochman, review of *Viktor Frankl: A Life Worth Living,* p. 38.
Bulletin of the Center for Children's Books, March, 2007, Hope Morrison, review of *Viktor Frankl,* p. 307.
Publishers Weekly, November 6, 2006, review of *Viktor Frankl,* p. 63.
School Library Journal, December, 2006, Rita Soltan, review of *Viktor Frankl,* p. 168.

ONLINE

Anna Redsand Home Page, http://www.annaredsand.com (October 29, 2007).
Houghton Mifflin Web site, http://www.houghtonmifflin books.com/ (October 29, 2007).
Internet Bookwatch, http://www.midwestbookreview.com/ (October 29, 2007), review of *Viktor Frankl.*
Jewish Book World Online, http://www.amazon.com/gp/pdp/profile/ABOG5L9W7JU5C (December 10, 2007).

*   *   *

REED, Kit 1932-
(Kit Craig, Shelley Hyde)

Personal

Born June 7, 1932, in San Diego, CA; daughter of John Rich (a lieutenant commander in the U.S. Navy) and Lillian (Hyde) Craig; married Joseph Wayne Reed, Jr. (a writer, painter, printmaker, and professor), December 10, 1955; children: Joseph McKean, John Craig, Katherine Hyde. *Education:* College of Notre Dame of Maryland, B.A., 1954.

Addresses

Home—45 Lawn Ave., Middletown, CT 06457. *Agent*—Charlotte Sheedy Literary Agency, 65 Bleecker St., New York, NY 10012.

Kit Reed (Reprinted with permission of John Halpern.)

Career

St. Petersburg Times, St. Petersburg, FL, reporter and television editor, 1954-55; *Hamden Chronicle,* Hamden, CT, reporter, 1956; *New Haven Register,* New Haven, CT, reporter, 1956-59. Book reviewer for *Hartford Courant* and *St. Petersburg Times;* freelance author of fiction. Visiting writer in India, 1974; Wesleyan University, Middletown, CT, visiting professor of English, then adjunct professor of English, 1974-2007. American coordinator, Indo-U.S. writers exchange, 1990—; speaker, First Mussoorie International Writers' Festival, U.A., India, 2007.

Member

Writers Guild, PEN, National Book Critics Circle (board member, 1991-95), Authors League Fund (board member).

Awards, Honors

Named New England Newspaper Woman of the Year, New England Women's Press Association, 1958, 1959; Abraham Woursell Foundation literary grant, 1965-70; Guggenheim fellowships, 1964-65, 1968; Rockefeller fellow, Aspen Institute, 1976; Best Books for Young Adults designation, American Library Association (ALA), 1979, for *The Ballad of T. Rantula*; Best Catholic Short Story of the Year Award, Catholic Press Association; Alex Award, ALA, for *Thinner than Thou*; James W. Tiptree Award finalist, for *Little Sisters of the Apocalypse* and *Weird Women, Wired Women.*

Writings

NOVELS

Mother Isn't Dead, She's Only Sleeping (for young adults), Houghton (Boston, MA), 1961.
At War as Children, Farrar, Straus (New York, NY), 1964.
The Better Part (for young adults), Farrar, Straus (New York, NY), 1967.
Armed Camps (science fiction), Faber & Faber (London, England), 1969, Dutton (New York, NY), 1970.
Cry of the Daughter, Dutton (New York, NY), 1971.
Tiger Rag, Dutton (New York, NY), 1973.
Captain Grownup, Dutton (New York, NY), 1976.
The Ballad of T. Rantula, Little, Brown (Boston, MA), 1979.
Magic Time (science fiction), Berkley (New York, NY), 1980.
(Under pseudonym Shelley Hyde) *Blood Fever* (science fiction), Pocket Books (New York, NY), 1982.
Fort Privilege (science fiction), Doubleday (Garden City, NY), 1985.
Catholic Girls, Donald I. Fine (New York, NY), 1987.
(Under name Kit Craig) *Gone* (thriller), 1992.
Little Sister of the Apocalypse (science fiction), Fiction Collective Two (Boulder, CO), 1994.
J. Eden, University Press of New England (Hanover, NH), 1996.
@expectations, Forge (New York, NY), 2000.
Thinner than Thou, Tor (New York, NY), 2004.
The Baby Merchant, Tor (New York, NY), 2006.

Also author, under name Kit Craig, of *Twice Burned* and four other psychological thrillers published in England.

SHORT STORIES

Mister Da V. and Other Stories (science fiction), Faber & Faber (London, England), 1967, Berkley (New York, NY), 1973.
The Killer Mice (science fiction; for young adults), Gollancz (London, England), 1976.
Other Stories and . . . The Attack of the Giant Baby (science fiction), Berkley (New York, NY), 1981.
The Revenge of the Senior Citizens Plus a Short Story Collection (science fiction), Doubleday (New York, NY), 1986.
Thief of Lives, University of Missouri Press (Colombia, MO), 1992.
Weird Women, Wired Women, University Press of New England (Hanover, NH), 1998.
Seven for the Apocalypse, University Press of New England, 1999.
Dogs of Truth: New and Uncollected Stories, Tor (New York, NY), 2005.

Contributor of short stories to more than sixty anthologies in the United States, Great Britain, Italy, and France, including *Winter's Tales* and *Norton Anthology of Contemporary Fiction.* Contributor of short fiction to

Yale Review, Transatlantic Review, Cosmopolitan, Journal, Missouri Review, Magazine of Fantasy and Science Fiction, Redbook, Tampa Review, Texas Review, Voice Literary Supplement, Omni, Nova, Argosy, Town, and *She.*

OTHER

When We Dream (for children), illustrated by Yutaka Sugita, 1965, Hawthorne (New York, NY), 1966.
(Compiler) *Fat* (anthology), Bobbs-Merrill (Indianapolis, IN), 1974.
The Bathyscaphe (radio play), National Public Radio, 1979.
Story First: The Writer as Insider (textbook; contains exercises by husband, Joseph W. Reed), Prentice-Hall (Englewood Cliffs, NJ), 1982, revised edition published as *Mastering Fiction Writing,* Writer's Digest (Cincinnati, OH), 1991.
George Orwell's 1984, Barron's Book Notes (Woodbury, NY), 1984.
Revision, Writer's Digest (Cincinnati, OH), 1989.

Sidelights

Kit Reed's publications are of interest to both adults and teenage readers. As the author once said, "Although I write primarily for adult readers, a great many teens seem to wander into my novels, perhaps because I do not believe there is an enormous difference between adults and young people." Reed's writing falls into a variety of categories: "Some of her stories are realistic, some impressionistic, some fantasy, some science fiction," indicated C.W. Sullivan III in the *St. James Guide to Science-Fiction Writers.* "Reed does not write hard, or technologically oriented, science fiction," explained Sullivan. Instead, she "seems to deal primarily with the people and to use the science fiction elements as another writer might use a car or truck—as a detail necessary to the story. . . . The two main themes of her work [are] the impact of technology on people's lives and the plight of senior citizens." Sullivan, who noted that "one of [Reed's] strongest pieces of social criticism is 'Golden Acres,' about a home for the elderly," commented that, in "the final analysis, it is Reed's characters that carry her fiction—science fiction, fantasy, or mainstream. To be sure, the other aspects of her writing are not found wanting, but her characters—especially the women struggling to find themselves in an indifferent or hostile society, or struggling against various institutions—remain in the reader's mind."

Reed described her genre-crossing writing this way: "Most people write what they want to read. In my case this mean a lot of early science fiction because, starting with the Oz books, I loved stories that departed from reality. Now I am more interested in what seems real. Sometimes I go for reality in a completely everyday way, as in *Captain Grownup* and *The Ballad of T. Rantula,* and at other times, as in *Magic Time,* from a position halfway up the wall. The work that pleases me most combines both elements." She commented on her tendency to write across genres to Gwyneth Jones for *Infinity Plus* online, noting: "I'm easily bored. . . . Brian Aldiss said I was a 'psychological novelist,' if that helps . . . As in, my central concern is why and how we are the way we are." As she commented to online interviewer Matthew Cheney for *SF Site,* "Both agents and editors will tell me after the fact that a book is satirical or socially concerned or . . . or . . . In fact, all I know about it is whether whatever drove me in the first place has gotten the novel to where it's going."

The Ballad of T. Rantula, deals with the thirteen-year-old hero's attempts to come to terms with the fact of his parents' divorce. According to Anne Tyler, writing in the *New York Times Book Review,* Reed's protagonist is "a stable, honest, earnest human being, the living center of a richly satisfying book." In "an era rampant with novels on marital bustups, Kit Reed's comes as refreshingly different, bringing with it a new point of view," claimed a *West Coast Review of Books* critic. "Told through the eyes of young Fred . . . during his last year at elementary school, the narrative avoids the cute and the obvious, rather it is brilliantly, uncannily accurate."

Captain Grownup is an adult novel about a newspaper reporter experiencing a mid-life crisis. After his wife kicks him out of their house, the man gives up his job to become an English teacher in a small town high school. Perceiving himself as a person who can help bring out young talent, he becomes platonically involved with a female student. Tyler called the book "a wry story about a 41-year-old man still trying to take the final steps to adulthood."

During the 1990s Reed released a number of works, including *J. Eden,* a novel that "shows us the extent to which people can hurt one another and still be loved and go on," related Molly E. Rauch in the *Nation.* The "cleverly assembled and often insightful" story portrays "four New York families shar[ing] a milestone summer in a New England country farmhouse," according to a *Publishers Weekly* critic, the reviewer complimenting Reed's dialogue while noting that "some readers may find that the bulk of the novel meanders too slowly through predictable lives." Calling *J. Eden* the "most ambitious . . . [and] slowest" novel by Reed to date, a *Kirkus Reviews* writer stated that the tale's "suspense hangs on the question of who's sleeping with whom and what everyone is thinking about aging, parenthood, mortality, etc." Telling the story from ten different viewpoints "gets us through in one piece," asserted Rauch, the critic adding that "the sustained hatred and doubt would be devastating otherwise." In *Entertainment Weekly* Suzanne Ruta similarly praised Reed for getting her readers to empathize with the story's "self-absorbed boomers and their desperately precocious offspring."

A veteran of online communication, Reed tells the tale of a woman whose internet life becomes more real and important to her than her daily existence in

@expectations. Jenny is a devoted wife, stepmother, and successful therapist. However, she is also plagued by dissatisfaction and troubles, and she sheds these when she goes online and becomes Zan, a resident of the resort St. Elene. She consorts with her online lover, "Reverdy," and tries to provide support to nineteen-year-old "Lark"; when Reverdy disappears, Jenny and Lark embark on a real-world journey to find him. "Reed makes Jenny's slide into an online world seem nearly plausible in this up-to-the-minute alternative love story," wrote a *Publishers Weekly* contributor. While noting the plot's sudden acceleration near the end of the novel, *New York Times Book Review* contributor J.D. Biersdorfer felt that "Reed manages to make a success of *@expectations* by zeroing in on that fascinating feeling one can get when leaving a mundane life to recreate the self in an alternative reality."

Though Reed is not one to get on "the soapbox, tub-thumping political aspect" of issues she cares about, as she explained to Jones for *Infinity Plus,* her novels and stories often contain social criticism. Many of her short stories have been considered feminist by critics—though Reed herself prefers the term "womanist"—and in *Thinner than Thou* she comments directly on the worship of body image embraced by the U.S. media. In the novel, an order of nuns known as the Dedicated Sisters act as a sort of body police and escort people to their convent in order for them to heal. One of their associates, Reverend Earl, runs a supposed luxury spa that is, in reality, a prison camp for obese individuals who have eating disorders or other body issues. "Reed provides much food for thought and reaffirms her position as one of our brightest cultural commentators," wrote a *Publishers Weekly* contributor of the novel. A *Kirkus Reviews* contributor called *Thinner than Thou* "unsettling, sometimes appalling: satire edging remorselessly toward reality." Owen McNally, writing in the *Hartford Courant,* described Reed's prose as "lean, fat-free and frequently seasoned with zesty turns of phrase. . . . Reed serves a feast of entertaining food for thought."

In *The Baby Merchant,* extremely likeable Tom Starbird is extremely good at his job: he kidnaps "unwanted" children and places them in loving families. Jake Zorn, a newsman, comes to Starbird for a child, but instead of business as usual, he threatens to ruin Starbird if he doesn't come through on his end of the deal. When Starbird's chosen unwed mother, Sasha, runs away from the group home where she's been living, Starbird has to revise his plans. Praising the role of Sasha, Collette Bancroft wrote in the *St. Petersburg Times:* "Trust Kit Reed to break the mold for an action hero," casting in the part "a nine-months-pregnant graduate student on the run from a man whose business is stealing babies." "Reed writes a fast-paced thriller with a consummate sense of style," wrote Regina Schroeder in *Booklist.*

Along with her novels, Reed has also published short fiction. *Weird Women, Wired Women,* is a collection of nineteen short stories focusing on the mother-daughter

relationships and women's role in a male-dominated society. "Covering more than 30 years of her darkly speculative fiction. . . . the volume offers a definitive, indispensable sampling of Reed in top form," reported a *Kirkus Reviews* contributor. "Anger, resentment, love, and obligation blur in tales that blend pathos and irony with the downright weird," summarized *Library Journal* contributor Eleanor J. Bader of the anthology. Crediting Reed as a "versatile" and "prolific" author, Ted Leventhal praised *Weird Women, Wired Women* for its "humorous, ironic prose." However, the *Booklist* critic also contended that *Weird Women, Wired Women* "suffers from repetition." Reed's "crisp and to the point" text collection contains "unrelenting obsessiveness," determined a *Publishers Weekly* reviewer, the critic similarly concluding that the "lack of contrast to offset the prevailing darkness becomes unnerving." In contrast, Bader judged *Weird Women, Wired Women* to be "fresh" and "refreshing."

Like her other collections, *Seven for the Apocalpyse* is a mix of science fiction, mainstream, and "womanist" writings, "sometimes all these things at once," according to Roberta Johnson in *Booklist.* In the longest story, "The Little Sisters of the Apocalypse," Reed depicts motorcycle riding nuns, protecting a group of women abandoned by their men when the men went to war. When the men return, the women must consider whether or not they want them back. Other tales feature a home security device in love with her owner, a man coping with his wife's Alzheimer's disease, a penal colony disguised as a living history tourist trap, and a retelling of the old fairy tale, "The Juniper Tree," retitled "The Singing Marine." According to a *Publishers Weekly* contributor, "Reed's stories are strikingly imagined and tautly written." Of the last story in the collection, Elizabeth Hand wrote in the *Magazine of Science Fiction and Fantasy* that "it leaves the reader thirsty for more, which is a good way, maybe the best way, to end any book."

Reed's more recent story collection, *Dogs of Truth: New and Uncollected Stories,* was deemed "a set of marvelous glimpses of the darker side of everything" by Schroeder. Many of the dystopian tales in this volume feature scary children and teenagers: one couple is stalked by a baby stroller, and in another tale, high schoolers revolt against their almost military enclosure of a high school—until they get bored and their revolt trails off. "Reed's humor is as sharp and cool as the edge of an icicle. These *Dogs of Truth* have bite," wrote Colette Bancroft in the *St. Petersburg Times.*

Discussing her writing process with *SF Site* interviewer Cheney, Reed noted: "I've always been a visceral writer. . . . I don't have an intellectual approach, twelve steps or twelve things you need to put in to make a story, any of that; I sit down in the morning most days and do what I have to do, whatever that is." Rob Bedford, interviewing Reed for the *SFF World Web* site, asked the author what drew her to become a writer. "I've been telling stories since I was four and a half," she explaine. "It's all I ever wanted to do; by the time I was in first grade I was writing them instead of dictating to my mother. It's who I am."

Biographical and Critical Sources

BOOKS

St. James Guide to Science-Fiction Writers, 4th edition, St. James Press (Detroit, MI), 1996.

PERIODICALS

Booklist, March 15, 1998, Ted Leventhal, review of *Weird Women, Wired Women,* p. 1203; May 15, 1999, Roberta Johnson, review of *Seven for the Apocalypse,* p. 1682; August, 2000, Whitney Scott, review of *@expectations,* p. 2108; June 1, 2004, Paula Leudtke, review of *Thinner than Thou,*"" p. 1713; April 1, 2005, Gillian Engberg, The Alex Awards, 2005, p. 1355; September 1, 2005, Regina Schroeder, review of *Dogs of Truth: New and Uncollected Stories,* p. 76; April 1, 2006, Regina Schroeder, review of *The Baby Merchant,* p. 29.

Entertainment Weekly, March 15, 1996, Suzanne Rutta, review of *J. Eden,* p. 59.

Hartford Courant"" (Hartford, CT), June 9, 2004, Owen McNally, The Land of Bodily Bliss.

Kirkus Reviews, January 15, 1996, review of *J. Eden;* February 1, 1998, review of *Weird Women, Wired Women;* April 15, 2004, review of *Thinner than Thou,* p. 368.

Library Journal, February 1, 1998, Eleanor J. Bader, review of *Weird Women, Wired Women,* p. 115; June 15, 2004, Jackie Cassada, review of *Thinner than Thou,* p. 62.

Magazine of Science Fiction and Fantasy, September, 1999, Elizabeth Hand, review of *Seven for the Apocalypse,* p. 30.

Nation, April 22, 1996, Molly E. Rausch, review of *J. Eden,* p. 36.

New York Times Book Review, July 4, 1976, Anne Tyler, review of *Captain Grownup;* June 17, 1979, Anne Tyler, review of *The Ballad of T. Rantula;* April 21, 1996, review of *J. Eden;* October 29, 2000, J.D. Biersdorfer, You've Got Males, p. 38; January 1, 2006, Sarah Ferguson, Fiction Chronicle, p. 17.

People, July 5, 2004, Lynn Andriani, review of *Thinner than Thou,* p. 47.

Philadelphia Inquirer (Philadelphia, PA), August 16, 2006, Martha Woodall, review of *The Baby Merchant.*

Publishers Weekly, December 18, 1995, review of *J. Eden,,* p. 39; February 9, 1998, review of *Weird Women, Wired Women,* p. 75; May 24, 1999, review of *Seven for the Apocalypse,* p. 65; July 31, 2000, review of *@expectations,* p. 67; May 10, 2004, review of *Thinner than Thou,*"" p. 41, Melissa Mia Hall, Abandon Flesh All Ye Who Enter Here, p. 42; July 25, 2005, review of *The Dogs of Truth,* p. 53; September 12, 2005, review of *Bronze: A Tale of Terror,* p. 46; March 13, 2006, review of *The Baby Merchant,* p. 46.

Review of Contemporary Fiction, spring, 1999, Irving Malin, review of *Weird Women, Wired Women,* p. 199.

St. Petersburg Times (St. Petersburg, FL), September 11, 2005, Colette Bancroft, Stories with Teeth, p. P7; June 11, 2006, Colette Bancroft, Fiction that Feels like Foreshadowing, p. P6.

West Coast Review of Books, September, 1979, review of *The Ballad of T. Rantula.*

ONLINE

Infinity Plus Web site, http://www.infinityplus.co.uk/ (May 18, 2007), Gwyneth Jones, interview with Reed.

Kit Reed Home Page, http://www.kitreed.net (May 18, 2007).

SFF World Web site, http://www.sffworld.com/ (May 25, 2006), Rob Bedford, interview with Reed.

SF Site, http://www.sfsite.com/ (May 18, 2007), Matthew Cheney, interview with Reed.

Wesleyan University Web site, http://www.wesleyan.edu/ (May 18, 2007), Kit Reed.

Autobiography Feature

Kit Reed

K it Reed contributed the following autobiographical essay to *SATA:*

At three I got lost at an intersection in downtown San Francisco, but only for a minute. Crossing the street, my panicky parents looked back and saw me planted on the curb. Adults streamed past on either side as I sat there, resolutely trying to jam an object into a box that was too small for it.

It's the story of my life.

A lifetime later a friend saw me reviving a defunct coffee maker. He suggested gently that it was beyond hope. I stopped long enough to say, "I never give up."

Then I admitted, "Sometimes you get tired of being the kind of person who never gives up."

It is, on the other hand, the engine that drives my work. For a writer, talent is only the beginning. Writers have to be tough, persistent, and alert to the world outside their heads.

Mine changed constantly. We moved a dozen times before I finished college.

I was born in San Diego, California, but I'm not from anywhere. The Naval officer's tour of duty was about two years—until war changed everything. I used to think it was the ideal way to live. If life in a given place went sour, the inconvenience was only temporary. Soon enough, there would be crates in the living room. A new school in a new place.

I used to wonder whether I'd be any good at living in the same town for long. Where I come from, if things aren't going right you can always move.

We had moved from California to Honolulu, to New London and back to Honolulu by the time I was four. Landscapes changed all the time. My parents and the Navy were the constants in my life: Mummy and Daddy and Harbor Wilson, the plush Easter bunny who started my career.

Wherever we moved certain objects followed, to be uncrated and set up in living rooms from Honolulu to Washington, DC to Panama and later to St. Petersburg, Florida, and on and on. These were the treasures Naval officers' families shored up against their ruin: camphor wood chest, chow bench, brass table; the Chinese rug and the teakwood desk.

There were treasures just like them in hundreds of other Navy living rooms. Come into one of our houses anywhere and you were at home. I still have some of these loyal objects. More important, Harbor sits in state in our upstairs hall. She is wearing three medals that followed her starring role in my first novel: one an American Library Association award for *Thinner than Thou,* two from the New England Newspaperwomen's Association for work I did for the *New Haven Register.*

In Honolulu, we lived in a bungalow perched on a mountainside. We had a Japanese maid. Daddy built me a playhouse out of a furniture crate. I sat my mother down and dictated my first novel. She printed it on paper folded to make a book. I was four and a half. She read it back, including a (parenthetical) question I had asked, which she had dutifully transcribed. I told her it didn't belong and covered the erasure with a drawing of

Kit at age three (Courtesy of Kit Reed.)

Harbor and her friend Bobby Jones. I titled the book "Harbor Plots Her Plans."

Three other bunnies, Bobby, Miz Peter, and Pitty Pat, ended up somewhere on the road down Diamond Head; they fell off the running board where I'd lined them up before my father left for the base at Pearl Harbor, where the U.S.S. *Neches* was docked. Later he was detached and sent to the Navy Department, which gave us two years of ordinary American life in Washington, DC.

I fell in love with Mikey in first grade. The big kids made me walk on flypaper in Helen Simmel's tent. My mother lost a baby, not the first and not the last. The RH factor was still a problem waiting to be solved. I wrote and illustrated the second "Harbor" book. My father was crestfallen because instead of waiting to be read to, I read the next "Oz" book to myself. I read *Beowulf* in the bathroom one long night while a gullible baby sitter waited for me to come out.

Daddy and I went for a walk on Thanksgiving, just the two of us, in the snow. He took me for my first haircut, freeing me from the bondage of my mother's laboriously tended Shirley Temple curls, and he probably sat me on the roving photographer's pony when he took my picture in front of our neat little house. When my new kitten gave Daddy hives they bought me a Scottie; I wanted a dog just like Fala. I had an accordion I didn't want to play, a bunny fur coat with matching muff.

In DC I was bowled over by *The Spirit.* Comics! Big Little Books. My mother's anxieties were catching. Radio accounts of bubonic plague and black widow spiders left me feeling my armpits for buboes, looking for spiders marked by the red hourglass and, incidentally, worrying about appendicitis. My mother subscribed to a religious newsletter, perhaps looking for a cure to ailments she could not name. I loved the gruesome details of all those heinous afflictions miraculously cured by St. Anne de Beaupré.

Ordinary wasn't quite ordinary, although I didn't know it; one day Daddy came home and destroyed all the toys marked MADE IN JAPAN. We were about to move.

In a childhood marked by frequent moves and changing scenery, there was another constant: the long-running story inside my head.

We were still in Honolulu when I began it, after my parents had turned out the lights and closed the door. It took the sting out of being put to bed. My story featured blond twins just about my age named Dick and Daisy, who lived on a ranch. It continued night after night until the three of us were old enough to start thinking about sex. One of us wasn't ready to be that person, and the stories stopped. The cast included Brad and Brenda, who had dark hair. Then I added red-headed Rusty; I was in love with him.

Kit with her parents, Lillian and John Craig, adorned with leis in Honolulu, 1939 (Courtesy of Kit Reed.)

By that time we were back in to snowy New London, where my father took command of the R-17. An aspiring flier who washed out at Pensacola, he turned to what the Navy called the Silent Service: submarines. The adventures of Harbor escalated. In "Harbor and Shamrock Wilson," Harbor's plane crashed in the jungle and she met her colored sister, a tribal princess. Together, they came back to America and became best friends. We moved to Panama and then, abruptly, back to New London before Christmas. That was the year I started over in St. Joseph's in New London twice, at a nuns' school in Panama and in St. Paul's school in Florida—all in fourth grade.

I asked for a gaudy Carmen Miranda doll that Christmas, but found the economy model stashed in a closet early that December. On Sunday morning the phone rang. Daddy answered it. Japanese planes had bombed Pearl Harbor and his brother Jimmy, an officer on the Pennsylvania, was dead. If I'd known enough to *worry,* I thought, none of this would have happened. Things would work out, as long as I had a plan. If they attacked New London I would crouch by the stairs and bash them with my alarm clock as they came in. On our last Christmas together, Santa brought the big Carmen Miranda doll instead.

By January the three of us and Toughy, the Scottie, were on our way to St. Petersburg, Florida, the safe place my father had chosen for my mother to sit out the war. Where I was used to hills, Florida was dauntingly flat, with staggering 360-degree skies. Spongy Bermuda grass battled for survival in sandy gray dirt. Sand spurs scratched my ankles and stuck in Toughy's paws. It was like landing on Mars. I used to stare out at sunny winter landscapes, praying for snow.

We said goodbye to Daddy at the Atlantic Coast Line station in downtown St. Petersburg—one of those wide places in the road where trains stopped on their way back to the real world. I remember hugging him and turning away stoically because in a life of change there was yet another constant: officers' children don't cry.

They think. And they worry. And they plan. God, do they plan. Do this right next time, or do it differently; expect the worst and the worst won't happen; watch out what you trust in and the next time, there won't be a war.

A Naval Academy graduate from Jacksonville, Florida, John R. Craig went where the Navy sent him, right up to the end. He went to the Pacific as skipper of the U.S.S. *Grampus,* a submarine that landed coast watchers during World War Two and destroyed several enemy ships in the Coral Sea. I still have his Navy Cross and his Bronze Star. Chief (VADM K.S.) Masterson, an Academy classmate and one of my first adult friends, told me years later that he and his wife Charlotte saw Jack for the last time in San Francisco the night before he shipped out. I can't bear to look at his letters home from that period but I cherish his exit line:

"If you see me lying drunk in the gutter turn me over. I don't want them to see the brass buttons on the uniform."

He was a gentle, funny man who used what spare time he had making intricate ship models, an inlaid cribbage board, a record cabinet, a teakwood album that he filled with snapshots lovingly captioned in white ink. He subscribed to *Popular Mechanics,* which I loved, and until I protested that I could read the next Oz book faster by myself, he read to me. I often wonder what I would have been like if he had lived.

Jack was one of three children, the second son born to James E. Craig and Clara Belle Rich Craig, who was—literally—the first white child born in Deland, the Florida town her parents founded in 1874. I imagine that going South, Union Army Captain John Rich invited a few freemen and their families along to help him settle the new land. Interesting that the Deland website revises history, calling Grandmother the "first child" born there. Widowed by the time I knew her well, my grandmother Craig was smart, funny and tough as nails. Contemporary photos indicate that as a girl, she was also beautiful.

She rated films for the Florida State Board of Censors and was—I fear—a leader in the D.A.R. But she was kind and she cooked, and, in sharp contrast to my mother, she loved to do it. Role model? Probably. Except for the D.A.R.

Jack Craig was a small man, neatly put together and, according to his superior officers, one who could be counted on to follow orders without question, even under fire. As an ensign he met and married a Jacksonville girl, Lillian Hyde. She was brought up in a tradition that died before she came of age: ladies talked in euphemisms. And ladies didn't work, although when Jack met her she was teaching school. The Hydes grew up in their own little Tara with white columns on the big front porch and servants' quarters behind the house; a bronze nymph raised a lamp high above the newel post in the front hall. There were nine children if you counted Uncle LeRoy, who burned to a cinder playing with matches under the back porch.

The family had pretensions. Because some America-bound ancestor had missed his tax bill, my mother said, his property in central London was "escheated to the crown." Hyde Park. She spent years scouring libraries for proof that she was descended from the patroon of Staten Island. After she died I handed her burden off to the archivist at the University of Florida.

Marie, the oldest sister, made her debut in Charleston at the St. Cecelia's Ball, well before the family lost its money in the 1923 Florida real estate crash. Older brothers moved on before I was old enough to visit the house, leaving three single sisters and Marie's orphaned daughter in a house full of hotly contested furniture.

The street had gone downhill since the glory days when, my mother reported glowingly, "John [the cook] said, 'Miss Lillian, you're poor to carry' and cut me an extra piece of pie," and, "Nurse used to take us out in the pony cart. People would say, 'I just know you're Forrest Hyde's children. I can tell by the eyes.'" For her, 553 May Street was always "home"—unlike anyplace she lived afterward, with what remained of our shrinking nuclear family.

Interesting, that she idealized an experience that must have been miserable. Lillian was the shy one, who only got attention when she was sick. She didn't much like her siblings, whom I was expected to love. Except for a few ceremonial visits when I was small, we avoided Jacksonville until my mother was widowed.

Later she felt guilty because the night the telegram came ("missing in action and presumed lost") she told me it was from her brother Forrest, and sent me back to bed. The next morning she broke the news—and put me to bed. The day after, we got up and got dressed and carried on as if everything was going to be all right (they'd find him) and nothing had changed. It was what you did. The alternatives were too grim.

At school, however, I was marked. The only kid without a father. As though it was something I did. Every time a new boy came into the class I studied him greedily, hoping he was like me. A former neighbor greeted me in tears, "Oh you poor child, you have lost your father." I despised the old lady for treating me like an aberration when I was working hard to be just like everybody else.

For the survivors, Missing in Action is both better and worse than dead. For a long time I imagined Daddy was a prisoner, or marooned on a desert island; as an adult I wondered what would happen if, mysteriously, he came back. What would he be like? Would he be proud of me? When my mother died I found letters of inquiry to the Navy Department, to Academy classmates. She tracked down leads well into the 1960s. Like me, she never gave up—on that, at least.

We moved into a room in somebody else's house. Later we had two rooms in a larger house, and next, a garage apartment. Toughy went with us. Harbor and my other stuffed rabbits did too. Made from cartons, their houses lined the sidewalk wherever we moved. Their town was named Bunny Ridge. "Harbor Comics" replaced the "Harbor" books.

Finally my mother went against the advice of crusty Forrest the financier and went into capital, what little there was. She bought us a house and saw it through renovation. It was necessary, to give me an apparently normal life.

We went to the christening of the U.S.S. *John R. Craig,* DD 885. Instead of a father, I had a ship.

It was probably good for me to grow up with an anxious hypochondriac. A cough bought me freedom for days. A polio scare kept me home for most of sixth grade, and I loved it. I read through the "Oz" books for the dozenth time, hung on the radio, wrote ("good heavens, Deanna ejaculated"), and drew, all in the comfort and security of my very own bed.

I already knew that the solution to life's problems was *not* lying down. Except when sidelined by childbirth or major surgery, I have never spent a day in bed.

I also learned, by negative example, that it did *not* matter what people said about what you wore or what you did. With her social aspirations, my mother taught me the converse: to value meritocracy. You are what you achieve. Poor little only mother, bringing up an only child. She was a mass of social anxieties. She never outgrew her fear that I would mortify her. "You can't go out wearing/saying/doing that," she'd say, guaranteeing that I would do anything to prove her wrong. "What will people think?"

When my bio turned up in *Who's Who,* she assumed it was only for that year. When I juggled work and family, she was afraid I'd "overdo." Ladies didn't work.

I should, however, add that she was essentially sweet, good at turning my anger into laughter. She had a formidable vocabulary. In her own tentative, frightened way, she was strong. When I got thrown from a horse in summer camp she engineered riding lessons. During the war she drove us up and down the Eastern Seaboard to see relatives in Jacksonville and Bronxville—and in Washington, the Mastersons, whose sons were the nearest things to siblings that I had. She managed our finances so carefully that I was a senior in college before I learned how tight things were.

She believed certain material wasn't suitable for children. Just as well she didn't know what I read, from her Book-of-the-Month-Club selections to *Forever Amber* and other parents' sex manuals—on the sly at the houses of friends. At twelve I went to *The Story of Dr. Wassell,* the first movie I'd been allowed to see where everything did *not* come out all right in the end. Watching Gary Cooper fight to the death as Dr. Wassell, I understood for the first time that if heroes could die on the screen, then my father might not come back.

Walking to school behind the big kids, I heard a boy telling a story—*a story!*—about something that had happened. It was better than radio. He did all the voices. Rapt, I thought: *I want to be that person.*

In the new house I began a novel about a girl and a horse. By then I was writing flap copy for the book I expected to publish, and soon. "Kitten Craig is twelve years old and has her own horse."

I did. My mother bought me an old cow pony with a sagging lip; until zoning caught up with us, he lived in the garage. Phlegmatic Satin was replaced by Rex, a skittish five-gaited horse with a barbwire scar on his haunch.

The visits to Jacksonville accelerated. I thanked God for the Craigs. Grandmother expected me to be tough. She had to be, with both sons killed in the war. Aunt Lydia was thirteen years younger than my father, and I saw him in her face. She was an air traffic controller when women weren't accepted. Being with them was an emotional boot camp: shape up or ship out. It was good for me. Great Aunt Ruth Rich was a journalist who kept on typing after she went blind. I re-read Oz books at their house; I read condensed novels in Grandmother's Omnibook; I read anything I found in every house we stayed in.

The Hydes were another story, one I transformed in my fourth novel, *Cry of the Daughter.* They were indeed a southern novel, just not that one. Fuse Faulkner at tremendous speeds with *Gone with the Wind* and you get the idea. On May Street I read books my aunts had on hand, including *Native Son* and *Scarlet Sister Mary,* which I hid under a sofa cushion so I wouldn't get caught.

Even without the Navy to prod her, my mother moved us to Parris Island, South Carolina, the summer I turned fifteen. She may have bought into the myth—that the right move would change her life. Or, she sometimes thought, the right operation: for the deviated septum, the defective toe joint, the malady she could not diagnose and would never cure—depression, because she never stopped grieving for him.

I fell in love with the Carolina landscape—dense marsh grass in the Inland Waterway; magnificent live-oaks shrouded in Spanish Moss. I fell in love with the human landscape: desperate Marine recruits running the obstacle course behind the Officers' Guest House where we lived; public high school, that microcosm of aspiration and politics, sex and violence. Classes were mediocre but going to Beaufort High was a powerful lesson in life.

To survive, a military kid learns to look and listen. Walk the walk and talk the talk or the pack will find out you are different and turn on you. Going into each new place, I learned to absorb social configurations without being told, move fast and join in conversations that had been going on for years. "Hey," I said in Beaufort, with its tidewater vocabulary and country cadences; it was never "Hi." Constant moves sharpened my ear for dialogue. It serves me to this day. I hear my characters coming before I see them.

At Beaufort High I blended—for a while.

We lived on the base, where my mother managed the Officers' Club until she declared for the last time, "This job is untenable," and quit. By then she and a boy from Wilder's stable had driven to St. Petersburg with a horse trailer to bring Rex back: five-foot woman, loading a horse that stood fifteen-and-a-half hands high.

Life on the base was exciting. Privileged. There were free movies at the Odeon, where dependents sat in a special section behind platoons of boots with shaved heads. There was a bowling alley. There was the club. I could swim in the pool all weekend, flirt with junior officers at dinner, sign a chit for apple pie for breakfast on Mondays before I left for school. In splendid isolation, seven of us rode the forty-five minutes from the base to Beaufort on a city bus painted regulation green. I never stopped reading, but in Beaufort, I wrote only for class.

"Oh," Mrs. Combs said, delivering Part One of the Chinese curse: "You are so fa-*ceel.*"

I had two boyfriends—the first an incipient stalker and the second a country boy who dumped me because I wouldn't put out. At the time I thought it was because I was funny, too brash. Also true. Lesson taken: don't let them know you're smart.

It was harder to hide the fact that I couldn't hit the ball. On the third strike Coach Askew loomed, drawling, "Gurl, ain't yew got no screw-ples?" Probably not.

We spent an extra year in Beaufort because after years of repression in parochial schools, I was out riding around in cars with boys and for a while, at least, they thought I was cute.

We lived on Federal Street in the town where Captain John Rich and his wife Clara buried their first baby before they went south. By that time the local kids were on to me. I was the same stupid, vulnerable stiff who didn't belong anywhere.

I read lurid historical novels in that house, and during study halls I raced through the library's run of Edna Ferber, a crash course in construction and suspense. Book reviews in *Time* magazine opened a new world to me. There were dozens of new novels every month. I wanted to read them all—and write about them. Imagine. I was sixteen.

My cousin Marie came to live with us, toting a baby of her own, and in her own wonderful, easygoing way, she put certain things in perspective. "You know, sometimes your mother can be a bitch." Decades later my daughter alleviated years of filial guilt by suggesting Marie was right.

I fell into a posture of rebellion; it was time. I was an adult with a family of my own when my mother's best friend told me, "Your mother was very brave, letting you live your own life instead of hanging on to you." That too.

Maybe that's why we moved back to Washington, DC at the end of my junior year at Beaufort High. Unless she feared the impossible, that her clueless, virginal daughter was having sex. Mystified, I found out by accident why I had been hauled into the base dispensary. The doctor reassured her and sent us home.

Although I hadn't thought about getting into college, my mother had. The formidable Sister Mary Leonard let me into Georgetown Visitation Convent in Washington, and from a world of boys who might—just might—fall in love with me, I moved into a girls' boarding school where Dobermans were posted at the bottom of the stairs every night, although it was never clear whether they were to keep out intruders, or keep us in. Reading *The Count of Monte Cristo,* I felt like Edmund Dantes, jailed in the Chateau d'If.

I knew we'd have to leave the horse behind when we left Beaufort. We left my dog!

Visitation was good for me, but not the way my mother hoped. Instead of polishing my manners, the school encouraged me to let the people know I had brains. Once again I came late to the feast; the boarders had been together for years. It went better for me than for the colonel's daughter, who claimed the Virgin came to her in the chapel with orders for the nuns to send her back to Colorado, where she belonged.

On weekends, my mother and I went calling on my father's classmates in their snug houses with their complete families: parents, children. Intact. They were generous when we came to call.

One day the senior class got on a bus and went to National Cathedral School to take S.A.T.'s. In vocabulary, I score in the ninety-ninth percentile—I just do, but there was a hitch. Leonard looked down her aristocratic nose. "My dear, with your math scores, you'll be fortunate if you get into any college at all." Mandatory G.R.E.s two years later confirmed it. In math I scored in the fourth percentile.

The College of Notre Dame in Baltimore was kind enough to take me. Later, Sister Maura Eichner let me submit short stories in lieu of a footnoted thesis. I roomed with the talented, temperamental daughter of the *Washington Post*'s answer to Ann Landers. In a conventional college we found the outsider culture, along with another good friend who later became a nun.

With meals and housekeeping taken care of, the sisters thought women could do anything: be scientists, scholars, artists. My favorite was the incendiary Sister Ignatius, who moderated the college paper. Her temper was like the weather. Violent, unpredictable. We asked survivors: "How is she today?"

The Ig was a precisionist, tougher than any city editor. She chose me to edit the yearbook, not the obvious A student. When the creator of *Pogo* came to speak I did the interview. The clipping got me my first job.

As freshmen, we were bussed to Annapolis for tea fights at the Naval Academy. I was in love with the Navy, from the craggy bust of Tecumseh to the photo of my father's gym team enshrined in Dahlgren Hall. I could show you the exact location of the initialed brick among thousands in front of Bancroft Hall. I went to hops with sons of my father's classmates. I thought I'd marry into the Navy. It was home.

But meanwhile. Meanwhile! The house in St. Petersburg was between tenants and needed work the summer after my freshman year. I was painting kitchen cabinets when my mother's college roommate invited us to dinner. Her son Jimmy had a hot date, but his mother barred the door. "You have to get a date for Kitten too." He dug up a high school classmate, a scholarship student at Yale who was, I was warned, "smart." I imagined a weedy character with glasses. He produced Joe Reed.

Attacking *War and Peace* that summer, I had read as far as the Battle of Austerlitz. I never finished the book.

We went dancing at the Bath Club where as a kid I'd been watched over by the club's fatherly headwaiter, B.C. A dance band played on the terrace by the pool. Joe and I danced well together; we still do. On the way

"In senior year I knitted a Dramat muffler for Joe," Baltimore, Maryland, 1954 (Courtesy of Bill Rettberg Photography.)

home one of us quoted T.S. Eliot's sober instructions about wiping your hand across the mouth. . . . In a flash the other provided the second line, and it is significant that I don't remember who said which.

Jimmy never scored with that hot girl, but Joe and I were bonded for life. We had just turned nineteen.

The next summer my mother pushed me into typing school—liberating for someone whose wretched handwriting could never keep pace with her thoughts. They taught me how to type.

Joe gave me the Modern Library Faulkner. He introduced me to *Vile Bodies*. Along with Scott Fitzgerald and Graham Greene, William Faulkner and Evelyn Waugh taught me how to write.

Decades later I marveled. "How did we find each other?"

He said, "How do two giraffes find each other in a field of zebras?"

My mother noted mildly that we might not have much in common, all we ever did was go to the movies, but she reckoned without the hours we spent parked on the Vinoy fill or in front of the house. There have been thousands of movies since, and in spite of her fears, we never run out of things to talk about.

His mother, I learned later, didn't approve of me. Where she wanted him to marry up, a Catholic girl would burden him with babies. I could only drag him down. She'd have moved heaven and earth to stop the wedding, but she couldn't budge Joe.

My mother worried because we fought. We fight like tigers. Growing up with a woman who would brood until I begged her to tell me what I'd done wrong, I vowed to get it out and get it over with. Fight. Negotiate. Resolve.

Being a long-distance landlord tired my mother, who had quit the government job that brought her to Washington. She'd tried selling insurance and real estate without success. It wasn't hard to convince her to move back to St. Petersburg. Friends lived there. So did the Reeds.

College life went on, but with a difference. There were the letters, days that there weren't letters, weeks of saving up for trips. Days at Notre Dame unfolded in black-and-white. The movie turned to Technicolor the minute I got off the train in New Haven. Although he was an English major whose work-study job put him to work for the noted Boswell scholar Frederick A. Pottle, Joe's life revolved around the Dramat, center of the outsider culture at Yale. He loved building sets and he loved running things. He was president in his senior year.

I went to every show. At the parties afterward, there was the ritual. Sam Pottle played mad piano while people sang drunken, outrageous songs. We were nothing like the preppy drunks going past outside on Fraternity Row with girls from Wellesley/Vassar/Smith with their cashmere sweaters and perfect hair.

It was a good fit for a Navy junior who didn't belong anywhere.

Compared to childhood, adult life is a dream. Unlike children, grownups make the decisions. Adults are in control of what they do, and what comes next. While Joe joined the U.S.S. *Macon* as an ensign in the reserve, I applied to the *St. Petersburg Times*. I got to the heart of the personality test, choosing answers that made me look inventive, creative, aggressive, naturally curious. All true.

Outside the Society department, which was its own kind of ghetto, there were five women—a record for newspapers in those days. Lorna Carroll, the religion editor, was an ex-showgirl. Assigned to a story about a crop duster, she cried, "Lash me to the plane." A neophyte who never went to journalism school, I was hired to answer the phone.

I loved it. I was being paid for what I did! I went into the newsroom on my days off for the sheer pleasure of hanging out with people who, like me, observed and recorded details about a world where they didn't necessarily belong.

Soon I was editing copy. I "enterprised" a feature about a sidewalk bank teller—my first. I convinced the desk to let me review new television shows. In short order I was a TV columnist. Unthinkable now, but nobody did it on a regular basis then.

Chick Ober was city editor, stern and businesslike. With work, I could make him smile. The newsroom was dominated by men, all busy and obviously more important than I could hope to be, pounding on klunky standard typewriters. I would have done anything to impress those guys.

I wrote well but moved too fast; after I overlooked a writ in Circuit Court I ended up on Obits, where I spent six dismal weeks phoning funeral homes. Lorna went on a two-week vacation and I dummied and wrote headlines and most of the copy for the weekly church page. I chose a pseudonym: Fidelia Kirk. In the composing room, I threw out blocks of hot type and rearranged columns with the best of them. I learned to read in reverse.

"Well," said my boss on the project, "you just passed Journalism 101." Sandy Stiles took notice and had me design and write for the TV section in his new Sunday magazine. From answering the phone, I had moved up fast. By that time I had inherited Great Aunt Ruth's typewriter. I remember starting and abandoning one short story at home.

I read C.S. Lewis's theological science-fiction trilogy, starting with *Out of the Silent Planet*. For a child who grew up on the "Oz" books, SF was the route into imaginary adult worlds. It fed my appetite for the weird.

A year later Joe came home on leave and we were engaged. Back on the *Macon,* he broke the news to his skipper, then-Captain Vernon L. Lowrance. When he told my father's classmate that he was marrying Jack Craig's daughter, Rebel laughed. "Get out of here, you make me feel old." Although Joe's mother is not smiling in the wedding photos, we were married that December. We moved to Great Lakes Naval Training Center for his last six months in the service.

Bottom line? I lost my job.

I went from struggling star, still rising, at the country's best independent newspaper to the editorship of the District Public Works Office house organ, *The Right*

Kit and Joe leave the Sunset Country Club after their wedding, December 10, 1955 (Courtesy of Graham Photography.)

Angle. I didn't know it was the ideal career move. With a job I could do in two days and a month of eight-hour work days to do it in, I wrote.

What was I reading? I remember *Miss Lonelyhearts,* which I read standing up in a drugstore because I couldn't afford the paperback. Shirley Jackson. J.D. Salinger. I remember an early fight over what belonged on our first bookshelf. I held out for my favorites, no matter how battered. Joe was a bindings snob. We split the difference.

I wrote a dozen stories in that period, sent them out to a pay-by-the-read "literary agent" and discovered that the operation was a scam. Ten dollars for the reading. If you wanted further notes on your story, you paid more. Life was too short. Joe pointed me to two amazing details in Herodotus. I wrote a story called "To Be Taken in a Strange Country."

My mother met a writer at the Bath Club. She said, "Oh, my daughter's a writer too." He offered to put me in touch with his agent at Curtis Brown. Emilie Jacobson liked my work but thought "To Be Taken" was too strange to show. She asked to see more. It would be a while.

We were moving to New Haven. Joe was preparing for graduate school at Yale. I was never happier to lose a job. After three tense months on area weeklies owned

by the spoiled son of a St. Louis newspaper scion, I moved to the *New Haven Register.* In a newsroom with exactly one other woman, I was hired to answer the phone. But not for long. I did rewrites. Then I did a couple of obits. I did a story. Then I did another one.

I followed a visiting nurse through her day in the poorest neighborhood in New Haven. With a photographer riding post, I covered a drug bust. I was learning how a city works.

Whenever an author came to town, I did the interview. I went in without an agenda. After the first question, I built questions on their answers. Avid for any detail that would help me become a writer, I took notes. With my head bent over the notebook, I was invisible. They opened up as if to their psychiatrists.

Composing on the typewriter taught me discipline. There was a lot of tearing out and crumpling pages and starting over from the top. As I hammered away at the lead, the rest of the story organized itself. Fiction unfolds for me in the same way. Writing and re-writing, I discover the tone, the point of view, the cadences of my characters. I find out what I'm doing in the process of getting it down, and getting it *right.*

I learned more from crusty newsmen than any writing program could teach. Precision and accuracy were the rule. There was no place in the newsroom for prima donnas. Excel and Chick or Bart or Al might mutter, "Good story." High praise. At the *Register,* Charlie McQueeney pulled me into the composing room, where the clatter of the Mergenthalers would keep the news that he was giving me a raise from reaching his staff.

Perhaps the most valuable lesson was in working on deadline. Now I work according to deadlines I set for myself.

Interviewing the news editor's wife, Kaatje Hurlbut, who had just sold her first short story to *Mademoiselle,* I learned that she'd been writing for eight hours a day for fifteen years. Inspired, I came home and pulled out "To Be Taken in a Strange Country." Bob Mills at *Venture* rejected it but sent me to Anthony Boucher at *The Magazine of Fantasy and Science Fiction,* who took it. That first sale was like a dealer's sample of a powerful drug. With no time to write, I finished long days in the newsroom and wrote short stories at night.

In the era of the happy housewife, Joe and I had agreed that a woman with a career was more interesting than one without. I put him through graduate school; since then he has supported my work, whether or not it pays. As resident critic, he reads every line of fiction I write.

At work, I was covering juvenile court. We were the first paper to do it. Assistant managing editor Al Sizer made an arrangement with the judge, agreeing to mask the young offenders' identities. Again, I was the invisible reporter: observing, recording, astonished by how many cases were custody matters— placing children when there were no responsible adults. Many ended up in the state school, batched with serious offenders. My third novel, *The Better Part,* reflects some of what I learned.

Four boys from the projects mugged and murdered an old man for a watch and some pocket change. Al assigned me to an in-depth series. I talked to families, to police and social workers, trying to find out what turned them into killers. The New England Newspaperwomen of America named me best reporter of the year. Picking up my second medal the following May, I asked about the last year's winner. "Died in childbirth," I was told. I was pregnant, although it didn't show.

One week in August, I interviewed Cary Grant and covered a talk by Eleanor Roosevelt. That Friday Charlie said he was afraid I'd deliver in the newsroom and sent me home. The guys in the newsroom took up a collection for a farewell present. I bought a desk. I thought I had a week to get ready, but that night I went to the hospital and by Saturday night, Joe and I had a boy.

Once more, I was out of a job.

In my life as a novelist, I have honored a tacit agreement that I will never write about my children, but it's important to name them here. We have three, Joseph McKean Reed, John Craig Reed and Katherine Hyde Reed. We used to come home early from parties because they were more fun to hang out with than most adults. They are grown now, pair-bonded in much the same way we are, Mack to Kristina Reed, John to Germàn Angulo-Salom and Katy to Ko Maruyama; Cooper and Miranda Reed and Jack and Reed Maruyama complete the group. Our joy is that our adult children are friends and colleagues who still like to hang out with us.

After five years in newsrooms, however, motherhood came as a shock. Where other Yale wives were getting together over morning coffee, I had been at work. Dumped into the new world with nothing to steer by but a copy of *Dr. Spock.* I was in culture shock. For the first time ever, I was physically weak. I had this small person to take care of, I hurt all over *and* I lost my job.

Recovery was swift after my mother left for home; she was intent on housekeeping, when all I wanted to do was sleep. The baby's schedule arranged itself and set my work times. After the morning bath, he slept for at least two hours. At four weeks I wrote a short story and (thanks Mom, for sewing lessons when I was twelve) made a skirt. At six weeks I started a novel and made a suit.

I read through Lawrence Durrell's *Alexandria Quartet* during that period. I discovered Ray Bradbury and Theodore Sturgeon and Ian Fleming; I read *Jude the Ob-*

scure and A.E. Ellis's response to *The Magic Mountain,* a scorching novel called *The Rack.* I was reviewing fiction for the *Register* in exchange for the book.

As a reporter committed to accuracy, I used to lie awake worrying. Had I gotten the facts wrong, had I misquoted a source? Fiction opened the door to freedom. As Joe's mentor at Yale, Frederick Hilles, said cheerily, "You don't have to worry. You can make it all up."

Examining life, I could shape lives on the page. Writing was my way of making life make sense. What's more, I could invent. Emmy Jacobson had no interest in weirdness, but sold my more reality-driven stories to *Redbook* and *Cosmopolitan.* The others, I sent out on my own.

Developing writers often write what they like to read. I was torn between Waugh and Faulkner, Fitzgerald and Salinger—and SF. Speculative fiction let me learn how to write without touching my central material. I mailed dozens of stories to genre magazines. My favorite rejection came from H.L. Gold, who in response to my question, "How does this grab you?" wrote back, "Right down the throat and by the lunch." My second favorite came from Emmy, who said of my story "Winter," "If you can sell this I'll pin a medal on you."

"Winter" appeared in MacMillan of London's *Winter's Tales* along with pieces by Ted Hughes and Sylvia Plath. It has been widely anthologized, most recently in *The Norton Anthology of Contemporary Literature.*

Peter Parsons, who edited a town-gown issue of the *Yale Literary Magazine* used a story. Mimicking author notes I'd read, I said it was part of a novel. Peter thought his uncle, a publisher, might want to see it. How much did I have? I wrote five chapters and an outline on Aunt Ruth's plum-colored Smith Corona, tapping away on a card table in the front hall. I entered the Houghton Mifflin contest. Robert Stone won, but I got a contract for *Mother Isn't Dead She's Only Sleeping.* By the time we arrived at Wesleyan University in Middletown, Connecticut for Joe's first job, the manuscript was done.

A dramatic change after Yale and New Haven, the small-town campus looked like a magazine cover by Norman Rockwell. Wholesome youths in Zelan windbreakers gathered around pep-rally bonfires across the street from our house. The first of our student roomers-cum-babysitters demonstrated that they were more interesting than they looked.

Infant naptimes eroded and we paid a local woman to watch the baby five mornings a week. It set my work schedule: work mornings, Monday through Friday. Take nights and weekends off. Routine serves me well. Sit down at the same time every day and sooner or later, something will happen. Now work time expands into the afternoons.

Young parents Kit and Joe, with son Joseph McKean "Mack," 1960 (Courtesy of Graham Photography.)

Transatlantic Review took two stories during this period, but I was also selling to the *Magazine of Fantasy and Science Fiction*. I was either blessed or cursed by a darker imagination than most and then and now, I am like the witch on the weather house. Sometimes the sensitive realist comes out; sometimes it's the witch. All my life I have worked to prove that they are the same person, but in publishing, you go where they take you. Editors of speculative fiction have always welcomed me.

At a party for my second novel, a faculty wife told my friend Jessie that it was obscene for me to be locked away upstairs working while downstairs, another woman watched my son. She was telling the wrong person: a mother of three who is also an M.D.

I was never cut out to be a housewife. I did what I did, took care of my baby and kept to myself. I rewrote the Ilg/Ames child care columns for the Hall Syndicate. I interviewed Richard Wilbur and Paul Horgan and John Cage for the New Haven *Register*. Dick was taken aback

by the pace of the questions. "When you're interviewing, you turn into somebody else."

The dean's wife looked hurt when I shrugged off the faculty wives' club; the chaplain's wife eyed me suspiciously: *Are you going to write about us?* Years later a religionist's unhappy wife confessed, "We thought you were crazy, sitting up there typing while we were outside with our babies, but. . ." Sigh. "Now you're *somebody* and I'm not."

A friend told us we had arrived "in the year of dancing and petty flirtation." The year before, an irate speech teacher had tried to kill an innocent professor who happened to look like the man who had seduced his wife. A member of the Dutch Resistance in World War Two, the wife of the real culprit had turned the cuckold with the pistol away from the door by implicating the wrong man.

Wow, *this* was interesting.

Throughout the Sixties and Seventies the college community lived out its own comic strip, writing new chapters every day. People went running down the street with children, pounding on windows of houses from which they had been exiled. I was told that our next-door neighbor, who happened to be Joe's boss, resented me because I wouldn't flirt. He was a ludicrous popinjay, flaunting his key to the Playboy Bunny Club. Joe got tenure anyway.

Faculty parties were a revelation; turn a corner at any gathering and find somebody surprising rubbing up against somebody they weren't married to. Didn't they know how silly they looked? Marriages crumbled, or cracked and got glued back together, but for us it was a remarkable spectator sport.

In more than one way, novelist and historian Paul Horgan was the saving grace. As director of the Center for Advanced Studies, he brought Jean Stafford and Herbert Reed to town, Martin D'Arcy, Frank Kermode and Daniel Patrick Moynihan. Faculty seemed uneasy with eminent outsiders. At Paul's behest, we entertained them all in our half of a college duplex. Edmund Wilson came to dinner and seemed delighted and grateful to be sitting down with us, even though we were only kids.

With his style and humor, Paul made clear that there was a whole world beyond the small academic community with its feverish attempts at festivity. He liked us. He liked my work.

After *Mother Isn't Dead She's Only Sleeping,* Houghton Mifflin wanted to send me to Breadloaf to network. There were two drawbacks. First, I didn't want to go away to write; I worked at home. Second, I was pregnant again.

I turned in *At War as Children,* my elegiac response to my childhood and to the suicide of Switch Masterson. Houghton Mifflin expected a second comic novel. Rejecting the manuscript, my editor wrote, "I predict a long and interesting career."

Part Two of the Chinese curse slid into place.

The Reed and Maruyama families, 2007: (standing) the author's daughter-in-law, Kristina Reed, with son Mack; son-in-law Ko Maruyama, with daughter, Kate; (sitting) Kit and Joe, with grandchildren Cooper Reed, Jack Maruyama, Kit Reed, Joseph Reed, Miranda Reed, and Reed Maruyama
(Courtesy of Kit Reed.)

I've never written the same thing twice, a problem in a publishing world where readers like to know what they're getting when they buy a book. I am too easily bored.

Paul liked the manuscript and took *At War as Children* to Bob Giroux of Farrar, Straus, who published the book. When galleys came I discovered that a pushy copy editor had inserted her own word choices and arbitrary punctuation into my text. In the days of hot type, corrections on proofs were expensive. The author was usually billed. To Bob's credit, the house covered the cost of restoring my copy.

As a precisionist, I care passionately about the way the text looks on the page. Every line has been through several drafts and I resent the outsider who, on the basis of one reading, decides that I'd prefer their changes to my careful work.

Except for one poisonous review, good things followed the publication of *At War:* a Guggenheim, a paperback sale, the knowledge that there were more books to come. In the realm of Chinese curses, I was my own self-fulfilling prophecy. I disappointed Bob with a collection of SF short stories under the title *Mr. Da V.*

After a Guggenheim trip to South Carolina, we settled in for a summer taking care of the Pottles' house. A painter who has had shows in New York, Washington and New Delhi, Joe got his start there. He painted a pair of herbals for the bathroom we redecorated for the Pottles as a thank-you gift.

I broke my heart over a long, complex novel nobody wanted to publish and on the rebound wrote *The Better Part.* A reviewer said it "made Holden Caulfield sound like Little Lord Fauntleroy." We took our two little boys to London. By the time Farrar, Straus engineered my invitation to a party for "cool people under 35," I was too pregnant to go. Our daughter came that May. At Paul's Center dinner that night, Joe says, fellows Stephen Spender and Frank Kermode toasted her.

On that first trip to London, I met Hilary Rubinstein of A.P. Watt, who took Joe and me to lunch at Simpson's in the Strand and in the most gentlemanly way possible, talked about how we might make money together. He sold *Mr. DaV.* and *Armed Camps,* my fourth novel, to Charles Monteith at Faber & Faber, the house where T.S. Eliot had worked.

Although *Armed Camps* satisfied Faber, my version of *Why are We in Vietnam* didn't sit well with the Farrar, Straus image of the sensitive literary writer, Kit Reed. It was time to reinvent myself. Agent Carl Brandt helped me do the job, convincing John MacRae of Dutton to buy *Armed Camps* and *Cry of the Daughter.* He would go on to publish *Tiger Rag* and *Captain Grownup* before we parted ways.

Friends from New York came to the house with their children—the nearest thing to cousins that our children have. Bob Giroux and Charlie Reilly came. Piers Paul Read and his wife came, as did Joan and Harry Harrison. Students who would become friends came.

We went: to Boston, to upstate New York, to Manhattan and Washington, DC.

Nicholas Ray came to the house, half-blind and lugging cans of film documenting the trial of the Chicago Seven. He imagined a movie of *The Better Part* would bring Oscar nominations like his picture, *Rebel without a Cause.* We heard Nick on the wall phone in our kitchen, desperately trying to reach his money. His money refused to pick up the phone.

Fred Pottle came into the Boswell office where Joe was working on volume ten of the papers and said he'd nominated me for an award. The letter came in German. The Abraham Woursell Foundation gave five-year literary grants; I was the first American grantee.

We bought a new car. We got a Scottie. We made the down payment on a house. The woman who never belonged anywhere has lived at the same address since 1971.

Meanwhile Wesleyan was in flux. In the wake of the first Kennedy assassination, the Sixties had rolled in like an eighteen-wheeler, carrying every drug in the pharmacy and a new kind of student. Creative. Inventive. Unconventional. People like us. Someone said, "You attract the arties," and we did, although we said no thank you when they came bearing drugs. Post-revolution Wesleyan brought us friends like television director Alan Metzger, who shot the first student film made at Wesleyan; Internet guru John Perry Barlow; producer Laurence Mark.

After the Kent State shootings, previously square faculty members let their hair grow and donned flashy flares. The women's revolution gathered force. At consciousness-raising sessions, faculty wives vented about their lives. I was too busy with career and family to take the time.

Our friends outside Wesleyan were in flux too. As the country moved into the *Ice Storm* era, marriages we believed in started busting up. When these things happened we felt like the kids in the sad song where the folks sit them down to break the bad news. Baffled. Maybe we were the only people around who were surprised.

The year our daughter was born I stood in for a writing teacher sidelined by a heart attack. I taught his class in my living room with Joe standing by, in case. He was, after all, the teacher. I'd never done it before. In the mid-Seventies the college wanted a writer to teach one class a year. They turned to me. Sure, I said. I didn't mind doing it, but just until my ship came in.

Boarding the ferry to Robben Island in Cape Town, South Africa, 2006: Joe and Kit with Germàn Angulo-Salom and son John (Courtesy of Kit Reed.)

I've been teaching ever since. Stephen Alter and I cooked an Indian dinner when Hilary and Helge Rubinstein came from London; Hilary sold Steve's first novel to Diana Athill at Cape. Other students who are friends and colleagues include Peter Blauner and Suzanne Berne, Daniel Handler, Cheryl Sucher and Matt Tyrnauer, Alisa Kwitney and Alexander Chee. There are more, just beginning to publish.

My first class was coming up when Pat Moynihan phoned from India, where he was ambassador, to find out whether Joe and I would come, but there was no splitting the job of cultural attaché. We chose the short visit, a U.S.I.S. lecture tour, and went for three weeks. Ignoring our bank balance, we bought tickets for the children. Joe was chairing the English department. I was recovering from the non-response to *Tiger Rag.* Time to reinvent myself. I began my second comic novel, *Captain Grownup,* on our return. Peter Prescott, who later became a dear friend, called to tell me *Newsweek* was reviewing the novel. I said, "Thank God." I knew the movie deal wouldn't work out when I found out the producers wanted my male reporter to be a photographer, played by Diane Keaton.

The following summer we were Mellon fellows at the Aspen Institute. Everybody went except the Scottie. In

one seminar an oil executive asked me how much I made. I told him, not admitting that most of it came from teaching. The next question staggered me. "Writing," he asked, "is this a hobby with you?"

It's my *life.*

Meanwhile, friends' marriages were crumbling all around us, a complex problem I addressed first in *The Ballad of T. Rantula,* published by Genevieve Young at Little, Brown in 1979. It was a good year for me. Carl convinced David Hartwell at Berkley to buy a collection and a novel. John Madden directed an adaptation of my story "Pilots of the Purple Twilight" on National Public Radio.

In movies, there is a unit called The Last Good Time. As our sons entered college, I plunged into yet another long, complicated novel that nobody would buy. In the Eighties I kept a morbid journal of submissions: short stories sent out and accepted, and novels and short stories returned. I remember one page marked: ZERO YEAR. Doubleday published two books in the Eighties but to cut costs, never produced bound galleys.

Wesleyan offered a special deal on computers to faculty. Joe was buying one. Like most writers at the time, I thought the "word processor" was a monstrosity. It would only ruin my work. As part of an M.I.T. project involving playwrights, Arthur Kopit became a cyber-evangelist. Clare Brandt sat us down at her Kaypro. It looked easy enough. Born competitive, I knew that if Joe had a computer, to save our marriage, I had to get one too. Our Digital Rainbows came with inscrutable instructions. We were like gorillas, trying to figure out how to open our coconuts.

By the time computer classes started a week later, I had written a short story. I went from composing on a Royal Standard office model typewriter to the fluidity of a computer, but it didn't change the way I work. I don't work any faster. Spared the mechanical effort of throwing the carriage, I don't declare a passage is finished because I'm exhausted. Instead of making eleven or twelve passes, I can keep going until I have it right.

Editors admired my big novel, but nobody made an offer. Once again, it was time to reinvent myself. I wrote my third comic novel, *Catholic Girls.* It came out in 1987, the year my mother began the downhill slide into death. The next five years were punctuated by trips to Florida, where I wove a few lines of personal history into *Little Sisters of the Apocalypse,* an SF novel about biker nuns.

The phrase "track record" crept into my conversations with Carl. I was having what a friend called "a midlist crisis." I began a psychological thriller about a submariner's widow who vanishes one day. I was writing to save my life. In 1990 Carl and I had what Clare called "the friendliest divorce I've ever seen." They are still dear friends. Richard Pine masterminded my reincarnation, selling *Gone* under my maiden name.

Between foreign, paperback and film rights, Kit Craig made more money than all those years of Kit Reed put together. A second thriller followed. A six-figure offer for two more. But. But . . . I was deep in yet another long, complex novel that may never be published. Remember the Chinese curse. I declined.

Four more thrillers appeared in the U.K. before I closed the door on that chapter. *J. Eden,* the long, complex novel I began in the late Eighties came out in 1996 from the University Press of New England. As a regular reviewer for the *Hartford Courant,* I joined the National Books Critic Circle, and for four years, served on the board.

Kit and Joe Reed, 2005 (Courtesy of Kit Reed.)

Meanwhile, I was leading a double life. My friend Stew the nun had plumbed the Internet. She gave me the Telnet address of an amazing place: an online gathering place for some 9,000 people from all over the world. I got a character on LambdaMOO, the text-based grandfather of Second Life. Although the community is dwindling, I'm still there.

I needed time off from Wesleyan. I was granted a year to design an online writing course. Patterned after LambdaMOO, my little virtual community allows student writers to workshop stories in a real-time, text-based environment where nobody knows what they look like and nobody can see them blush. Until the last class at my house, they don't know who each other are.

It seemed logical to write about the cyber-life. Fascinated by the power of text and performative utterance, I began @*expectations*, published in 2000. Two more novels followed, both departures from the expected and both billed as S.F. At this writing, *The Baby Merchant* is the most recent, unfolding in a near future that is, essentially, already here.

Beginning this summary of a long career, I talked about anxieties and planning ahead, both essential to my survival. In college, where I was labeled an under-achiever, a clueless teacher asked me to summarize my philosophy of life. It was an outrageous request. I didn't have one, at least nothing I could articulate, but I can say this.

As a fatherless kid reared by an anxious mother, I dealt in worst-case scenarios. If X happened, I could always do Y. I think of it as protective pessimism. The protective pessimist is always prepared, never disappointed and often pleasantly surprised. Like Paul Horgan, I always have a work in progress by the time a novel comes out. For a writer, this is essential. Whatever happens, it won't be so bad if you have a backup plan.

Like everything that has ever happened to me, thinking in worst-case scenarios taught me how to write. My fiction grows out of a profusion of *what-ifs*. What if X happened to this character? What would I do in his place?

To finish a biography neatly, the obliging subject needs to rise to fame—or die. I haven't accomplished the first and am not about to try the second. At this writing, I am beginning a new novel. The work goes on.

* * *

REYNOLD, Ann
See BERNARDO, Anilú

RICHTER, Jutta 1955-

Personal

Born 1955, in Burgsteinfurt, Westphalia, Germany. *Education:* College degree, c. 1978.

Addresses

Home—Hamburg, Germany. *E-mail*—Post@juttarichter. de.

Career

Author of books for children.

Awards, Honors

City of Soltau literary prize, 1983; Rattenfänger literary prize, 2000; Luchs de Monats prize, and German youth literature prize. both 2001, both for *Der Tag, als ich lernte die Spinnen zu zähmen;* Luchs des Monats prize, and LesePeter award, both 2004, and Katholischer Kinder-und Jugendbuchpreis, 2005, all for *Hechtsommer.*

Writings

Popcorn und Sternbenbanner: Tagebuch einer Austauschschülerin, Herder (Freiburg, German), 1975.

Dad Geraniengefängis (novel), Beltz & Gelberg (Weinheim, Germany), 1980.

Die Puppermütter, Anrich (Modautal-Neunkirchen, Germany), 1980.

Herr Oska und das Zirr, illustrations by Barbara Schumann, Middelhauve (Munich, Germany), 1998.

Der Hund mit dem gelben Herzen oder die Geschichte vom Gegenteil, Carl Hanser (Munich, Germany), 1998.

Es lebte ein Kind auf den Bäumen, illustrated by Konstantin Wecker and Katrin Engelking, Carl Hanser (Munich, Germany), 1999.

Der Tag, als ich lernte die Spinnen zu zähmen, Carl Hanser (Munich, Germany), 2000.

Hinter dem Bahnhof liegt das Meer, C. Hanser (Munich, Germany), 2001.

Annabella Klimperauge, illustrated by Ulrike Möltgen, Carl Hanser (Munich, Germany), 2002.

An einem großen stillen see, illustrated by Susanne Janssen, Carl Hanser (Vienna, Austria), 2003.

Hechtsommer, illustrated by Quint Buchholtz, Carl Hanser (Munich, Germany), 2004, translated by Anna Brailovsky as *The Summer of the Pike,* Milkweed Editions (Minneapolis, MN), 2006.

Sommer und Bär. Eine Liebesgeschichte, photographs by Nomi Baumgartl, Sanssouci (Munich, Germany), 2006.

Die Katze oder Wie ich die Ewigkeit verloren habe, illustrated by Rotraud Susanne Berner, Carl Hanser (Munich, Germany), 2006, translated by Anna Brailovsky as *The Cat; or, How I Lost Eternity,* Milkweed Editions (Minneapolis, MN), 2007.

All das wünsch ich dir, Sanssouci (Munich, Germany), 2007.

Biographical and Critical Sources

PERIODICALS

Booklist, January 1, 2007, Carolyn Phelan, review of *The Summer of the Pike,* p. 104.
Kirkus Reviews, October 15, 2006, review of *The Summer of the Pike,* p. 1078.
Publishers Weekly, December 11, 2006, review of *The Summer of the Pike,* p. 70.
School Library Journal, December, 2006, Alison Follos, review of *The Summer of the Pike,* p. 152.

ONLINE

Jutta Richter Home Page, http://www.juttarichter.de (November 15, 2007).*

* * *

ROBERTS, Diane 1937-

Personal
Born 1937; married; husband's name Jim; children: three.

Addresses
Home and office—Fort Worth, TX. *E-mail*—DRaccoon@aol.com.

Career
Storyteller, puppeteer, and author.

Awards, Honors
Made You Look was nominated for several state book awards, 2005-06.

Writings

Made You Look, Delacorte (New York, NY), 2003.
Puppet Pandemonium, Delacorte (New York, NY), 2006.

Sidelights
Children's writer Diane Roberts got the idea for her first book, *Made You Look,* through her experience as a game-show contestant. As she noted on her home page, Roberts "won sixty pairs of shoes and a bright red coat." In *Made You Look* she creates "Masquerade Mania," a trivia game show that Jason, the main character in her novel, is dying to try out. When his family plans a vacation to California, Jason figures this will be his chance to accomplish his dream. Jason's quest is not quite that simple, however, because his parents decide to drive a camper from Texas to California rather than fly. Catastrophe follows catastrophe, from the instant the camping gear is attached to the roof of the family's SUV to Jason's mother turning everyone's underwear pink. "This light, fun fiction marks a solid start," wrote a *Publishers Weekly* critic, and Genevieve Gallagher maintained in *School Library Journal* that *Made You Look* "will be a big hit" because the "over-the-top elements . . . fit perfectly in this funny book."

In addition to her work as a writer, Roberts is a puppeteer. For thirty-seven years she and her puppets, led by Ricky Raccoon, have entertained groups at birthday parties, carnivals, and schools. Through puppetry, Roberts teaches children about energy conservation and the importance of reading. This interest in puppetry figures in her book *Puppet Pandemonium,* which introduces a new kid in town named Baker. Baker misses his old home, his grandmother, and his friends. Gram had him a ventriloquist puppet before he moved away,

Cover of Diane Roberts' middle-grade novel **Made You Look,** *featuring artwork by Matt Phillips.* (Illustration © 2004 by Matt Phillips. Used by permission of Random House Children's Books, a division of Random House, Inc.)

Cover of Roberts' Puppet Pandemonium, *featuring artwork by David Sheldon.* (Illustration © 2006 by David Sheldon. Reproduced by permission of Dell Publishing, a division of Random House, Inc.)

and Baker now discovers that not only are kids in his new home town not as different from his old friends as he feared, but the puppet may be the key to helping him make new friends. Although Sadie Mattox noted in *School Library Journal* that the theme of being the new kid has been done before, "kids interested in puppetry might pick up a few tips." A *Kirkus Reviews* contributor concluded of *Puppet Pandemonium* that Roberts' inclusion of "gentle humor makes [the novel] . . . an easy, comfortable read."

Biographical and Critical Sources

PERIODICALS

Kirkus Reviews, October 15, 2006, review of *Puppet Pandemonium,* p. 1078.
Publishers Weekly, May 6, 2003, review of *Made You Look,* p. 70.
School Library Journal, September, 2003, Genevieve Gallagher, review of *Made You Look,* p. 220; December, 2006, Sadie Mattox, review of *Puppet Pandemonium,* p. 114.

ONLINE

Diane Roberts Home Page, http://www.dianeroberts.com (October 11, 2007).*

* * *

ROBERTS, Priscilla 1955-

Personal

Born July 6, 1955, in Aldershot, England; daughter of Donald (a Royal Air Force officer and seedsman) and Barbara May (a teacher) Roberts. *Education:* King's College Cambridge, B.A., 1976, M.A., 1980, Ph.D., 1981.

Addresses

Home—Hong Kong. *Office*—Department of History, University of Hong Kong, Pokfulam Rd., Hong Kong. *E-mail*—proberts@hkucc.hku.hc.

Career

University of Hong Kong, lecturer in history, 1984-2006, associate professor, 2006—. Northeastern University, Shenyang, China, adjunct professor, 2002; Fulbright Scholar at George Washington University Institute for European, Russian, and Eurasian Studies, 2003.

Awards, Honors

Arthur Miller Prize for best British article in American studies, British Association for American Studies, 1997; appointed honorary professor, Shanghai International Studies University, 2005; numerous research grants.

Writings

FOR ADULTS

(Editor and author of introduction) *Sino-American Relations in the Twentieth Century,* Centre of Asian Studies, University of Hong Kong (Hong Kong), 1991.
(Editor) *Window on the Forbidden City: The Beijing Diaries of David Bruce, 1973-1974,* Centre of Asian Studies, University of Hong Kong (Hong Kong), 2001.
(Editor) *Behind the Bamboo Curtain: China, Vietnam, and the World beyond Asia,* Stanford University Press (Stanford, CT), 2006.

Guest editor, *Journal of Oriental Studies*; assistant editor of *Encyclopedia of the Korean War: A Political, Social, and Military History,* ABC-Clio, 2000; *The Encyclopedia of World War II: A Political, Social, and Military History,* ABC-Clio, 2004; *World War II: A Student Encyclopedia,* ABC-Clio, 2005; *The Encyclopedia of World War I: A Political, Social, and Military His-*

Priscilla Roberts (Courtesy of Priscilla Roberts.)

tory, ABC-Clio, 2005; and *World War I: A Student Encyclopedia,* 2006. Contributor to anthologies, including *Studies in the American Jewish Experience,* 1984; *The United States and the Asia-Pacific Region in the Twentieth Century,* 1993; *Essays in Economic and Business History,* 1998; *Twentieth-Century Anglo-American Relations,* 2001; *Essays in Economic and Business History,* 2002; *The Human Tradition in America since 1945,* 2003; *The Korean War at Fifty: International Perspectives,* 2004; *Re-reading America: Changes and Challenges,* 2004; *Return of the Dragon: U.S.-China Relations in the 21st-Century-Asia Pacific Horizon,* 2005; and *The Most Dangerous Years: The Cold War 1953-1975,* 2005; and to encyclopedias. Contributor of articles to periodicals, including *American Jewish Archives Journal, Australian Journal of Politics and History, Business History Review, Diplomacy and Statecraft, Historian, Journal of American Studies, Journal of Military History, Journal of Orient Studies, Journal of Transatlantic Studies,* and *Tamkang Journal of International Affairs.* Contributor of numerous reviews to professional journals.

Author's works have been translated into Chinese.

Biographical and Critical Sources

PERIODICALS

Choice, September, 2005, E.F. Konerding, review of *The Encyclopedia of World War II: A Political, Social, and*

Military History, p. 80; June, 2007, C.C. Lorett, review of *Behind the Bamboo Curtain: China, Vietnam, and the World beyond Asia,* p. 1809.
School Library Journal, August, 2005, Madeleine G. Wright, review of *The Encyclopedia of World War II,* p. 78.*

*   *   *

ROOT, Phyllis 1949-

Personal

Born February 14, 1949, in Fort Wayne, IN; daughter of John Howard and Esther Root; married James Elliot Hansa (a mason); children: Amelia Christin, Ellen Rose. *Education:* Valparaiso University, B.A., 1971. *Hobbies and other interests:* Canoeing, sailing, gardening, reading.

Addresses

Home—3842 Bloomington Ave. S., Minneapolis, MN 55407. *E-mail*—rootx005@tc.umn.edu.

Career

Writer. Has worked as architectural drafter, costume seamstress, bicycle repair person, and administrative assistant. Vermont College, instructor in M.F.A. in Writing for Children Program, 2002—.

Member

Society of Children's Book Writers and Illustrators.

Awards, Honors

Children's Books of the Year citation, Child Study Association of America, and Bologna International Children's Book Fair selection, both 1985, both for *Moon Tiger;* Minnesota Picture Book Award, 1997, for *Aunt Nancy and Old Man Trouble;* Best Books of the Year, *School Library Journal,* 1998, for *What Baby Wants;* Top-Ten Easy Readers selection, *Booklist,* 2002, for *Mouse Has Fun,* and 2003, for *Mouse Goes Out; Boston Globe/Horn Book* Picture Book Award, 2003, for *Big Momma Makes the World.*

Writings

FOR CHILDREN

Hidden Places, illustrated by Daniel San Souci, Carnival Press (Milwaukee, WI), 1983.
(With Carol A. Marron) *Gretchen's Grandma,* illustrated by Deborah K. Ray, Carnival Press (Milwaukee, WI), 1983.
(With Carol A. Marron) *Just One of the Family,* illustrated by George Karn, Carnival Press (Milwaukee, WI), 1984.

(With Carol A. Marron) *No Place for a Pig,* illustrated by Nathan Y. Jarvis, Carnival Press (Milwaukee, WI), 1984.

My Cousin Charlie, illustrated by Pia Marella, Carnival Press (Milwaukee, WI), 1984.

Moon Tiger, illustrated by Ed Young, Holt (New York, NY), 1985.

Soup for Supper, illustrated by Sue Truesdell, Harper (New York, NY), 1986.

Great Basin, Carnival/Crestwood (Mankato, MN), 1988.

Glacier, Carnival/Crestwood (Mankato, MN), 1989.

Galapagos, Carnival/Crestwood (Mankato, MN), 1989.

The Old Red Rocking Chair, illustrated by John Sanford, Arcade (New York, NY), 1992.

The Listening Silence, illustrated by Dennis McDermott, Harper (New York, NY), 1992.

Coyote and the Magic Words, illustrated by Sandra Speidel, Lothrop (New York, NY), 1993.

Sam Who Was Swallowed by a Shark, illustrated by Axel Scheffler, Candlewick Press (Cambridge, MA), 1994.

Aunt Nancy and Old Man Trouble, illustrated by David Parkins, Candlewick Press (Cambridge, MA), 1996.

Mrs. Potter's Pig, illustrated by Russell Ayto, Candlewick Press (Cambridge, MA), 1996.

Contrary Bear, illustrated by Laura Cornell, HarperCollins/ Laura Geringer Books (New York, NY), 1996.

One Windy Wednesday, illustrated by Helen Craig, Candlewick Press (Cambridge, MA), 1996.

Rosie's Fiddle, illustrated by Kevin O'Malley, Lothrop (New York, NY), 1997.

The Hungry Monster, illustrated by Sue Heap, Candlewick Press (Cambridge, MA), 1997.

Turnover Tuesday, illustrated by Helen Craig, Candlewick Press (Cambridge, MA), 1998.

What Baby Wants, illustrated by Jill Barton, Candlewick Press (Cambridge, MA), 1998.

One Duck Stuck: A Mucky Ducky Counting Book, illustrated by Jane Chapman, Candlewick Press (Cambridge, MA), 1998.

Aunt Nancy and Cousin Lazybones, illustrated by David Parkins, Candlewick Press (Cambridge, MA), 1998.

Grandmother Winter, illustrated by Beth Krommes, Houghton Mifflin (Boston, MA), 1999.

Hey, Tabby Cat!, illustrated by Katherine McEwen, Candlewick Press (Cambridge, MA), 2000.

All for the Newborn Baby, illustrated by Nicola Bayley, Candlewick Press (Cambridge, MA), 2000.

Kiss the Cow!, illustrated by Will Hillenbrand, Candlewick Press (Cambridge, MA), 2000.

Here Comes Tabby Cat, illustrated by Katherine McEwen, Candlewick Press (Cambridge, MA), 2000.

Meow Monday, illustrated by Helen Craig, Candlewick Press (Cambridge, MA), 2000.

Foggy Friday, illustrated by Helen Craig, Candlewick Press (Cambridge, MA), 2000.

Soggy Saturday, illustrated by Helen Craig, Candlewick Press (Cambridge, MA), 2001.

Rattletrap Car, illustrated by Jill Barton, Candlewick Press (Cambridge, MA), 2001.

(With Michelle Edwards) *What's That Noise?,* illustrated by Paul Meisel, Candlewick Press (Cambridge, MA), 2002.

Mouse Goes Out, illustrated by James Croft, Candlewick Press (Cambridge, MA), 2002.

Mouse Has Fun, illustrated by James Croft, Candlewick Press (Cambridge, MA), 2002.

Big Momma Makes the World, illustrated by Helen Oxenbury, Candlewick Press (Cambridge, MA), 2002.

Oliver Finds His Way, illustrated by Christopher Denise, Walker (New York, NY), 2002.

The Name Quilt, illustrated by Margot Apple, Farrar, Straus, and Giroux (New York, NY), 2003.

Ten Sleepy Sheep, illustrated by Susan Gaber, Candlewick Press (Cambridge, MA), 2004.

Baby Ducklings, illustrated by Petra Mathers, Candlewick Press (Cambridge, MA), 2004.

Baby Bunnies, illustrated by Petra Mathers, Candlewick Press (Cambridge, MA), 2004.

If You Want to See a Caribou, illustrated by Jim Meyer, Houghton Mifflin (Boston, MA), 2004.

Hop!, illustrated by Holly Meade, Candlewick Press (Cambridge, MA), 2005.

The House That Jill Built (pop-up book), illustrated by Delphine Durand, Candlewick Press (Cambridge, MA), 2005.

Quack!, illustrated by Holly Meade, Candlewick Press (Cambridge, MA), 2005.

Who Said Boo?, illustrated by Ana Martín Larraífaga, Little Simon (New York, NY), 2005.

Looking for a Moose, illustrated by Randy Cecil, Candlewick Press (Cambridge, MA), 2006.

Lucia and the Light, illustrated by Mary GrandPré, Candlewick Press (Cambridge, MA), 2006.

Aunt Nancy and the Bothersome Visitors, illustrated by David Parkins, Candlewick Press (Cambridge, MA), 2007.

FOR ADULTS

Gladys on the Go, photographs by Kelly Povo, Conari Press (York Beach, ME), 2004.

Hot Flash Gal, photographs by Kelly Povo, Conari Press (York Beach, ME), 2004.

Ask Gladys: Household Hits for Gals on the Go, photographs by Kelly Povo, Conari Press (Boston, MA), 2005.

Dear Hot Flash Gal: Every Answer to a Gal's Every Question, photographs by Kelly Povo, Conari Press (Boston, MA), 2005.

Sidelights

Popular with young readers, Phyllis Root is perhaps best known for creating picture books that range from retellings of Native-American stories and tall tales to celebrations of intergenerational relationships and the small, intimate moments of childhood. As Kelly Milner Halls noted in *Booklist,* Root "has carved a niche for herself by using homespun observations and the playful use of rural undertones." Working with illustrators such as Helen Craig, Paul Meisel, Jill Barton, Will Hillenbrand, Susan Gaber, Mary GrandPré, and Helen Oxenbury, the award-winning author has produced such

Phyllis Root tells a humorous story about a family and their beloved—but none too reliable—automobile in **Rattletrap Car,** *illustrated by Jill Barton.* (Candlewick Press, 2001. Illustrations © 2001 by Jill Barton. Reproduced by permission of Candlewick Press, Inc., Cambridge, MA.)

popular titles as *One Windy Wednesday, Ten Sleepy Sheep, What Baby Wants, Kiss the Cow!, Big Momma Makes the World,* and *Looking for a Moose.*

Although Root began writing professionally in the late 1970s, she has been writing for fun as long as she can remember. "I made up stories, poems, and songs," she once told *SATA.* "In first grade, I wrote a poem about love and a dove, and in second grade, I won a class essay contest for my four-sentence story about the Sahara desert. In fifth grade, I had a remarkable and wonderful teacher, Mrs. Keller, who encouraged me to write. It was in her class that I decided I would be an 'authoress' when I grew up."

Root went on to attend college at Valparaiso University, earning a bachelor's degree in 1971; she did not begin writing professionally for another eight years, after taking course work in the tools of the writing trade, learning important book-writing skills, such as creating plots, settings, tension, and characters.

One of Root's earliest published works, *Gretchen's Grandma,* was co-written with colleague Carol A. Marron. The 1983 picture book tells the story of Gretchen and her "Oma," or grandmother, who is visiting from Germany. At the beginning of the visit, the language barrier is troublesome, but eventually grandmother and grandchild overcome their verbal problems through pantomime and affection. Ilene Cooper, writing in *Booklist,* described *Gretchen's Grandma* as "a gentle

story that could be used as [a] starting point for some preschool discussion."

Another early picture book, *Moon Tiger,* was described by a *Bulletin of the Center for Children's Books* writer as "the stuff of which dreams are made," and Nancy Schmidtmann dubbed it a "heavenly treat" in her *School Library Journal* review. *Moon Tiger* follows a young girl's imaginative journey as she dreams of being rescued from the task of babysitting her pesky younger brother by a magical tiger. When the tiger offers to eat the boy, however, the sister declines, admitting that she might actually miss her brother after all.

Root's whimsical humor shines through in picture books such as *The Old Red Rocking Chair, The Hungry Monster, Sam Who Was Swallowed by a Shark, Contrary Bear,* and *Looking for a Moose.* In *The Old Red Rocking Chair* a discarded rocking chair is rescued time and time again from the garbage by various eagle-eyed dump-pickers. Each new owner takes from the chair different pieces and discards the remains, until what was once a chair evolves into a blue footstool which is sold to its original—and oblivious—owner at a garage sale. In *The Hungry Monster* a hungry little alien finds that his hunger cannot be satisfied until a little Earthling offers him a banana, peel and all. "While the premise is hardly new . . . Root's cheerfulness and lucid logic" animate the text of *The Old Red Rocking Chair,* in the opinion of a *Publishers Weekly* critic, and in *Kirkus Reviews* a writer praised *The Hungry Monster* as a "silly story that includes a dash of suspense" as well as "a just-right read-aloud for board-book graduates."

A "cheery tale of compromise," according to a *Publishers Weekly* writer, *Mrs. Potter's Pig* focuses on a neat freak who learns to appreciate the joy of mud when she has to rescue her dirt-loving daughter from a pigpen. *Contrary Bear* finds a toy blamed for its owner's obstinate behavior. Contrary Bear takes the rap for making loud train whistles during naptime and wanting a bigger piece of cake, but the last straw for Dad is when the stuffed toy supposedly splashes water all over the bathroom. Finally relegated to the clothesline to dry out, Contrary Bear watches his penitent owner promise to help the toy "try harder to be good tomorrow."

In *Sam Who Was Swallowed by a Shark* readers meet a rat who is determined to build a boat and sail the sea, despite the nay-saying of his rodental neighbors. When he finally accomplishes his goal and leaves, the neighbors assume the worst when they do not hear from him, although Sam is actually having the time of his life. A *Publishers Weekly* critic hailed Root's "understated prose" and "chipper dialogue," and noted that "the even pacing underlines [Sam's] quiet persistence and progress."

Brought to life in humorous illustrations by Randy Cecil, *Looking for a Moose* takes story-hour participants on "an engaging romp," according to *Booklist* contributor Connie Fletcher. In the story, listeners follow four children on a hunt through the forest. When they reach their goal and stumble upon the moose that have been following THEM all along, Root's "infectious" onomatopoeic rhyming text comes full circle, according to a *Publishers Weekly* critic, and a *Kirkus Reviews* writer concluded that the author's "buoyant, rhymed text makes for a stellar read-aloud." Similar in theme, *If You Want to See a Caribou* also features a poetic text, this time drawing readers into a balsam forest in search of a caribou mother and calf. Gentler in tone, the book pairs Root's "subtle" poetry with illustrator Jim Meyer's "serene, expansive" block-printed illustrations, according to *Booklist* reviewer Gillian Engberg.

The author collaborates with artist Jill Barton on *What Baby Wants,* a "farmyard tale of an implacable baby," according to a contributor to *Publishers Weekly.* In Root's tale, an entire family tries to help when Mother has difficulty getting her crying infant to sleep. Each family member thinks that the fussy baby needs something different, but ultimately it is the younger brother who knows the trick: all Baby wants is a big cuddle. In *Booklist* Stephanie Zvirin deemed *What Baby Wants* a "sweet, simple charmer." Author and illustrator team up again for *Rattletrap Car,* a cumulative story about the humorous mini-disasters that befall a family during a summertime outing to the lake. As a *Publishers Weekly* reviewer commented, "Root and Barton prove that they know how to convey mounting comic mayhem" in the humorous picture book, and Ilene Cooper concluded in *Booklist* that *Rattletrap Car* "passes the fun test with flying fizz."

Root addresses some universal childhood fears in *What's That Noise?* and *Oliver Finds His Way.* In the first title, a "story of how imagination can run amok," according to *School Library Journal* critic Susan Marie Pitard, two little brothers hear noises in the night. While at first frightened, they learn to calm their fears by making up a silly song that classifies each of the scary sounds. Similarly, *Oliver Finds His Way* explores the fear of getting lost and the consequent relief in finding one's way home again. Baby bear Oliver loses his way one warm day while his parents are busy. He follows a leaf as eddies of air carry it farther and farther away from his home, finally leading him into the shadowy woods. Eventually, the resilient bear is able to find his way back again by calling out to his parents and then following the sound of their returning calls. A critic for *Publishers Weekly* praised both Root and illustrator Christopher Denise for bringing "a fresh poignancy to the familiar theme," and Kathleen Simonetta wrote in *School Library Journal* that the "happy ending" in *Oliver Finds His Way* "will leave readers smiling."

Like many authors, Root has mined her own family experiences for many picture-book ideas. *Soup for Supper* was the result of a thunderstorm. "I had gotten up to comfort my daughter Amelia," she once recalled to *SATA,* "and remembered how, when I was a child, my sister and I had sat on the bed with our parents, watching the lightning and rain. 'Don't let the thunder scare you,' they reassured us. 'It's just the noise potatoes

make spilling out of the giant's cart.' Listening to the thunder with my own daughter, I suddenly saw the giant with his cart of vegetables and a wee small woman chasing after him. The next morning I wrote down the first draft of *Soup for Supper.*" The result is "an original story with a folkloric ring," as described by a *Bulletin of the Center for Children's Books* writer, which is "dandy [for] reading aloud because of the simple rhymes, name-calling, and sound effects." The wee small woman of Root's tale vigorously defends her garden against the Giant Rumbleton's attempts to plunder it. After an energetic confrontation, the two enemies discover a common culinary goal and become friends as together they make vegetable soup. Root even includes music for the giant's song at the end of the book.

Root called on her then-ten-year-old daughter for help with *One Windy Wednesday,* part of a series of books illustrated by Helen Craig that detail various days of the week. In the humorous tale, a day comes when the wind is so strong that it blows the sound right out of some farm animals and into others. When the wind subsides, the lamb are left quacking, the ducks start mooing, and the cow starts oinking, leaving Bonnie Bumble to hitch the right critter to the right call. Hazel Rochman, writing in *Booklist,* described *One Windy Wednesday* as a "simple, funny story." Other books in the series include *Turnover Tuesday,* which finds Bonnie Bumble literally turning over after making plum turnovers; and *Meow Monday,* in which Bonnie's pussy willow sprout some real pussycats who are hungry for milk from the milkweed plant. *Foggy Friday* catches Bonnie napping when her faithful rooster forgets to crow, and in *Soggy Saturday* a heavy rain has washed the blue from the sky onto the animals on Bonnie's farm. Lynda Ritterman, writing in *School Library Journal,* cited the "winning combination of spare, well-chosen words and lively, crisp pacing" in *Meow Monday,* and a *Kirkus Reviews* critic praised the "beguiling simplicity" of *Soggy Saturday.*

More rural settings are served up in the concept books *One Duck Stuck: A Mucky Ducky Counting Book* and *Ten Sleepy Sheep.* In the first book, when a poor fowl gets stuck in the mud, it is helped in turn by varying numbers of fish, crickets, and frogs. Shirley Lewis, writing in *Teacher Librarian,* called it a "delightful picture book," and in *Booklist* Helen Rosenberg predicted that *One Duck Stuck* is "great fun and sure to become an instant favorite among the toddler crowd." Another counting book, *Ten Sleepy Sheep,* shows readers that counting sheep in order to fall asleep can sometimes be challenging, especially when the sheep are not sleepy themselves. Fortunately, one by one, the frisky lambs nod off to sleep amid the cozy setting created by illustrator Susan Gaber.

In *Kiss the Cow!,* illustrated by Will Hillenbrand, Root returns again to a farm setting, this time to find little Annalisa watching her mother milk the family's cow. Without a kiss on the nose, Luella the cow refuses to give milk, but when Annalisa attempts to perform the milking herself, she needs some convincing before she can bring herself to touch Luella's damp cow nose with her lips. In *Booklist* Carolyn Phelan commented on the

Another rural-themed story is served up by Root in **Kiss the Cow!,** *a picture book featuring nostalgic illustrations by Will Hillenbrand.* (Candlewick Press, 2003. Illustration © 2000 by Will Hillenbrand. Reproduced by permission of Candlewick Press, Inc., Cambridge, MA.)

"satisfying folksy sound" of Root's narrative and commended Hillenbrand's artwork for its "style and panache." Anne Knickerbocker wrote in *School Library Journal* that the book's "flowing language makes it a fun read-aloud," while a reviewer for *Horn Book* called *Kiss the Cow!* "an original story of magic and mischief."

In *The Listening Silence* Root draws on Native-American traditions and creates a "strong, believable" heroine, according to Ruth S. Vose in *School Library Journal.* Kiri is a young, orphaned girl who is raised in a tribe whose healer recognizes her ability to send her spirit inside of both people and animals. Reluctant to use her power, Kiri goes on a vision quest to discover her true calling and eventually uses her gift to heal a

young man she encounters. While Vose praised the "smooth, lyrical, language" in *The Listening Silence,* a *Kirkus Reviews* writer hailed Root's "spare, carefully honed narration." Much like J.R.R. Tolkien did in his classic *Lord of the Rings,* Root invents names for the woodland plants and animals, creating what Kathryn Pierson Jennings described in the *Bulletin of the Center for Children's Books* as "a fantasy culture . . . [that] is orderly and compelling and may inspire young creative writing students who need a more modest fantasy world than Tolkien."

In *Coyote and the Magic Words* Root employs elements of Native-American folklore, including the use of a coyote as a trickster. As she explained, the book is "a story about storytelling, about how to create worlds with nothing more than our words." In the tale, Maker-of-All-Things uses words to speak her creations into existence and grants her creatures the power to meet their own needs simply by speaking into existence what they want. Coyote grows bored with this easy way of life, however, and begins to incite mischief using the magic words. To punish him, Maker-of-All-Things takes away the magic of the words, except the ones Coyote uses in storytelling. Karen Hutt, writing for *Booklist,* characterized the tale as "simple but satisfying," and a *Kirkus Reviews* critic observed that "Root's Coyote is appropriately childlike; her lively narration is well-honed and agreeably informal, just right for oral sharing."

The "Aunt Nancy" of *Aunt Nancy and Old Man Trouble,* published in 1996, does not refer to the Aunt Nancy of the "Anansi" storytelling tradition; however Root's story, like many others she written, possesses a folklore flair. Using a down-home dialect, Root describes Aunt Nancy and the way she outsmarts Old Man Trouble when he dries up her well. When he shows up at her door and causes more mischief, Aunt Nancy finds a way to turn trouble into a blessing. Old Man Trouble falls for her ruse and, determined not to cause good to come from his actions, restores the well before he leaves, again hoping to quash Aunt Nancy's good spirits. Deborah Stevenson, writing in the *Bulletin of the Center for Children's Books,* commented that Root's story of the "victory of the underestimated" is a "kid-pleasing version with some bite to it."

Aunt Nancy returns in *Aunt Nancy and Cousin Lazybones.* In this episode, she is not looking forward to a visit from her Cousin Lazybones, whose laziness is legendary. Instead of going to get water from the well, Lazybones simply sets a bucket outside the door and then hopes for rain. Fed up with the slacker, Aunt Nancy decides to fight fire with fire; she becomes as lazy as her cousin. When more and more housework falls to him, Cousin Lazybones decides to cut his visit short. In *Publishers Weekly* a reviewer noted of *Aunt Nancy and Cousin Lazybones* that "Root brings generous dollops of humor and homespun flavor to her folktale." Similar praise came from *Booklist* contributor John Peters, who predicted that "youngsters will delight in this battle of wits and look forward to Aunt Nancy's next visitor." In *Horn Book* Lolly Robinson also enjoyed the book, commenting that Root and illustrator David Parkins "have created another original tall tale that sounds as though it's been told for years." Robinson also praised Root's "rhythmic" text, noting that it "begs to be read aloud."

Root's adaptation of an American folk tale in *Rosie's Fiddle* "bursts with vitality and spunk," according to a *Kirkus Reviews* critic. Her story features the devil himself, as he enters a fiddling contest with Rosie after he hears of her stellar fiddling reputation. After three rounds, Rosie fiddles the devil into a puff of smoke, wins his golden instrument, and saves her own soul from the devil's hands. A *Publishers Weekly* critic commented that "the folksy prose and stormy spreads convey the tale's intensity—the only thing missing is a

Root's picture-book text for **Lucia and the Light** *is paired with evocative paintings by noted artist Mary GrandPré.* (Illustration © 2006 by Mary GrandPré. Reproduced by permission of Candlewick Press, Inc., Cambridge, MA.)

Helen Oxenbury's detailed illustrations bring to life Root's creation story **Big Momma Makes the World.** (Candlewick Press, 2002. Illustration © 2002 by Helen Oxenbury. All rights reserved. Reproduced by permission.)

bluegrass soundtrack." Janice M. Del Negro, writing in the *Bulletin of the Center for Children's Books,* also offered a favorable estimation of *Rosie's Fiddle,* asserting that "Root's adaptation of this traditional motif has a fine readaloud rhythm and a thoroughly satisfying progression as the devil gets his musical due."

Inspired by a traditional Norwegian legend about Saint Lucia Day, *Lucia and the Light* explains what must happen in order for the days to begin to lengthen in the dead of winter. In her adaptation, Root brings readers to a cabin in the mountains, where Lucia lives with her mother and younger brother, as well as Cow and White Cat. All is well until one winter, when the sun appears less and less frequently until it disappears altogether, leaving no way for Lucia to mark night from day. Determined to restore the sun, the brave girl and her cat ski off up the mountain, where she ultimately frees the sun from a band of evil trolls. Noting the story's underlying message about loyalty and cooperation, *Booklist* contributor of Gillian Engberg added that "Root's rich language and well-paced story are sure to capture a young crowd of eager listeners." In *Publishers Weekly* a contributor noted how award-winning illustrator Mary GrandPré's "incandescent pastel art" evokes the story's Nordic setting, and in *School Library Journal* Tamara E. Root wrote that, "with its terrifying trolls and triumphant travails," *Lucia and the Light* will spark the imagination of young listeners.

Again taking inspiration from traditional sources, Root adapts a German fairy-tale character in *Grandmother*

Winter and provides a new take on the creation story in *Big Momma Makes the World,* two picture books featuring strong female protagonists. The eponymous heroine of *Grandmother Winter* proves to be the harbinger of the cold season. All summer long she gathers the fallen feathers from her white geese; when autumn comes, she uses them to stuff a feather comforter. Fluffing up the comforter, feathers fall, transforming into snowflakes as they fall from the sky. A reviewer for *Horn Book* commended Root's "cadenced" and "lyrical" text in this folktale remake. Kay Weisman, writing in *Booklist,* also felt that the book would be "a wonderful choice for primary units on seasons or winter," and a *Publishers Weekly* critic called *Grandmother Winter* "a cozy mood-setter."

Big Momma Makes the World, illustrated by Helen Oxenbury, is a "sassy creation myth that tweaks the first chapter of Genesis," according to a contributor for *Publishers Weekly.* In Root's rendition, Big Momma creates the world and surveys her creation with satisfied, folksy expressions. "Root infuses her tale with a joyful spirit, and her lyrical vernacular trips off the tongue," a *Publishers Weekly* critic further commented. In *Booklist,* Cooper dubbed the tale "a raucous, joyous version of the creation story," while a *Kirkus Reviews* critic called it a "paean to the Earth and to motherhood."

A grandmother full of memories and traditional stories of her own is at the center of *The Name Quilt,* in which a little girl elicits family tales from her grandmother each night by picking a name embroidered on the patchwork quilt on her bed. When the quilt is swept away by a fierce wind, the young girl is disconsolate. Finally her grandmother suggests they make a new quilt together, and this time the young girl's name is in the center of it. Mary Elam, writing in *School Library Journal,* noted that Root "stitches together generations, memories, and traditions in this tale of a much-loved family treasure."

Like her character in *The Name Quilt,* Root's goal as a writer has also been to "stitch" tales together, crafting books that entertain and teach gentle lessons. As the author once commented to *SATA:* "My hope is to keep writing and to keep having stories to tell." In an online interview with Cynthia Leitich Smith on *Cynsations,* Root also addressed aspiring writers. "Read lots and lots and lots and lots of picture books, read them aloud, type out the ones you like best to get a manual feel for how the words look on a page," she advised, "dummy up your stories to get a feel for the shape of a picture book . . . and write and write and write and rewrite and rewrite and rewrite." "Tell the stories you have to tell the best way you know how," she added, "always remembering for whom you are telling them: children. And write from your heart."

Biographical and Critical Sources

PERIODICALS

Booklist, January 1, 1984, Ilene Cooper, review of *Gretchen's Grandma,* p. 684; July, 1986, p. 1616; November

15, 1993, Karen Hutt, review of *Coyote and the Magic Words,* p. 633; October 15, 1996, Hazel Rochman, review of *One Windy Wednesday,* p. 437; April, 1998, Helen Rosenberg, review of *One Duck Stuck: A Mucky Ducky Counting Book,* p. 1333; September 15, 1998, Stephanie Zvirin, review of *What Baby Wants,* p. 240; October 15, 1998, Ilene Cooper, review of *Turnover Tuesday,* p. 429; November 15, 1998, John Peters, review of *Aunt Nancy and Cousin Lazybones,* p. 597; November 15, 1999, Kay Weisman, review of *Grandmother Winter,* p. 637; September 1, 2000, Gillian Engberg, review of *All for the Newborn Baby,* p. 134; November 15, 2000, Kelly Milner Halls, reviews of *Meow Monday* and *Foggy Friday,* and Carolyn Phelan, review of *Kiss the Cow!,* all p. 650; December 1, 2001, Ilene Cooper, review of *Soggy Saturday,* pp. 650-651; January 1, 2002, review of *Rattletrap Car,* p. 768; January 1, 2003, Ilene Cooper, review of *Big Momma Makes the World,* p. 88; March 15, 2003, Carolyn Phelan, review of *The Name Quilt,* p. 1333; April 15, 2004, Gillian Engberg, review of *If You Want to See a Caribou,* p. 1449; September 1, 2006, Gillian Engberg, review of *Lucia and the Light,* p. 45; October 1, 2006, Connie Fletcher, review of *Looking for a Moose,* p. 60.

Bulletin of the Center for Children's Books, January, 1986, review of *Moon Tiger,* p. 95; July-August, 1986, review of *Soup for Supper,* p. 216; March, 1992, Kathryn Pierson Jennings, review of *The Listening Silence,* p. 191; March, 1996, Deborah Stevenson, review of *Aunt Nancy and Old Man Trouble,* p. 240; April, 1997, Janice M. DelNegro, review of *Rosie's Fiddle,* p. 293; December, 1998, Betsy Hearne, review of *Aunt Nancy and Cousin Lazybones,* p. 144; October, 1999, Fern Kory, review of *Grandmother Winter,* p. 66; February, 2001, Kate McDowell, review of *Foggy Friday* and *Meow Monday,* pp. 235-236.

Horn Book, January-February, 1999, Lolly Robinson, review of *Aunt Nancy and Cousin Lazybones,* p. 55; September-October, 1999, review of *Grandmother Winter,* p. 599; January-February, 2001, review of *Kiss the Cow!,* p. 85; May-June, 2004, Lauren Adams, review of *Ten Sleepy Sheep,* p. 319.

Kirkus Reviews, May 1, 1992, review of *The Listening Silence,* p. 616; September 1, 1993, review of *Coyote and the Magic Words,* p. 1151; May 15, 1996, p. 749; January 1, 1997, review of *The Hungry Monster,* p. 63; February 1, 1997, review of *Rosie's Fiddle,* p. 227; September 15, 2001, review of *Soggy Saturday,* p. 1366; July 1, 2002, review of *What's That Noise?,* p. 953; August 1, 2002, review of *Oliver Finds His Way,* p. 1141; January 15, 2003, review of *Big Momma Makes the World,* p. 146; March 1, 2003, review of *The Name Quilt,* p. 397; August 1, 2005, review of *The House That Jill Built,* p. 857; July 15, 2006, review of *Looking for a Moose,* p. 729; October 15, 2006, review of *Lucia and the Light,* p. 1079.

Language Arts, March, 2003, review of *Rattletrap Car,* p. 317.

Publishers Weekly, May 18, 1992, review of *The Old Red Rocking Chair,* p. 68; May 30, 1994, review of *Sam Who Was Swallowed by a Shark,* pp. 55-56; May 13, 1996, review of *Contrary Bear,* p. 75; June 10, 1996, review of *Mrs. Potter's Pig,* p. 99; November 4, 1996, p. 74; January 13, 1997, review of *Rosie's Fiddle,* pp.

75-76; May 4, 1998, review of *One Duck Stuck,* p. 211; September 14, 1998, review of *What Baby Wants,* p. 67; October 26, 1998, review of *Aunt Nancy and Cousin Lazybones,* p. 66; August 30, 1999, review of *Grandmother Winter,* p. 82; April 30, 2001, review of *Rattletrap Car,* p. 77; June 17, 2002, review of *What's That Noise?,* p. 64; August 19, 2002, review of *Oliver Finds His Way,* p. 87; November 25, 2002, review of *Big Momma Makes the World,* p. 66; January 13, 2003, review of *The Name Quilt,* p. 59; September 18, 2006, review of *Looking for a Moose,* p. 53; November 27, 2006, review of *Lucia and the Light,* p. 50.

School Library Journal, December, 1985, Nancy Schmidtmann, review of *Moon Tiger,* p. 81; June, 1992, Ruth S. Vose, review of *The Listening Silence,* p. 125; June, 1998, Heide Piehler, review of *One Duck Stuck,* pp. 118-119; September, 1998, Kathy M. Newby, review of *What Baby Wants,* p. 180; November 1, 1998, Gale W. Sherman, review of *Turnover Tuesday,* p. 94, and Barbara Elleman, review of *Aunt Nancy and Cousin Lazybones,* p. 94; September, 1999, Maryann H. Owens, review of *Grandmother Winter,* p. 201; August, 2000, Anne Knickerbocker, review of *Here Comes Tabby Cat,* p. 164; October, 2000, review of *All for the Newborn Baby,* p. 62; November, 2000, Lynda Ritterman, review of *Meow Monday,* p. 130; December, 2000, Anne Knickerbocker, review of *Kiss the Cow!,* p. 124; June, 2001, Adele Greenlee, review of *Rattletrap Car,* p. 128; December, 2001, Ann Cook, review of *Soggy Saturday,* p. 110; October, 2002, Kathleen Simonetta, review of *Oliver Finds His Way,* p. 126; December, 2002, Susan Marie Pitard, review of *What's That Noise?,* p. 94; March, 2003, Laurie von Mehren, review of *Big Momma Makes the World,* p. 206; May, 2003, Mary Elam, review of *The Name Quilt,* p. 129; October, 2006, Kara Schaff Dean, review of *Looking for a Moose,* p. 124; December, 2006, Tamara E. Richman, review of *Lucia and the Light,* p. 114.

Teacher Librarian, September, 1998, Shirley Lewis, review of *One Duck Stuck,* p. 47.

Times Educational Supplement, March 26, 1999, Ted Dewan, review of *What Baby Wants,* p. 23; February 23, 2001, Ted Dewan, review of *Kiss the Cow!,* pp. 19-20.

ONLINE

Book Jackets Web site, http://www.bookjackets.com/ (September 8, 2003), "Phyllis Root."

Cynsations, http://cynthialeitichsmith.blogspot.com/ (March 23, 2006), Cynthia Leitich Smith, interview with Root.

Minnesota Authors and Illustrators Web site, http://www.metrolibraries.net/ (July 18, 2006), "Phyllis Root."*

*   *   *

RUBY, Lois 1942-
(Lois F. Ruby)

Personal

Born September 11, 1942, in San Francisco, CA; daughter of Philip (an artist) and Eva (an apartment manager)

Lois Ruby (Reproduced by permission.)

Fox; married Thomas Ruby (a psychologist), August 29, 1965; children: David, Kenn, Jeff. *Education:* University of California, Berkeley, B.A., 1964; San Jose State College (now California State University, San Jose), M.A., 1968. *Politics:* "Liberal Democrat." *Religion:* Jewish. *Hobbies and other interests:* Jewish survival ("a miracle!"), youth advocacy, First Amendment issues, "pigs!"

Addresses

Home and office—Albuquerque, NM. *Agent*—Susan Cohn, Writers House, 21 W. 26th St., New York, NY 10010. *E-mail*—loisruby@comcast.net.

Career

Librarian, author, and educator. Dallas Public Library, Dallas, TX, young-adult librarian, 1965-67; University of Missouri, Columbia, art and music librarian, 1967-68; freelance writer, beginning 1973; Wichita Jewish Community School, Wichita, KS, director, 1989-90; youth group adviser, 1976-91; creative writing instructor, 1985—; Temple Emanu-el of Wichita, librarian, 1975-93. Board president, Homeless Services of Inter-Faith Ministries, 1992-96, and Wichita Civil Rights and Services Board, 1994-97; member of board, Wichita Public Library.

Member

American Library Association, Society of Children's Book Writers and Illustrators, Association of Jewish Libraries, ALAN, Kansas Center for the Book (member, advisory board), New Mexico Library Association.

Awards, Honors

Best Books for Young Adults designation, American Library Association, 1977, for *Arriving at a Place You've Never Left,* and 1994, for *Miriam's Well;* Notable Children's Trade Book in the Field of Social Studies designation, National Council for the Social Studies/Children's Book Council (NCSS/CBC), 1982, for *Two Truths in My Pocket,* and 1995, for *Steal Away Home;* First Prize for fiction, Kansas Authors' Club, 1987, and honorable mention, *Writer's Digest* short-story competition, 1991, both for "Jubilee Year"; Books for the Teen Age designation, New York City Public Library, 1994, for *Miriam's Well,* 1995, for *Skin Deep,* 1996, for *Steal Away Home;* Young Adult Choice selection, International Reading Association, 1996, for *Steal Away Home;* Professionals Celebrate Literacy Award, Wichita Area Reading Council, 1996; Kansas Notable Book designation, 2007, for *Shanghai Shadows.*

Writings

Arriving at a Place You've Never Left (short stories), Dial (New York, NY), 1977.
What Do You Do in Quicksand?, Viking (New York, NY), 1979.
Two Truths in My Pocket (short stories), Viking (New York, NY), 1982.
This Old Man, Houghton (Boston, MA), 1984.
Pig-Out Inn, Houghton (Boston, MA), 1987.
Miriam's Well, Scholastic (New York, NY), 1993.
Steal Away Home, Macmillan (New York, NY), 1994.
Skin Deep, Scholastic (New York, NY), 1994.
Soon Be Free, Simon & Schuster (New York, NY), 2000.
Swindletop, Eakin Press (Austin, TX), 2000.
The Moxie Kid, Eakin Press (Austin, TX), 2002.
Anita Diamant's The Red Tent, Spark (New York, NY), 2003.
Journey to Jamestown, Kingfisher (Boston, MA), 2005.
Shanghai Shadows, Holiday House (New York, NY), 2006.

Contributor to books, including *Words on the Page, the World in Your Hands,* edited by Catherine Lipkin and Virginia Solotaroff, Harper, 1990, and *The VOYA Reader,* edited by Dorothy M. Broderick, Scarecrow Press, 1990. Contributor of short fiction to *Writer's Digest,* and one-act play to *Today I Am,* edited by Sandra Fenichel Asher.

Sidelights

In her novels and short stories for young adults, Lois Ruby confronts and addresses issues that shape many of her readers' lives in a society far different that that of their parents and teachers. According to Sharon Clontz Bernstein in *Twentieth-Century Young-Adult Writers,* "Ruby's skillful incorporation of [controversial] themes into detailed story lines . . . and the strength of her characters in confronting [such] dilemmas head on— sometimes with the help of traditional faith, but often not—results in compelling fiction that is relevant to today's young people." Celebrated as a perceptive writer who tackles difficult issues while remaining impartial,

Ruby places great value in showing teens "how important it is to be open to ideas, feelings, and new experiences," as she once explained to SATA. "It's often a lonely world we live in, and if we can touch and be touched by others, we cross that chasm between strangers."

Ruby was born in San Francisco in 1942, and was raised in an urban environment. "As a city child, I led a breathlessly exciting life," she once recalled to SATA. "I walked ten blocks to the library at least twice a week and read all the books about doctors. Early on, leprosy became a sentimental favorite of mine. Sometimes I took the trolley downtown, or the bus out to the beach, where you'd freeze to death, and no one dared swim because of the sharks. The big attraction at the beach midway was the Laughing Lady. She was obese and had bad skin and a boring job. I never could understand how she could laugh all the time. I guess it got me wondering about how people who laugh on the outside feel deep within themselves."

A reserved person, Ruby played the role of observer through much of high school, a role common to many budding writers. "I watched all the coolest of my classmates, to see if I could figure out what they had that I didn't. Since I couldn't figure it out, I did what I could do: I began [writing] parodies of them," she once explained to SATA. Unfortunately, her writing abilities got her into some trouble. "My mother sent one such embarrassment to a teen magazine, which actually paid fifty dollars to publish the story," the author remembered. "When it came out in bold black print, and when all the 'Cool Kids' read it, any hope I once harbored of being 'IN' was out." Dauntless, Ruby kept on writing, regardless of what others might think.

She continued to write through college, as well as through her marriage and after the birth of her three children, although she did not summon the courage to submit anything to a publisher until the early 1970s, a period during which realistic stories were in vogue with both publishers and the reading public. Ruby became confident that she could spin an honest yarn—"about kids who had something more important going on in their lives than a new gown for the prom or a new crankshaft for the jalopy," she once told SATA. Her prose did not pull any punches, despite the fact that her audience was youthful: "I was sure that teenagers weren't a separate species of animal, but that they were just like other humans—with problems, triumphs, heartbreaks, fears, dreams. Actually," Ruby added, "my approach hasn't changed much since then."

Ruby's first published book was the 1977 short-story collection *Arriving at a Place You've Never Left.* Containing seven short works that focus on teens attempting to cope with the crises in their lives, the book received enough positive critical response to encourage its author to pursue her writing further. While noting that "some of the stories are diffuse in structure or weak

in endings," a reviewer for the *Bulletin of the Center for Children's Books* added that Ruby's short fiction contains "diversity and drama," and that her "writing style shows promise." A reviewer for *Booklist* agreed, noting that "Ruby's first book is indeed an impressive achievement."

Ruby's first young-adult novel, *What Do You Do in Quicksand?,* was published in 1979 and features Leah, an unhappy teen living with her widowed stepfather. When sixteen-year-old Matt moves in next door with his infant daughter, Leah quickly offers to help out with the baby. Matt, pressured by efforts to support his family, keep up with schoolwork, and cope with the demands of an infant, is grateful for Leah's help, until she attempts to steal the baby in an effort to fill the emotional void in her own life. Dubbing the work "far from a run-of-the-mill-novel," a critic in the *Bulletin of the Center for Children's Books* praised Ruby's portrayal of the increasingly obsessed Leah, calling *What Do You Do in Quicksand?* "strong and moving . . . well structured and paced, with good characterization and dialogue and a candid exploration of human relationships." A *Publishers Weekly* reviewer called the novel "Ruby's amazing feat," adding that it "spotlights not only the actions but the emotions of characters who couldn't be more real and affecting."

What Do You Do in Quicksand? was followed by *Two Truths in My Pocket,* a collection of short stories that center on Jewish teenagers. *Voice of Youth Advocates* contributor Sari Feldman noted that Ruby "has done a beautiful job of combining the universal elements of adolescence with the unique experience of Jews in America," while in *Horn Book* Ann A. Flowers asserted that the "strength of centuries of religious observance and the power of belief shine through every story." The author then wrote several other novels that confront controversial topics of interest to teens, including sexual molestation, prostitution, racism, and religious controversy. For example, in *Skin Deep,* Laurel Grady and Dan Penner become high school sweethearts at the beginning of their senior year, but the stresses of school, athletics, and family push Dan into acting out his personal frustrations by joining a local white-supremacist group. Abandoning Laurel for the acceptance of his new friends, Dan eventually realizes that he is no longer acting in accordance with his own personal beliefs and must now attempt to refocus his life. A *Kirkus Reviews* commentator maintained that Ruby "portrays skinhead culture and racial hatred with terrifying clarity in this well-written novel," and in *Publishers Weekly* a critic called the story's conclusion "satisfying without offering easy answers." *Booklist* critic Frances Bradburn, noting the depth in both Laurel and Dan, called *Skin Deep* "a complex novel, one that is hardly 'skin deep'!"

In *Miriam's Well,* Ruby explores the concept of religious freedom through the relationship of two classmates, shy Miriam Pelham, a Christian fundamentalist, and Adam Bergen, a popular, outgoing Jewish boy.

When Miriam is diagnosed with bone cancer, her fundamentalist sect disallows medical care for religious reasons, but as a minor the courts order her to accept treatment. As Miriam and her family cope with the legal and philosophical issues involved in the young woman's situation, Adam becomes increasingly drawn into her life as well. As his understanding and acceptance of Miriam's religious values grow, "the reader becomes more knowledgeable about Fundamentalist and Jewish beliefs and customs," according to Barbara Flottmeier in the *Voice of Youth Advocates.* Flottmeier concluded that *Miriam's Well* presents two diverse religious philosophies "with clarity and compassion" as well as with "teen appeal." In the *Bulletin of the Center for Children's Books,* Betsy Hearne noted that Ruby explores "some controversial issues of religion and civil rights, without making her characters mouthpieces," a "real achievement" for the writer.

Steal Away Home started out "as a bunch of bones rattling around in my head," Ruby once recalled. "As I interviewed the bones, it became clear that they were the remains of a runaway slave in 1856, and that led me to the research, and *that* led me to more characters and their conflicts, and then all I had to do was record the story as the movie in my mind rolled before my eyes." Combining history with an engaging story, *Steal Away Home* follows twelve-year-old Dana Shannon as she discovers a skeleton in a hidden room of the old Kansas house she and her parents are restoring. An old diary dating from the pre-Civil War Era provides the parallel tale of the Weavers, a Quaker family who lived in Dana's house more than 140 years ago and who helped guide escaped slaves to freedom as part of the Underground Railroad. The diary gives Dana clues as to the skeleton's origins and helps the police solve a century-old mystery; it also gives teen readers insight into the issues surrounding the institution of slavery in the United States. Ruby's "skillfully rendered book will appeal to a wide audience," noted Margaret A. Bush in *Horn Book.* Writing in the *Voice of Youth Advocates,* Patsy H. Adams noted that the author's "fluid transition and realistic portrayal of life in the present and the past make [*Steal Away Home*] . . . one of the best young adult books I have read in a long time."

The story begun in *Steal Away Home* continues in *Soon Be Free.* Like *Steal Away Home,* half of the sequel is told from Dana's perspective. The alternating chapters continue the story of James Weaver, who, at Dana's age, made decisions on behalf of escaping slaves that sometimes made him question his own loyalties. In *Soon Be Free,* James decides to hide a treaty between the United States and the Delaware Indians, endangering the cause of the Delaware people to protect the escaping slaves. Although characterizing the switch between narratives as sometimes "confusing," Hazel Rochman noted in *Booklist* that "both worlds are complex." Referencing the difficult decision James makes in the novel, a reviewer wrote in *Horn Book* that "Dana's

Cover of Ruby's teen novel Soon Be Free, *featuring an illustration by Jean François Podevin.* (Illustration © 2000 by Jean François Podevin. Reproduced by permission of Aladdin Paperbacks, an imprint of Simon & Schuster Macmillan.)

parallel story illustrates the enduring consequences of long-ago decisions."

To flee Nazi Austria in 1939, Ilse Shpann and her family flee to Shanghai in *Shanghai Shadows,* another of Ruby's historical novels. Though Ilse is at first preoccupied with her own woes—her family lives as refugees, and the only possession they have is her father's violin—she begins to realize the importance of freedom. The citizens of Shanghai are struggling under Japanese occupation, and Ilse's mother is eventually arrested by the Japanese government. Soon afterward, Ilse joins a resistance movement, befriends a street urchin and another refugee, and struggles not only to survive but to strive toward freedom. Noting that the Jewish exodus to Shanghai is a little-told part of World War II history, Bradburn wrote that Ruby's story combines "careful research, courageous characters, low-key descriptions of fear and misery, and understated examples of love, friendship, and courage."

In addition to her novels and stories for young adults, Ruby is the author of *Pig-Out Inn,* a middle-grade novel that describes how the operation of a restaurant/truck

186 • RUBY
Something about the Author, Volume 184

Cover of Ruby's young-adult novel Shanghai Shadows, *featuring an illustration by Jonathan Barkat.* (Illustration © 2006 by Jonathan Barkat. Reproduced by permission of Holiday House, Inc.)

stop run by fourteen-year-old Dovi and her mother leads to a custody battle for a nine-year-old boy left behind by his trucker father. A *Publishers Weekly* reviewer called *Pig-Out Inn* a "warm and funny novel" in which Ruby "has created a memorable and original situation."

Geared for middle-grade readers, *The Moxie Kid* tells the story of Jonathan's summer before sixth grade. He wishes for excitement and fun, and misses his friend Randy, who is away at church camp. Although Jonathan is Jewish, he contemplates joining his friend so he will not be left out. Adventures start to happen, however, when Jonathan meets Mr. Caliberti, an aging neighbor who tells the preteen that he has "moxie." "The fast-paced plot features a humorous, convincing first-person narrative," wrote Laura Scott in a *School Library Journal* review.

For Ruby, the process of writing a book begins long before research trips to the library or setting down plot outlines on paper. As the author once told *SATA,* "a book starts in my mind as a character who taps me on the shoulder and says, 'Hey, lady, check me out. If you ask me the right questions, I might just have a story to

tell you.' So, I bombard this mental pest with a hundred questions, and if I'm intrigued by the answers, I write the story."

"I hope that kids will like the stories I write," Ruby once told *SATA,* "but to be honest, I write them to please myself first. I like to do stories that are emotional roller coasters. You leap over a peak, your heart in your throat, and plunge down into a valley with your stomach doing flip-flops. Then you coast for a while until the next peak catches you off guard." Although she writes to please herself, Ruby is also aware of her audience. She told an interviewer for the *Raven Stone Press Web site:* "With every word and thought I put to paper, I'm conscious of the enormous responsibility of writing for young people. These are the things I worry about: Did I model proper English with at least one character in my story? Did I get the facts right? . . . Am I out of touch, or are there stories and values that transcend time and place and generation gaps? Despite these worries, I'm ultimately aware of the great privilege I have in doing the work I love most and seeing young people read and think robustly about my stories."

In teaching the craft of writing to others, Ruby discounts the old adage "Write what you know." "I say, write what you *want* to know," she once explained to *SATA,* "then find out all you can about it." Her own practice is to research a book for months, sometimes even years, collecting piles of notecards, drawers full of files, and things tacked up on the walls and stacked in piles on the floor of her office. "Sometimes I cower under the load of all those details," the author admitted. "I have to be careful not to pack too many of them into my stories. Fiction needs to be true, that is, true to the way the human heart behaves, but not absolutely factual."

Ruby also offered the following advice to young writers on her home page: "Read everything . . . . Read out loud to hear how words sound, how they feel rolling around on your tongue and not just on the back of your eyelids. Spy on conversations. Feed your curiosity. . . . Keep a journal. Jot down fascinating tidbits. . . . Use them. Don't censor your work as you write. Write down your first thoughts fast, without worrying about spelling or grammar or punctuation. Then go back and fix it all up carefully. Let somebody you trust give you feedback. Most important: write and write and write. . . ."

Biographical and Critical Sources

BOOKS

Bernstein, Sharon Clontz, *Twentieth-Century Young Adult Writers,* St. James Press (Detroit, MI), 1994.
Gallo, Donald R., editor, *Speaking for Ourselves,* National Council of Teachers of English, 1993.

PERIODICALS

Booklist, October 1, 1977, review of *Arriving at a Place You've Never Left,* p. 282; November 15, 1994, Frances Bradburn, review of *Skin Deep,* p. 595; June 1, 2000, Hazel Rochman, review of *Soon Be Free,* p. 1882; November 1, 2006, Frances Bradburn, review of *Shanghai Shadows,* p. 45.

Bulletin of the Center for Children's Books, December, 1977, review of *Arriving at a Place You've Never Left,* p. 68; February, 1980, review of *What Do You Do in Quicksand?,* p. 117; May, 1993, Betsy Hearne, review of *Miriam's Well,* pp. 294-295; February, 1995, review of *Steal Away Home,* p. 214; July, 2000, review of *Soon to Be Free,* p. 415; March, 2007, Elizabeth Bush, review of *Shanghai Shadows,* p. 307.

Horn Book, October, 1982, Ann A. Flowers, review of *Two Truths in My Pocket,* pp. 522-523; March-April, 1995, Margaret A. Bush, review of *Steal Away Home,* p. 195; September, 2000, review of *Soon Be Free,* p. 581.

Kirkus Reviews, February 1, 1993, review of *Miriam's Well,* p. 153; November 11, 1994, review of *Skin Deep,* p. 1542; October 1, 2006, review of *Shanghai Shadows,* p. 1023.

Publishers Weekly, October 15, 1979, review of *What Do You Do in Quicksand?,* p. 67; April 24, 1987, review of *Pig-Out Inn,* p. 72; March 22, 1993, review of *Miriam's Well,* p. 80; September 19, 1994, review of *Skin Deep,* p. 72.

School Library Journal, May, 1993, review of *Miriam's Well,* p. 128; February, 1995, Bruce Anne Shook, review of *Steal Away Home,* p. 112; March, 1995, Margaret Cole, review of *Skin Deep,* p. 225; July, 2000, review of *Soon Be Free,* p. 415; February, 2003, Laura Scott, review of *The Moxie Kid,* p. 147; June, 2005, Christina Stenson-Carey, review of *Journey to Jamestown,* p. 168.

Voice of Youth Advocates, October, 1982, Sari Feldman, review of *Two Truths in My Pocket,* p. 45; June, 1993, Barbara Flottmeier, review of *Miriam's Well,* p. 94; April, 1995, Patsy H. Adams, review of *Steal Away Home,* p. 27; August, 2000, review of *Soon Be Free,* p. 193; February, 2007, Florence H. Munat, review of *Shanghai Shadows,* p. 531.

ONLINE

Lois Ruby Home Page, http://www.loisruby.com (November 17, 2007).

Raven Stone Press Web site, http://www.ravenstonepress. com/ (November 17, 2007), "Lois Ruby."

*   *   *

RUBY, Lois F.
See RUBY, Lois

S

SABERHAGEN, Fred 1930-2007
(Fred T. Saberhagen, Fred Thomas Saberhagen, Frederick Thomas Saberhagen)

OBITUARY NOTICE— See index for *SATA* sketch: Born May 18, 1930, in Chicago, IL; died of prostate cancer, June 29, 2007, in Albuquerque, NM. Science fiction and fantasy writer. In the late 1950s and early 1960s, Saberhagen worked by day as an electronics technician in Chicago, while at night his imagination roamed free. He published his first science-fiction novel in 1964 and his first short-story collection in 1965, but it was his "Berserker" series, launched with an eponymous short-story collection in 1967, that determined his future. Overall Saberhagen published dozens of science-fiction, fantasy, and quasi-horror titles, most often grouped into series. "Berserker" introduced a fleet of giant, computer-automated warships from outer space, housing aliens determined to conquer the universe by destroying all organic life forms. The theme of the series was complex and highly developed enough to spawn more than a dozen successful sequels over nearly forty years. Critics routinely praised the author for action-packed, philosophical—even mystical—adventures, populated by aliens whose "characters" were as sharply defined as those of their human opponents. Another popular series was Saberhagen's "Dracula" books, a collection of at least eight titles, published between 1975 and 1994, in which Saberhagen looked at the classical vampire myth from the point of view of the count himself. He also used this device in novels about Frankenstein, King Arthur, the assassin of Abraham Lincoln, and other historical and literary topics. The author's re-creation of historical events and settings earned him substantial praise from the critics, especially reviewers of the novel *Merlin's Bones.* The "Swords" trilogy and "Lost Swords" series were also well received. There are twelve swords, according to Saberhagen's premise, each endowed with a single supernatural attribute: wound-healer, stonecutter, farslayer, and so forth. Together they are supposed to possess the power to destroy the gods who made them. The series offered enough variety, in Saberhagen's hands, to generate at least a dozen stories, if only the author had lived long enough to write them all. Saberhagen's other series include "Empire of the East," a trilogy published between 1967 and 1973 and supplemented by a final volume, *Ardneh's Sword,* published in 2006; and the "Books of the Gods" series, offering up stories of Apollo, Hercules, and other giants of myth, published between 1997 and 2002. Saberhagen also published a number of titles that stand alone.

OBITUARIES AND OTHER SOURCES:

PERIODICALS

New York Times, July 9, 2007, p. A17.

* * *

SABERHAGEN, Frederick Thomas
See SABERHAGEN, Fred

* * *

SABERHAGEN, Fred T.
See SABERHAGEN, Fred

* * *

SABERHAGEN, Fred Thomas
See SABERHAGEN, Fred

SALONEN, Roxane Beauclair 1968-

Personal

Born September 2, 1968, Lovell, WY; daughter of Robert E. (an English teacher) and Jane E. (an elementary school teacher) Beauclair; married Troy J. Salonen (a music retail store owner), November 23, 1991; children: Christian, Olivia, Elizabeth, Adam, Nicholas. *Education:* Moorhead State University, B.S. (mass communications/music minor), 1991.

Addresses

Home—Fargo, ND. *E-mail*—rbsalonen@cableone.net.

Career

Writer. Newspaper reporter in Washington for five years.

Member

Society of Children's Book Writers and Illustrators, National Federation of Press Women, North Dakota and Fargo-Moorhead Professional Communicators.

Awards, Honors

Flicker Tale Award in Upper-Grade-Level Book Category, 2006, and first-place award, North Dakota Professional Communications contest, and third-place award, National Federation of Press Women contest, all for *P Is for Peace Garden.*

Writings

First Salmon, illustrated by Jim Fowler, Boyds Mills Press (Honesdale, PA), 2005.

P Is for Peace Garden: A North Dakota Alphabet, illustrated by Joanna Yardley, Sleeping Bear Press (Chelsea, MI), 2005.

Editor of *The Selling Gap* (nonfiction), 2007.

Sidelights

Roxane Beauclair Salonen told *SATA:* "In second grade, I presented my teacher with a hand-bound (stapled) book I'd both illustrated and written. After reading it, she told me, 'You should write books someday.' I never told anyone else what she'd said, but I kept her words close to my heart. About thirty years later, the dream she'd planted in my mind became a reality. But it took time. First, I had to finish my education. That took me

Roxane Beauclair Salonen (Courtesy of Roxane Beauclair Salonen.)

down the path of journalism. My first career job out of college was as a newspaper reporter, and that experience helped me hone my writing skills and gain confidence in myself as a writer. Eventually, my husband and I welcomed children into our fold, and reading to them got me thinking more seriously again about my dream of becoming an author. Because I love children and children's literature and had always been surrounded by both (in part through growing up with parents as teachers), it clicked: this is the kind of book writing I am meant to pursue.

"My goal as a writer is to help children see the continued value of picking up a book and reading; of finding those stories that bring them to laughter and/or tears. I want children to see themselves in story, and to take the energy from those words and apply them to their lives in a positive way. I want them to know that books can change their lives. I want them to know that every good writer I know is also a voracious reader. I want them to know that it's hard work but, ultimately, the work of a writer—or any creative pursuit—is extremely rewarding. I consider my work as a writer and author to be a gift, and I hope to share that gift with many people, big and little, whose paths I cross on this journey."

North Dakota writer Salonen introduces readers to the life of a child living in the far north in First Salmon, *a picture book featuring illustrations by* **Jim Fowler.** (Boyds Mills Press, 2005. Illustration © 2005 by Jim Fowler. Reproduced by permission.)

Biographical and Critical Sources

PERIODICALS

Booklist, October 15, 2005, Hazel Rochman, review of *First Salmon,* p. 60.
School Library Journal, November, 2005, Angela J. Reynolds, review of *First Salmon,* p. 106.

ONLINE

Roxane Beauclair Salonen Home Page, http://www.roxane salonen.com (November 12, 2007).

* * *

SANDOM, J.G.
See WELSH, T.K.

* * *

SANDOM, J. Gregory
See WELSH, T.K.

* * *

SANTAMARÍA, Benjamín 1955-

Personal

Born August 6, 1955, in Mexico City, Distrito Federal, Mexico; immigrated to Canada, 2002; son of Iola Daphne Ochoa de Enrríquez (an educator and professional dancer); children: Shakti Paluna Santamaría Crast, Ivana Nansal Santamaría Crast. *Religion:* "Friendly to socialism (non-extremism)." *Hobbies and other interests:* Zen martial arts, initiatic traditions of spirituality, human rights and social justice.

Addresses

Home—Toronto, Ontario, Canada; Mexico Tenochtitlan, Mexico.

Career

Storyteller, writer, educator, actor, and activist. Storyteller, under name El Rey Mono ("The Monkey King"), and actor in popular and sacred theatre, beginning 1970; writer and educator, beginning 1971. Writer-in-residence at Champlain College, Trent University; writer-in-exile-in-residence at George Brown College, Acadia University. Appointed ombudsman for children in Durango, Mexico, 1979, and countrywide, 1997; freelance articulist for *La Journada (niños)* (newspaper) and Canal 1 television, Mexico, 1980; Instituto Goethe and Alianza Francesa, Cordoba, Argentina, acting teacher, 1983. Yoga instructor.

Member

PEN Canada (writer in exile).

Writings

No se olvida (México 68) (novel), Plaza y Janés, 1999.
(Reteller) *Tales of the Monkey King* (stories), illustrated by Brian Deines, Tundra Books (Toronto, Ontario, Canada), 2005.

Also author of text book *Colorea tus derechos,* 1999; author of *Valors, derechos y responsabilidades de las niñez* ("The Rights of Boys and Girls [Only for Those under 18 Years Old]"; child-friendly version of U.N. Convention on the Rights of Children).

Biographical and Critical Sources

PERIODICALS

Books in Canada, December, 2005, Olga Stein, review of *Tales of the Monkey King,* p. 39.
Canadian Book Review Annual, Stacey Penney, review of *Tales of the Monkey King,* p. 461.
Resource Links, October, 2005, review of *Tales of the Monkey King.*
School Library Journal, December, 2005, Margaret A. Chang, review of *Tales of the Monkey King,* p. 121.*

*   *   *

SCHLITZ, Laura Amy

Personal

Female. *Education:* Goucher College, B.A. (aesthetics). *Hobbies and other interests:* Theatre, reading, music, crafts.

Addresses

Home—Baltimore, MD. *E-mail*—lschlitz@parkschool. net.

Career

Librarian, storyteller, and author. Park School, Baltimore, MD, lower school librarian; professional storyteller.

Awards, Honors

Great Lakes Good Books Award for Nonfiction, for *The Hero Schliemann;* Judy Lopez Honor Book designation, 2006, and Cybils Award for Children's Literature in Middle-School Fiction Category, 2007, both for *A Drowned Maiden's Hair;* Cybils Award for Poetry nomination, *School Library Journal* Best Books designation, and *Booklist* Editor's Choice designation, all 2007, and Newbery Medal, Association for Library Service to Children, 2008, all for *Good Masters! Sweet Ladies!*

Writings

A Drowned Maiden's Hair: A Melodrama, Candlewick Press (Cambridge, MA), 2006.
The Hero Schleimann: The Dreamer Who Dug for Troy, illustrated by Robert Byrd, Candlewick Press (Cambridge, MA), 2006.
Good Masters! Sweet Ladies! Voices from a Medieval Village (monologues), illustrated by Robert Byrd, Candlewick Press (Cambridge, MA), 2007.
(Adaptor) *The Bearskinner: A Tale of the Brothers Grimm* (based on "Der Bärenhäuter"), illustrated by Max Grafe, Candlewick Press (Cambridge, MA), 2007.

Also author of short plays for children that have been produced throughout the United States.

Sidelights

Laura Amy Schlitz made a name for herself in 2006, when her first two books were published to widespread critical acclaim. A librarian at Park School in Baltimore, Maryland, Schlitz had been writing for many years when Candlewick Press decided to release her novel *A Drowned Maiden's Hair: A Melodrama* as well as her nonfiction title *The Hero Schleimann: The Dreamer Who Dug for Troy.* Described by *Horn Book* contributor Kathleen Isaacs as an "irreverent" look back at the life of the German who, in 1870 rediscovered the ancient city of Troy by following the directions set down in Homer's epic Iliad, *The Hero Schleimann* "attempts to disentangle" the legends from the facts surrounding Heinrich Schleimann's colorful life, Isaacs added, writing that the cartoon illustrations provided by Robert Byrd "add to the appeal of the gently humorous text." Noting Schlitz's inclusion of information regarding archeological techniques of a past era, Gillian Engberg predicted that *The Hero Schleimann* will likely "spark interesting class discussions about how history is made and slanted over time."

Cover of Laura Amy Schlitz's highly praised novel A Drowned Maiden's Hair, *featuring artwork by Tim O'Brien.* (Illustration © 2006 by Tim O'Brien. Reproduced by permission of Candlewick Press, Inc., Cambridge, MA.)

As its subtitle unabashedly pronounces, *A Drowned Maiden's Hair* is an old-fashioned melodrama in which an unsuspecting heroine finds herself in the clutches of a ne'er-do-well until, despite the odds, she ultimately escapes. In Schlitz's story, which is set in 1909, the heroine is an eleven-year-old orphan named Maud Flynn. Headstrong Maud is considered a troublesome child by the staff at the Barbary Asylum for Orphans, so no one is more surprised than she when she is selected to be adopted by three unmarried sisters of obvious financial means. Moving to the Hawthorne sisters' large home, she is given pretty dresses and good food. Oddly, though she must remain hidden from the many people who come to visit. Soon Maud realizes why: the sisters make their living as spiritualists, performing mechanically orchestrated séances in order to tap into the bank accounts of sad, lonely, and grieving people. Because of her resemblance to the recently deceased daughter of a wealthy widow, Maud is expected to join in their plan to con the woman of her money. Although her gratitude for her material comforts and her desire for love motivate Maud to willingly join in the scheme, as events progress she begins to have second thoughts. Ultimately, a taste of freedom and her growing friendship with the sisters' deaf housemaid, Muffet, inspires the girl to take her life into her own hands.

"Schlitz's well-written narrative . . . captures melodrama at its best," concluded a *Kirkus Reviews* writer in a review of *A Drowned Maiden's Hair*, the critic commenting in particular on the author's detailed account of how the fake spiritualists created optical illusions during their pretend séances. Calling Maud a "charismatic, three-dimensional character" whose moral battle is believable, Melissa Moore added in her *School Library Journal* review that the novel "will find an audience with fans of gothic tales," and *Horn Book* reviewer Anita L. Burkham maintained that "Schlitz realizes both characters and setting . . . with unerring facility." "People throw the word 'classic' about rather a lot, but *A Drowned Maiden's Hair* genuinely deserves to become one," concluded Meghan Cox Gurdon in her review for the *Wall Street Journal,* and Elizabeth Spires wrote in the *New York Times Book Review* that Schlitz's "delightful" debut novel "provides a satisfying, if slightly creepy, look behind the scenes at how spiritualists accomplished some of their haunting effects. But it is also about love in all of its guises, deceptions and disappointments."

A storyteller and playwright as well as a fiction writer, Schlitz has also published a selection of her short dramas. In *Good Masters! Sweet Ladies! Voices from a Medieval Village* she brings to life a roster of fascinating characters ranging in age from ten to fifteen. By adopting the persona of the leading role in "Jack, the Half-wit," "Mariot and Maud, the Glassblower's Daughters," or "Hugo, the Lord's Nephew," a performer gains an intimate understanding of what life was like on an English manorial estate during the thirteenth century. Writing that Schlitz's book "gives teachers a refreshing option for enhancing the study of the European Middle Ages," Deirdre F. Baker added in *Horn Book* that *Good Masters! Sweet Ladies!* also features "pristine, elegant" watercolor art by Robert Byrd. "Bolstered by lively asides and unobtrusive [author's] notes," Schlitz's twenty-two monologues successfully "bring to life a prototypical English village in 1255," concluded a *Publishers Weekly* reviewer.

Discussing her work as a writer during an online interview for the *Cybils Award Web site,* Schlitz noted of the vivid characters she creates: "I'm not sure why, but I almost never write about people I know. On those rare occasions that I use real people as models, they're people that I don't understand. I think in order to write about something, you have to find it mysterious. Too much knowledge leaves the writer at a disadvantage."

Biographical and Critical Sources

PERIODICALS

Booklist, June 1, 2006, Gillian Engberg, review of *The Hero Schleimann: The Dreamer Who Dug for Troy,* p. 100; December 15, 2006, Hazel Rochman, review of *A Drowned Maiden's Hair: A Melodrama,* p. 43.

Bulletin of the Center for Children's Books, October, 2006, Elizabeth Bush, review of *The Hero Schleimann,* p. 93; November, 2006, Elizabeth Bush, review of *A*

Drowned Maiden's Hair, p. 144; September, 2007, review of *Good Masters! Sweet Ladies! Voices from a Medieval Village,* p. 51.

Horn Book, July-August, 2006, Kathleen Isaacs, review of *The Hero Schleimann,* p. 469; November-December, 2006, Anita L. Burkam, review of *A Drowned Maiden's Hair,* p. 725; November-December, 2007, Deirdre F. Baker, review of *Good Masters! Sweet Ladies!,* p. 699.

Kirkus Reviews, July 15, 2006, review of *The Hero Schleimann,* p. 730; October 15, 2006, review of *A Drowned Maiden's Hair,* p. 1079; July 15, 2007, review of *Good Masters! Sweet Ladies!*

Magpies, March, 2007, Rayma Turton, review of *A Drowned Maiden's Hair,* p. 40.

New York Times Book Review, December 3, 2005, Elizabeth Spires, review of *A Drowned Maiden's Hair,* p. 66.

Publishers Weekly, August 27, 2007, review of *Good Masters! Sweet Ladies!,* p. 90.

School Library Journal, September, 2006, Rita Soltan, review of *The Hero Schleimann,* p. 236; October, 2006 Melissa Moore, review of *A Drowned Maiden's Hair,* p. 170; August, 2007, Alana Abbott, review of *Good Masters! Sweet Ladies!,* p. 138.

Wall Street Journal, November 11, 2006, Meghan Cox Gurdon, review of *A Drowned Maiden's Hair.*

ONLINE

Cybils Award Web site, http://dadtalk.typepad.com/cybils/2007/ (March 12, 2007), interview with Schlitz.

Park School Web site, http://www.parkschool.net/ (August 29, 2007), "Laura Amy Schlitz, Librarian, Receives National Attention for *A Drowned Maiden's Hair.*

School Library Journal Online, http://www.schoollibraryjournal.com/ (November 5, 2007), Elizabeth Bird, interview with Schlitz.

*   *   *

SCHONGUT, Emanuel

Personal

Male. *Education:* Pratt Institute, B.F.A. and M.F.A.

Addresses

Home—San Francisco, CA. *E-mail*—eschongut@yahoo.com.

Career

Illustrator and educator. Freelance editorial, advertising, and book illustrator; Pratt Institute, New York, NY, member of faculty for six years. *Exhibitions:* Work included in shows staged by Graphic Arts Guild, Communication Arts, *Print* magazine, and Society of Illustrators. Solo shows include at Beck Gallery and Delaware Valley Arts Alliance and Somarts Gallery, San Francisco, CA.

Writings

SELF-ILLUSTRATED BOARD BOOKS

Look Kitten, Walker (London, England), 1983.
Play Kitten, Walker (London, England), 1983.
Wake Kitten, Walker (London, England), 1983.
Catch Kitten, Walker (London, England), 1983.

ILLUSTRATOR

Eileen Rosenbaum, *The Kidnapers Upstairs,* Doubleday (Garden City, NY), 1968.

Lillie D. Chaffin, *John Henry McCoy,* Macmillan (New York, NY), 1971.

Anne Merrick Epstein, *Stone Man, Stone House,* Doubleday (Garden City, NY), 1972.

Georgess McHargue, *Elidor and the Golden Ball,* Dodd, Mead (New York, NY), 1973.

Betty Virginia Doyle Boegehold, *What the Wind Told,* Parents' Magazine Press (New York, NY), 1974.

Seon Manley and Gogo Lewis, compilers, *Baleful Beasts: Great Supernatural Stories of the Animal Kingdom,* Lothrop, Lee & Shepard (New York, NY), 1974.

Seon Manley and Gog Lewis, *Bewitched Beings: Phantoms, Familiars, and the Possessed in Stories from Two Centuries,* Lothrop, Lee & Shepard (New York, NY), 1974.

Georgess McHargue, *The Talking Table Mystery,* Doubleday (Garden City, NY), 1977.

Seon Manley, *The Ghost in the Far Garden, and Other Stories,* Lothrop, Lee & Shepard (New York, NY), 1977.

Jenny Hawksworth, *The Lonely Skyscraper,* Doubleday (Garden City, NY), 1980.

Mary Stewart, *A Walk in Wolf Wood: A Tale of Fantasy and Magic,* Morrow (New York, NY), 1980.

Andrew Taylor, *The Private Nose,* Candlewick Press (Cambridge, MA), 1993.

Andrea Vlahakis, *Christmas Eve Blizzard,* Sylvan Dell (Mt. Pleasant, SC), 2005.

Jennifer Keats, *Turtles in My Sandbox,* Sylvan Dell (Mt. Pleasant, SC), 2006.

Contributor of illustrations to periodicals, including *Parents, Children's Digest, Vogue, Cosmopolitan, Harper's, Pushpin Graphic, Long Island Newsday, New York,* and *New York Times.*

Biographical and Critical Sources

PERIODICALS

Kirkus Reviews, October 15, 2006, review of *Turtles in My Sandbox,* p. 1068.

Publishers Weekly, February 1, 1993, review of *The Private Nose,* p. 95.

School Library Journal, March, 1993, Jeanette Larson, review of *The Private Nose,* p. 202.

Small Press Bookwatch, December, 2005, review of *Christmas Eve Blizzard;* November, 2006, review of *Turtles in My Sandbox.*

ONLINE

Emanuel Schongut Home Page, http://www.eschongut.com (November 15, 2007).

* * *

SCHWARTZ, Virginia Frances 1950-

Personal

Born December 14, 1950, in Stoney Creek, Ontario, Canada; married Neil Eric Schwartz (an educator), January, 1978. *Education:* Waterloo Lutheran University (now Wilfrid Laurier University), B.A.; Pace University, M.S. *Politics:* Democrat.

Addresses

Home—Flushing, NY. *E-mail*—virginiafschwartz@yahoo.com.

Career

Children's book author and educator. Registered nurse in New York, NY, and in Canada, 1975-88; elementary school teacher in New York, NY, 1988-94; elementary school writing teacher in New York, NY, beginning 1994.

Member

Society of Children's Book Writers and Illustrators.

Awards, Honors

Gold Award in fiction category, Parents' Choice, 2000, Best Book for Young Adults selection, American Library Association, Notable Book for a Global Society selection, International Reading Association, Top Shelf Fiction for Middle School Readers selection, *Voice of Youth Advocates,* and Books for the Teen Age selection, New York Public Library, all 2001, all for *Send One Angel Down;* Silver Birch Award for Historical Fiction, for *If I Just Had Two Wings.*

Writings

YOUNG-ADULT HISTORICAL FICTION

Send One Angel Down, Holiday House (New York, NY), 2000.
If I Just Had Two Wings, Stoddart Kids (Toronto, Ontario, Canada), 2001.

Virginia Frances Schwartz (Courtesy of Virginia Frances Schwartz.)

Messenger, Holiday House (New York, NY), 2002.
Initiation, Fitzhenry & Whiteside (Markham, Ontario, Canada), 2003.
Four Kids in 5E and One Crazy Year, Holiday House (New York, NY), 2006.

Sidelights

Born in eastern Canada, Virginia Frances Schwartz now makes her home in New York state, where she has taught elementary-grade students since the late 1980s. In her historical novel *Messenger* Schwartz draws on family history to tell a story about an immigrant farming family moving from Eastern Europe to rural Canada during the early twentieth century, while her other novels focus on slavery and the lives of Native Americans prior to the arrival of Europeans.

Based on the experiences of Schwartz's mother and grandmother, *Messenger* follows a widowed Croatian woman as she brings her family to Canada in the hopes of giving her children a better life. Set in central Ontario during the depression years of the late 1920s and 1930s, the novel finds narrator and oldest daughter Frances attempting to help her overworked mother while also helping to raise her two younger brothers. Threading her story with Croatian customs and folklore, Schwartz follows her young heroine as Frances attempts to hold the fragile family together as they move from the farm to a boarding house her mother plans to operate in an Ontario mining town. In *Kirkus Reviews,* a critic noted the novel's uplifting ending and praised *Messenger* as a "lyrically written" tale that is "rich in emotional nuance." A *Publishers Weekly* critic cited the book's prose, which the critic called "strongly atmospheric" despite Frances's "detached" narration.

Other historical novels by Schwartz include the award-winning *Send One Angel Down* and *If I Just Had Two Wings*, as well as *Initiation*, a story about Kwakiutl twins Nana and Nanolatch. As the siblings reach adulthood in west-coast Canada during the 1440s, they must accept the destiny that awaits them as the children of a chieftain. "Schwartz is able to weave" Kwakiutl culture and history into "a compelling, mythical" coming-of-age tale, noted *Resource Links* critic Teresa Hughes in her review of *Initiation*. Reviewing *If I Just Had Two Wings*, which finds two three slaves determined to escape from their life picking cotton via the Underground Railway, *Kliatt* critic Paula Rhorlick praised Schwartz for crafting a "well-written and exciting story" that includes numerous facts about what it was like to make this historic flight to freedom. Schwartz draws on actual slave recollections gathered by the Federal Writers Project during the 1930s in her novel *Send One Angel Down*, which also introduces readers to the day-to-day

Cover of Schwartz's middle-grade novel Messenger, *featuring an illustration by Greg Spalenka.* (Holiday House, 2002. Illustration © 2002 by Greg Spalenka. Reproduced by permission.)

life of Southern slaves. The winner of numerous awards, *Send One Angel Down* was also praised by *Resource Links* critic Gail de Vos as "a strong novel with authentic, charismatic characters."

In a change of pace, Schwartz's middle-grade novel *Four Kids in 5E and One Crazy Year* is a humorous story in which a special teacher changes the lives of four special-ed students during their fifth-grade school year. Framed as a journal that interweaves entries by Gio, Max, Destiny, and Willie, *Four Kids in 5E and One Crazy Year* was cited by *School Library Journal* contributor Carly B. Wiskoff as "a promising motivational book for reluctant readers." In *Kirkus Reviews* a reviewer asserted that, in a text that "goes straight to the heart," Schwartz tells a story that will provide "inspiration to . . . those who struggle with life or literacy." *Booklist* contributor Hazel Rochman also viewed Schwartz's novel favorably, dubbing *Four Kids in 5E and One Crazy Year* a "beautiful story" about the enduring legacy of an inspiring teacher.

Cover of Schwartz's entertaining 2006 novel Four Kids in 5E and One Crazy Year, *featuring an illustration by Eric Brace.* (Holiday House, 2006. Illustration © 2006 by Eric Brace. Reproduced by permission of Holiday House, Inc.)

Schwartz once told *SATA:* "I knew I wanted to be a writer by the time I went to school. School gave me the written word, but, long before that, the environment in which I was raised prepared me to write. It provided me with certain qualities: beauty, space, endless time to daydream, storytelling, and access to books.

"I grew up in Canada in the heart of the fruit belt that stretched across southern Ontario from Niagara Falls to Toronto. When I was young, it was completely rural, 'like a slice of heaven' as my grandfather says in my latest novel about my family, *Messenger*. My backyard was a twenty-acre orchard of blossoming fruit trees where I played, daydreamed, and read. My mind traveled to a million places as I dangled upside down, played dress-up, and spent every moment I could, even throughout the long, snowy winters, outside. Beauty and space were essential for me to become a writer.

"I lived in a multicultural neighborhood of immigrants who came from all areas of Europe—Croatia, Serbia, Italy, England, Scotland, Italy, Sicily, France, and Ireland. They spoke with strong accents, ate delicious foods, looked and dressed differently, all of which mesmerized me. Their traditions, like ours, were shared orally. Something in their voices sparked so many images in my mind about their characters and the countries they had left behind. In the afternoons, when our neighbors dropped over for a scone and tea, they spilled their stories into my ears. We had no television in our house until I was twelve, but we always had entertainment. On hot summer evenings, spread out on a blanket beneath the cherry trees and the Milky Way, my grandparents, aunts, uncles, and parents competed to tell the stories of their lives: spooky stories like my grandmother's, funny stories like my father's, and of course, great fishing stories and jokes from Uncle Phillip. I became a listener, a sponge, at an early age.

"Storytelling was the fuel. Reading provided the fire. By sheer luck, the one library in the whole county was built a block away from my house. I had a new place to explore then. When I read everything in the juvenile section, the librarian secretly allowed me access to that intermediary section, on a landing between the kids' books in the basement and the real adult books on the sunny upper floor. This was 'young adult,' for teenagers, a collection of historical fiction and mysteries that fed my imagination. I had reached a new land, and the best part was getting there while I was still a fourth-grader.

"Although I did write as a child, I did not take writing all that seriously. Perhaps that was because it came easily to me to write the required essays and assignments. But I didn't venture out on my own much. The stories were still locked in my head. It wasn't until I was an adult that I could finally focus on writing. I began a teaching career in the fourth and fifth grades. I loved teaching writing and reading the most. I used to say to my fellow teachers, 'If only I could just teach writing all day!' My wish came true. I was sent by my district to Columbia University to be trained as a teacher of 'The Writing Process.' Each day, I visited classrooms to inspire and train young writers from kindergarten to grade six. Side by side with the children, we read great stories from Cynthia Rylant, Gary Paulsen, Eloise Greenfield, and Donald Crews. We wrote in writers' notebooks every day and learned the steps of drafting, revision, editing, and proofreading. You can't imagine how lucky I felt working each day to transform children into writers. It fed something deep inside. I felt as if I was facing the child in me who dreamed of becoming a writer, but had no idea how to do it. It was during my tenure as a writing teacher that my first book was accepted for publication.

"In life, I always root for the underdog, the one who is left behind in some way, the one I recognize as having so much potential that is covered or perhaps crushed. They often sat in my classroom: girls so shy they never looked up, boys who stuttered, new immigrants lost without the words and friendships to make them feel at home, kids who stumbled over math, students who, at eight years of age, had dark worry-circles beneath their eyes. I wanted them to succeed and realize the tremendous power they had inside them. I wanted the other children to learn tolerance, to know that others can be different from you on the outside, but that inside we are all the same. It is no surprise to me that I write about slaves, immigrants, and Native Americans. These groups suffered tremendous hardships and injustices. In my novels I give them hope and a different life.

"One of the ways in which I have dealt with suffering in my own life was developing into a spiritual person. That means that I look to a higher place than just my own mind for everyday guidance. The songs and prayers of the slaves in *Send One Angel Down* and *If I Just Had Two Wings* mirror the spiritual belief that helped slaves endure centuries of degradations. In *Messenger*, the fatherless narrator is soothed by prayer, literature, poetry, and a belief in the afterlife. These books explore ways to nourish a spirit that has been crushed by abuse and overwhelming family or social problems. Spirituality, or thinking about God, helps us recognize our true selves and develop our potential.

"As a writer, I sit down at my desk, or lie in a field studying clouds in the sky, and listen carefully to the words in my head, the same way I did as a child. I try to get them down as fast as I can at first and do a lot of revision later. The words often come in a rush and my hand moves so fast that it hurts. I keep a notebook by my bedside because ideas often come just before I fall asleep. My characters seem to find me. I did not decide, for instance, to write about slavery. One evening, as I was falling asleep, a girl's face appeared in my mind. At once I knew she was a slave. What drew me into her was her extreme pain and urgency. She had a story to tell. All I had to do was listen. That character was Phoebe and her story became *If I Just Had Two Wings*. Slavery is obviously something that needs to be talked about in the new millennium. America needs racial healing.

"What I realize is that to be a children's author today is to take responsibility for the ways in which children think and grow. I'd like to help make the world a healing place for all races, religious, and cultures."

Biographical and Critical Sources

PERIODICALS

Booklist, June 1, 2000, Debbie Carton, review of *Send One Angel Down;* December 1, 2001, Michael Cart, review of *If I Just Had Two Wings,* p. 638; December 1, 2006, Hazel Rochman, review of *Four Kids in 5E and One Crazy Year,* p. 50.

Canadian Review of Materials, September 19, 2003, review of *Initiation.*

Horn Book, July, 2000, review of *Send One Angel Down,* p. 465.

Kirkus Reviews, October 1, 2002, review of *Messenger,* p. 1480; October 1, 2006, review of *Four Kids in 5E and One Crazy Year,* p. 1024.

Kliatt, January, 2002, Paula Rohrlick, review of *If I Just Had Two Wing.*

Publishers Weekly, May 1, 2000, review of *Send One Angel Down,* p. 71; October 21, 2002, review of *Messenger,* p. 77.

Resource Links, December, 2003, Teresa Hughes, review of *Initiation,* p. 41; June, 2005, Gail de Vos, review of *Send One Angel Down,* p. 23.

School Library Journal, August, 2000, Bruce Anne Shook, review of *Send One Angel Down,* p. 188; December, 2001, Farida S. Dowler, review of *If I Just Had Two Wings,* p. 143; March, 2004, Carol A. Edwards, review of *Initiation,* p. 220.

Voice of Youth Advocates, December, 2002, review of *Messenger,* p. 391.*

*   *   *

SHEARING, Leonie 1972-

Personal

Born March 4, 1972, in England. *Education:* Anglia Polytechnic University, B.A. (illustration; with honours), 1994.

Addresses

Home—3, Toronto Terrace, Brighton, East Sussex BN2 9UW, England. *Agent*—Philippa Milnes-Smith, LAW, 14 Vernon St., London W14 0RJ, England. *E-mail*—info@leonieshearing.com.

Career

Illustrator.

Awards, Honors

Macmillan Children's Book Awards runner up, 1992; Bisto Book of the Year Ellis Dillon Award, and Bisto Merit Award, both 2000.

Illustrator

Marita Conlon-McKenna, *Granny MacGinty,* Orchard (London, England), 1999.

Marilyn McLaughlin, *Fierce Milly,* Mammoth (London, England), 1999.

Pippa Goodhart, *Frankie's House-Tree,* Mammoth (London, England), 2000.

Beth Wyllyams, *I Don't Want To!,* Egmont (London, England), 2000.

Beth Wyllyams, *Please Be Gentle!,* Egmont (London, England), 2000.

Marilyn McLaughlin, *Fierce Milly and the Amazing Dog,* Mammoth (London, England), 2001.

Marilyn McLaughlin, *Fierce Milly and the Biggest Conker Ever,* Egmont (London, England), 2001.

Marilyn McLaughlin, *Fierce Milly and the Demon Saucepan,* Egmont (London, England), 2002.

Marilyn McLaughlin, *Fierce Milly and the Swizzled Eyes,* Egmont (London, England), 2002.

Jillian Powell, *Izzie's Idea,* Franklin Watts (London, England), 2003, Picture Window Press (Minneapolis, MN), 2005.

Marni McGee, *The Noisy Farm,* Bloomsbury Children's (New York, NY), 2004.

Nursery Rhyme Treasury, Marks & Spencer (Chester, England), 2004.

Claire Freedman, *Squabble and Squawk,* Simon & Schuster (New York, NY), 2006.

Franzeska Ewart, *Starting School,* Paragon, 2006.

Also illustrator of *It's Fall; Ben's Ten Hens,* by Mandy Ross; and *Ron's Race,* by Jillian Powell.

Biographical and Critical Sources

PERIODICALS

Kirkus Reviews, May 15, 2004, review of *The Noisy Farm,* p. 495; October 15, 2006, review of *Squabble and Squawk,* p. 1070.

School Library Journal, October, 2004, Maryann H. Owen, review of *The Noisy Farm,* p. 122.

ONLINE

Leonie Shearing Home Page, http://www.leonieshearing.com (November 15, 2007).*

*   *   *

SHOVELLER, Herb

Personal

Born in Sudbury, Ontario, Canada; married; wife's name Joanne (a university vice president). *Education:* University of Western Ontario, B.A. (philosophy; with honours), M.A. (journalism).

Addresses

Home—Guelph, Ontario, Canada.

Career

Author and consultant. *London Free Press,* London, Ontario, Canada, journalist and business editor until 2005.

Awards, Honors

Disney Adventures Book Award shortlist, and Parents' Choice Recommended designation, both 2006, and Reiser Award, Metro Atlanta Corporate Volunteer Council, Notable Social Studies Trade Books for Young People designation, Notable Books for a Global Society designation, and *ForeWord* Book of the Year Award shortlist, all 2007, all for *Ryan and Jimmy and the Well in Africa That Brought Them Together.*

Writings

Ryan and Jimmy and the Well in Africa That Brought Them Together, Kids Can Press (Toronto, Ontario, Canada), 2006.

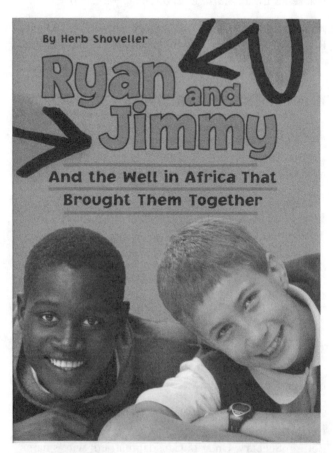

Cover of Herb Shoveller's true-life story Ryan and Jimmy and the Well in Africa That Brought Them Together, *which features artwork by Bill Grimshaw.* (Photograph © by Bill Grimshaw. Used by permission of Kids Can Press Ltd., Toronto.)

(Coauthor) Lincoln M. Alexander, *"Go to School, You're a Little Black Boy": The Honourable Lincoln M. Alexander: A Memoir,* Dundurn Press (Toronto, Ontario, Canada), 2006.

Sidelights

Before becoming a published children's author and a freelance writer/editor, Herb Shoveller worked for the *London Free Press* for two decades. His award-winning *Ryan and Jimmy and the Well in Africa That Brought Them Together* is based on a true story of a boy's campaign to help bring clean drinking water to Third-World countries. An Ontario native, Ryan Hreljac first learned about the lack of clean drinking water in Africa from his first-grade teacher. Hoping to do his part in bringing water to this region, Hreljac donated seventy dollars, which he earned by completing a variety of chores, to the WaterCan Foundation which constructs wells in impoverished countries. When Hreljac learned that his donation would only be enough to purchase a single water pump, he was inspired to collect enough money to fund the construction of an entire well. Over the next decade, the boy, with his community's help, raised two thousand dollars, ultimately funding the construction of a well within a small town in Uganda.

Shoveller had a special interest in Hreljac's story: he is the boy's uncle. He tells his nephew's story by combining a photo essay with a "text-heavy narrative" that successfully conveys Hreljac's "inspiring story," as a *Publishers Weekly* critic noted. In *Resource Links,* Joanne de Groo commented that while *Ryan and Jimmy and the Well in Africa That Brought Them Together* is "longer than a standard picture book," Shoveller's work should appeal to elementary-grade readers because it "is informally written and often feels like it is being narrated by a young person."

Biographical and Critical Sources

PERIODICALS

Kirkus Reviews, October 1, 2006, review of *Ryan and Jimmy and the Well in Africa That Brought Them Together,* p. 1025.
Publishers Weekly, November 20, 2006, review of *Ryan and Jimmy and the Well in Africa That Brought Them Together,* p. 59.
School Library Journal, November, 2006, Genevieve Gallagher, review of *Ryan and Jimmy and the Well in Africa That Brought Them Together,* p. 164.

ONLINE

Hackmatack Web site, http://www.hackmatack.ca/ (November 12, 2007), "Herb Shoveller."
London Free Press Web site, http://lfpress.ca/ (January 20, 2007), Kathy Rumleski, "Oprah Gives Ex-Londoner's Book Nod."*

SHULMAN, Mark 1962-

Personal

Born 1962, in Rochester, NY; married, wife's name Kara; children: Hannah, Solomon. *Education:* University of Buffalo, degree.

Addresses

Home—New York, NY. *Office*—Oomf, Inc., 420 W. 24th St., Ste. 10E, New York, NY 10011. *Agent*—Susan Cohen, Writers House, 21 W. 26th St., New York, NY 10010. *E-mail*—mark@oomf.com.

Career

Writer and publisher. Worked as an advertising creative director, radio news broadcaster, restaurant maître d', and licensed New York City tour guide; Oomf, Inc. (children's book packaging company), New York, NY, director, 2000—.

Cover of Mark Shulman's Mom and Dad Are Palindromes, *featuring quirky illustrations by Adam McCauley.* (Illustration © 2006 by Adam McCauley. Used by permission of Chronicle Books, LLC, San Francisco. Visit ChronicleBooks.com.)

Writings

Colorful Illusions: Tricks to Fool Your Eyes, Sterling Publishing (New York, NY), 2000.

Secret Hiding Places (for Clever Kids), Sterling Publishing (New York, NY), 2001.

You Poser! 101 Percent Genuine Fake I.D.s, Scholastic (New York, NY), illustrated by Joe Bartos, 2002.

How I Built Rusty and You Can, Too, Scholastic (New York, NY), illustrated by Philip Fickling, 2002.

Shamu and the Adventurous Seal Pup, Busch Entertainment (Clayton, MO), 2002.

The Voodoo Revenge Book: An Anger Management Program You Can Really Stick With, illustrated by Joe Bartos, Main Street Press (New York, NY), 2002.

Colors: There's No Blue on a Bagel, photographs by Bill Milne, Grosset & Dunlap (New York, NY), 2002.

Counting: I'll Take a Dozen, photographs by Bill Milne, Grosset & Dunlap (New York, NY), 2002.

Opposites: Big Bagel, Little Bagel, photographs by Bill Milne, Grosset & Dunlap (New York, NY), 2003.

Shapes: My Square Breakfast, photographs by Bill Milne, Grosset & Dunlap (New York, NY), 2003.

Super Sports, illustrated by Jenny B. Harris, Sterling Publishing (New York, NY), 2003.

Jazzy Jobs, illustrated by Jenny B. Harris, Sterling Publishing (New York, NY), 2003.

Amazing Animals, illustrated by Jenny B. Harris, Sterling Publishing (New York, NY), 2003.

Some Pigs, illustrated by Vincent Nguyen and Joe Bartos, Barron's (Hauppauge, NY), 2003.

Some Ducks, illustrated by Vincent Nguyen and Joe Bartos, Barron's (Hauppauge, NY), 2003.

Some Cows, illustrated by Vincent Nguyen and Joe Bartos, Barron's (Hauppauge, NY), 2003.

Wacky Weekend, Sterling Publishing (New York, NY), 2004.

(With Hazlitt Krog) *Attack of the Killer Video Book: Tips and Tricks for Young Directors,* illustrated by Martha Newbigging, Annick Press (Toronto, Ontario, Canada), 2004.

Flashlight Dinosaurs: Terrors in Time!, illustrated by John S. Dykes, Barron's (Hauppauge, NY), 2004.

Flashlight Monsters: Invade Hollywood!, illustrated by John S. Dykes, Barron's (Hauppauge, NY), 2004.

Fillmore and Geary Take Off!: The Adventures of a Robot Boy and a Boy Boy, illustrated by Phillip Fickling, Chronicle Books (San Francisco, CA), 2004.

(With Melissa Heckscher) *The Explorer's Gazette: Amazing Stories of Thirty Real-life Journeys,* Scholastic (New York, NY), 2004.

(With Aki Nurosi) *Colorful Optical Illusions,* Main Street Press (New York, NY), 2004.

Stella the Star, illustrated by Vincent Nguyen, Walker (New York, NY), 2004.

Spooky Spider, illustrated by Patti Jennings, Sterling Publishing (New York, NY), 2004.

Batty Bat, illustrated by Patti Jennings, Sterling Publishing (New York, NY), 2004.

The Mini-Voodoo Revenge Book: An Anger Management Program You Can Really Stick With, illustrated by Joe Bartos, Main Street Press (New York, NY), 2004.

Big Cat, illustrated by Sally Chambers, Tiger Tales (Wilton, CT), 2004.

Foxy Fox, illustrated by Sally Chambers, Tiger Tales (Wilton, CT), 2004.

(With Aki Nurosi) *Artful Illusions: Designs to Fool Your Eyes,* Main Street Press (New York, NY), 2005.

Aa Is for Aardvark, illustrated by Tamara Petrosino, Sterling Publishing (New York, NY), 2005.

Louis and the Dodo, illustrated by Vincent Nguyen, Sterling Publishing (New York, NY), 2005.

(Adaptor) *Madagascar* (sound storybook), Meredith Books (Des Moines, IA), 2005.

A Is for Zebra, illustrated by Tamara Petrosino, Sterling Publishing (New York, NY), 2006.

Not Another Tea Party, illustrated by Vincent Nguyen, Sterling Publishing (New York, NY), 2006.

Mom and Dad Are Palindromes: A Dilemma for Words . . . and Backwards, illustrated by Adam McCauley, Chronicle Books (San Francisco, CA), 2006.

(With Oscar de la Hoya) *Super Oscar: The Made-Up Adventures of Oscar de la Hoya,* illustrated by Lisa Kopelke, Simon & Schuster (New York, NY), 2006.

The Brainiac Box: 600 Facts Every Smart Person Should Know, Kaplan Publishing (New York, NY), 2006.

Nutsy the Robot Goes to School, illustrated by Katie Boyce, School Specialty Publishing (Grand Rapids, MI), 2006.

Nutsy the Robot Goes to Bed, illustrated by Katie Boyce, School Specialty Publishing (Grand Rapids, MI), 2006.

Flip-O-Matic: Instant History for Grades 6/7/8, Kaplan Publishing (New York, NY), 2006.

Flip-O-Matic: Instant Math for Grades 6/7/8, Kaplan Publishing (New York, NY), 2006.

Flip-O-Matic: Instant Science for Grades 6/7/8, Kaplan Publishing (New York, NY), 2006.

Flip-O-Matic: Instant Language Arts for Grades 6/7/8, Kaplan Publishing (New York, NY), 2006.

The Incredible Hulk: Hulk vs. Hulk, illustrated by Louie De Martinis, Meredith Books (Des Moines, IA), 2006.

The Wicked Wit and Wisdom of Ben Franklin: More than 500 Quotes, Sayings, and Proverbs, Random House (New York, NY), 2007.

Dino in the Jungle!, illustrated by Sarah Massini, Barnes & Noble Books (New York, NY), 2007.

Wicked Weather: When Everything Goes Right, It Goes So Wrong (Discovery Channel), Meredith Books (Des Moines, IA), 2007.

Shark Attack: Top-Ten Attack Sharks (Discovery Channel), Meredith Books (Des Moines, IA), 2007.

"STORYTIME STICKERS" SERIES

Horsing Around, illustrated by Susan Nethery, Sterling Publishing (New York, NY), 2005.

Car and Truck Show, illustrated by Phillip Small, Sterling Publishing (New York, NY), 2005.

Magic Fairy Forest, illustrated by Kathy Wilburn, Sterling Publishing (New York, NY), 2005.

Dinosaurs Then and Wow!, illustrated by Bob Ostrom, Sterling Publishing (New York, NY), 2005.

Enchanted Princess Castle, illustrated by David Wenzel, Sterling Publishing (New York, NY), 2005.

The Insect Invaders, illustrated by Mark Collins, Sterling Publishing (New York, NY), 2005.

Flower Girls, illustrated by Maggie Swanson, Sterling Publishing (New York, NY), 2006.

UFO Alien Invaders, illustrated by Ed Shems, Sterling Publishing (New York, NY), 2006.

Spooky Halloween House, illustrated by Bob Ostrom, Sterling Publishing (New York, NY), 2006.

Santa's on His Way, illustrated by Kathy Wilburn, Sterling Publishing (New York, NY), 2006.

Undersea Adventures, illustrated by Terri Chicko, Sterling Publishing (New York, NY), 2007.

Easter Bunny, illustrated by Maggie Swanson, Sterling Publishing (New York, NY), 2007.

Sidelights

Mark Shulman, the founder of Oomf, Inc., a children's book packaging company, is also the author of a number of highly regarded picture books for young readers. In one of his earliest efforts, *Secret Hiding Places (for Clever Kids),* Shulman offers suggestions for finding, using, and building a variety of hiding places, in addition to making codes, maps, and more. "Future spies, and probably present spies, can benefit from the painstaking instructions found here," noted *Children's Literature* contributor Danielle Williams in a review of the work.

Two friends from the planet Zada build a canine companion in *Fillmore and Geary Take Off!: The Adventures of a Robot Boy and a Boy Boy.* When Fillmore and his robot pal Geary decide they want a pet of their own, they head to the Invention Room to construct Sbot; unfortunately, their creation acts more like a robot than a dog. Borrowing a spaceship, the trio set out across the galaxy in search of proper canine role models. According to Lisa Gangemi Kropp, writing in *School Library Journal,* Phillip Fickling's "computer-generated cartoons are perfect for the narrative's futuristic feel." In *Stella the Star,* a youngster lands a role in her first school play, causing her parents to go overboard with excitement. "More a satire, this tale is best appreciated by an older reader," a *Kirkus Reviews* critic observed of the book.

Shulman and coauthor Hazlitt Krog present advice for aspiring filmmakers in *Attack of the Killer Video Book: Tips and Tricks for Young Directors.* The humorous text, accompanied by cartoon-style illustrations, discusses the fundamentals of video production, including storyboarding, composition, sound, lighting, and editing. "Ideas are progressively presented in clear concise hip language," noted *Resource Links* critic Anne Hatcher, and *Booklist* reviewer GraceAnne A. DeCandido predicted that "young Spielbergs and Sofia Coppolas will probably mine useful nuggets."

In *Louis and the Dodo,* a fantasy for preschoolers, a lonely little boy and his songbird friends rescue a dodo that is being mistreated by the owner of a circus. A contributor in *Kirkus Reviews* described the work as a "dreamy, oddball episode." A bossy youngster almost loses her best friends to a chameleon in *Not Another Tea Party.* The "absurdist quality" of Shulman's story appealed to a critic writing in *Kirkus Reviews.*

Shulman has also published a pair of unusual alphabet books: *Aa Is for Aardvark* and *A Is for Zebra.* In the former, Shulman and illustrator Tamara Petrosino present words with repeated letters; the page featuring "TT," for example, includes a "little kitten." A reviewer in *Publishers Weekly* stated that "there are indeed laughs to be had in these silly, often inventive pages," and *School Library Journal* critic Steven Engelfried noted that Petrosino's colorful scenes "lend the right touch of wackiness to the visual presentation." In *A Is for Zebra,* which also features Petrosino's art, the author highlights a word's final letter. "A fresh, delightful take on an alphabet book," is how Hazel Rochman described the book in her *Booklist* review.

In another book devoted to wordplay, *Mom and Dad Are Palindromes: A Dilemma for Words . . . and Backwards,* young Bob becomes obsessed with language when he realizes palindromes are all around him, including his race car, his sister, Anna, and his pup, Otto. Shulman's "text crackles with cleverly integrated palindromes," noted a *Kirkus Reviews* critic, and a contributor in *Publishers Weekly* praised the story, "which slyly promotes a catchy spelling game."

Biographical and Critical Sources

PERIODICALS

Booklist, May 15, 2004, GraceAnne A. DeCandido, review of *Attack of the Killer Video Book: Tips and Tricks for Young Directors,* p. 1618; March 15, 2006, Hazel Rochman, review of *A Is for Zebra,* p. 51.

Kirkus Reviews, April 1, 2004, review of *Stella the Star,* p. 338; October 1, 2004, review of *Fillmore and Geary Take Off!: The Adventures of a Robot Boy and a Boy Boy,* p. 969; December 1, 2005, review of *Louis and the Dodo,* p. 1280; April 15, 2006, review of *Super Oscar: The Made-Up Adventures of Oscar De La Hoya,* p. 404; June 1, 2006, review of *Mom and Dad Are Palindromes: A Dilemma for Words . . . and Backwards,* p. 580; October 15, 2006, review of *Not Another Tea Party,* p. 1080.

Publishers Weekly, December 13, 2004, review of *Fillmore and Geary Take Off!,* p. 67; November 14, 2005, review of *Aa Is for Aardvark,* p. 68; March 6, 2006, review of *Super Oscar,* p. 73; July 10, 2006, review of *Mom and Dad Are Palindromes,* p. 81.

Resource Links, June, 2004, Anne Hatcher, review of *Attack of the Killer Video Book,* p. 31.

School Library Journal, August, 2001, Augusta R. Malvagno, review of *Zany Rainy Days: Indoor Ideas for Active Kids,* p. 173; May, 2004, Maryann H. Owen, review of *Stella the Star,* p. 124; June, 2004, Jeffrey Hastings, review of *Attack of the Killer Video Book,* p. 174; January, 2006, Amy Lilien-Harper, review of *Louis and the Dodo,* p. 113; February, 2006, Steven Engelfried, review of *Aa Is for Aardvark,* p. 109; June, 2006, Grace Oliff, review of *Mom and Dad Are Palindromes,* p. 126.

ONLINE

Annick Press Web site, http://www.annickpress.com/ (October 31, 2007), "Mark Shulman."

Children's Literature Online, http://www.childrenslit.com/ (December 1, 2001), Danielle Williams, review of *Secret Hiding Places (for Clever Kids).*

Chronicle Books Web site, http://www.chroniclebooks.com/ (October 31, 2007), "Mark Shulman."

Publishers Marketplace Web site, http://www.publishersmarketplace.com/ (October 31, 2007), "Mark Shulman."

*   *   *

SILIN-PALMER, Pamela

Personal

Married Patrick Palmer; children: four daughters.

Addresses

Home—Mendocino, CA.

Career

Illustrator, decorative artist, and designer of furniture, textiles, and housewares. Faunus School of Decorative Art, CA, cofounder, 1976, and designer for Rabbits of the Rainbow brand.

Illustrator

Paul Mandelstein, *The Nightingale at the Wind,* Rizzoli (New York, NY), 1994.

Molly Coxe, *Bunny and the Beast,* Random House (New York, NY), 2001.

Emily Snowell Keller, reteller, *Sleeping Bunny,* Random House (New York, NY), 2003.

Mallory Loehr, *Unicorn Wings,* Random House (New York, NY), 2006.

Biographical and Critical Sources

PERIODICALS

Booklist, January 1, 2003, Ilene Cooper, review of *Sleeping Bunny,* p. 899.

Kirkus Reviews, November 15, 2002, review of *Sleeping Bunny,* p. 1696; October 15, 2006, review of *Unicorn Wings,* p. 1073.

Publishers Weekly, June 6, 1994, review of *The Nightingale and the Wind,* p. 65; January 8, 2001, review of *Bunny and the Beach,* p. 66; November 25, 2002, review of *Sleeping Bunny,* p. 65.

San Francisco Chronicle, March 25, 2001, review of *Bunny and the Beast.*

School Library Journal, May, 2001, Linda M. Kenton, review of *Bunny and the Beast,* p. 140; March, 2003, Joy Fleishhacker, review of *Sleeping Bunny,* p. 220; February, 2007, Susan Lissim, review of *Unicorn Wings,* p. 92.

ONLINE

Pamela Silin-Palmer Home Page, http://www.pamelasilinpalmer.com (November 15, 2007).*

*   *   *

SMITH, Gordon 1951-

Personal

Born 1951, in Upper Darby, PA; children: one daughter. *Education:* Antioch College, B.S. (fine arts), 1973.

Addresses

Home and office—San Francisco, CA. *E-mail*—info@beatriz.co.uk.

Career

Graphic designer and author. Tower Advertising, Sacramento, CA, art director, 1980-85; graphic designer; Tremain & Smith (graphic design firm), Berkeley, CA, partner, 1985-89; *California Lawyer* (magazine), San Francisco, art director, 1989-95; freelance graphic designer, beginning 1999; School Wise Press, San Francisco, CA, design director, 2005-07.

Awards, Honors

New York Public Library Books for the Teen Age designation, 2007, for *The Forest in the Hallway;* Society of Illustrators citation for art direction; Western Publications Association Maggie Award.

Writings

The Forest in the Hallway, Clarion Books (New York, NY), 2006.

Sidelights

Gordon Smith began his career as a graphic designer and art director working for publishers, magazines, and corporate enterprises. The year 2006 marked a career shift, however, when Smith made his authorial debut.

Based on a story he told to his daughter over the course of their daily commute to her middle school, *The Forest in the Hallway* focuses on a fourteen-year-old girl named Beatriz. When her parents mysteriously disappear, Beatriz is sent to live with her uncle, a man who lives in a strange and magical New York City apartment complex which holds a portal to another world. On the nineteenth floor of her uncle's apartment building is a hallway that magically transfers her into a dark forest in a magical realm. When Beatriz passes out of her own world and into the world beyond the hallway, the adventure she has there allows her to unravel the mystery of her parents' disappearance.

Featuring elements familiar to fans of C.S. Lewis's "Chronicles of Narnia" books, Smith's middle-grade novel was hailed as an auspicious start by several critics. In *Kliatt* Donna Scanlon regarded *The Forest in the Hallway* as an "engaging debut" and "a delight from start to finish." Although the novel is not illustrated, Smith's use of words evokes a visual element within the story, according to Scanlon. "Smith's prose is so vivid and evocative that one might believe that the book is illustrated," the critic maintained. Likewise, *Booklist* reviewer Shelle Rosenfeld praised *The Forest in the Hallway* for featuring both "creative characters and a story line that will keep readers engaged." Beatriz continues her adventures in a sequel, *Beatriz and the Crazed Librarians from the Future,* which Smith completed in 2007.

Biographical and Critical Sources

PERIODICALS

Booklist, November 15, 2006, Shelle Rosenfeld, review of *The Forest in the Hallway,* p. 61.

Bulletin of the Center for Children's Books, February, 2007, April Spisak, review of *The Forest in the Hallway,* p. 267.

Kirkus Reviews, October 15, 2006, review of *The Forest in the Hallway,* p. 1080.

Kliatt, November, 2006, Donna Scanlon, review of *The Forest in the Hallway,* p. 15.

School Library Journal, December, 2006, Connie Tyrrell Burns, review of *The Forest in the Hallway,* p. 155.

ONLINE

Children's Bookwatch Web site, http://www.midwest bookreview.com/ (December 1, 2006), review of *The Forest in the Hallway.*

Gordon Smith Home Page, http://www.beatriz.co.uk (November 7, 2007).

SPIEGEL, Beth 1957-

Personal

Born 1957. *Education:* California Institute of the Arts, B.F.A. (film graphics and film); attended Academy for Applied Art (Vienna, Austria).

Addresses

Home and office—Altadena, CA. *E-mail*—bethspiegel@ sbcglobal.net.

Career

Film editor, artist, and illustrator. Editor of documentary and animated films for producers including National Geographic, Turner Productions, Nature, Disney, and Wonderworks, including *Wolf: Return of a Legend,* 1993; *Patagonia: To the End of the World; The Dragons of Galapagos,* 1998; *Lost World of the Holyland,* 2003; *In the Land of Milk and Honey,* 2004; *Strange Days on Planet Earth: Invaders,* 2005; and *Arctic Tale,* 2007. *Exhibitions:* Paintings exhibited at Barnsdall, Los Angeles County Museum of Art, Sun Valley Center for the Humanities, and Museum of Tolerance.

Member

Society of Children's Book Writers and Illustrators.

Beth Spiegel's art is a feature of Mary Ann Rodman's humorous picture book **First Grade Stinks!,** *which focuses on a less-than-enthusiastic young student.* (Peachtree, 2006. Illustration © 2006 by Beth Spiegel. Reproduced by permission.)

Illustrator

Barbara Bottner, *Rosa's Room,* Peachtree (Atlanta, GA), 2004.

Mary Ann Rodman, *First Grade Stinks!,* Peachtree (Atlanta, GA), 2006.

Julie Kaplow and Donna Pincus, *Samantha Jane's Missing Smile: A Story about Coping with the Loss of a Parent,* Magination Press (Washington, DC), 2007.

Sidelights

As a college student, Beth Spiegel studied film graphics at the California Institute of the Arts in preparation for embarking on what has become a successful career as an award-winning documentary film editor. In her job, she has traveled frequently, spending time in many U.S. cities as well as in the Yucatan and South Africa. As a child, Spiegel was fond of drawing and painting, and these creative interests have inspired her second career as a children's-book illustrator. Beginning with Barbara Bottner's 2004 picture book *Rosa's Room,* she has contributed illustrations to books by Mary Ann Rodman and collaborators Julie Kaplow and Donna Pincus. In addition to her work as a book illustrator, Spiegel has also exhibited her paintings at galleries and institutions such as the Los Angeles County Museum of Art.

Spiegel's illustrations for Rodman's humorous *First Grade Stinks!* focus on a young girl who is none too pleased with the day-to-day realities of life as an elementary-school student. From the very first day of first grade Haley is disappointed by the things her school lacks. For instance, there is only one recess, her classroom seems dull and undecorated, and her teacher is not nearly as affectionate as her own mom. However, when Haley tests the limits by throwing a temper tantrum, she learns to appreciate her new teacher and the opportunities that await her in first grade. In a review of *First Grade Stinks!* in *Booklist,* Stephanie Zvirin wrote that Spiegel's pen-and-ink illustrations, with their incor-

poration of "splashy" water color, "perfectly convey" the worries of Rodman's young heroine. Also praising the illustrator's work, a *Publishers Weekly* critic concluded of the book that "Spiegel's winsome watercolors keeps this lively tale on track."

Biographical and Critical Sources

PERIODICALS

Booklist, April 1, 2004, Connie Fletcher, review of *Rosa's Room,* p. 1368; August 1, 2006, Stephanie Zvirin, review of *First Grade Stinks!,* p. 96.

Bulletin of the Center for Children's Books, September, 2006, Deborah Stevenson, review of *First Grade Stinks!,* p. 31.

Kirkus Reviews, March 1, 2004, review of *Rosa's Room,* p. 219; September 1, 2006, Mary Ann Rodman, review of *First Grade Stinks!,* p. 912.

Library Media Connection, February, 2007, Gregory A. Martin, review of *First Grade Stinks!,* p. 70.

Publishers Weekly, March 1, 2004, review of *Rosa's Room,* p. 68; June 12, 2006, review of *First Grade Stinks!,* p. 50.

School Library Journal, May, 2004, Linda Staskus, review of *Rosa's Room,* p. 102; August, 2006, Marge Loch-Wouters, review of *First Grade Stinks!,* p. 96.

ONLINE

Beth Spiegel Editing Web site, http://bethspiegelediting.com/ (November 7, 2007).

Beth Spiegel Home Page, http://www.bethspiegel.com (November 7, 2007).

Children's Bookwatch Web site, http://www.midwestbookreview.com/ (August, 2007), review of *Samantha Jane's Missing Smile: A Story about Coping with the Loss of a Parent.**

T-Z

THOMPSON, Richard 1951-

Personal

Born January 7, 1951, in Edmonton, Alberta, Canada; son of an oilfield worker; married Maggee Spicer (a teacher and writer); children: Jesse (daughter). *Education:* College of New Caledonia B.A. (early childhood education), 1980.

Addresses

Home—Prince George, British Columbia, Canada. *Home and office*—195 Allstate Parkway, Markham, Ontario L3R 4TB, Canada.

Career

Children's book author and storyteller. Formerly worked as a restaurant cook and daycare worker; Oscar O's Family Daycare, operator for six years; Story Vine Nursery School, teacher until 1989; full-time writer and storyteller, beginning 1989. Member, Prince George Storytellers Roundtable; speaker at schools and libraries throughout North America.

Writings

FOR CHILDREN

Jenny's Neighbours, illustrated by Kathryn E. Shoemaker, Annick Press (Toronto, Ontario, Canada), 1987.

Sky Full of Babies, illustrated by Eugenie Fernandes, Annick Press (Toronto, Ontario, Canada), 1987.

Foo, illustrated by Eugenie Fernandes, Annick Press (Toronto, Ontario, Canada), 1988.

I Have to See This!, illustrated by Eugenie Fernandes, Annick Press (Toronto, Ontario, Canada), 1988.

The Last Story, the First Story, illustrated by Ruth Ohi, Annick Press (Toronto, Ontario, Canada), 1988.

Gurgle, Bubble, Splash, illustrated by Eugenie Fernandes, Annick Press (Toronto, Ontario, Canada), 1989.

Effie's Bath, illustrated by Eugenie Fernandes, Annick Press (Toronto, Ontario, Canada), 1989.

Zoe and the Mysterious X, illustrated by Ruth Ohi, Annick Press (Toronto, Ontario, Canada), 1990.

Jesse on the Night Train, illustrated by Eugenie Fernandes, Annick Press (Toronto, Ontario, Canada), 1990.

Frog's Riddle, and Other Draw-and-Tell Stories, Annick Press (Toronto, Ontario, Canada), 1990.

Maggee and the Lake Minder, illustrated by Eugenie Fernandes, Annick Press (Toronto, Ontario, Canada), 1991.

The Gastank of My Heart (story collection), Caitlin Press (Prince George, British Columbia, Canada), 1991.

Tell Me One Good Thing: Bedtime Stories, illustrated by Eugenie Fernandes, Annick Press (Toronto, Ontario, Canada), 1992.

Jill and the Jogero, illustrated by Françoise Durham-Moulin, Annick Press (Toronto, Ontario, Canada), 1992.

Don't Be Scared, Eleven, illustrated by Eugenie Fernandes, Annick Press (Toronto, Ontario, Canada), 1993.

The Ice Cream Bucket Effect (story collection), Caitlin Press (Prince George, British Columbia, Canada), 1993.

Who, illustrated by Martin Springett, Orca (Victoria, British Columbia, Canada), 1993.

Cold Night, Brittle Light, illustrated by Henry Fernandes, Orca (Victoria, British Columbia, Canada), 1994.

(With wife, Maggee Spicer) *Fishes in the Ocean,* Fitzhenry & Whiteside (Toronto, Ontario, Canada), 1998.

Then and Now, illustrated by Barbara Hartman, Fitzhenry & Whiteside (Toronto, Ontario, Canada), 1999.

There Is Music in a Pussy Cat, illustrated by Barbara Hartmann, Fitzhenry & Whiteside (Toronto, Ontario, Canada), 1999.

The Follower, illustrated by Martin Springett, Fitzhenry & Whiteside (Markham, Ontario, Canada), 2000.

(With Maggee Spicer) *We'll All Go Sailing,* illustrated by Kim LaFave, Fitzhenry & Whiteside (Toronto, Ontario, Canada), 2001.

(With Maggee Spicer) *We'll All Go Flying,* illustrated by Kim LaFave, Fitzhenry & Whiteside (Toronto, Ontario, Canada), 2002.

The Night Walker, illustrated by Martin Springett, Fitzhenry
& Whiteside (Markham, Ontario, Canada), 2002.

(With Maggee Spicer) *We'll All Go Exploring,* illustrated
by Kim LaFave, Fitzhenry & Whiteside (Toronto, Ontario, Canada), 2003.

(With Maggee Spicer) *When They Are Up . . . ,* illustrated
by Kirsti Anne Wakelin, Fitzhenry & Whiteside (Toronto, Ontario, Canada), 2004.

OTHER

(Self-illustrated) *Draw and Tell: Reading, Writing, Listening, Speaking, Viewing, Shaping,* Annick Press (Toronto, Ontario, Canada), 1988.

Adaptations

*Foo, Sky Full of Babies, I Have to See This!, Jesse on
the Night Train,* and *Gurgle, Bubble, Splash* were
adapted for audiocassette, Annick Press, 1990.

Sidelights

Devoting his career to inspiring young children with a
love of story, Richard Thompson worked as a day-care
provider and even started his own nursery school, until
his family's prodding and the acquisition of a computer
convinced him to devote his full time to writing and
telling stories. Beginning in 1989, Thompson created
dozens of tales for young children, and also spent sixteen weeks a year traveling throughout his native
Canada and the United States to share his stories and
his creative ideas with school and library groups. "My
school visits have given me a chance to explore new
storytelling ideas and to find out first hand what 'works'
for both myself and my audiences," he noted on his
home page. "And, of course, sharing stories with enthusiastic and appreciative audiences is a very rewarding
process in itself."

Among Thompson's books for young children are picture books and beginning readers for younger children
such as *Then and Now, The Follower, Fishes in the
Ocean,* and *When They Are Up . . . ,* the last two coauthored by his wife, Maggee Spicer. Story collections for
older elementary-graders include *The Gastank of My
Heart* and *The Ice Cream Bucket Effect.* Praising the
coauthors' adaptation of a traditional nursery rhyme in
When They Are Up . . . , Bina Williams described the
work in *School Library Journal* as a "merry book [that]
will make an active storyhour even more fun." A
slightly scary mystery that offers up clues on every
page, *The Follower* was praised by *Booklist* contributor
Shelle Rosenfeld as a "charming, not-too-spooky story."
In her *School Library Journal* review of the same book,
Margaret Bush wrote that, with its nighttime "images
richly rendered" in both Thompson's text and Martin
Springett's "surreal" art, *The Follower* serves up "fine
read-aloud fare."

In the trio of books that include *We'll All Go Sailing,
We'll All Go Flying,* and *We'll All Go Exploring,* Thompson's rhyming text, with its singsong question-and-

answer structure, follows the adventures of the young
narrator and his friends Maggee and Jesse (characters
named after Thompson's wife and daughter). In *We'll
All Go Sailing,* which features bold, heavily outlined art
by award-winning illustrator Kim LaFave, the three
sailors launch their small boat and discover a host of
amazing sea creatures, introducing children to basic
color concepts along the way. *We'll All Go Flying* finds
the trio soaring up through the clouds and then into
outer space in their hot air balloon, while hiking is the
preferred form of transportation in *We'll All Go
Exploring.* "The repetitive verses and simple rhymes
will make this a favorite of young naturalists," concluded a *Kirkus Reviews* writer in an appraisal of *We'll
All Go Exploring.* Noting that the lift-the-flap pages of
the book allow Thompson to expand his introduction to
various forest ecosystems, Kathleen Kelly McWilliams
wrote in *School Library Journal* that the collaboration
between author and artist serves as an effective way to
"introduce basic ecology" while "maintaining a lighthearted appeal."

Although retiring from his work as a traveling storyteller in 2006, Thompson continues to inspire children
and teachers alike through his interactive home page,
www.drawandtell.com, which includes word games,
puzzles, magic tricks, and other mind-stretchers, as well
as draw-and-tell tales and other stories for use in story-
hour groups.

Biographical and Critical Sources

PERIODICALS

Booklist, December 15, 2000, Shelle Rosenfeld, review of
The Follower, p. 823; May 15, 2001, Carolyn Phelan,
review of *We'll All Go Sailing,* p. 1755; May 1, 2003,
Carolyn Phelan, review of *We'll All Go Exploring,* p.
1603; September 1, 2003, Shelle Rosenfeld, review of
The Night Walker, p. 131.

Canadian Review of Materials, June 8, 2001, review of
There Is Music in a Pussycat; June 22, 2001, Catherine Hoyt, review of *We'll All Go Sailing;* November
29, 2002, review of *The Night Walker.*

Kirkus Reviews, December 15, 2002, review of *The Night
Walker,* p. 1858; April 1, 2003, review of *We'll All Go
Exploring,* p. 540.

Publishers Weekly, June 4, 2001, review of *We'll All Go
Sailing,* p. 82.

Quill & Quire, October, 2000, review of *Follower,* p. 44;
April, 2001, review of *We'll All Go Sailing,* p. 33.

Resource Links, February, 1999, review of *Fishes in the
Ocean,* p. 2; December, 2000, review of *The Follower,*
p. 41; June, 2001, Linda Ludke, review of *We'll All
Go Sailing,* p. 6; December, 2002, Isobel Lang, review of *We'll All Go Flying,* p. 18; February, 2003,
Ann Ketcheson, review of *The Night Walker,* p. 7; October, 2003, Kathryn McNaughton, review of *We'll All
Go Exploring,* p. 9; April, 2004, Lori Lavallee, review
of *When They Are Up . . . ,* p. 8.

School Library Journal, December, 2000, Margaret Bush, review of *The Follower,* p. 126; July, 2001, DeAnn Tabuchi, review of *We'll All Go Sailing,* p. 100; December, 2002, Carol L. Mackay, review of *We'll All Go Flying,* p. 110; April, 2003, Kathy Piehl, review of *The Night Walker,* p. 140; May, 2003, Kathleen Kelly MacMillan, review of *We'll All Go Exploring,* p. 129; May, 2004, Bina Williams, review of *When They Are Up . . . ,* p. 136.

ONLINE

Richard Thompson Home Page, http://www.drawandtell. com (November 15, 2007).*

* * *

TROTTER, Deborah W.

Personal

Born in CA; married; children: four.

Addresses

Home and office—Moraga, CA.

Career

Author.

Writings

How Do You Know?, illustrated by Julie Downing, Clarion Books (New York, NY), 2006.

A Summer's Trade/Shiigo Na'iini', Navajo translation by Lorraine Begay Manavi, illustrated by Irving Toddy, Salina Bookshelf (Flagstaff, AZ), 2007.

Sidelights

California author Deborah W. Trotter has loved reading since childhood, but she did not turn to writing until after the birth of her fourth child. Trotter's first picture book, *How Do You Know?,* follows a young girl named Polly as she awakes to discover that a thick fog has blanketed the land around her home, making everything strangely unfamiliar. A walk with her mother into this strange misty world prompts discussions of questions such as how someone knows that a thing exists if that thing cannot be seen. In her story, Trotter makes a unique connection between fog and the concept of faith, as Martha Simpson noted in her *School Library Journal* review. Ilene Cooper, citing this same connection in her review for *Booklist,* remarked that the author successfully describes "a bit of natural phenomenon and then link[s] . . . it to emotions." A *Kirkus Reviews* critic deemed *How Do You Know?* a "heartwarming look at

the bond between an inspiring mother and her child," and Simpson made special note of Julie Downing's "lovely" watercolor illustrations, which accompany Trotter's text.

Written for older children, Trotter's *A Summer's Trade/ Shiigo Na'iini'* focuses on Tony, a Navajo boy who works in a New Mexico trading post. The son of a rancher, Tony hopes to save enough money to buy his own saddle, so that he can help his father round up the family's sheep and goats on horseback. When his grandmother goes to desperate lengths to acquire much-needed cash and then becomes ill, Tony has to decide whether to continue to save toward his goal of a saddle or use his savings to help the elderly woman. Told in a parallel English and Navajo text and illustrated by Navajo artist Irving Toddy, Trotter's story "has a quiet dignity that makes Tony's actions all the more poignant," in the opinion of *School Library Journal* contributor Joy Fleishhacker.

Biographical and Critical Sources

PERIODICALS

Booklist, December 15, 2006, Ilene Cooper, review of *How Do You Know?,* p. 52.

Boy's Quest, February-March, 2005, review of *Full House,* p. 40.

Kirkus Reviews, October 15, 2006, review of *How Do You Know?,* p. 1080.

School Library Journal, November, 2006, Martha Simpson, review of *How Do You Know?,* p. 114; September, 2007, Joy Fleishhacker, review of *A Summer's Trade,* p. 177.*

* * *

WELLS, Robert E.

Personal

Married; wife's name Karen; children: Kim, Jeffrey; Kurt (stepson).

Addresses

Home—WA.

Career

Author and illustrator of children's books.

Awards, Honors

Outstanding Science Trade Book for Children designation, Children's Book Council (CBC)/National Science Teachers Association, 1996, for *What's Smaller than a Pygmy Shrew?;* Children's Choice selection, CBC/

International Reading Association, 1998, for *What's Faster than a Speeding Cheetah?;* Gold Seal Award, Oppenheim Toy Portfolio, 2000, for *Can You Count to a Googol?;* Gold Seal Award, 2003, for *How Do You Know What Time It Is?*

Writings

SELF-ILLUSTRATED

Is a Blue Whale the Biggest Thing There Is?, Albert Whitman (Morton Grove, IL), 1993.

What's Smaller than a Pygmy Shrew?, Albert Whitman (Morton Grove, IL), 1995.

How Do You Lift a Lion?, Albert Whitman (Morton Grove, IL), 1996.

What's Faster than a Speeding Cheetah?, Albert Whitman (Morton Grove, IL), 1997.

Can You Count to a Googol?, Albert Whitman (Morton Grove, IL), 2000.

How Do You Know What Time It Is?, Albert Whitman (Morton Grove, IL), 2002.

What's Older than a Giant Tortoise?, Albert Whitman (Morton Grove, IL), 2004.

Did a Dinosaur Drink This Water?, Albert Whitman (Morton Grove, IL), 2006.

Several of Well's books have been published in Spanish translation.

Sidelights

Robert E. Wells, the author and illustrator of a number of well-regarded nonfiction picture books for children, made his literary debut with *Is a Blue Whale the Biggest Thing There Is?* In the 1993 work, Wells "delivers a healthy, age-appropriate jolt to common assumptions about proportion and numbers," observed a *Publishers Weekly* contributor. Beginning with a comparison of a blue whale to an elephant, Wells illustrates the relative sizes of Mount Everest, Earth, the sun, and other celestial bodies. According to Carolyn Phelan in *Booklist,* the book's strength is "making the inconceivable more imaginable through original, concrete images," such as a drawing of a crate of sun-sized oranges dwarfed by the red supergiant star Antares.

In a related work, *What's Smaller than a Pygmy Shrew?,* Wells looks at the infinitesimal, contrasting the tiny pygmy shrew with a ladybug and continuing with paramecium, bacteria, molecules, and atoms. The author's

Robert E. Wells gears his self-illustrated picture book Did a Dinosaur Drink This Water? *to young dino-fans looking to increase their supply of dino-facts.* (Albert Whitman, 2006. Illustration © 2006 by Robert E. Wells. Reproduced by permission.)

"lighthearted treatment is fine for the familiar," remarked *School Library Journal* critic Frances E. Millhouser, although the reviewer noted that younger readers might be confused by Wells' description of single-celled organisms. Phelan stated, however, that the author "introduces a challenging concept in a way that will entertain and intrigue" his audience.

Wells examines simple machines in *How Do You Lift a Lion?* Here his illustrations depict children using levers, wheels, and pulleys to raise a lion off the ground, haul a panda, and transport bananas to a group of hungry baboons. In *What's Faster than a Speeding Cheetah?* he explores the swiftness of a falcon, the rapidness of a jet plane, and the acceleration of a meteoroid. "Always in sync with the way children think, Wells takes each concept and makes it concrete, vivid, and understandable," Phelan commented.

The number system is the focus of *Can You Count to a Googol?* Wells creates humorous drawings, including a band of ice-cream-loving penguins, as well as more-realistic depictions of dollar bills to show how numbers increase exponentially. Ultimately, he explains a googol, represented by the number one followed by one hundred zeros. "The switch from fanciful to factual in these examples is somewhat jarring," remarked *School Library Journal* critic Adele Greenlee, "but the pen-and-acrylic cartoons do adequately illustrate the growing numbers." Phelan offered a more positive assessment of the title, stating that *Can You Count to a Googol?* "encourages young children to stretch their minds a bit."

In *How Do You Know What Time It Is?,* Wells offers "a succinct, child-friendly history of how time came to be measured," wrote Wanda Meyers-Hines in *School Library Journal.* Among the devices the author considers are the sundial, the pendulum, and the atomic clock. According to *Booklist* reviewer Hazel Rochman, Wells's "picture-book format . . . roots the concepts in daily experience." The author takes readers on a trip through time in *What's Older than a Giant Tortoise?* In his exploration of a sequoia tree, the pyramids, and fossilized mammoths, Wells "manages to boggle the mind in a way that is stimulating rather than confusing," Phelan stated. In *Did a Dinosaur Drink This Water?* Wells examines Earth's water cycle in a "simple text [that] asks good questions and offers clearly worded answers," as Phelan observed.

Biographical and Critical Sources

PERIODICALS

Booklist, December 15, 1993, Carolyn Phelan, review of *Is a Blue Whale the Biggest Thing There Is?,* p. 759; August, 1995, Carolyn Phelan, review of *What's Smaller than a Pygmy Shrew?,* p. 1953; October 1,

1997, Carolyn Phelan, review of *What's Faster than a Speeding Cheetah?,* p. 335; March 1, 2000, Carolyn Phelan, review of *Can You Count to a Googol?,* p. 1249; December 1, 2002, Hazel Rochman, review of *How Do You Know What Time It Is?,* p. 686; October 15, 2004, Carolyn Phelan, review of *What's Older than a Giant Tortoise?,* p. 409; December 1, 2006, Carolyn Phelan, review of *Did a Dinosaur Drink This Water?,* p. 63.

Publishers Weekly, October 11, 1993, review of *Is a Blue Whale the Biggest Thing There Is?,* p. 86; February 21, 2000, review of *Can You Count to a Googol?,* p. 88.

School Library Journal, May, 1995, Frances E. Millhouser, review of *What's Smaller than a Pygmy Shrew?,* p. 117; January, 1997, Virginia Opocensky, review of *How Do You Lift a Lion?,* p. 110; May, 2000, Adele Greenlee, review of *Can You Count to a Googol?,* p. 165; January, 2003, Wanda Meyers-Hines, review of *How Do You Know What Time It Is?,* p. 132; January, 2005, Deborah Rothaug, review of *What's Older than a Giant Tortoise?,* p. 118; February, 2007, Christine Markley, review of *Did a Dinosaur Drink This Water?,* p. 114.*

*   *   *

WELSH, T.K. 1956-
[A pseudonym]
(J. Gregory Sandom, J.G. Sandom)

Personal

Born December 19, 1956, in Chicago, IL; son of Zane Joseph (a financial services executive) and Else (a cosmetics industry manager) Sandom; married Julia Clare Pendleton Gallagher (an advertising executive), June 9, 1987; children: one daughter. *Education:* Amherst College, B.A. (English and philosophy), 1978.

Addresses

Home—Hopewell, NJ.

Career

Novelist, copywriter, and in public relations. Hill & Knowlton, Inc., New York, NY, account executive/public relations, 1978-79; Rowland Company, New York, NY, account executive/media consultant, 1979-80; Sandom Company, New York, NY, marketing consultant, 1980-86; Einstein & Sandom, Inc. (multi-media marketing and interactive advertising agency), chief executive officer and creative director, beginning 1986; freelance writer.

Awards, Honors

Academy of American Poets prize, 1978, for "The First Time"; *Washington Post* Top Ten Children's Book designation, and Cybils Literary Award nomination, both

2006, and Association of Jewish Libraries Notable Book for Teens designation, and American Library Association Best Book for Young Adults designation, both 2007, all for *The Unresolved.*

Writings

YOUNG-ADULT NOVELS

The Unresolved, Dutton (New York, NY), 2006.
Resurrection Men, Dutton (New York, NY), 2007.

ADULT NOVELS; UNDER NAME J.G. SANDOM

Gospel Truths, Doubleday (New York, NY), 1992.
The Hunting Club, Doubleday (New York, NY), 1993.
The Wave, Lulu.com, 2007.

Biographical and Critical Sources

PERIODICALS

Booklist, March 15, 1992, Margaret Flanagan, review of *Gospel Truths,* p. 1342; May 15, 1993, Mary Frances Wilkens, review of *The Hunting Club,* p. 1677.
Bulletin of the Center for Children's Books, October, 2006, Elizabeth Bush, review of *The Unresolved,* p. 100; May, 2007, Elizabeth Bush, review of *Resurrection Men,* p. 390.
Horn Book, July-August, 2006, Vicky Smith, review of *The Unresolved,* p. 453.
Kirkus Reviews, August 1, 2006, review of *The Unresolved,* p. 798; March 1, 2007, review of *Resurrection Men,* p. 233.
Kliatt, March, 2007, Paula Rohrlick, review of *Resurrection Men,* p. 20.
Library Journal, January, 1992, Rex E. Klett, review of *Gospel Truths,* p. 181; June 15, 1993, Darryl Dean James, review of *The Hunting Club,* p. 98.
Publishers Weekly, January 20, 1992, review of *Gospel Truths*; June 7, 1993, review of *The Hunting Club,* p. 52; May 15, 2007, review of *Resurrection Men,* p. 56.
School Library Journal, September, 2006, Lisa Prolman, review of *The Unresolved,* p. 221.
Voice of Youth Advocates, April, 2007, Dotsy Harland, review of *Resurrection Men,* p. 58.

ONLINE

J.G. Sandom Home Page, http://www.JGSandom.com (November 15, 2007).
T.K. Welsh Home Page, http://www.TKWelsh.com (November 15, 2007).*

*   *   *

WILLEY, Bee

Personal

Female.

Addresses

Home and office—Suffolk, England.

Career

Illustrator and commercial artist.

Member

Society of Children's Book Writers and Illustrators.

Awards, Honors

Kate Greenaway Medal shortlist, 2003, Chartered Institute of Library and Information Professionals, for *Bob Robber and Dancing Jane.*

Writings

(With Susannah English, and Rhian Nest James) *In the Town,* Ginn (Aylesbury, England), 1993.
Geraldine McCaughrean, *The Golden Hoard: Myths and Legends of the World,* Orion (London, England), 1995.
Anne Cassidy, *Spider Pie,* Hamish Hamilton (London, England), 1995.
Geraldine McCaughrean, *The Silver Treasure: Myths and Legends of the World,* Orion (London, England), 1996.
Edward Lear, *Nonsense Songs,* Orion (London, England), 1996.
Michael Rosen, *The Zoo at Night: Verses,* Tradewind (London, England), 1996.
Michael Rosen, *Michael Rosen's ABC,* Millbrook Press (Brookfield, CT), 1996.
John Mole, *Copy Cat,* Kingfisher (London, England), 1997.
Karen Wallace, *Blue Eyes,* Hodder Children's (London, England), 1997.
Geraldine McCaughrean, *The Bronze Cauldron,* Orion (London, England), 1997.
Leon Rosselson, *Emiliano's Wickedness,* Macdonald Young (Hove, England), 1997.
Geraldine McCaughrean, *The Crystal Pool: Myths and Legends around the World,* Orion (London, England), 1998.
Lori Reid, *Sweet Dreamer: A Guide to Understanding Your Dreams,* Element Children's (Shaftesbury, England), 1998.
Sandra Ann Horn, *Rory McRory,* Macdonald Young (Hove, England), 1998.
Meredith Hooper, *The Pear Tree: An Animal Counting Book,* Macmillan Children's (London, England), 1998.
Maddie Stewart, *Peg,* Mammoth (London, England), 1999.
Grace Nichols, *The Poet Cat,* Bloomsbury Children's (London, England), 2000.
Meredith Hooper, *River Story,* Walker (London, England), 2000.
Geraldine McCaughrean, *One Hundred World Myths and Legends,* Orion (London, England), 2001.
Ita Daly, *Irish Myths and Legends,* Oxford University Press (Oxford, England), 2001.

John Mole, *The Wonder Dish: Poems,* Oxford University Press (Oxford, England), 2002.

Andrew Matthews, *Bob Robber and Dancing Jane,* Jonathan Cape (London, England), 2003.

Geraldine McCaughrean, *The Jesse Tree,* Lion (Oxford, England), 2003.

Shahrukh Husain *Egypt,* Evans (London, England), 2004.

Shahrukh Husain, *Rome,* Evans (London, England), 2004.

Shahrukh Husain, *Greece,* Evans (London, England), 2004.

Joan Aiken, *The Wooden Dragon,* Jonathan Cape (London, England), 2004.

Shahrukh Husain, *Indian Myths,* Evans (London, England), 2005.

Shahrukh Husain, *The Vikings,* Smart Apple Media (North Mankato, MN), 2005.

Shahrukh Husain, *African Myths,* Evans (London, England), 2006.

Meredith Hooper, *Celebrity Cat,* Frances Lincoln (London, England), 2006.

Sidelights

Bee Willey has illustrated over twenty children's books in addition to her work creating art for companies such as Mattel and the British Royal Mail. Willey typically incorporates digitally produced elements into her illustrations, and then offsets these computer images with her original ink line drawings. Her stylistic art has been credited for its eccentric and energetic design. For example, her contributions to Meredith Hooper's *Celebrity Cat* features human-like felines with large eyes. A *Kirkus Reviews* critic acknowledged the book's artwork for incorporating "unusual details." Carolyn Phelan, in a review of *Celebrity Cat* for *Booklist,* observed Willey's ability to subtlety change her artistic method between pages and commented that the illustrations in *Celebrity Cat* diverge "in style, with areas of clearly delineated drawings and other places softened to fuzziness." Willey's use of bold color is another characteristic of her art, according to Carolyn Janssen, the critic remarking in her *School Library Journal* review of *Celebrity Cat* that "bright colors and smooth surfaces give a luminescence to the pages."

Willey takes on another feline-centered project in illustrating *Copy Cat,* a picture book with a text by John Mole. The book centers on a cat that mimics the actions of a young boy named Oliver. The tables are turned, however, when Oliver starts copying the cat's actions by climbing up trees and jumping up onto tabletops. Willey's creative usage of colors in this project was cited by a *Publishers Weekly* critic who commented that her "energetic gouache paintings in blacklight purple, chartreuse and flame orange lend the book an electric flair."

Biographical and Critical Sources

PERIODICALS

Booklist, May 1, 1996, Hazel Rochman, review of *The Golden Hoard: Myths and Legends of the World,* p. 1501; April 1, 1997, Carolyn Phelan, review of *Nonsense Songs,* p. 1335; April 15, 1997, Karen Morgan, review of *The Silver Treasure: Myths and Legends of the World,* p. 1424; June 1, 1997, Kathleen Squires, review of *Michael Rosen's ABC,* p. 1712; May 15, 1998, John Peters, review of *The Bronze Cauldron,* p. 1624; May 15, 1999, John Peters, review of *The Crystal Pool: Myths and Legends of the World,* p. 1694; July, 2000, Michael Cart, review of *River Story,* p. 2038; June 1, 2001, Jennifer Mattson, review of *Irish Myths and Legends,* p. 1866; October 1, 2005, Jennifer Mattson, review of *The Jesse Tree,* p. 70; November 16, 2006, review of *Celebrity Cat,* p. 53.

Book Report, November-December, 2001, Heather Hepler, review of *Irish Myths and Legends,* p. 68.

Bulletin of the Center for Children's Books, July, 1996, review of *The Golden Hand,* p. 379; June, 1997, review of *The Silver Treasure,* p. 366; July, 1998, review of *The Bronze Cauldron,* p. 403; September, 1999, review of *The Crystal Pool,* p. 22.

Horn Book, May-June, 1996, Maria B. Salvadore, review of *The Golden Hoard,* p. 211.

Kirkus Reviews, September 1, 2003, review of *Bob Robber and Dancing Jane,* p. 1127; January 1, 2005, review of *The Wooden Dragon,* p. 73; October 15, 2006, Meredith Hooper, review of *Celebrity Cat,* p. 1072.

Publishers Weekly, April 15, 1996, Cheri Estes, review of *The Golden Hoard,* p. 211; March 3, 1997, review of *Michael Rosen's ABC,* p. 77; June, 1997, Kathleen Whalin, review of *Nonsense Songs,* p. 109; September 1, 1997, review of *Copy Cat,* p. 103; May 11, 1998, review of *Sweet Dreamer,* p. 70; May 11, 1998, review of *The Bronze Cauldron,* p. 68; May 10, 1999, review of *Telling Tales,* p. 69; June 10, 2000, review of *River Story,* p. 106; May 10, 1999, review of *The Celebrity Cat,* p. 100; August 29, 2005, review of *The Jesse Tree,* p. 60.

School Library Journal, March, 1996, Cheri Estes, review of *The Golden Hoard,* p. 165; December, 1996, review of *The Golden Hoard,* p. 31; April, 1997, Patricia Lothrop-Green, review of *The Silver Treasure,* p. 153; March, 1997, Tana Elias, review of *Michael Rosen's ABC,* p. 165; July, 1998, Angela J. Reynolds, review of *The Bronze Cauldron,* p. 108; August, 2000, Judith Constantinides, review of *River Story,* p. 170; June, 1997, Kathleen Whalin, review of *Nonsense Songs,* p. 109; Sally R. Dow, September, 1997, review of *Copy Cat,* p. 188; August, 1999, Angela J. Reynolds, review of *The Crystal Pool,* p. 174; May, 2005, Judith Constantinides, review of *Egypt,* p. 109; January, 2006, Linda L. Walkins, review of *The Jesse Tree,* p. 106; December, 2006, Carolyn Janssen, review of *Celebrity Cat,* p. 100.

Times Educational Supplement, February 2, 1996, review of *Michael Rosen's ABC,* p. 12; November 7, 1997, review of *Myths and Legends of the World,* p. 8; February 26, 1999, review of *The Pear Tree: An Animal Counting Book,* p. 23; September 22, 2000, review of *River Story,* p. 9; January 26, 2001, review of *The Poet Cat,* p. 20.

ONLINE

Candy Gourlay Web site, http://candygourlay.com/ (April 4, 2006), "Illustrator Bee Willey."

Illustration Web site, http://www.illustrationweb.com/ (November 11, 2007), "Bee Willey."

Walker Books Australia Web site, http://www.walkerbooks. com.au/ (November 11, 2007), "Bee Willey."*

*   *   *

WINDHAM, Sophie

Personal

Married Bruce Robinson (a film director and writer); children: Lily, Willoughby.

Addresses

Home and office—London, England.

Career

Author and illustrator.

Awards, Honors

Kate Greenaway Award shortlist, Chartered Institute of Library and Information Professionals, 1997, for *Unicorns! Unicorns!*

Writings

Paula Yates, *A Tale of Two Kitties,* Quartet (London, England), 1983.

The Twelve Days of Christmas, Putnam (New York, NY), 1986.

Illustrator Sophie Windham creates detailed paintings that bring to life the fresh version of a traditional tale presented in Vivian French's 2006 picture book **Henny Penny.** (Bloomsbury, 2006. Illustration © 2006 by Sophie Windham. Reproduced by permission.)

Noah's Ark: A Peek-through-the-Window Book, G.P. Putnam's Sons (New York, NY), 1988.

Read Me a Story: A Child's Book of Favorite Tales, Scholastic (New York, NY), 1991.

The Orchard Book of Nursery Stories, Orchard (London, England), 1991.

Down in the Marvelous Deep: A Book of Sea Poems, Orchard Books (London, England), 1994.

(Compiler) *The Mermaid and Other Sea Poems,* Scholastic (New York, NY), 1996.

Geraldine McCaughrean, *Unicorns! Unicorns!,* Holiday House (New York, NY), 1997.

Bruce Robinson, *The Obvious Elephant,* Bloomsbury Children's Books (New York, NY), 2000.

Bruce Robinson, *Harold and the Duck,* Bloomsbury Children's Books (London, England), 2005.

Vivian French, *Henny Penny,* Bloomsbury Children's Books (New York, NY), 2006.

Sidelights

While growing up, Sophie Windham benefited from the creative environment she experienced as part of a family full of artists and musicians. Not surprisingly, she also pursued a job in the arts, and has established a successful career as an illustrator and author of books for children. Windham's artwork, which has been paired with texts by writers such as Gerald McCaughrean and Vivian French in addition to her own stories, was accorded a special honor when her illustrations for McCaughrean's *Unicorns! Unicorns!* were shortlisted for the prestigious Kate Greenaway Medal. Windham has also collaborated with her husband, filmmaker Bruce Robinson, on the humorous picture books *The Obvious Elephant* and *Harold and the Duck,* both of which feature a text by Robinson that is paired with Windham's engaging art.

Critics often compliment Windham for her use of color and her ability to incorporate telling details into her illustrations. In her contributions to French's folk-tale retelling *Henny Penny,* Kristen Cutler commented in *School Library Journal* that Windham creates "brightly colored and skillfully drawn" images that "balance perfectly with the delightful text and draws readers into their depths." GraceAnne A. DeCandido, in her review for *Booklist,* also cited the artist for her choice of palette, noting that the book's art is "richly burnished with the late-summer reds, golds, russets, and greens." Windham's use of color for *Unicorn! Unicorn!* was also recognized by a *Publishers Weekly* critic who took special note of the book's "exquisite watercolors" and Carolyn Phelan commented in her *Booklist* review that in *Unicorns! Unicorns!* Windham "illustrates the tale with quiet beauty, gentle rhythm, and depth of feeling."

Biographical and Critical Sources

PERIODICALS

Booklist, February 1, 1996, Carolyn Phelan, review of *The Mermaid and Other Sea Poems,* p. 931; November

15, 1997, Carolyn Phelan, review of *Henny Penny,* p. 566; September 15, 2002, Susan Dove Lempke, review of *The Obvious Elephant,* p. 242; August 1, 2006, GraceAnne A. DeCandido, review of *Unicorns! Unicorns!,* p. 86.

Bulletin of the Center for Children's Books, December, 1997, review of *Unicorns! Unicorns!,* p. 133.

Kirkus Reviews, August 1, 2002, review of *The Obvious Elephant,* p. 1140; June 15, 2006, review of *Henny Penny,* p. 633.

Publishers Weekly, September 26, 1986, review of *Twelve Days of Christmas,* p. 72; December 9, 1988, review of *Noah's Ark: A Peek-through-the-Window Book,* p. 61; March 25, 1996, review of *The Mermaid and Other Sea Poems,* p. 84; August 25, 1997, review of *Unicorns! Unicorns!,* p. 71; June 17, 2002, review of *The Obvious Elephant,* p. 64; August 7, 2006, review of *Henny Penny,* p. 57.

School Librarian, November, 1991, review of *The Orchard Book of Nursery Stories,* p. 143; February, 1995, review of *Down in the Marvellous Deep,* p. 30; November, 1997, Trevor Dickinson, review of *Harold and the Duck,* p. 190; November, 1997, review of *Unicorns! Unicorns!,* p. 192; winter, 2006, review of *Henny Penny,* p. 182.

School Library Journal, October, 1986, review of *Twelve Days of Christmas,* p. 111; May, 1996, Margaret Bush, review of *The Mermaid and Other Sea Poems,* p. 128; October, 1997, Kathy Piel, review of *Unicorns! Unicorns!,* p. 104; August, 2002, Shawn Brommer, review of *The Obvious Elephant,* p. July, 2006, Kristen Cutler, review of *Henny Penny,* p. 77.

Times Educational Supplement, December 26, 1997, review of *Unicorns! Unicorns!,* p. 22.

ONLINE

Bloomsbury Web site, http://www.bloomsbury.com/ (November 11, 2007), "Sophie Windham."

Laura Cecil Literary Agent Web site, http://www.lauracecil.co.uk/ (November 11, 2007), "Sophie Windham."*

*   *   *

WINTER, Jeanette 1939-

Personal

Born 1939, in Chicago, IL; married Roger Winter (an artist); children: Jonah, Max. *Education:* Attended Art Institute of Chicago; University of Iowa, B.F.A.

Addresses

Home—New York, NY.

Career

Author and illustrator.

Awards, Honors

Notable Children's Trade Book in the Field of Social Studies designation, National Council for Social Studies/Children's Book Council (NCSS/CBC), and

Jeanette Winter (Reproduced by permission.)

Notable Children's Trade Book in Language Arts designation, National Council of Teachers of English (NCTE), both 1988, both for *Follow the Drinking Gourd; New York Times* Best Illustrated Book citation, Parent's Choice Award, and Notable Children's Trade Book in the Field of Social Studies designation, NCSS/CBC, all 1991, all for *Diego* by Jonah Winter; *New York Times* Notable Book citation, 1991, for *Eight Hands Round* by Ann Whitford Paul; Teacher's Choice citation, IRA/CBC, and Parent's Choice Award, both 1992, both for *Klara's New World; Hungry Mind Review* Book of Distinction designation, 1993, for *A Fruit and Vegetable Man;* Notable Children's Trade Book in the Field of Social Studies designation, NCSS/CBC, 1994, for *Shaker Boy;* Children's Choice Award, IRA/CBC, 1994, for *The Christmas Tree Ship;* Parent's Choice Honor citation, 1995, for *Cowboy Charlie;* Best Book of the Year citation, *Publishers Weekly,* Notable Children's Book citation, American Library Association (ALA), Editor's Choice, *Booklist,* Notable Book in Language Arts, NCTE, 100 Titles for Reading and Sharing designation, New York Public Library, and Best Book citation, Bank Street College of Education, all 1998, all for *My Name Is Georgia;* Notable Book citation, *New York Times,* and Parent's Choice silver medal, both 2002, both for *Emily Dickinson's Letters to the World;* Parent's Choice Honor citation, Best Books citation, Bank Street College, and Notable Children's Trade Book in the Field of Social Studies designation, NCSS/

CBC, all 2003, all for *Niño's Mask;* Notable Children's Book selection, ALA, Flora Stieglitz Straus Award for Nonfiction, Bank Street College of Education, Notable Children's Trade Book in the Field of Social Studies designation, NCSS/CBC, and Middle East Outreach Council honorable mention citation, all for *The Librarian of Basra; Boston Globe/Horn Book* Honor designation, 2006, for *Mama.*

Writings

SELF-ILLUSTRATED

(Reteller) Peter Christen Asbjørnsen, *The Christmas Visitors,* Pantheon Books (New York, NY), 1968.

(Reteller) *The Girl and the Moon Man: A Siberian Tale,* Pantheon (New York, NY), 1984.

Come out to Play, Knopf (New York, NY), 1986.

(Reteller) *The Magic Ring* (based on the story by the Brothers Grimm), Knopf (New York, NY), 1987.

Follow the Drinking Gourd, Knopf (New York, NY), 1988.

Klara's New World, Knopf (New York, NY), 1992.

The Christmas Tree Ship, Philomel Books (New York, NY), 1994.

Cowboy Charlie: The Story of Charles M. Russell, Harcourt (San Diego, CA), 1995.

Josefina, Harcourt (San Diego, CA), 1996.

My Name Is Georgia, Silver Whistle (San Diego, CA), 1998.

Sebastian: A Book about Bach, Harcourt (San Diego, CA), 1999.

The House That Jack Built, Dial (New York, NY), 2000.

My Baby, Frances Foster Books (New York, NY), 2001.

Emily Dickinson's Letters to the World, Frances Foster Books (New York, NY), 2002.

Niño's Mask, Dial (New York, NY), 2003.

Beatrix: Various Episodes from the Life of Beatrix Potter, Farrar, Straus & Giroux (New York, NY), 2003.

Elsina's Clouds, Farrar, Straus & Giroux (New York, NY), 2004.

September Roses, Farrar, Straus & Giroux (New York, NY), 2004.

Calavera Abecedario: A Day of the Dead Alphabet Book, Harcourt (Orlando, FL), 2004.

The Librarian of Basra: A True Story from Iraq, Harcourt (Orlando, FL), 2004.

Mama: A True Story in Which a Baby Hippo Loses His Mama during the Tsunami, but Finds a New Home and a New Mama, Harcourt (Orlando, FL), 2006.

Angelina's Island, Farrar, Straus & Giroux (New York, NY), 2007.

The Tale of Pale Male: A True Story, Farrar, Straus & Giroux (New York, NY), 2007.

ILLUSTRATOR

Ann Cameron, *Harry (The Monster),* Pantheon Books (New York, NY), 1980.

Carol Greene, *Hinny Winny Bunco,* Harper & Row (New York, NY), 1982.

Hush Little Baby, Pantheon Books (New York, NY), 1984.

Barbara Diamond Goldin, *The World's Birthday: A Rosh Hashanah Story,* Harcourt (San Diego, CA), 1990.

Jonah Winter, *Diego* (bilingual book), Spanish translation by Amy Prince, Knopf (New York, NY), 1991.

Ann Whitford Paul, *Eight Hands Round: A Patchwork Alphabet,* HarperCollins (New York, NY), 1991.

Selma Lagerlöf, *The Changeling* (originally published as *Bortbytingen*), translated by Susanna Stevens, Knopf (New York, NY), 1992.

Kathleen Hershey, *Cotton Mill Town,* Dutton (New York, NY), 1993.

Hanna Bandes, *Sleepy River,* Philomel (New York, NY), 1993.

Roni Schotter, *A Fruit and Vegetable Man,* Joy Street Books (Boston, MA), 1993.

Mary Lyn Ray, *Shaker Boy,* Harcourt (San Diego, CA), 1994.

Steve Sanfield, *Snow,* Philomel Books (New York, NY), 1995.

Tony Johnston, *Day of the Dead,* Harcourt (San Diego, CA), 1997.

Nancy Willard, *The Tortilla Cat,* Harcourt (San Diego, CA), 1998.

Hey Diddle Diddle, Harcourt (San Diego, CA), 1999.

The illustrations Winter creates for her picture book **Angelina's Island** ***showcase the author/illustrator's talent as a graphic artist.*** (Illustration © 2007 by Jeanette Winter. Reprinted by permission of Farrar, Straus & Giroux, LLC.)

Rock-a-Bye Baby, Harcourt (San Diego, CA), 1999.

Jonah Winter, *Once upon a Time in Chicago: The Story of Benny Goodman,* Hyperion (New York, NY), 2000.

Jane Taylor, *Twinkle, Twinkle Little Star,* Red Wagon Books (San Diego, CA), 2000.

The Itsy-Bitsy Spider, Harcourt (San Diego, CA), 2000.

Jonah Winter, *The Secret World of Hildegard,* Arthur A. Levine Books (New York, NY), 2007.

"WITCH, GOBLIN, AND GHOST" SERIES; ILLUSTRATOR

Sue Alexander, *Witch, Goblin, and Sometimes Ghost,* Pantheon Books (New York, NY), 1976.

Sue Alexander, *More Witch, Goblin, and Ghost Stories,* Pantheon Books (New York, NY), 1978.

Sue Alexander, *Witch, Goblin, and Ghost in the Haunted Woods,* Pantheon Books (New York, NY), 1981.

Sue Alexander, *Witch, Goblin, and Ghost's Book of Things to Do,* Pantheon Books (New York, NY), 1982.

Sue Alexander, *Witch, Goblin, and Ghost Are Back,* Pantheon Books (New York, NY), 1985.

Sidelights

Jeanette Winter is an award-winning author and illustrator of works for young readers whose original self-illustrated stories include *Shaker Boy, My Name Is Georgia, The Librarian of Basra: A True Story from Iraq,* and *Angelina's Island.* "I always wanted to be an artist," Winter remarked on the *Farrar, Straus & Giroux* Web site. "I wanted to make pictures that told stories. But it wasn't until college, when I saw a Kate Greenaway book for the first time, that I knew I would make books for children."

Although Winter's self-illustrated titles have been praised for their evocative narratives, according to critics the most notable aspect of her work is her distinctive painting style. Her simple, uncluttered illustrations feature little shading and a minimal use of depth of field, which makes them appear flat rather than realistic. This approach has led many to term Winter's style "folk art," although some critics view it as more complex than that. In a profile of Winter for *Riverbank Review,* Susan Marie Swanson elaborated upon the illustrator's style, writing that "Winter achieves perspective by overlapping shapes and by composing her pictures in such a way that the view looks from one layer through to the next—looking through doorways and windows, for example, past desert to mountains, through scaffolding to mural." Winter also frequently makes use of unique, brilliant color schemes that are more vivid than life: rich aqua grass, for example, or skies that range from pink to green.

According to *Horn Book* reviewer Nancy Vasilakis, the "stylized folk quality" of Winter's art serves as an excellent complement to Mary Lyn Ray's text in *Shaker Boy.* The book narrates the life of Caleb, a boy who is raised in a Shaker community after his father is killed in the U.S. Civil War and his mother leaves to earn a living in the textile mills of Lowell, Massachusetts. At first, Caleb has trouble adjusting to the community's many rules, but he eventually adapts to this new way of life. As an adult, Caleb becomes the deacon of the apple orchard, where he oversees the work of growing and picking the fruit. The Shakers are famous for their close-knit, collaborative way of life, and as Vasilakis noted, "Winter's full-color paintings reflect that sense of order and community." A *Publishers Weekly* reviewer also praised *Shaker Boy,* calling it "a work of craftsmanship on all levels: exceptionally well written, elegantly designed, and lovingly illustrated."

Day of the Dead, written by Tony Johnston and illustrated by Winter, join Winter's own *Calavera Abecedario: A Day of the Dead Alphabet Book* and *Niño's Mask* in taking various Mexican holidays as its subject. "The visual spontaneity and directness of Mexican crafts have been a big influence on my work," the author/illustrator noted in her *Harcourt Books* interview. "It is an artist's way of relating to the world, and it resonates with me so strongly." In *Day of the Dead,* a book about the holiday known as Día de los muertos, a day for honoring dead ancestors, Winter uses her signature bright colors, accenting each illustration with a thick black border. Her pictures for the book are studded with colorful motifs such as the red chili peppers used to make food for the holiday picnic and the yellow-orange marigold petals that are traditionally scattered on the road to help spirits find their way. The book's paintings are "gem-like," wrote a *Publishers Weekly* reviewer, and *Booklist* critic Hazel Rochman maintained that Winter's distinctive style effectively conveys "the magic realism that is part of the ceremony under the stars." *Calavera Abecedario,* a work based on the Spanish alphabet, follows the members of a Mexican family as they construct the papier-mâché skeletons known as *calaveras,* a holiday tradition. Once finished, their creations represent different characters, including a *bruja* (witch) and a *vaquero* (cowboy). "This is a lovely book that approaches the Day of the Dead from an unusual angle," Cooper Renner wrote in his *School Library Journal* review.

In *Niño's Mask* a little boy longs to play a part in his town's celebration of *El Tigre.* During the traditional celebration, older boys get to wear masks and pretend to be a *conejo* (rabbit) or *ciervo* (deer), but Niño's father says that he is not yet old enough to join in. Undiscouraged, Niño decides to carve his own mask. He makes his mask a *perro* (dog), the character which will catch el tigre and save the day. The story is told entirely through dialogue, and "Winter neatly slots her crisp prose into speech bubbles, lending the outing an inviting look and a rapid pace," noted a *Publishers Weekly* reviewer. Besides being an engaging story, the book also teaches young readers many Spanish words, the meaning of which can easily be discerned by looking at the illustrations. According to *Horn Book*'s Joanna Rudge Long, *Niño's Mask* "is an affectionate portrayal of a Mexican tradition."

Winter retells an African folk story in **My Baby,** ***and brings it to life in ethnic-inspired art.*** (Illustration © 2001 by Jeanette Winter. Reprinted by permission of Farrar, Straus & Giroux, LLC.)

In the self-illustrated *My Baby,* Winter introduces readers to the Malian art form *bogolan,* in which mud is used to paint designs on fabric. The story follows one bogolan artist, a girl named Nakunte Diarra, as she grows to become the premiere bogolan maker of her village. Eventually Nakunte marries, and as she waits for her first child to be born she sets out to make the best bogolan ever for her baby. As she paints, the woman talks to her unborn child about the things that inspire her designs, such as drums, leopards, crocodiles, and calabash flowers. "The designs . . . appear in charming frames surrounding each wonder as [Nakunte] details its uniqueness," Rosalyn Pierini explained in *School Library Journal.* "Older children, who can better appreciate both the techniques and emotions, are probably the book's best audience," commented *Booklist* critic Ilene Cooper, "but many readers—from little ones to adults—will be enthralled by the illustrations" in *My Baby.*

In addition to fiction, Winter has written and illustrated child-friendly biographies of artists and authors such as Mexican muralist Diego Rivera, English author/illustrator Beatrix Potter, and Baroque composer Johann

Sebastian Bach. Focusing on individuals who would perhaps not normally be known to young children, these books are notable, as *Horn Book* critic Lolly Robinson wrote in a review of *Beatrix: Various Episodes from the Life of Beatrix Potter,* because "Winter's goal . . . seems to be to capture the spirit of her subject rather than provide every salient fact for report writing." Winter's biographies are written in short, simple sentences, with a minimal amount of text on each page. In both *Beatrix* and *My Name Is Georgia,* the latter a biography of painter Georgia O'Keeffe, the author weaves quotations from her subject's own writings into her first-person narrative. Winter's design for *Beatrix* echoes the small, square format of Potter's own books for children. The focus of the text is Potter's childhood, when she sketched, talked to animals, and studied art and science to assuage her loneliness, and a *Publishers Weekly* reviewer predicted that the author's description of Potter's lonely childhood is "likely to be of interest to a young audience."

In *My Name Is Georgia* Winter introduces the noted painter in "words as clear, spare, and rhythmic as the painter's compositions," according to *Booklist* contribu-

In Winter's self-illustrated Beatrix *she introduces one of the most beloved picture-book characters of all time.* (Illustration © by Jeanette Winter. Reprinted by permission of Farrar, Straus & Giroux, LLC.)

tor Carolyn Phelan. As with *Beatrix,* reviewers noted that *My Name Is Georgia* is "a biography only in the broadest, sparest sense," as Roger Sutton wrote in *Horn Book.* Although focusing more on O'Keeffe's creative vision than on the details of her life, Winter covers the span of the artist's life, from art lessons during her childhood in Wisconsin through her years studying art in Chicago and New York City, to the decades she spent living in New Mexico in the shadow of Pedernal Mountain, a frequent subject of her paintings. Commenting upon "Winter's poetic text," a *Publishers Weekly* reviewer declared *My Name Is Georgia* to be an "outstanding biography" as well as "a superb and inspiring introduction for children to an exceptional American artist."

In the picture-book biography *Cowboy Charlie: The Story of Charles M. Russell* "Winter invitingly describes Russell's journey . . . in a concise text," as Ellen Mandel noted in her *Booklist* review. The book describes how, as a boy in St. Louis, Russell dreamed about the American West. His parents finally allowed him to spend a month working in Montana when he was fifteen, and he never looked back. For decades, Russell worked on the open range, until crowding on the frontier and the introduction of the barbed-wire fence put an end to the cowboy way of life. At that point, he dedicated himself to documenting the disappearing old West in paintings and sculpture. Winter's paintings for *Cowboy Charlie* are "reminiscent of folk art, though far more sophisticated in picture design," according to *Horn*

Book contributor Margaret A. Bush. The author/illustrator updates her folk-art designs with rich, unusual colors, using shades of mauve, purple, blue, and green not typically associated with prairie art. The effects of this combination are "both timeless and cutting edge," in the view of a *Publishers Weekly* reviewer.

Winter's picture book titled *The Librarian of Basra* was inspired by an article published in the *New York Times.* The work concerns Alia Muhammad Baker, a daring woman who saved some 30,000 books from destruction in war-torn Iraq after her library was converted into a military outpost and ultimately destroyed in a fire. "Alia's story gave me a much-needed sense of optimism during this dark period of war," Winter told an interviewer on the Harcourt Books Web site. "With so much destruction all around her, and no help from either side in this war, Alia had the will to defy her surroundings and act with remarkable courage," she added. "The optimism of the human spirit, even in inhuman conditions, is a wonderful inspiration." *The Librarian of Basra* earned strong reviews for its discriminating approach to a sensitive subject. "Winter represents the terrors of war realistically but not graphically," observed *Horn Book* contributor Susan Dove Lempke, and in *School Library Journal* Marianne Saccardi similarly noted that the author "artfully achieves a fine balance between honestly describing the casualties of war and not making the story too frightening for young children."

In *Mama: A True Story in Which a Baby Hippo Loses His Mama during the Tsunami, but Finds a New Home and a New Mama* Winter uses her signature acrylic paintings and a simple two-word narrative to recount the tale of unlikely animal companions. After a young hippo is separated from its mother during a tsunami, it washes ashore, winds up in an animal sanctuary, and adopts a 130-year-old tortoise as its surrogate parent. Although some critics noted that the young protagonist's brush with tragedy might prove troubling to younger readers, *Horn Book* reviewer Margaret A. Bush maintained that Winter's book "pleases the eye and touches the heart." In *Publishers Weekly* a critic stated that *Mama* "reassuringly portrays how friendship can ease a devastating loss." Winter chronicles another real-life animal adventure in *The Tale of Pale Male: A True Story,* about a red-tailed hawk and his mate that take up residence atop an apartment building in downtown Manhattan. "Winter's luminous, hieratic style, with its velvety rich color and carefully shaped geometry, is eminently suited" for the story, remarked a *Kirkus Reviews* critic.

A young Jamaican immigrant now living in New York City longs to return to her homeland in *Angelina's Island.* When Angelina's mother learns that a carnival celebration will be held in Brooklyn, she helps her daughter design a sparkling costume and learn to perform a traditional dance. Rochman praised Winter's "simple, poetic text and small, framed, brilliantly col-

In **The Librarian of Basra** *Winter tells a true story about the librarian who worked to save her town's library in war-torn Iran.* (Illustration © 2005 by Jeanette Winter. Reproduced by permission of Harcourt Brace & Company.)

ored pictures," and a *Publishers Weekly* reviewer wrote of *Angelina's Island* that Winter's young readers "will easily sense—and share—the girl's gradually lightening spirits and final exuberance."

Biographical and Critical Sources

PERIODICALS

American Visions, December, 1991, Walter Dean Myers, review of *Follow the Drinking Gourd,* pp. 31-32.

Booklist, January 1, 1992, Hazel Rochman, review of *The Changeling,* p. 826; July, 1992, Stephanie Zvirin, review of *Klara's New World,* p. 1940; February 1, 1993, Stephanie Zvirin, review of *Cotton Mill Town,* p. 989; September 1, 1993, Hazel Rochman, review of *A Fruit and Vegetable Man,* p. 71; October 15, 1993, Janice Del Negro, review of *Sleepy River,* pp. 448-449; August, 1994, Stephanie Zvirin, review of *The Christmas Tree Ship,* p. 2053; November 15, 1994, Carolyn Phelan, review of *Shaker Boy,* p. 613; November 1, 1995, Ellen Mandel, review of *Cowboy Charlie: The Story of Charles M. Russell,* p. 475; October 15, 1996, Annie Ayres, review of *Josefina,* p.

423; September 15, 1997, Hazel Rochman, review of *Day of the Dead*, p. 242; March 1, 1998, Hazel Rochman, review of *The Tortilla Cat*, p. 1136; October 15, 1998, Carolyn Phelan, review of *My Name Is Georgia*, p. 418; April 1, 1999, Hazel Rochman, review of *Sebastian: A Book about Bach*, p. 1409; February 15, 2001, Ilene Cooper, review of *My Baby*, p. 1158; March 1, 2001, Stephanie Zvirin, review of *My Name Is Georgia*, p. 1280; March 1, 2002, Gillian Engberg, review of *Emily Dickinson's Letters to the World*, p. 1148; February 1, 2003, Julie Cummins, review of *Niño's Mask*, p. 1002; March 1, 2003, Susan Dove Lempke, review of *Beatrix: Various Episodes from the Life of Beatrix Potter*, p. 1208; March 1, 2004, Hazel Rochman, review of *Elsina's Clouds*, p. 1199; November 1, 2004, Julie Cummins, review of *Calavera Abecedario: A Day of the Dead Alphabet Book*, p. 487; December 1, 2004, Jennifer Mattson, review of *Mama: A True Story in Which a Baby Hippo Loses His Mama during a Tsunami, but Finds a New Home and a New Mama*, p. 649; April 1, 2006, Jennifer Mattson, review of *The Librarian of Basra: A True Story from Iraq*, p. 649; February 1, 2007, Hazel Rochman, review of *Angelina's Island*, p. 61; February 15, 2007, Abby Nolan, review of *The Tale of Pale Male: A True Story*, p. 86; October 1, 2007, Ilene Cooper, *The Secret World of Hildegard*, p. 72.

Bulletin of the Center for Children's Books, May, 2006, Deborah Stevenson, review of *Mama*, p. 402; March, 2007, Deborah Stevenson, review of *The Tale of Pale Male*, p. 313.

Horn Book, June, 1981, Virginia Haviland, review of *Witch, Goblin, and Ghost in the Haunted Woods*, p. 295; March-April, 1988, Elizabeth S. Watson, review of *The Magic Ring*, p. 220; May-June, 1992, Carolyn K. Jenks, review of *The Changeling*, pp. 337-338; January-February, 1994, Hanna B. Zeiger, review of *A Fruit and Vegetable Man*, p. 66; January-February, 1995, Nancy Vasilakis, review of *Shaker Boy*, pp. 52-53; January-February, 1996, Margaret A. Bush, review of *Cowboy Charlie*, pp. 95-96; September-October, 1998, Roger Sutton, review of *My Name Is Georgia*, p. 627; July, 1999, review of *Sebastian*, p. 487; March-April, 2003, Joanna Rudge Long, review of *Niño's Mask*, p. 208; May-June, 2003, Lolly Robinson, review of *Beatrix*, pp. 371-372; March-April, 2004, Susan Dove Lempke, review of *Elsina's Clouds*, p. 177; January-February, 2005, Susan Dove Lempke, review of *The Librarian of Basra*, p. 119; May-June, 2006, Kitty Flynn, review of *Mama*, p. 351; March-April, 2007, Joanna Rudge Long, review of *The Tale of Pale Male*, p. 216; May-June, 2007, review of *Angelina's Island*, p. 275; September-October, 2007, Lauren Adams, review of *The Secret World of Hildegard*, p. 600.

Instructor, May, 1989, Lynn Minderman, review of *Follow the Drinking Gourd*, p. 49.

Instructor and Teacher, May, 1981, Allan Yeager, review of *Witch, Goblin, and Ghost in the Haunted Woods*, p. 59; October, 1982, Allan Yeager, review of *Witch, Goblin, and Ghost's Book of Things to Do*, p. 24.

Kirkus Reviews, December 15, 2002, reviews of *Niño's Mask* and *Beatrix*, pp. 1859-1860; March 15, 2006,

review of *Mama*, p. 303; January 15, 2007, review of *The Tale of Pale Male*, p. 82; April 1, 2007, review of *Angelina's Island*.

New York Times, July 13, 2003, DeRaismes Combes, review of *Beatrix*, p. 20.

New York Times Book Review, August 26, 1984, review of *Hush Little Baby*, p. 23; May 19, 1991, Patricia T. O'Conner, review of *Eight Hands Round: A Patchwork Alphabet*, p. 29; January 12, 1992, Grace Glueck, review of *Diego*, p. 20; November 8, 1992, Ruth J. Abram, review of *Klara's New World*, p. 58; December 4, 1992, review of *The Christmas Tree Ship*, p. 76; May 19, 2002, Martha Davis Beck, "They're Somebody! Who Are You?: Jeanette Winter Acquaints Young Readers with Emily Dickinson," p. 33; December 8, 2002, p. 74.

Pittsburgh Post-Gazette, October 3, 2006, Bob Hoover, interview with Winter.

Publishers Weekly, March 21, 1980, review of *Harry (The Monster)*, p. 69; August 20, 1982, review of *Witch, Goblin, and Ghost's Book of Things to Do*, p. 72; March 30, 1984, review of *Hush Little Baby*, pp. 56-57; September 7, 1984, review of *The Girl and the Moon Man: A Siberian Tale*, p. 79; June 27, 1986, review of *Come out to Play*, p. 84; October 14, 1988, review of *Follow the Drinking Gourd*, p. 73; August 31, 1990, review of *The World's Birthday: A Rosh Hashanah Story*, pp. 64-65; August 9, 1991, review of *Diego*, pp. 57-58; December 6, 1991, review of *The Changeling*, p. 73; August 10, 1992, review of *Klara's New World*, pp. 70-71; January 18, 1993, review of *Cotton Mill Town*, p. 468; September 6, 1993, review of *Sleepy River*, pp. 96-97; September 20, 1993, review of *A Fruit and Vegetable Man*, p. 71; September 19, 1994, review of *The Christmas Tree Ship*, p. 30; October 17, 1994, review of *Shaker Boy*, p. 80; August 14, 1995, review of *Cowboy Charlie*, p. 84; October 28, 1996, review of *Josefina*, p. 81; September 1, 1997, review of *Day of the Dead*, p. 103; March 2, 1998, review of *The Tortilla Cat*, pp. 68-69; September 14, 1998, review of *My Name Is Georgia*, p. 69; October 19, 1998, "In the Studio with Jeanette Winter"; April 5, 1999, review of *Sebastian*, p. 241; May 22, 2000, review of *The House That Jack Built*, p. 91; September 11, 2000, review of *Day of the Dead*, p. 93; January 1, 2001, review of *My Baby*, p. 91; January 7, 2002, review of *Emily Dickinson's Letters to the World*, p. 65; January 20, 2003, reviews of *Niño's Mask* and *Beatrix*, p. 81; April 19, 2004, review of *Elsina's Clouds*, p. 60; December 20, 2004, review of *The Librarian of Basra*, p. 57; February 13, 2006, review of *Mama*, p. 87; January 29, 2007, review of *The Tale of Pale Male*, p. 70; April 2, 2007, review of *Angelina's Island*, p. 56; August 27, 2007, review of *The Secret World of Hildegard*, p. 94.

Reading Teacher, March, 1998, review of *Josefina*, pp. 504-512.

Riverbank Review, winter, 2002-2003, Susan Marie Swanson, "Jeanette Winter," pp. 11-14.

San Francisco Chronicle, October 26, 1997, Susan Faust, review of *Day of the Dead*, p. 10.

School Library Journal, May, 1980, Joan McGrath, review of *Harry (The Monster)*, pp. 51-52; March, 1985,

Carol Kolb Phillips, review of *The Girl and the Moon Man*, p. 160; December, 1985, review of *Witch, Goblin, and Ghost Are Back*, p. 108; September, 1986, Mary Lou Budd, review of *Come out to Play*, p. 118; September, 1987, Mary B. Nickerson, review of *Hush Little Baby*, p. 104; March, 1988, Helen Gregory, review of *The Magic Ring*, p. 186; May, 1989, Kathleen T. Horning, review of *Follow the Drinking Gourd*, p. 95; February, 1991, Micki S. Nevett, review of *The World's Birthday*, p. 69, and Elise Wendel, review of *Follow the Drinking Gourd*, pp. 53-54; July, 1991, Kathy Piehl, review of *Eight Hands Round*, p. 70; January, 1992, Ruth Semrau, review of *Diego*, p. 107; April, 1992, Susan Scheps, review of *The Changeling*, p. 118; September, 1992, Denise Anton Wright, review of *Klara's New World*, p. 214; November, 1992, Kevin Wayne Booe, review of *Diego*, p. 51; March, 1993, Ellen Fader, review of *Cotton Mill Town*, p. 129; May, 1993, Fritz Mitnick, review of *Follow the Drinking Gourd*, p. 62; October, 1993, Cynthia K. Richey, review of *A Fruit and Vegetable Man*, p. 112; November, 1993, Marianne Saccardi, review of *Snow*, p. 81; October, 1994, Jane Marino, review of *The Christmas Tree Ship*, p. 45; November, 1994, Marie Clancy, review of *Shaker Boy*, pp. 89-90; December, 1995, Claudia Cooper, review of *Cowboy Charlie*, p. 101; October, 1996, Pam Gosner, review of *Josefina*, p. 109; September, 1997, Ann Welton, review of *Day of the Dead*, p. 184; March, 1998, Ann Welton, review of *The Tortilla Cat*, p. 190; April, 1999, Jane Marino, review of *Sebastian*, p. 128; May, 2000, Christine Lindsey, review of *The House That Jack Built*, p. 158; April, 2001, Rosalyn Pierini, review of *My Baby*, p. 126; March, 2002, Nancy Menaldi-Scanlan, review of *Emily Dickinson's Letters to the World*, p. 224; March, 2003, Kathy Piehl, review of *Beatrix*, p. 225; December, 2003, Daryl Grabarek, review of *Niño's Mask*, p. 131; April, 2004, Mary N. Oluonye, review of *Elsina's Clouds*, p. 127; January, 2005, Marianne Saccardi, review of *The Librarian of Basra*, p. 118; May, 2005, Coop Renner, review of *Calavera Abecedario*, p. 116; March, 2006, John Peters, reviews of *September Roses* and *The Librarian of Basra*, p. 88; May, 2006, Wendy Lukehart, review of *Mama*, p. 106; March, 2007, Kathy Piehl, review of *The Tale of Pale Male*, p. 202; June, 2007, Julie R. Ranelli, review of *Angelina's Island*, p. 127.

ONLINE

BookPage, http://www.bookpage.com/ (October 31, 2007), Heidi Henneman, "The Heroic Story of an Iraqi Librarian."

Farrar, Straus & Giroux Web site, http://www.fsgkidsbooks.com/ (October 31, 2007), "Jeanette Winter."

Harcourt Web site, http://www.harcourtbooks.com/ (October 31, 2007), interview with Winter.*

*   *   *

WU, Liz
(Elizabeth Wu)

Personal

Female. *Education:* University of Cincinnati, B.A. (jazz performance), 2002. *Hobbies and other interests:* Jazz music performance, making jewelry.

Addresses

Home and office—Cincinnati, OH.

Career

Author and journalist.

Writings

Rosa Farm: A Barnyard Tale, illustrated by Matt Phelan, Alfred A. Knopf (New York, NY), 2006.

Contributor of articles to Cincinnati, OH, *CityBeat* online, under name Elizabeth Wu.

Sidelights

A native of Cincinnati, Ohio, where she works as a journalist for a local newspaper, Liz Wu is also a world traveler, jazz musician, and jewelry artist. The influences of Wu's global travels can be seen in her first children's title, the chapter book *Rosa Farm: A Barnyard Tale*, which was inspired by Wu's visit to Portugal.

In *Rosa Farm* readers are introduced to Gallileon, a young rooster who has to take his father's place as the morning crower at a family farm. Gallileon takes this new responsibility very seriously and his crowing awakens every creature within earshot every morning at sunrise. One day, however, the young rooster's schedule becomes confused when his mother assigns Gallileon's younger sister, Pepina the chicken, to help him. A series of adventures ensues, including the kidnapping of Pepina after rooster and chicken are targeted by a gang of ducks led by a bullying goose named Prattle. In a review of Wu's children's-book debut, a *Kirkus Reviews* critic cited *Rosa Farm* for containing a charming if over-busy plot that features "amusing moments." In her review for *School Library Journal*, Melissa Christy Buron applauded Wu's eventful storyline and noted that the author's "plot is quick paced and will keep the interest of readers new to chapter books."

Biographical and Critical Sources

PERIODICALS

Bulletin of the Center for Children's Books, February, 2007, Hope Morrison, review of *Rosa Farm: A Barnyard Tale*, p. 273.

Kirkus Reviews, October 15, 2006, review of *Rosa Farm*, p. 1081.

Cover of Liz Wu's debut novel **Rosa Farm,** *featuring artwork by Matt Phelan.* (Illustration © 2006 by Matt Phelan. Used by permission of Alfred A. Knopf, an imprint of Random House Children's Books, a division of Random House, Inc.)

School Library Journal, January, 2007, Melissa Christy Buron, review of *Rosa Farm,* p. 111.

ONLINE

Children's Bookwatch Web site, http://www.midwest bookreview.com/ (March, 2007), review of *Rosa Farm.*
CityBeat Online (Cincinnati, OH), http://citybeat.com/ (November 11, 2007), "Liz Wu."
Random House Web site, http://www.randomhouse.ca/ (November 11, 2007), "Liz Wu."*

*   *   *

WU, Elizabeth
See WU, Liz

*   *   *

ZEISES, Lara M. 1976-
(Lola Douglas)

Personal

Surname rhymes with "vices;" born January 20, 1976, in Philadelphia, PA; daughter of Nancy Stone. *Education:* University of Delaware, B.A. (with advanced honors), 1997; Emerson College, M.F.A., 2001.

Addresses

Home—Wilmington, DE. *Agent*—c/o George Nicholson, Sterling Lord Literistic, 65 Bleecker St., New York, NY 10012. *E-mail*—zeisgeist@aol.com; lola@loladouglas. com.

Career

Writer. Worked as an intern for *Baltimore Sun* and *News Journal;* also worked briefly as a features reporter in Indiana and Delaware.

Member

Society of Children's Book Writers and Illustrators.

Awards, Honors

Honor book award, Delacorte Press Contest for First Young-Adult Novel, 2001, and Best Book for the Teen Age selection, New York Public Library, 2003, both for *Bringing up the Bones.*

Writings

YOUNG-ADULT NOVELS

Bringing up the Bones, Delacorte (New York, NY), 2002.
Contents under Pressure, Delacorte (New York, NY), 2004.
Anyone but You: A Novel in Two Voices, Delacorte (New York, NY), 2005.

Coauthor of play produced by Delaware Theater Company. Contributor of fiction and nonfiction to periodicals, including *Jewish Education News* and *Kliatt.*

UNDER NAME LOLA DOUGLAS

True Confessions of a Hollywood Starlet, Razorbill (New York, NY), 2005.
More True Confessions of a Hollywood Starlet, Razorbill (New York, NY), 2006.

Sidelights

Lara M. Zeises writes fiction under her own name, and has created a second identity as a young-adult novelist under the pen name Lola Douglas. As Zeises explained In an interview for *Kliatt,* "I never intended to write for teenagers. But as I became more fully immersed in the genre, and learned that there are far fewer boundaries in writing for children than one may imagine, I realized that the stories I wanted to tell were the ones I wished I had found when I was a teenager myself."

Zeises's first novel, *Bringing up the Bones,* is the story of nineteen-year-old Bridget, whose first love, Benji, breaks up with her via a letter she receives just weeks before he is killed in a car accident. Bridget has trouble coping with the tragedy, and after what she intends to be a one-night stand with a young man named Jasper, she finds herself beginning to heal as she becomes a part of Jasper's life. "Zeises dishes out a heavy slice of realism, suggesting that happily-ever-after endings don't come easily," wrote a critic for *Publishers Weekly.* Noting the depth of the novel's secondary characters, a *Kirkus Reviews* contributor wrote that, "without shifting the focus from Bridget, the author surrounds her with characters that enrich and authenticate her emotional journey." Susan W. Hunter, writing for *School Library Journal,* noted that "the open ending" of *Bringing up the Bones* brings a satisfying sense of realism."

Contents under Pressure is the story of Lucy, a teen who has always admired her successful older brother Jack. When Jack drops out of school and brings home a pregnant girlfriend, Lucy resents the change and is astonished by her beloved brother's continually selfish behavior. "Zeises presents these people and this situation without stereotypes," wrote Claire Rosser, reviewing the novel in *Kliatt.* The "novel takes a mature approach to many issues surrounding young people and sex, managing at the same time to be both light-handed and earnest," according to a critic for *Publishers Weekly.* Linda Bindner, reviewing *Contents under Pressure* for *School Library Journal,* called Lucy a "fully realistic heroine who's confused and scared."

Raised as siblings, Seattle and Critter have to face the changes in their lives as they traverse their teen years in *Anyone but You: A Novel in Two Voices.* Critter, age seventeen, has always thought of Seattle as his own little sister since her father abandoned Seattle along with Critter's own mother. But now that Seattle is fifteen, Critter feels himself becoming attracted to her as something more. Seattle is not sure what she feels, but when she gets extremely jealous over Critter's new girlfriend, she leaps into the arms of another boy. "Pitch-perfect narration and a meandering plot give this story real life appeal," wrote a contributor to *Kirkus Reviews,* while Rosser maintained that "Zeises manages family relationships with acute precision."

Using the pseudonym Lola Douglas, Zeises moves away from realistic family drama and steps into a world of Hollywood gossip. *True Confessions of a Hollywood Starlet* is narrated by Morgan, a movie star who is going through rehab. In order to fully recover before leaping back into the Hollywood scene, Morgan goes undercover in Indiana, trying to live like a "normal" teen on a less-than-Hollywood budget. "This engaging read with a promised sequel will be popular," wrote Suzanne

Gordon in *School Library Journal.* While noting that the theme of addiction is dealt with in a serious fashion, a *Kirkus Reviews* contributor added that because Zeises frames her "narrative . . . in chatty diary form," *True Confessions of a Hollywood Starlet* "is light, breezy and lots of fun."

Morgan rejoins readers in *More Confessions of a Hollywood Starlet.* No longer undercover, but still attending school in Indiana, Morgan finds that her relationships change once her identity is revealed. When she makes a brief return to Hollywood, she is paired by the media with a celebrity she detests because, years before, he raped her. Zeises "manages the lightest of styles while delving into deep issues for adolescents," wrote a contributor to *Kirkus Reviews* in reviewing the sequel, while Rosser concluded of *More Confessions of a Hollywood Starlet:* "Much of it is nearly over the top, but it is appealing," Claire Rosser concluded in *Kliatt.* On the *Lola Douglas Home Page,* Zeises discussed how she started writing about Morgan. "I wanted to write a diary format book, because it seemed fun and challenging," she explained. "But it's not exactly a novel concept (no pun intended), so I tried to think of whose diary I'd want to read. Of course, I immediately thought of Drew Barrymore, and on a long drive at 2 a.m. I fleshed out the basics of the story."

In an interview with a contributor for *Down Home Books Online,* Zeises talked about her decision to give up journalism. "When I made the decision to quit journalism and go to grad school for writing, it was sort of my way of giving myself permission to write. It was without a doubt the best decision I've ever made," she explained. Asked to give advice to aspiring writers by Debbie Michiko on Michiko's home page, Zeises replied, "Grow thick skin. Read everything you can get your hands on. Be curious about people, both real and imaginary. Never give up."

Biographical and Critical Sources

PERIODICALS

Booklist, November 15, 2002, Gillian Engberg, review of *Bringing up the Bones,* p. 596; March 15, 2004, Ilene Cooper, review of *Contents under Pressure,* p. 1301; December 15, 2005, Shelle Rosenfeld, review of *Anyone but You: A Novel in Two Voices,* p. 42.

Bulletin of the Center for Children's Books, January, 2003, review of *Bringing up the Bones,* p. 215; March, 2006, Karen Coates, review of *Anyone but You,* p. 332.

Horn Book, March-April, 2004, Lauren Adams, review of *Contents under Pressure,* p. 192.

Kirkus Reviews, September 15, 2002, review of *Bringing up the Bones,* p. 1404; March 15, 2004, review of *Contents under Pressure,* p. 279; October 15, 2005, review of *Anyone but You,* p. 1149; October 15, 2005, review of *True Confessions of a Hollywood Starlet,* p. 1136; October 15, 2006, review of *More Confessions of a Hollywood Starlet,* p. 1068.

Kliatt, November, 2002, Claire Rosser, review of *Bringing up the Bones,* p. 16; March, 2004, Claire Rosser, review of *Contents under Pressure,* p. 17; May, 2004, Claire Rosser, review of *Bringing up the Bones,* p. 25; November, 2005, Claire Rosser, review of *Anyone but You,* p. 1; November, 2005, Myrna Marler, review of *True Confessions of a Hollywood Starlet,* p. 5; November, 2006, Claire Rosser, review of *More Confessions of a Hollywood Starlet,* p. 8.

Library Media Connection, April-May, 2003, Leslie Schoenherr, review of *Bringing up the Bones,* p. 77; January, 2006, Brenda Ethridge Ferguson, review of *Anyone but You,* p. 75.

Publishers Weekly, October 7, 2002, review of *Bringing up the Bones,* p. 74; March 15, 2004, review of *Contents under Pressure,* p. 76; December 19, 2005, review of *Anyone but You,* p. 66.

School Library Journal, November, 2002, Susan W. Hunter, review of *Bringing up the Bones,* p. 178; April, 2004, Linda Bindner, review of *Contents under Pressure,* p. 163; December, 2005, Suzanne Gordon, review of *True Confessions of a Hollywood Starlet,* p. 144; January, 2006, Kathy Lehman, review of *Anyone but You,* p. 145.

Voice of Youth Advocates, December, 2002, review of *Bringing up the Bones,* p. 393; June, 2004, Cynthia Winfield, review of *Contents under Pressure,* p. 138.

ONLINE

Debbie Michiko Florence Web site, http://www.debbi michikoflorence.com/ (October 29, 2007), Debbie Michiko Florence, interview with Zeises.

Down Home Books Web site, http://www.downhomebooks. com/zeises.htm (October 29, 2007), interview with Zeises.

Lara M. Zeises' Blog, http://zeisgeist.livejournal.com/ (October 29, 2007).

Lara M. Zeises Home Page, http://www.zeisgeist.com/ (October 29, 2007).

Lola Douglas's Blog, http://loladouglas.livejournal.com/ (September 21, 2007).

Lola Douglas Home Page, http://www.loladouglas.com (October 8, 2007).

Random House Web site, http://www.randomhouse.com/ (October 29, 2007), profile of Zeises.

Teen Reads Web site, http://www.teenreads.com/authors/ au-douglas-lola.asp (November 8, 2005), interview with Lola Douglas.

YA Books Central Web site, http://www.yabookscentral. com/ (October 29, 2007), interview with Zeises.*

DATE DUE